Middle Childhood Version

Student Study Guide

CHILDREN

third edition

John W. Santrock
University of Texas at Dallas

Prepared by

Allen H. Keniston
University of Wisconsin–Eau Claire

Blain F. Peden
University of Wisconsin–Eau Claire

WCB Brown & Benchmark
PUBLISHERS

Madison, Wisconsin • Dubuque, Iowa • Indianapolis, Indiana
Melbourne, Australia • Oxford, England

A Times Mirror Company

ISBN 0-697-17119-1

Printed in the United States of America by Wm. C. Brown Communications, Inc., 2460 Kerper Boulevard, Dubuque, Iowa, 52001

10 9 8 7 6 5 4 3 2

Brief Contents

Brief Contents

To the Student

You are about to undertake the challenging and, we hope, exciting task of learning about physical and psychological development from conception through adolescence. This study guide will help you (a) learn and memorize basic course content and (b) learn to be actively involved in and to think critically about your study of child development. To help you learn course content, we have provided detailed learning objectives, chapter summaries, key terms, guided reviews, key term matching exercises, and self-tests. To help you learn actively and think critically, we have included critical thinking exercises, research projects, and challenging essay questions. In sum, each chapter of this study guide contains ten sections designed to help you master the corresponding chapters in John Santrock's *Children,* third edition.

Learning Objectives

Each chapter of the study guide starts with a detailed set of learning objectives. We have organized these objectives by major chapter heading and numbered them accordingly. For example, "Images of Children" is section 1.0 in each chapter; the associated objectives are numbered 1.1, 1.2, and so forth. These objectives cover all material in the chapter, including chapter introductions and boxed materials. They indicate as specifically and behaviorally as possible what you should be able to do after you have read and mastered the material.

Chapter Summary

Chapter summaries, also numbered by major chapter heading, present an overview of the main points of each chapter. Read the summary before reading a chapter for a general outline of what you will be learning (but remember that you must read the chapter itself for detailed coverage of the material!). Also read the summary after reading the chapter for a quick review before classes or exams.

Key Terms

Key terms follow each chapter summary. These include all bold-faced items in a chapter and a few more. These "few more" include words that are not emphasized in the text, but which are terms you need to understand in order to fully understand the material. They also include key terms from other chapters that you may need to review.

We recommend that you study these terms by preparing your *own* definitions of them based on your understanding of the text's definitions. This is important because you will not know whether you really understand a term until you can define it in your own way. Also, when we wrote test items for these terms, we did not copy the definitions given in the textbook, but instead worded definitions in different ways. You will have difficulty with test items about the key terms if you have only memorized a specific definition that you are not sure that you understand.

Guided Review

The guided review is a second chapter summary with fill-in-the-blank items to help you test your memory for a chapter after you have read it. You will be tempted to look at the answers to the guided review statements as you read, but we urge you to use the review as a self-test by covering up the answers with a sheet of paper and not looking at them until you have tried to fill in the blanks. Also, mark the items that you missed and review the relevant material in the textbook after you have worked through the guided review.

Key Terms Matching Exercise

To do this exercise, match each key term with its definition. This will test your knowledge of key terms and concepts and provide a chapter glossary for study and review. Check your work with the answers given at the end of the exercise. We also encourage you to figure out which learning objective each match achieves. Annotate each item with the number of the corresponding learning objective. This is another way to determine whether you understand the material.

Self-Tests

Because there is a good chance that you will take multiple choice tests to measure your learning of chapter material, we have provided two sample 20-item tests. After you have completed the activities we have suggested above you may want to take Test A to see how well you are learning the material. Or you may want to do some or all of the additional exercises described below before you attempt a test. In either case, use Test A (or Test B) to find out how well you have learned the material, use the items you missed as indicators of what you need to review, and use Test B to find out whether you have improved after a review.

Please note the following features of these tests: (a) The items on each are like the items that will probably be used on tests your instructor gives you. Notice that some of them ask you to recall facts, others test your understanding of concepts, and still others ask you to apply a concept. Items also vary in difficulty. Use your self-test performances to determine what types of items are especially difficult for you. This knowledge may help you to study more effectively, or may help you to ask your instructor specific questions about how to improve your test performance. (b) The items sample material evenly from each chapter, *but they do not cover every learning objective.* This is very important for you to remember. Taking these tests will give you a relative idea about how well you have mastered course material. Be sure to notice what material in a chapter the tests cover and what material they do not, and be sure to study the omitted material as well. (c) The self tests cover some of the same material and some different material. A good idea is to identify which of the learning objectives each item tests. Annotate self-test items with the numbers of the objectives relevant to each. This will help you to identify material that you have not reviewed by taking the tests, and possibly will suggest questions you can ask your instructor when you need help.

Critical Thinking Exercises

To the best of our knowledge, the critical thinking exercises for *Children* are unique. They are exercises we have created to help you to think about the material you are studying in deeper and more analytic ways. We use exercises like these as regular assignments in our courses and have suggested to your instructors that they do likewise, but even if they do not, we urge you to try doing them anyway.

What are critical thinking exercises? As we define them, they are problems in a multiple choice format that require you to identify a best answer, explain why it is the best answer, and explain why the other answers are not as good. We have developed various kinds of problems for you to solve as you read and study *Children*, third edition. For example, many exercises ask you to analyze material in terms of the "nature of development" presented in Chapter 1. You may be asked which of several aspects of development are illustrated by material in the text, or to identify which of several developmental themes receives greatest emphasis in particular topics. A second type of exercise requires you to integrate material within chapters. For example, an exercise for Chapter 12 asks you to identify which of five statements about physical development or children's health provides the basis of the most compelling criticism of the Chinese sports schools sketched early in the chapter. A third type of exercise requires you to interpret the figures or tables used throughout *Children*, third edition to supplement and illustrate the text. Finally, a fourth type of exercise requires you to learn how to recognize assumptions and distinguish them from inferences and observations. This last type of exercise probably represents what is most widely viewed as critical thinking, but we believe critical thinking also involves using and analyzing information that you study. **The important activity common across all of the exercises is giving reasons for answers.**

If you are like our students, you will find these exercises quite difficult to do at first. They are probably different from anything you have been asked to do before with the exception of some of the tasks you may have performed to write essay questions or term papers. Despite the difficulty, persist in doing the assignments. Do not expect to do them perfectly at first, because you need to learn how to do them. (After all, did you ever do anything perfectly the first time?). As you gain experience the exercises will begin to be easier. Furthermore, we have made many suggestions in your instructor's course planner about how to teach about and discuss the exercises.

We have also included a key for each exercise in the instructor's course planner. If your instructors are not using the exercises as assignments, laboratory exercises, or guides for discussion, you may want to ask them for copies of the keys. But please note this: We have identified what we think are the best answers. Once in a while, however, some of our students disagree with us and have very good reasons for claiming that another answer is either just as good—or better!

To repeat a point we made earlier, the important aspect of the critical thinking exercises is giving *reasons* for answers. This represents what it really means to know child psychology, and in fact, the exercises represent what child psychologists do with their expertise. In any case, use the exercises to interact with what you are learning constructively and creatively. Research on how people learn and remember suggests that doing them will enhance your ability to remember what you have studied. We hope they will also deepen your understanding and expand your learning skill.

Student Research Projects

Each chapter of the study guide contains at least two suggested research projects (Chapter 3 has just one). These projects usually are simple types of systematic observation that you can do in everyday settings such as playgrounds, stores, or malls. Occasionally they call for interviews, questionnaires, or small experiments. (Read Chapter 1 to understand these terms better!).

Your instructors may require you to do some or many of these projects, but we strongly recommend that you do these activities on your own if they do not. Our main reason for urging you to do this is that it is hard to learn how tentative, fragile, and difficult to generate knowledge is until you have attempted to create some of it on your own. It is also important for you to examine your own unstructured, unavoidably biased everyday experience in light of more systematic and objective study. Your most difficult task in learning child psychology is to come to grips with the fact that what you personally have experienced is not the best and most valid source of information about children. Attempting to do structured, purposeful data collection may help you to acquire more objective and scientific attitudes about knowledge.

In any event, doing the research projects will make you more aware of the pleasures and pains of data collection, and will also give you first-hand experience with children. The projects may also make readings, lectures, and other class activities more interesting.

An important concern is that your projects follow guidelines for ethical research. Each of these projects is safe, but read the essay "Ethics, Human Subjects, and Informed Consent" that follows this preface to better understand and apply guidelines for ethical research.

Essay and Critical Thinking Questions

Just before Self-Test B in each chapter of your study guide there are two sets of questions. The first of these is a "traditional" set of questions intended to test your comprehension of textbook material. These questions typically require you to define and distinguish terms, show how concepts relate to each other, discuss and evaluate evidence for hypotheses, or apply concepts to aspects of your own life. The main resource for these questions should be the text (and possibly lectures) and your own experiences. There are ten of these comprehension questions for each chapter.

The second set of questions is more rigorous and systematic. They are more rigorous because they require you to go beyond textbook or lecture material. They are more systematic because five different types of questions occur in every chapter, except Chapter 1. The first question asks you to design a study to answer a question not answered by the text. The focus of these questions is application of "the science base of child development" (see Chapter 1). The second question asks you to analyze material in each chapter in terms of the five issues that define "the nature of development" presented in Chapter 1 of the text. The third question asks you to analyze and interpret a specific topic presented in a chapter in terms of the six major approaches to child development presented in Chapter 2. (We did not write a question like this for Chapter 1.) The fourth question focusses your attention on information that is not covered in a chapter, and asks you to speculate on why a given topic was omitted. Finally, the fifth question asks you to research one of the many quotes from famous people found in the margins of each chapter of *Children,* third edition. You must find out something about each author and explain why the quote is important, what the quote means, and how it relates to the material presented in the chapter. More detailed instructions about answering these critical thinking essay questions appear on page 16.

We included these questions in the instructor's course planner and suggested a number of ways for your instructors to use them. But even if your instructor does not use them in any way obvious to you, use the questions to guide your study of your textbook and to prompt you to look beyond your textbook. Outline or write a short answer for the more traditional questions, or use them for study sessions with your friends. The more challenging critical thinking questions may require too much effort to do them on a regular basis, but they may provide useful suggestions for term paper topics or other projects that you may have to do for this or other courses you are taking.

Some Final Thoughts . . .

. . about studying: We designed this study guide to give you activities that we believe will enhance your ability to learn, remember, analyze, and critique knowledge about child psychology. However, effective studying involves more than the specific things you do to learn the material; it includes developing good general study habits, plans, and strategies. To help you develop these skills, we are including the following essay, "How to be a Better Student," written by Michael G. Walraven for the third edition of a study guide that accompanied another Santrock text, *Life Span Development.* Take time to read it—the investment will pay off!

. . about active learning: We have included critical thinking exercises, research projects, and challenging essay questions in your study guide because we firmly believe that you should be actively involved in your own learning. Indeed, research has shown that the other study aids we have provided do not really help unless you use them in a very active way (e.g., working through the guided review without yielding to the temptation to look at the answers, and checking the material you could not remember). If you agree with us, we hope that all of the activities in this study guide will be useful both as ready-made suggestions for study, and as models for activities that you invent on your own to help you achieve your own course goals and objectives. In fact, we are interested to learn about your reactions to these activities. Please tell us about your experiences by writing us at the Department of Psychology, University of Wisconsin-Eau Claire, Eau Claire, Wisconsin 54702-4004. Also, send samples of additional activities, exercises, or assignments that have enhanced your learning, or that represent the kind of learning tools you like. We look forward to hearing from you!

Allen H. Keniston

Blaine F. Peden

How to Be a Better Student

Everyone who goes to college wants to be a good student. As you chose your college or university, and perhaps even an area of major interest or concentration, you had certain goals in mind. I would be willing to bet that three of them were to do well in school, earn good grades, and graduate.

Unfortunately, many students find that they do not do as well in college as they had hoped and expected. There are several reasons for this disappointment, and in examining them it is possible to see how to avoid them. It is possible, in other words, to know how to be a good student, and to guide our behavior so we improve the chances of achieving our goals.

The oldest known definition of education is "how people learn stuff." For most of our history, educators have focused on the "stuff." Teachers were required to be masters of their respective academic fields. Even today, some states have requirements which speak only to the need to be qualified in the subject matter one teaches.

In the 1960s, we became more interested in the "people" part of the definition, a movement made manifest by fads like open classrooms and free universities. The idea was that people just naturally learn, and need only the opportunity to do so. These experiments were dismal failures, but they taught us something.

The key to the definition of education is the word "how." Today, thanks to a wealth of research on the principles which guide the phenomenon of learning, and on the nature of learning and memory, we know a considerable amount about how learning occurs and how we can make it better. It is by the application of these principles that we can become better students.

Formulating the Plan

Anything worth having is worth planning for. Whether you hope to learn to teach, to fly, to write for profit, or to change diapers correctly, you have in mind a goal.

From the earliest days in elementary school, many students are asked what they want to be when they grow up. This usually means what they want to do as work when they reach adulthood. Although I have been teaching at the college level for almost 15 years, may father still asks me when I am going to get a steady job! The answer to these questions is one way of formulating a goal. Now that you are a college student, many people will expect that you know what you want to do for a profession or career. Yet, you may not have the foggiest notion, or you may have an idea which is still slightly foggy. That is OK. What is clear, however, is that you want to succeed in your college courses. This is a relatively long-range goal, and as such can serve a purpose in keeping you on track.

But our day-to-day behavior is often hard to connect to our long-range goals. We need short-term goals to keep us organized, and to be sure that the flow of our activities is in the correct direction.

I suggest that as students, we need three types of short-term (relatively speaking) goals. First, we need goals for the semester or term; second, goals for the week; and third, goals for the day. Let's look at each of these separately.

Goals for the Semester

At the beginning of each semester, we find ourselves immersed suddenly in many new courses. Often, we are confronted by several new professors with whom we have not worked before. It is difficult to sort out the expectations and demands of these several courses. However, organizing this information is critical to effectively completing all these requirements, and to success.

If you can, obtain a large wall calendar, and mark on it all the dates of tests, exams, and term paper due dates. But sure to write on the calendar for which course the date applies. Now, estimate how long it will take you make final preparations for those exams, and mark those dates as warning or alert dates. Look over the dates on which papers are due, and see if they are bunched together. If your college is typical, they are. You can help yourself to avoid the last minute all-nighters, if you will simply determine a spread of due dates for yourself, and mark those on the calendar too. As you do this step, please be sure to avoid any days which have personal significance for you, such as birthdays, anniversaries, and the like. This calendar gives you an overview of major dates in your semester.

Goals for the Week

Students who are successful in college also schedule their time weekly. Sometime during the course of registration, you undoubtedly made up a schedule showing your classes arrayed over the week. If you also have a part-time or full-time job, you must allow time for that, too. And, everyone needs some time for relaxing, eating, and sleeping, not to mention life's essentials: ice cream and love. With all these things in mind, it is no wonder we find very little time to study.

But good students do all these things, too, yet they study. Do they have more time? No, we all have the same amount of time. But successful students schedule their time carefully. So, make up a weekly schedule and block off time for all these necessary events: classes, work, relaxation, eating, sleeping, loving, ice cream, and studying. Is there any time left? If so, appoint a committee to decide what to do with it. If not, consider yourself a student.

As you make up your weekly schedule, you may find your study time in a large block. If this is true, please remember to take a short break every 20 to 30 minutes. This is called distributed practice and is far more efficient than studying for hours on end. After the first twenty or thirty minutes, most of us become much less efficient anyway.

Goals for Today

It is also helpful to keep a daily checklist, as a reminder of what must be done that day. Check off the things as you accomplish them. A pocket calendar is most helpful for this task.

If you have followed this carefully, you now have a large semester calendar plastered on your wall, a weekly schedule of major life events, classes, and study times taped over your desk, and a daily check list of must-do items in your pocket or purse. We have to hurry now; it's time to go to class!

Attending Classes

Many students believe that, since they are in college, they can decide whether to go to class at all. They are correct. Some students believe further that attendance in class is not important to their grade. They are misled! Some instructors even announce that they do not adjust grades based on attendance. But they do not have to! Students who do not attend class sessions almost always do more poorly on the tests and exams. Perhaps they were absent when a crucial item was discussed, or when the instructor lectured over the material this examination requires. Moreover, if you are not there, the instructor cannot get to know you (sorry, instructors are not telepathic), and therefore cannot give you the benefit of the doubt on your answers.

In study after research study, the data clearly show that those students who attend class regularly receive the highest grades and actually learn more, too! So, the first rule of effective studenthood is to attend classes. Besides, how else can you get your money's worth?

When you get to class, what do you do?

Benefiting from Lectures

Sometimes students attend lectures and just sit and pay attention. They reason that if they take notes, they will miss much of what the instructor says. But sitting and paying attention is difficult to do. For one thing, most people can think much faster than they can speak. While the instructor lectures at 80 words per minute, the student thinks at about 350 words per minute! If the student is using this extra "thinking capacity" to focus on what the instructor is saying, it is fine. This rarely lasts more than five minutes at a time, however. Most of the time, this extra "thinking capacity" is used in daydreaming!

Daydreaming can be helpful in resolving our emotional problems, planning the course of our lives, and avoiding work. Most of the time it is motivated by the desire to avoid work. For whatever motive, however, daydreaming is not compatible with attending a lecture. Human beings simply cannot attend to more than one stimulus at one time. And you have to admit, your daydreams can be ever so much more interesting than your professor's lectures.

Attending lectures is best done while taking notes. Use plenty of paper, and leave blank lines at regular intervals. You will use these lines later (they are not wasted!). If the instructor permits it, interrupt with questions if you do not understand what is being said. Lectures have a way of progressing. It is important to understand each point, or later points will be lost.

When you take notes, write out the major points, and try to just make simple notes on the supporting minor points. If you miss something, and you cannot ask a question about it, approach the instructor immediately afterward, when it is likely to still be fresh in both your minds.

Within one or two hours after the lecture, but for sure on the same day, go back over your notes, and do two things. First, fill in the rest of the minor points. This often amounts to completing the sentence or other element. Second, write brief summaries and any questions that you now have in the blank lines you left earlier (clever of you to leave those blank lines!). These few minutes spent reviewing and organizing your notes will pay off in greatly improved memory. The questions you have you can ask in class, or during the instructor's office hours, and reap two benefits. First, you will get the answers. Second, you will demonstrate that you are a serious student, and that will impress your instructor.

By the way, weren't we supposed to read something before the next class period? Oh yes, now where did I leave my textbook? I sure hope I can get through all those pages before I fall to sleep!

Reading for Learning

We all know how to read. You are proving it by reading these words. Hopefully, you are also realizing some ideas as a result of reading. If you are only reading words, please WAKE UP! STOP DAYDREAMING!

We can read a variety of things: newspapers, movie reviews, novels, sleazy paperbacks, and textbooks. Textbooks are unlike all the others, and must be read with a strategy all their own.

There are a multitude of reading and studying strategies, and all of them work to an extent. Perhaps you learned one or more in the course of going to high school. Perhaps you even took a how-to-study course as you entered college. If so, you probably learned one or two of these systems. If you have one you like, which works for you, keep it. If you are interested in learning a new one, read on.

The SQ3R Method

One of the most successful and most widely used methods of studying written material is the SQ3R method, first developed at Ohio State University. Researchers had noted that students who were more successful were more active readers. This method teaches you the same skills which have made many thousands of students successful. If you use this method when you read and study, you will be more successful, too. If not, there's always snake oil.

The S stands for **SURVEY**. After you have read the overview or chapter outline, and the list of learning objectives, you should survey the chapter in the text. This is also called skimming. Look at the headings and subheadings, and get the gist of the major points in this chapter. If you have an outline of the chapter (some books provide them), check off each point as you pass it in the pages of the text.

The Q stands for **QUESTIONS**. Reading is greatly enhanced if you are searching for the answers to questions. For this text, the study guide provides learning objectives which can serve as questions. For other texts, make up questions for yourself, based on the chapter overview or on your own survey of the chapter. Be sure that you have at least one question for each major unit in the chapter, or you will find less efficiency in studying those units for which you do not have questions.

The first of the three Rs is for **READ**. As you read, look for the answers to the questions you posed, or to the study or learning objectives furnished for you. When you find material which answers these questions, put a mark (X) in the margin next to that material. This will help now, since you are actively involved, and later, when you review. It is a good idea to wait to underline or highlight lines of text until after have read the entire chapter at least once, so you will know what is and what is not most important.

The second R is for **RECITE**. One of the oldest classroom techniques in the world (Aristotle used it) is recitation. In the classroom version, the teacher asks the questions and the students answer them. Unless you can get your teacher to study with you regularly, you'll have to play both roles. (Incidentally, if you do get your teacher to study with you regularly, please write and let me know how you accomplished it. Thanks.)

Stop periodically in your reading and say aloud (if possible) what the author is telling you. Try to put it in your own words, but be sure to use technical terms as you learn them. If you are not in a situation where you can recite out loud, do it in writing. Just thinking it is not enough.

People who do not use recitation usually forget half of what they read in one hour, and another half of the half they remembered by the end of the day. People who use recitation often remember from 75 to 90 percent of what they studied. This technique pays off. By the way, if anyone questions why you are talking to yourself, tell them that a psychologist recommended it.

When should you pause to recite? A good rule of thumb is that each time you come to the end of a major subheading, you should recite. I like to encourage my students to recite at least one sentence at the end of each paragraph, and two or three or more sentences at the end of each subunit (when you come to a new heading). Who ever said that students should be seen and not heard?

The third R (in SQ3R, remember?) is for **REVIEW**. You should review a chapter soon after you have studied it (using the SQ and first 2Rs). You should review it again the day or evening before a test. It is not usually helpful to cram the night before a test, and particularly not the day of the test! That type of study does not produce good memory, and is likely to make you more anxious during the test itself.

Taking Tests

One of the things students fear most is failure. Failure signifies that things are not going well, and alerts us to the possibility that we may not achieve our goals. Unfortunately, many students see tests and exams as opportunities to fail. They prepare by becoming anxious and fearful, and trying to cram as much as possible as near as possible to the exam itself. These students rarely do well on the exam. They often fail, thus accomplishing just what they feared. Perhaps they should learn to fear success?

Taking tests requires some strategy and planning. First, it is helpful to know what type of tests you will have. Your instructor probably told you during the first class meeting, or perhaps is waiting for you to ask. If you do not know, ask and find out.

If you are going to be taking essay exams, the best way to prepare is by writing essays. Before you do this, it is a good idea to find out what types of questions the instructor asks, and what is expected in a response. Again, it is helpful to ask the instructor for this material. Perhaps you can even see some examples of essay questions from previous years. By finding out what is expected, you can formulate a model against which you can evaluate your answers.

Now, using the learning objectives, or some essay questions you wrote, actually sit down and write out the answers. HINT: If you usually feel more anxious during a test, it may help you to practice writing your essays in the room in which the test will be given. Simply find a time when the room is vacant, and make yourself at home.

If your instructor gives multiple choice tests, then you should practice taking multiple choice tests. For each chapter, either use questions provided in the student study guide, or make up your own. You may find it helpful to work out an arrangement to pool questions with other students, thereby reducing the amount of work you have to do, and developing a network of friends. Good for you!

Whichever way you do it, the important thing is to prepare for tests and exams. Preparation is about 95 percent of the secret to getting a good grade. (Yes, there is some actual luck or chance involved in test scores, as even your instructor will admit!) Preparation is not only a good study and review technique, but also helps to reduce anxiety.

Dealing with Test Anxiety

Some students find that the prospect of a test or an examination produces a set of responses which leave them feeling helpless, very anxious, and certain of failure. They find it hard to read the questions, often leave the examination incomplete, have stomach pains and other somatic problems, and contemplate drastic measures, such as dropping out.

Other students are less severely affected. For some, a little anxiety gives them the "edge" they need to do well. In fact, anxiety can be a helpful drive, when it occurs in low levels. In 1908, Yerkes and Dodson showed that the amount of anxiety which could benefit performance was a function of the difficulty and complexity of the task. As the difficulty of the task rose, anxiety became less helpful and more likely to interfere with performance.

If you have even been so anxious in a test situation that you were unable to do well, even though you knew the information, you have test anxiety. If you get your exams back, and are surprised that you marked wrong answers when you knew the correct answers, or if you can only remember the correct answers after you leave the examination room, you too may have test anxiety. Short of dropping out of college, or seeing a professional counselor, what can you do? In fact, you can do three things.

Strategy Number One: Effective Study

Using study habits which promote learning and make the best use of time is a sure help. Such study strategies as we discussed above, including scheduling your time, and using the SQ3R system, reduce anxiety by increasing confidence. As you come to realize that you know the material, your confidence rises and anxiety retreats.

Strategy Number Two: Relaxation

Each of us develops a unique pattern of relaxation. Some people relax by going to a specific place, either in person or mentally. Others relax by playing music, by being with friends, by using autogenic relaxation phrases, or by meditating. Whatever you do, be aware of it, and try to practice relaxation techniques. If you are good at relaxing, try thinking about those situations which make you anxious, and relax while you think of them. To do this, allow yourself to think only briefly (15 to 30 seconds at a time) of the situation which makes you anxious, and then relax again. After a number of such pairings, you will find that thinking about that situation no longer makes you anxious. At this point, you may be surprised to find that the situation itself also no longer produces anxiety. You may find that it is helpful to think about these anxiety-provoking situations in a sequence from those which produce very little anxiety to those which are more anxiety-evoking. Such a list, from low to high anxiety, might look something like this:

1. Your instructor announces that there will be a test in four weeks.
2. Your instructor reminds you of the test next week.
3. As you study, you see on the course outline the word test, and remember next week's test.
4. One of your friends asks you if you want to study together for the test which is the day after tomorrow.
5. You choose not to go out with your friends because of the test tomorrow.
6. As you get up in the morning, you remember that today is the day of the test.
7. You are walking down the hall toward the classroom, thinking about what questions might be on the test.
8. The instructor enters the classroom, carrying a sheaf of papers in hand.
9. The instructor distributes the papers, and you see the word "test" or "exam" at the top.
10. After reading the first five questions, you have not been able to think of the answer to any of them.

If you work at it gradually and consistently, pairing these types of thoughts (briefly) with relaxation and remembering to let go and relax after each one will dispel test anxiety and make test taking a more productive and successful experience.

Strategy Number Three: Thinking Clearly

Most students who have test anxiety think in unclear and unproductive ways. They say to themselves things like: "I can't get these answers correct . . . I don't know this stuff . . . I don't know anything at all . . . I'm going to fail this test . . . I'm probably going to flunk out of school . . . I'm just a dumb schmuck." These thoughts share two unfortunate characteristics: they are negative and they are absolute. They should be replaced.

When we tell ourselves absolute and negative thoughts, we find it impossible to focus on the test material. The result is that we miss questions even when we know the answers. Our thinking prevents us from doing well.

A good strategy for replacing these negative and absolute thoughts is to practice thinking positive and honest thoughts, such as: "I may not know all the answers, but I know some of them . . . I don't know the answer to that right now, so I will go on to the next one and come back to that . . . I don't have to get them all right . . . I studied hard and carefully, and I can get some of them correct . . . I am a serious student, and have some abilities . . . I am prepared for this test, and know many of the answers . . . This test is important, but it is not going to determine the course of my entire life."

By thinking clearly, honestly, and positively, we quiet the flood of anxiety, and focus on the task at hand. Students who use this technique invariably do better on the tests. It takes practice to think clearly, but it is worth the effort. After a while, you will find that it becomes natural, and does not take any noticeable effort. And as anxiety is reduced, more energy is available for studying and for doing well on examinations. The eventual outcome is more enjoyment with learning, better learning, more success in college, and the achievement of your goals.

Answering Essay and Critical Thinking Questions

In Chapter 13, Santrock argues that children must learn to think critically. For Santrock, critical thinking is "grasping the deeper meaning of problems, keeping an open mind about different approaches and perspectives, and thinking reflectively rather than accepting statements and carrying out procedures without significant understanding and evaluation" (p. 403).

Learning to think critically requires activity rather than passivity on the part of students. To improve your critical thinking skills (e.g., developing problem-solving strategies, seeing things from multiple points of view, expanding your knowledge base, and becoming motivated to use newly acquired critical thinking skills in daily life), you must actively: (a) read, listen, and observe carefully, (b) identify or formulate questions, (c) organize your thoughts on an issue or topic, (d) note similarities and differences, (e) make deductions by reasoning from the general to the specific, and (f) distinguish between logically valid and invalid inferences.

In Chapter 16, Santrock provides an additional discussion of critical thinking by adolescents. Here he emphasizes that an aspect of critical thinking is being open-minded about issues and thoroughly examining both sides of an issue. Open-minded and thorough answers to questions or solutions to problems require you to present statements that are accurate and true, are relevant to the issue, and encompass all relevant issues.

In answering the essay and critical thinking questions, you should demonstrate each of these aspects of critical thinking and satisfy the following criteria regarding content, organization, and writing skills. *Appropriate content* includes a sentence that restates the question, and a sentence or paragraph answers to all parts of the question. Additional aspects of content include major points and supporting evidence that are accurate and related to the answer. Provide credit for information from others that you include in your response. Finally, end your response by restating the answer to the question and summarizing major points. *Appropriate organization* requires that your answer to the question appear near the beginning of your response. Major points and supporting evidence should be arranged in an order that is logical and coherent. The answer should be summarily restated at the end of your response. *Appropriate writing skills* require that you use complete sentences, correct punctuation, and other mechanics of good writing.

Ethics, Human Subjects, and Informed Consent

The following section presents information about the ethics involved in doing research with human subjects. It also provides information about what is involved in both a Human Subjects Review Committee Application and in an informed consent form.

It has been our experience that many students today are concerned with issues involving the risks to and the rights of potential subjects in psychological and other research. Many of them have had experience as subjects participating in our research projects. It is in their best interest and ours to provide them with information so that they can understand the issues involved.

Ethical Practices in Research with Human Subjects[1]

There are four issues of major importance in conducting research with human subjects:

1. Informed consent is required from the subject prior to any psychological testing. In doing research with children, written consent of the parents is required. Informed consent means that the purpose of the research and the procedures involved have been explained to the parents and that they understand what is involved and agree to allow their child to participate in the study. The procedures should then be explained to the child at the child's level of understanding, the child's cooperation should be enlisted, and an attempt should be made to maintain the child's interest during his or her participation in the project. Parents must be informed that both they and their child have the right to withdraw from participation at any time for any reason.

2. A Human Subjects Review Committee, by that or some similar name, exists at all institutions that do research with human subjects to evaluate the research projects and to safeguard the rights and the safety of potential subjects. Determinations of such review committees are usually based, in part, upon the possible use of deception and any potential risk to subjects. The concept of informed consent assumes that the real purpose of the experiment has been revealed to subjects and that the subjects are competent to decide whether or not to participate. This condition is violated when the experiment requires deception of the subject. None of the projects in this study guide require deception of the subjects. The second problem is possible risk to subjects. None of the projects presented here involve risk to the subjects. However, they do not provide positive benefits to the subjects either; they are neutral.

3. The requirement for informed consent is violated when coercion is used on subjects because, when coercion is used, subjects are not free to refuse to participate. This freedom to refuse must be guaranteed to the subjects. When working with children as subjects, it is necessary to make the study as playful and gamelike as possible to enlist the interest of the children. However, their rights to refuse to participate and to not be coerced must also be respected and protected.

4. Privacy and confidentiality must be guaranteed. It is important to inform the parents that, in any report of the information gained, their child will not be identified by name but only by averages or identifiers that cannot be traced to the individual child. The child's privacy will be protected. This requires that, when you present data in class, you report the data only by age and sex of the child, never by name.

---

[1]Carroll, M.A., Schneider, H.G., and Wesley, G.R., (1985) *Ethics in the practice of psychology.* Englewood Cliffs, N.J.: Prentice-Hall.

Human Subjects Information

Your school should have forms available to use for the submission of research studies to the Human Subjects Review Committee on your campus. The kind of information generally required on these forms includes:

1. A description of the purpose of the research and a detailed description of the procedures used, including potential hazards and benefits to the subjects.
2. A copy of the informed consent form that subjects will sign, along with a description of the way in which their consent will be elicited.
3. A description of any possible harm—physical, emotional or psychological—that might come from participation in the project.
4. A description of the subjects to be seen, including number, age, and other characteristics.

It is also possible that your school allows, as many do, for entire study guides such as this one to be submitted for consideration so that all the research exercises can be considered at once. This is a great convenience. Ask whether your school has such a policy.

Informed Consent Form

The informed consent form that parents sign should include several kinds of information:

1. A description of the procedures and the purpose of the study.
2. A statement of the rights of the subject to refuse to participate and to withdraw from participation at any time.
3. A statement guaranteeing the privacy and confidentiality of the results of the study. This usually involves a statement saying that results will not be reported by name and that any identifying information will be omitted from the report.
4. A description of any possible risks or discomforts that the subject might experience.
5. A description of any possible benefits to be expected for the subject. In the exercises presented in this study guide, the benefits tend to simply be the enjoyment of playing some of the games.

It is very likely that your school has such a form already prepared for use by faculty researchers. You can use the same form.

Chapter **1** **Introduction**

Objectives

1.0 *Images of Children: The Best of Times and the Worst of Times for Today's Children*
1.1 What observations indicate that it is the best (and the worst) of times for today's children?

2.0 *Why Study Children?*
2.1 Explain why it is important to study child development.

3.0 *Child Development—Today and Yesterday*
3.1 List three concerns that influence a contemporary understanding of children.
3.2 Identify characteristics of modern families that affect children.
3.3 Describe contemporary problems in education that affect children.
3.4 Discuss how sociocultural contexts of development can affect children.
3.5 List four key concepts that define a sociocultural context.
3.6 Define and distinguish between context and culture.
3.7 Explain the purpose of a cross-cultural study.
3.8 Compare child care practices in the United States and other countries.
3.9 Define ethnicity, and describe trends in ethnic diversity in the United States.
3.10 Understand why the term *minority* is unsatisfactory to some individuals or groups.
3.11 Define and distinguish between gender and sex.
3.12 Contrast historical accounts of child development during the Middle Ages, Renaissance, late nineteenth century, and contemporary times.
3.13 Explain how the assumptions and philosophies of original sin, tabula rasa, and innate goodness apply to an understanding of child development.
3.14 Explain how social policy influences children's lives.

4.0 *The Nature of Development*
4.1 Define development.
4.2 Describe the three major processes (biological, cognitive, and social) that shape child development.
4.3 Know the major developmental periods (prenatal period, infancy, early, middle, and late childhood, and adolescence).
4.4 List three major developmental issues.
4.5 Define and distinguish the maturation (nature) versus experience (nurture) explanations of development.
4.6 Define and distinguish the continuity versus discontinuity views of development.
4.7 Define and distinguish the stability versus change views of development.

5.0 *The Science Base of Child Development*
5.1 Define theory and scientific method.
5.2 List and explain the purpose of each step in the scientific method.
5.3 Define and distinguish between observations and inferences.

5.4 Explain the relationship between theory and method.

5.5 List and explain the strengths and limitations of the seven methods for collecting information scientifically (observations; interviews and questionnaires; case studies; standardized tests; cross-cultural research; physiological research; and the multimeasure, multisource, and multicontext approach).

5.6 Define dependent variable, independent variable, and random assignment, and compare and contrast the strengths and weaknesses of experimental and correlation strategies for collecting information scientifically.

5.7 Discuss the strengths and limitations of each strategy listed in 5.6.

5.8 Compare and contrast cross-sectional and longitudinal approaches.

5.9 Discuss the strengths and limitations of each approach in 5.8.

5.10 Understand how research on children can be sexist.

5.11 Indicate ways to reduce sexism in child development research.

5.12 Describe ethical concerns in research on child development.

6.0 *Careers in Child Development*

6.1 List career opportunities in child development.

6.2 Compare and contrast two or more careers in child development with respect to jobs, degrees, education, training, and work description.

6.3 Discuss opportunities for ethnic minorities in the field of child development.

Summary

1.0 Images of Children: The Best of Times and the Worst of Times for Today's Children

Contemporary children face greater opportunities, such as longer life spans and rapid global communication, and greater dangers, such as AIDS and crack cocaine, than those of previous generations. This situation provides new challenges and opportunities for child development research.

2.0 Why Study Children?

Children are, or will be, part of almost everyone's everyday life. Studying children produces responsible caretakers who better can deal with and help children become competent human beings.

3.0 Child Development—Today and Yesterday

Some Contemporary Concerns. The prominent concern with the well-being of children is reflected by the growing interest in family processes, education, and sociocultural issues. The family is changing, and the quality of child care now provided by single-parent families and by families in which both parents work may be problematic. The quality of education that children receive in American schools has come under attack. Finally, the American cultural tapestry has changed dramatically. Sociocultural issues arise with regard to context, culture, ethnicity, and gender. Context refers to the setting in which development occurs, a setting that is influenced by economic, social, and cultural factors. Culture refers to the behavioral patterns, beliefs, and all other products that one group of people transmit from generation to generation. Ethnicity encompasses cultural heritage, national characteristics, race, religion, and language. Gender is a sociocultural definition of female and male.

Historical Accounts of Childhood. The view of children and child development has changed throughout history. Aries used samples of art to conclude that, historically, development consisted of only two phases—infancy and adulthood. However, his conclusions have been called into question because ancient Egyptians, Grecians, and Romans held rich conceptions of children's development.

The three classic philosophical views of the child were original sin, which appeared during the Middle Ages, and the tabula rasa and innate goodness views, which appeared during the Renaissance. The original sin view reflected the philosophical perspective that children are inherently evil and that societal constraints and salvation are necessary for children to become mature adults. Locke's tabula rasa view saw the child as a blank slate upon which experience would write. Rousseau's innate goodness view conceived of children as basically good and stressed that children should be allowed to grow naturally, without constraints from parents or society.

Social Policy and Children's Development. Although we now conceive of childhood as highly eventful, political realities influence social policy. One goal of contemporary child development research is to produce knowledge that will lead to wise and effective social policies regarding children.

4.0 The Nature of Development

Biological, Cognitive, and Social Processes. Child development researchers explain the nature of development in terms of three processes. The biological processes include evolution, ethnology, genetics, neurological development, and physical growth. Cognitive processes include thought, perception, attention, problem solving, and language. Cognitive activities are considered to have causal influences on behavior. Experience alone does not determine a child's behavior but is tempered by how the child's cognitive processes interpret it. Social processes include interactions with other people in the environment and properties of the individual child such as self, gender roles, and morality.

Periods of Development. The periods of childhood development are the prenatal period (conception to birth), infancy (birth to 18-24 months), early childhood (the preschool years), middle and late childhood (the elementary school years), and adolescence (puberty to 18-21 years). Different developmental tasks are important at each of these stages, ranging from the physical characteristics that appear during the prenatal period to the formation of logical reasoning and abstract thought during adolescence.

Maturation and Experience (Nature and Nurture). One controversy concerns the issue of how much of development is explained by maturation (nature) and how much by the influence of the environment (nurture). The current view is that both nature and nurture are responsible for development.

Continuity and Discontinuity. A second controversy concerns the issue of whether development consists of gradual change from conception onward (continuity) or whether development entails distinct stages and qualitative changes (discontinuity).

Stability and Change. A third controversy concerns the issue of how much a child simply becomes an older version of her or his younger self (stability) and how much a child becomes different with age (change).

Evaluating the Developmental Issues. Most developmentalists recognize that extreme positions on these three issues are unwise. Nonetheless, spirited debate characterizes these issues.

Theory and the Scientific Method. Science is an accumulation of facts held together by theories. Theories, in turn, generate hypotheses that test specific predictions of the theory. The scientific method involves a number of steps: identifying the problem, collecting data, drawing conclusions, and revising the theory.

Collecting Information about Children's Development. All of the following methods for collecting information about children employ systematic observation under controlled conditions. Field studies and naturalistic observation provide information under less controlled conditions than laboratory settings, which allow the most control. Interviews may be informal or structured. Questionnaires resemble structured interviews, but can much more easily be given to large numbers of individuals. A case study allows an in-depth look at a person. Standardized tests compare an individual's characteristics with those of a large group of similar individuals. Cross-cultural research compares children from different cultures or different ethnic minority groups. Physiological research focuses on the biological basis of children's development. Because each method has certain limitations, researchers are most confident with converging conclusions derived from multimeasures, multisources, and multicontexts.

Strategies for Setting Up Research Studies. Correlational strategies are different from experimental strategies. The correlational strategy involves measuring the degree of relation between two variables, such as height and weight; however, causal statements cannot be made from correlational studies. In contrast, the experimental strategy can determine causal relations between variables. In an experiment, an independent variable is manipulated and a dependent variable is measured. Subjects are randomly assigned to receive a given level of the independent variable. For example, one group receives a certain level (experimental group) whereas a second group receives a zero level (control group). Differences between the groups on the dependent variable are attributed to the differences in the levels of the independent variable.

Time Span of Inquiry. Cross-sectional and longitudinal approaches examine the effects of age on behavior. In a cross-sectional study, groups of children in different age ranges are compared at the same time. This is easy and efficient; however, differences may be due to different generations rather than to age alone. In a longitudinal study, a group of same-age children are examined at two or more points in time. Although this consumes much time, this design can detect changes within individuals over time.

Reducing Sexist Research. Developmentalists now recognize that much psychological research has been male-oriented and male-dominated, and have begun to examine children's worlds from the perspectives of girls and women. Recommendations for conducting nonsexist research focus on gender stereotypical assumptions in research methods, appropriate analysis and interpretation of gender differences and similarities, and drawing conclusions appropriate to the scope of the study.

Ethics in Research in Child Development. There are four important ethical standards employed in child development research: (a) informed consent must be obtained from parents or guardians who have a complete description of the procedures to be used with their children. (b) Children have the right to refuse to participate, and the experimenter has an obligation to calm the child if any upset occurs during the procedure. (c) The benefits of the experience for the child must outweigh any chance of harm, and the psychologist must convince a peer review board of this before conducting the research. (d) Children should be treated with courtesy and respect.

6.0 Careers in Child Development

Many opportunities are available to those who want to pursue a career in the broad domain of child development. There is a special interest in involving ethnic minority individuals in the field of child development.

Key Terms

1.0 Images of Children: The Best of Times and the Worst of Times for Today's Children

2.0 Why Study Children?

3.0 Child Development—Today and Yesterday
context
culture
cross-cultural studies
ethnicity
ethnic minority
gender
original sin
tabula rasa
innate goodness
social policy
family policy
generational equity

4.0 The Nature of Development
development
biological processes
cognitive processes
social processes
prenatal period
infancy
early childhood
middle and late childhood
adolescence
maturation
nature-nurture controversy
continuity of development
discontinuity of development
stability-change issue
interaction

5.0 The Science Base of Child Development
theories
hypotheses
scientific method
data
systematic observation
interviews
questionnaires
case study
standardized test
physiological research
multimeasure, multisource, multicontext approach
correlational strategy
correlation coefficient
negative correlation
positive correlation
experimental strategy
experiment
cause and effect
random assignment
experimental group
control group
independent variable
dependent variable
cross-sectional approach
longitudinal approach
sexism
code of ethics
informed consent

6.0 Careers in Child Development
career

Guided Review

1.0 Images of Children

1. The prevalence of computers and drugs in modern society is an example of how this is the _____ _____ _____ of times for today's children.

   best and worst

2. A modern quandary for parents is how to spend _____ with their children and teach _____ to them.

   time
   values

2.0 Why Study Children?

1. The major premise of *Children* is that in order to parent or teach children effectively people need to _____ them.

   understand

2. To understand children is to know how they _____ when they grow and what _____ these changes.

   change
   causes

3.0 Child Development—Today and Yesterday

1. There are many changes in the structure of the family because often _____ parents have careers.

   both

2. Two-worker families bring up concerns over the quality of _____ _____ for their children.

   day care

3. Today we are concerned about reforming _____ to prepare our children for the future.

   schools

4. In order to reform schools effectively we need to understand how children _____, what _____ them, and how to _____ them.

   think
   motivates
   socialize

5. Demographic trends indicate that a major challenge for the immediate future is the increased _____ _____ of American culture.

   ethnic diversity

6. An important point to remember about ethnic groups is that they are comprised of very _____ individuals.

   diverse

7. Besides ethnicity, an important sociocultural variable is _____ _____.

   gender roles

8. Four important sociocultural concepts for the study of child development are _____, _____, _____, and _____.

   contexts, culture, ethnicity, gender

9. The setting in which development occurs is called the _____.

   context

6

10. The _____ _____, _____ _____ _____ of a people make up their culture.

behavior pattern
beliefs and products

11. One way to discover whether aspects of child development are universal is to do _____ _____.

cross-cultural studies

12. Religion and national characteristics are two features of an individual's _____.

ethnicity

13. The term _____ has fallen into disfavor because it implies _____, but developmentalists continue to use it because of its _____ on child development.

minority
inferiority
influence

14. Sex is the _____ aspect of being male or female, whereas _____ refers to the sociocultural aspect.

biological
gender

15. Aries (1962) presented the view that many societies in the past divided development into two periods: _____ and _____. However, this work was based largely on the work of _____, and recent work questions its validity.

infancy, adulthood
artists

16. During the Middle Ages it was generally believed that children were born filled with evil. This is known as the concept of _____ _____. _____ was the goal of child rearing at this time.

original sin, Salvation

17. During the Renaissance two other views appeared. John Locke believed the child's mind at birth is a _____ _____. He proposed the adult mind was constructed from _____.

tabula rasa
experience

18. During the eighteenth century, Rousseau suggested that children are _____ _____. Rousseau cautioned parents to impose no _____ on their children as they grow. He believed children should be allowed to grow _____.

innately good
constraints
naturally

19. Today we think of childhood as a time during which the child requires _____ and _____.

protection, training

20. Child developmentalists are currently doing research on what contributes to children's _____ in order to help shape _____ _____.

welfare
social policy

21. Two important political processes that influence social policy are _____ and _____.

negotiation, compromise

22. _____ shape social policy; a current attempt to express the value of children is the creation of a children's _____ ___ _____.

Values
bill of rights

23. The American public increasingly is concerned about _____ _____ _____ _____ issues.

day-care
and children's health

24. A new idea for improving childcare is to use _____ _____ for after-school childcare.

    public schools

25. An issue in _____ _____ is how to make care for children and the elderly more _____.

    family policy
    equitable

4.0 The Nature of Development

1. The type of process that stems from the genetic composition of the individual is called a _____ process.

    biological

2. The process that involves thinking is called a _____ process. The overall pattern of movement or change that is characteristic of the entire life span is called _____.

    cognitive

    development

3. The process involving social interaction with other individuals is a _____ process.

    social

4. The prenatal period extends from _____ to _____, and infancy extends from _____ to about _____ or _____ months of age.

    conception, birth
    birth, 18, 24

5. The period from the end of infancy to about _____ or _____ years is called early childhood.

    five, six

6. The elementary school years are divided into _____ and _____ childhood. The former extends from _____ to _____ years; the latter extends from _____ to _____ years.

    middle
    late, six
    eight, 8, 11

7. Adolescence is a period of transition from _____ to _____. It begins about _____ to _____ years of age and extends to about _____ years of age.

    childhood, adulthood
    11, 13
    21

8. Modern developmentalists believe that development is a _____ process.

    life-long

9. _____ is the sequence of changes that unfolds from the genetic blueprint. _____ refers to the effects of the environment.

    Maturation
    Experience

10. The debate about how much heredity versus environment influences development is called the _____ _____ issue. Nature refers to _____ and nurture refers to _____.

    nature-nurture
    heredity, environment

11. A part of the continuity versus discontinuity issue is the extent to which later development is dependent on _____ _____.

    earlier development

12. Psychologists who contend that development is a gradual process argue for the _____ of development. Those who argue for discontinuity in development assert that development involves a series of _____.

continuity

stages

13. Another expression of the continuity-discontinuity debate is the _____ _____ issue. Those on the side of continuity argue for _____ in the development, whereas those who argue for _____ assert that change is possible.

stability-change
stability
change

14. Developmentalists generally do not take _____ _____ on the three _____ _____.

extreme positions
developmental issues

15. A key idea in understanding how _____ contribute to development is the concept of interaction.

nature and nurture

5.0 The Science Base of Child Development

1. General beliefs that explain data or facts are called _____. _____ are predictions or guesses about the future that come from theories. Good hypotheses can be _____.

theories
Hypotheses
tested

2. _____ and _____ the problem comprise the first step in the scientific method.

Identifying, analyzing

3. The second step in the scientific method is collecting _____. Data are also called _____.

data
observations

4. Finally, we must draw _____ and revise _____. The former step may involve the use of _____ to aid the decision process.

conclusions, theories
statistics

5. An observation made according to a specific description of what to look for, the identity of the subject, and when and where the observations are to be made is called a _____ _____.

systematic observation

6. A set of questions used in a personal meeting with verbal responses is called a(n) _____. A(n) _____ is similar to a structured interview, but the subject reads the questions and marks the answers on a prepared sheet.

interview, questionnaire

7. An in-depth look at a particular individual is called a _____ _____.

case study

8. A special concern about case studies is to avoid making _____ from them.

overgeneralizations

9. Standardized tests provide a _____ of one child's performance with a large group. The test score frequently is presented as a _____.

comparison

percentile

10. Cross-cultural research helps us to determine to what extent aspects of development are _____ or _____ _____.

universal
culture-specific

11. In order to answer such questions as how hormones are related to juvenile delinquency, investigators use _____ _____.

physiological methods

12. In order to overcome the _____ of specific research methods, researchers may use a _____, _____, or _____ approach.

limitations
multimeasure,
multimethod, multicontext

13. The correlation coefficient is a statistic that measures the strength of the _____ between two variables. A correlation cannot be used to support the argument that a change in one variable _____ a change in another.

association or
relationship
caused

14. If high scores on one variable are associated with high scores on another, and low scores on one are associated with low scores on the other, the correlation coefficient will be _____. If high scores are associated with low scores and vice-versa, the correlation coefficient will be _____.

positive

negative

15. The strength of a relationship is indicated in the _____ of a correlation coefficient. The direction of the relationship is indicated by the _____ of the correlation coefficient.

size

sign

16. The most important advantage of the experimental strategy over the correlational strategy is that it demonstrates a _____ relationship between two variables.

causal

17. The variable manipulated by a researcher who is doing an experiment is called the _____ variable. The researcher measures the effect of this variable on the _____ variable.

independent
dependent

18. _____ _____ _____ _____ is a method used to assure that experimental groups do not differ in any systematic way.

Random assignment to
conditions

19. A cross-sectional study compares children of _____ _____. A longitudinal study examines effects related to age by testing a child at least _____.

different ages

twice

20. A limitation of cross-sectional research is that it provides no information about the _____ of development.

stability

21. A common problem in longitudinal research is that children _____ _____ and the sample becomes _____.

drop out, biased

22. An important problem with much research in child development is that it has been _____.

sexist

23. Three ways in which research has been sexist include _____ _____, _____ _____ _____, and _____ _____ _____ _____ _____ _____ _____.

subject sampling, reporting of results, generalizing from research on only one sex

24. According to the code of ethics of the American Psychological Association, before a child can participate in research the parents must provide _____ _____. The researcher must also have the consent of _____ _____.

informed consent
the child

25. It is essential that researchers weigh the potential _____ to the child against the potential _____.

risk or harm
benefit

26. The research must also adhere to accepted _____ _____ _____ and guard the child's _____.

standards of practice
privacy

6.0 Careers in Child Development

1. Careers in child development are very _____ and can be pursued with differing levels of _____.

diverse
education

2. To become a professor of child psychology one needs a _____; to become a child psychiatrist one needs a(n) _____; to become a school psychologist one needs a _____ _____ or _____.

Ph.D
M.D.
masters degree
D.Ed.

3. A major problem for the field of child psychology is the _____ _____ _____ _____.

underrepresentation of ethnic minorities

4. Ethnic minorities comprise fewer than _____ of the individuals practicing in all of the different careers in child psychology; the most poorly represented minority is _____ _____.

10%

Native Americans

Key Terms Matching Exercise

1. context
2. culture
3. cross-cultural studies
4. ethnicity
5. ethnic minority
6. gender

a. Research that compares or deals with two or more cultures, and identifies differences and similarities in them
b. A potentially objectionable term that refers to individuals with a distinctive cultural heritage, national characteristics, race, religion, or language
c. The social dimensions of being male or female
d. The circumstances or situation in which development occurs
e. Membership in a particular cultural group
f. Refers to the behavior patterns, beliefs, values, and others products that are learned and shared by a group, and that are transmitted from one generation to another

7. original sin
8. tabula rasa
9. innate goodness
10. social policy
11. family policy
12. generational equity

a. Action on the part of national governments that are intended to influence the welfare of its citizens
b. Philosophical view that children are basically evil and that only through the constraints of their upbringing will they become mature adults
c. An aspect of social policy that specifically addresses the welfare of families and family members
d. The view that an aging society is unfair to its younger members because older adults have the advantage of receiving an inequitably large allocation of resources
e. Philosophical view that children are born basically good and should be permitted to grow naturally, without constraints from parents
f. Philosophical view that the child's mind is a blank slate at birth, with experience determining the kind of adult the child becomes

13. development
14. biological processes
15. cognitive processes
16. social processes

a. Processes that include neurological development and growth
b. The period from birth to about 18 or 24 months
c. The period from conception to birth
d. Mental activities such as perception, attention, thought, problem solving, memory, and language

17. prenatal period
    e. A pattern of change or movement that begins at conception and continues through the entire life span

18. infancy
    f. The child's interactions with other individuals in the environment, as well as properties of the individual child such as the self, sex roles, gender identity, and morality

---

19. early childhood
    a. Period of transition from childhood to early adulthood

20. middle and late childhood
    b. Corresponds to the preschool years

21. adolescence
    c. Development is conceptualized as a gradual, cumulative change from conception to death

22. maturation
    d. Debate about whether development is influenced primarily by maturation or experience

23. nature-nurture controversy
    e. Corresponds to the elementary school years

24. continuity of development
    f. The orderly sequence of changes dictated by one's individual genetic blueprint

---

25. discontinuity of development
    a. Degree to which early characteristics of the child are characteristic of the same child at an older age

26. stability-change issue
    b. General beliefs that explain observed data and make predictions

27. interaction
    c. The process of obtaining information by identifying and analyzing the problem, collecting data, drawing conclusions, and revising theories

28. theories
    d. Assumptions that can be tested to determine their accuracy

29. hypotheses
    e. The combination of nature and nurture factors that influence human development

30. scientific method
    f. Development is conceptualized as distinct stages in the life span

---

31. data
    a. A set of questions put to an individual along with the responses

32. systematic observation
    b. A highly structured interview on paper in which a subject reads the question and then marks an answer on a sheet of paper

33. interviews
    c. A test developed to identify an individual's characteristics or abilities relative to those of a large group of similar individuals

34. questionnaires
    d. An in-depth examination of an individual

35. case study
    e. Information obtained about subjects from various research methods

36. standardized test
    f. Observations made according to a specific protocol or set of rules

37.	physiological research	a.	A mathematical measure of the strength of the relationship between two measured variables; it may range from -1.00 to +1.00
38.	multimeasure, multisource, multicontext approach	b.	A design to describe how strongly two or more events or characteristics are related
39.	correlational strategy	c.	A correlation that implies a direct relationship between two variables, such that a low score on one is associated with a low score on the other
40.	correlation coefficient	d.	Method of research that obtains biological measures of development
41.	negative correlation	e.	An approach to testing hypotheses that uses several different measures of behavior or development
42.	positive correlation	f.	A correlation that implies an inverse relationship between two variables, such that a high score on one is associated with a low score on the other

43.	experimental strategy	a.	A controlled context in which the factors that are believed to influence the mind or behavior are controlled or manipulated; causation can be concluded from the results
44.	experiment	b.	The event being manipulated and the behavior that changes because of the manipulation
45.	cause and effect	c.	The group of subjects in an experiment that receives zero level of the independent variable; also the comparison group in an experiment
46.	random assignment	d.	The variable in an experiment that is manipulated by the experimenter
47.	experimental group	e.	Placing subjects into groups by the luck of the draw
48.	control group	f.	This allows determining the causes of behavior precisely
49.	independent variable	g.	The group of subjects in an experiment that gets the independent variable or receives the treatment condition

50.	dependent variable	a.	Discriminating against an individual, particularly a woman, on the basis of sex
51.	cross-sectional approach	b.	The requirement that subjects in psychological and developmental research understand their rights and responsibilities, and the potential benefits and risks of their participation in research
52.	longitudinal approach	c.	One's chosen occupation or profession

53. sexism

54. code of ethics

55. informed consent

56. career

d. The rules or standards that govern psychologists who engage in research

e. A design that tests a single group of individuals of the same age at two or more separate times, and thus at two or more ages

f. The variable in an experiment that is measured

g. A design that compares groups of different children in different age ranges at the same time

Key Terms Matching Exercise
Answer Key

1. d	9. e	17. c	25. f	33. a	41. f	49. d
2. f	10. a	18. b	26. a	34. b	42. c	50. f
3. a	11. c	19. b	27. e	35. d	43. f	51. g
4. e	12. d	20. e	28. b	36. c	44. a	52. e
5. b	13. e	21. a	29. d	37. d	45. b	53. a
6. c	14. a	22. f	30. c	38. e	46. e	54. d
7. b	15. d	23. d	31. e	39. b	47. g	55. b
8. f	16. f	24. c	32. f	40. a	48. c	56. c

Self-Test A

1. Santrock lists all but one of the following as important contemporary concerns in the study of child development except
   a. education.
   b. the family.
   c. sociocultural contexts.
   d. human nature.

2. A developmental psychologist who studies teenagers' beliefs about their lives is studying an aspect of sociocultural influence called
   a. culture.
   b. context.
   c. ethnicity.
   d. cognition.

3. All but one of the following have been offered as criticisms of Aries's conclusions. Which one is the exception?
   a. represent existing perspectives on children
   b. reflect artistic style
   c. represent aristocratic subjects
   d. show an idealization of society

4. According to the text, rich conceptions of children's development
   a. originated in the Renaissance.
   b. date back to ancient Egypt.
   c. developed from interaction between the Greeks and the Romans.
   d. first appeared in the twentieth century.

5. The assumption that the child should be allowed to grow naturally without constraints from the parents is characteristic of which view?
   a. innate goodness
   b. *tabula rasa*
   c. original sin
   d. social learning view

6. The development of the concept of self is part of which process of development?
   a. biological/physical
   b. cognitive
   c. social
   d. maturation

7. The period of development that is characterized by physical changes in cells, and the development of new physical structures is
   a. the prenatal period.
   b. infancy.
   c. early childhood.
   d. adolescence.
8. Sarah is learning how to identify numbers and how to dress herself. She is likely to be in the period of development called
   a. infancy.
   b. early childhood.
   c. middle childhood.
   d. late childhood.
9. Piaget argued that an adult not only has more intelligence than a child, but also has a different kind of intelligence. This illustrates the argument for
   a. the nature-nurture controversy.
   b. the role of experience.
   c. stability of development.
   d. discontinuity in development.
10. General beliefs that explain facts and make predictions are termed
    a. hypotheses.
    b. theories.
    c. predictions.
    d. the scientific method.
11. The purpose of standardized tests is to
    a. gather information that would be unethical to gather experimentally.
    b. determine an individual's standing relative to a large group.
    c. provide an unstructured environment where the child can set the pace.
    d. remove the possibility of receiving socially undesirable responses.
12. An important advantage of the correlation strategy is that
    a. causal statements can be made.
    b. only one variable needs to be measured.
    c. the independent variable can be chosen by the researcher.
    d. variables that cannot be manipulated ethically can be studied.
13. Dr. Chang, a researcher, is interested in physical development. In the fall of 1992, she measured the height of boys and girls in the first, third, and fifth grades in an elementary school in a small town. She found that the oldest children were the tallest group and that the youngest children were the shortest group. The study exemplifies the research strategy called
    a. experimental.
    b. correlational.
    c. cross-sectional.
    d. case study.
14. Which variable in the study described in item 13 is best described as the independent variable?
    a. age
    b. sex
    c. height
    d. school size.
15. Which variable in the study described in item 13 is best described as the dependent variable?
    a. age
    b. sex
    c. height
    d. school size
16. The study described in item 13 is potentially confounded by differences in
    a. school size.
    b. subjects' ages.
    c. the amount of food subjects in the two age groups have eaten.
    d. the contexts in which subjects in the two age groups have grown.
17. One of the advantages of the cross-sectional method is that
    a. true developmental changes can be seen.
    b. cultural effects can be measured.
    c. it is relatively easy to do.
    d. causal statements can be made.
18. All but one of the following are ways that research in child development has been sexist. Which one is the exception?
    a. Gender differences have been exaggerated in research reports.
    b. Studies of one sex have been presented as representative of both sexes.
    c. Men dominate research in the field.
    d. Subject selection in research has been influenced by gender biases.

19. The ethical standards for working with children in psychological research include all of the following except
    a. the parents or guardian must give their consent for children to participate.
    b. a peer review board must review the project.
    c. the child must participate if the parents give consent.
    d. the child should be treated with courtesy and respect.

20. Individuals who want to have a career in child development usually have to
    a. obtain clinical training.
    b. teach children.
    c. undergo analysis of their own development to determine if they are suitable.
    d. do advanced work beyond their undergraduate training.

Self-Test Answers
Test A

1. d	4. b	7. a	10. b	13. c	16. d	19. c
2. a	5. a	8. b	11. b	14. a	17. c	20. d
3. a	6. c	9. d	12. d	15. c	18. c	

Critical Thinking Exercises

Exercise 1

Read the following description of a study that compared memory performances of children and adults:

Do adults remember more than children because they know more about what they are trying to remember? Would children remember more than adults if they knew more than adults did about a topic? These were questions Michelene Chi tried to answer by comparing the memory performances of children and adults with differing levels of knowledge about the information they tried to remember.

Chi asked children from grades three through eight who were experienced chess players to study either ten numbers or the positions of chess pieces in a chess game for ten seconds. The children then tried to remember all the numbers or all the chess positions, after which they viewed the items again for ten seconds. The look-recall cycle continued until the children remembered all the items. Memory performance was measured in two ways: the total number of items remembered on the first trial, and the number of trials that were needed to remember all the items.

Chi compared the children's performances on both tasks to the performances of adults who were novice chess players. The results suggested that knowledge of to-be-remembered material is important to memory. The child chess experts remembered more chess positions and needed fewer trials to achieve perfect recall, than the adult chess novices. On the other hand, adults—who presumably knew more about numbers than the children—outperformed the children in both ways when remembering the numbers (From Chi, M.T.H. (1978). Knowledge structures and memory development. In R.S. Siegler (Ed.), *Children's thinking: What develops?* Hillsdale, NJ: Erlbaum.)

Which of the following sets of terms best describes Chi's research? **Circle the letter of the best answer and explain why it is the best answer and why each other answer is not as good.**

A. cross-sectional, experimental study using interviews
B. longitudinal, correlational study using standardized tests
C. cross-sectional, correlational study using observations
D. longitudinal, experimental study using questionnaires
E. cross-sectional, experimental study using multiple measures

17

Exercise 2

In the introduction to Chapter 1 of your text, Santrock describes some contemporary concerns in the study of child development. These concerns reflect a larger emphasis on one of the following determinants or aspects of development than on the others. Which one is it? **Circle the letter of the best answer and explain why it is the best answer and why each other answer is not as good.**

A. cognitive processes
B. nurture
C. maturation
D. discontinuity
E. change

Exercise 3

Turn to Chapter 1 and read the first two paragraphs in the section titled "Sociocultural Contexts." This discussion about cultural diversity in the United States contains a number of observations, assumptions, and inferences. Which of the following statements constitutes an assumption rather than an inference or an observation? **Circle the letter of the best answer and explain why it is the best answer and why each other answer is not as good.**

A. Ethnic minority groups comprise 20% of the children and adolescents under the age of 17 in the United States.
B. There will be difficulties in the year 2000 because the balance of ethnicities will change.
C. Not all Hispanic children are Catholic.
D. Teachers and administrators in today's schools are not as sensitive as they should be to ethnic differences.
E. Knowing about different ethnicities will make teachers more sensitive to minority group members.

Research Project 1 Playground Observation of Social Interaction

This exercise has two purposes: (a) it teaches you to look at children, and (b) it introduces you to the process of systematic observation.

Go to a local playground or park with a classmate. Choose two children of the same sex (that is, either two girls or two boys). The first child should be three or four years old; the second child should be eight or nine years old. One of you should observe each child for five minutes while the other records the observations.

Observe the amount of social interaction in which the children engage. For each 30 seconds of the five minutes, record whether or not the child you are observing interacts with another person and whether that person is a child (C) or an adult (A). Use the following data sheet to record your observations. Then answer the questions that follow.

DATA SHEET

Time (seconds)	Child 1 (three to four years) SEX ___ AGE ___			Child 2 (eight to nine years) SEX ___ AGE ___		
0–30	0	C	A	0	C	A
31–60	0	C	A	0	C	A
61–90	0	C	A	0	C	A
91–120	0	C	A	0	C	A
121–150	0	C	A	0	C	A
151–180	0	C	A	0	C	A
181–210	0	C	A	0	C	A
211–240	0	C	A	0	C	A
241–270	0	C	A	0	C	A
271–300	0	C	A	0	C	A

Circle: 0 = No Social Interaction
C = Interacts with Child
A = Interacts with Adult

Questions

1. During how many time slots (from 0 to 10) did Child 1 (age three or four) interact with only a child? With only an adult? With both a child and an adult? With neither a child nor an adult?
2. During how many time slots (from 0 to 10) did Child 2 (age eight or nine) interact with only a child? With only an adult? With both a child and an adult? With neither a child nor an adult?
3. Are there any differences between the total number of intervals in which social interaction occurred for Child 1 and for Child 2? What is the nature of this difference (that is, who interacted more)?
4. Which child interacted more often with other children? Which child interacted more often with adults? Which child interacted more overall? (Your comparisons should be based only on the number of intervals in which an interaction occurred, not on your memory of the length of the interaction, which was not directly measured.)
5. What do you think is the explanation for the differences you found? Could any factors other than age account for the difference? Why were you instructed to observe two children of the same sex?

Research Project 2 Journal Article Critique

Part of conducting psychological research is reviewing and understanding published research studies. In this research project, you will choose one of the topics that will be covered in this course (e.g., play, gender roles, moral development, effects of television) and find a research report in a journal (e.g., *Adolescence, Journal of Developmental Psychology, Child Development, Family Therapy, Journal of Marriage and the Family*) on the chosen topic. Read the article and write a report about the article. Enclose a copy of the first page of the research article (include the abstract which briefly summarizes the entire research study) with your report. In addition to including the main points of the study, give your personal reactions to the research findings.

Questions

1. Can you use the title of the study to identify the independent and dependent variables? (Many titles are in this format: "The effects of IV on the DV.")
2. What did you learn from the introduction section? What is the historical background of the research topic? Which earlier research findings are given as most relevant to this study? What theoretical explanations are emphasized in this section? What is the hypothesis of the present study?
3. What did you learn from the methods section? Who were the subjects? What procedures (e.g., apparatus, directions, assessment tools) were used?
4. What did you learn from the results section? What kinds of statistical procedures were used? What did you learn from charts, frequency tables, and bar graphs? What results did the authors say were statistically significant?
5. What did you learn from the discussion section? How did the authors interpret their results? Did they provide alternative explanations? Did they talk about the limitations of the present research study? What future research studies were suggested?
6. What kinds of ideas did this article make you think about? Can you design a similar study on this topic?

Essay and Critical Thinking Questions

Comprehension and Application Essay Questions

We recommend that you follow either our guidelines for answering essay and critical thinking questions, or those guidelines provided by your instructor, in preparing your response. Your answers to the following ten questions demonstrate an ability to comprehend and think critically about concepts and topics discussed in this chapter.

1. Define and describe each of the three contemporary concerns for present-day child developmentalists (i.e., family issues, educational reform, and sociocultural issues).
2. What do you believe is the most important social policy issue involving children today? How would you persuade the government to improve children's lives related to this particular issue?
3. Describe each of the three historical, philosophical views about the nature of the child (i.e., tabula rasa, original sin, and innate goodness). Also explain how belief in each view might affect how or what a child developmentalist studies.
4. Provide illustrative examples as you explain what it means to ask whether the changes that appear during development take place gradually or in stages.
5. What is science? How does a scientific understanding of child development differ from an understanding produced by ordinary, everyday experiences with children?
6. Discuss important considerations that would influence your selection of a method from among the seven methods for scientifically collecting data about child development?
7. What are the strengths and weaknesses of the cross-sectional and longitudinal approaches to research? In what ways do cross-sectional and longitudinal designs differ from experimental strategies? What kinds of conclusions can be drawn from each? What do you gain and lose by using a correlational rather than experimental strategy in research?
8. Explain how research on children can be sexist. Also discuss ways to reduce sexism in child development research.
9. What precautions must be taken to safeguard the rights and welfare of a child who might be a psychological subject? In your answer, relate each precaution to a specific ethical concern. In addition, discuss at least two examples of other types of subjects who pose similar ethical difficulties for researchers.
10. Indicate your own abilities and interests, and then discuss the career in child development most suitable for you. Also discuss what factors will encourage or discourage you from pursuing this career.

Critical Thinking Questions

Your answers to the following kinds of questions reflect an ability to apply your critical thinking skills to a novel problem or situation that is *not* specifically discussed in this chapter.

1. At the end of Chapter 1, Santrock concludes that we need more individuals from ethnic minorities in the field of child development. Apply your knowledge about the scientific base of child development by designing a study to determine how ethnic affiliation affects the past, present, and/or future of child development: (a) What specific problem or question do you want to study? (b) What predictions would you make and test in your study? (c) What measures would you use (i.e., observation, interviews and questionnaires, case studies, standardized tests, physiological research, or multimeasure, multisource, and multicontext approaches) and how would you define each measure clearly and unambiguously? (d) What strategy would you follow—experimental or correlational, and what would be the time span of your inquiry—

cross-sectional or longitudinal? (e) What ethical considerations must be addressed before you conduct your study?

2. According to Chapter 1, five issues define the nature of development: (a) biological, cognitive, and social processes, (b) periods or stages, (c) the issue of maturation (nature) versus experience (nurture), (d) the issue of continuity versus discontinuity, and (e) the issue of stability versus change. Indicate your ability to think critically by (a) perusing your textbook for two examples of each of the five defining issues and (b) explaining how and why each of your examples illustrates one of the five defining issues.

3. One aspect of thinking critically is to read, listen, and observe carefully, and then ask questions about what is missing from a text, discussion, or situation. Fore example, one approach to writing a textbook is to study all of the different characteristics of successive developmental periods (e.g., infancy, early childhood, middle/late childhood, and adolescence). An alternative strategy is to study one particular aspect of development (e.g., body weight, cognition, or social interaction) chronologically from infancy through adolescence. Indicate your ability to think critically by (a) perusing your textbook to identify Santrock's approach, and (b) evaluating the pros and cons of what you would learn from each approach.

4. Santrock places several quotations in the margins of this chapter. One by Arthur Conan Doyle says, "Truth is arrived at by the painstaking process of eliminating the untrue." Another by Thomas Henry Huxley says "The chess-board is the world. The pieces are the phenomena of the universe. The rules of the game are what we call laws of nature." Indicate your ability to think critically by selecting one of the quotes and (a) learning about the author and indicating why this individual is eminently quotable (i.e., what was this individual's contribution to human knowledge and understanding), (b) interpreting and restating the quote in your own terms, and (c) explaining what concept, issue, perspective, or term in this chapter Santrock intended this quote to illuminate. In other words, about what aspect of issue in development does this quote make you pause and think reflectively?

Self-Test B

1. The fact that today's schools have powerful teaching tools and teach about topics such as AIDS illustrates that
    a. education is an important contemporary concern in child psychology.
    b. there are strong media effects on today's education.
    c. we need to return to traditional methods of education.
    d. it is the best of times and the worst of times for children.

2. An individual's national characteristics, race, religion, and language define her
    a. ethnicity.
    b. culture.
    c. sociocultural context.
    d. generation

3. The assumption that the child is a blank slate affected by experience is characteristic of which view?
    a. innate goodness
    b. *tabula rasa*
    c. original sin
    d. cognitive view

4. The assumption that nature is important in development is characteristic of which view?
    a. innate goodness
    b. *tabula rasa*
    c. social view
    d. learning

5. Attention is considered a part of the process of development called
    a. biological/physical.
    b. cognitive.
    c. social.
    d. philosophical.

6. Interactions with other people are part of the process of development called
   a. biological/physical.
   b. cognitive.
   c. social.
   d. reflexive.
7. Roberta is currently learning to write in cursive, do long division, and play the viola. She is likely to be in the stage of childhood called
   a. early childhood.
   b. middle childhood.
   c. pubescence.
   d. adolescence.
8. Which issue focuses on the extent to which early experiences influence an individual's behavior in later life?
   a. qualitative versus quantitative changes
   b. stages
   c. individual differences in development
   d. continuity versus discontinuity in development
9. The question of how much development is due to heredity and how much is due to environment is a component of which of the following debates?
   a. whether or not there are stages in development
   b. nature/nurture controversy
   c. continuity/discontinuity issue
   d. whether development is qualitative or quantitative
10. Systematic observation of children involves all of the following except
   a. changing what we observe from one moment to the next.
   b. knowing whom we are to observe.
   c. knowing when and where we are to observe.
   d. knowing how we will record our observations.
11. The purpose of an experiment is to
   a. gather information that would be unethical to get with systematic observation.
   b. determine an individual's standing relative to a large group.
   c. provide an unstructured environment where the child can set the pace.
   d. allow the determination of causal relations between variables.

12. An important advantage of the correlational method is that
   a. causal statements can be made from correlational data.
   b. variables that cannot be manipulated can be studied.
   c. it is the only way several different variables can be manipulated.
   d. the independent variable is assigned by the researcher.
13. Dr. Robin, a researcher, was interested in language development. In the fall of 1991 he measured the vocabulary of 12 two-year-old boys and girls in a small town. He measured their vocabulary again in the fall of 1992 when they were three. He found that the children's vocabulary had more than doubled. This study was an example of a research strategy called
   a. experimental.
   b. longitudinal.
   c. cross-sectional.
   d. case study.
14. The variable in the study described in item 13 that could best be called an independent variable was
   a. age.
   b. sex.
   c. vocabulary.
   d. town size.
15. The variable in the study described in item 13 that could best be called a dependent variable was
   a. age.
   b. sex.
   c. vocabulary.
   d. town size.
16. The study described in item 13 used a method called a(n)
   a. interview.
   b. case study.
   c. questionnaire.
   d. behavioral observation.
17. One of the advantages of the longitudinal method is that
   a. true developmental differences can be seen.
   b. sociocultural influences can be controlled.
   c. it is efficient to do.
   d. causal statements can be made.

24

18. A psychologist reports in her research that "... only 36 percent of boys had difficulty throwing a ball, but as many as 40 percent of girls had serious difficulty." What criticism would contemporary researchers make of this report?
   a. It is not representative of today's boys and girls.
   b. The work is unethical because it compares girls and boys.
   c. The report is sexist.
   d. These findings will hurt sport programs for girls.

19. The ethical standards for working with children in psychological research include which one of the following?
   a. The parents or guardian must give their consent.
   b. If the research question is important it should be done regardless of potential harm to the child.
   c. The child must participate if the parents give consent.
   d. Responsible psychologists are not required to present their research to a peer review board.

20. An unusual feature of training for a career in child development is that it
   a. prepares individuals for adult life.
   b. leads individuals into a narrow selection of specialties.
   c. places individuals in a field well-represented by diverse minorities.
   d. is relatively short for professional training.

Self-Test Answers
Test B

1. d	4. a	7. b	10. a	13. b	16. d	19. b
2. a	5. b	8. d	11. d	14. a	17. a	20. a
3. b	6. c	9. b	12. b	15. c	18. c	

Objectives

1.0 *Images of Children: Piaget and Erikson as Children*
1.1 Explain how one's experience might influence one's view of child development.
1.2 Justify the study of different theories of child development.

2.0 *Psychoanalytic Theories*
2.1 Identify the basic assumptions of psychoanalytic theory.
2.2 Define and distinguish among Freud's personality structures, and explain how each operates individually and how they function collectively.
2.3 Define the concept of a defense mechanism, and list six examples.
2.4 Define and distinguish among Freud's five stages of psychosexual development, and explain how conflicts at each stage contribute to the adult personality.
2.5 Summarize the sociocultural (culture- and gender-based) criticisms of Freud's theory.
2.6 Explain why Erikson formulated an alternative to Freud's psychoanalytic theory.
2.7 Compare and contrast Freud's and Erikson's theories.
2.8 Define and distinguish among Erikson's eight stages of psychosocial development and explain how crises at each stage contribute to the adult personality.
2.9 Evaluate psychoanalytic theories.

3.0 *Cognitive Theories*
3.1 Identify the basic assumptions of cognitive theory.
3.2 Define and distinguish between organization and adaptation, and between assimilation and accommodation.
3.3 Define and distinguish among Piaget's four stages of cognitive development.
3.4 Compare and contrast Piaget's cognitive theory with psychoanalytic theories.
3.5 Diagram the operations of a human mind according to information processing theory.
3.6 Explain the computer metaphor for information processing.
3.7 Identify questions about development raised by information processing theory.
3.8 Compare and contrast Piaget's theory and information processing theory.
3.9 Evaluate cognitive theories.

4.0 *Behavioral and Social Learning Theories*
4.1 Identify the basic assumptions of behavioral and social learning theories.
4.2 Define and distinguish among behavioral concepts such as operant conditioning, contingency, reinforcement, and punishment.
4.3 Explain why Bandura and Mischel developed an alternative to behavioral theory.
4.4 Define and distinguish among such key concepts in Bandura's and Mischel's social learning theory as behavior, cognition, and environment.
4.5 Evaluate behavioral and social learning theories.
4.6 Compare and contrast behavioral and social learning theories with one another and with psychoanalytic and cognitive theories.

5.0 *Phenomenological and Humanistic Theories*
5.1 Identify the basic assumptions of phenomenological and humanistic theories.
5.2 Define and distinguish key concepts in Roger's theory such as self-concept, unconditional positive regard, empathy, and genuineness.

Summary

1.0 Images of Children: Piaget and Erikson as Children

The life experiences of developmental theorists influence what aspects of development interest them and the methods of study they use. Erik Erikson's struggle to understand himself is reflected by his theory about the psychosocial stages of development. Jean Piaget's intellectual training and interest in the normal intellect is reflected by his theory about the stages of cognitive development. Each alternative theory of development contributes something to the understanding of children.

2.0 Psychoanalytic Theories

Psychoanalytic theory is a view of personality that emphasizes biological forces and the symbolic transformation of experience and the private, unconscious aspects of a person's mind.

Freud's Theory. Freud proposed a psychoanalytic model with three structures. The *id,* the source of psychic energy, is composed of unconscious sexual and aggressive instincts. It operates to maximize pleasure and avoid pain in accord with the pleasure principle. The *ego* is concerned with reality and operates according to the reality principle, which attempts to satisfy the pleasure needs of the id within the boundaries of reality. The ego is also seen as the seat of reason and logical thinking. The *superego* is the moral branch of the personality that arises through interactions with parents. Conflicts arise when the ego must balance the demands of the id and the requirements of the superego. The ego reduces conflicts with the id through the use of defense mechanisms, which express the desires of the id in disguised fashions. Defense mechanisms include repression, displacement, projection, sublimation, reaction formation, and regression.

Freud indicated that different areas of the body (i.e., erogenous zones) comprise the seat of pleasure at the different stages of development. Fixation can occur when a person does not pass from one stage into another, through under- or overgratification at that stage. In the oral stage, the mouth is the region of maximum pleasure. In the anal stage, the anus is the region of maximum pleasure. During the phallic stage, the child focuses on the genital region and experiences feelings of desire for the opposite-sex parent. During the latency stage, the child represses sexual feelings. The final psychosexual stage begins with the onset of puberty and is called the genital period. During this period, sexual interest is reawakened.

Erikson's Theory. Erikson's theory incorporates aspects of Freud's theory but sees development as psychosocial rather than psychosexual, and continuous throughout the life span. Erikson's stages are (a) trust versus mistrust, (b) autonomy versus shame and doubt, (c) initiative versus guilt, (d) industry versus inferiority, (e) identity versus identity confusion (diffusion), (f) intimacy versus isolation, (g) generativity versus stagnation, and (h) ego integrity versus despair.

Evaluating Psychoanalytic Theories. Strengths of the psychoanalytic approach include (a) emphasis on roles of the past, (b) discussion of the developmental course of personality, (c) the role of mental representation of the environment, (d) the role of the unconscious mind, (e) the emphasis on conflict, and (f) its influence on developmental psychology as a discipline. Weaknesses of the psychoanalytic approach include (a) difficulty in testing the concepts, (b) a lack of empirical evidence and reliance on self-reports of the past, (c) overemphasis on the unconscious mind and sexuality, (d) a negative and pessimistic view of human nature, and (e) too much emphasis on early experience. Recently, both culture- and gender-based criticism of Freud's theory have been made.

3.0 Cognitive Theories

Piaget's Theory. Jean Piaget was interested in zoology, and later in philosophy and psychology. His theory about the development of thought in children is biologically based, broad in scope, and has changed the course of developmental psychology.

Organization and adaptation are important concepts in Piaget's theory. Adaptation occurs through the dual processes of assimilation and accommodation. Assimilation occurs when a current cognitive structure is used to understand some aspect of the world, whereas accommodation occurs when a new feature of the environment is incorporated into a structure by modifying the structure. Cognition is qualitatively different at each stage of development.

There are four stages of cognitive development in Piaget's theory. *Infancy* comprises the sensorimotor stage when thought is characterized by sensory and perceptual processes and action. Thought is not symbolic. By the end of this stage, the ability to use simple symbols develops. During Piaget's *preoperational period,* stable concepts are formed, mental reasoning emerges, magical belief systems are constructed, and egocentrism is perceptually based. Piaget's *concrete operational period* extends from about seven years of age to the beginning of adolescence (approximately age 11). During this period, thought is characterized as reversible and decentered, but is limited to reasoning about the concrete world as it is. Thought is made up of operations, which are mental actions or representations that are reversible. The last stage of Piaget's theory is called *formal operational thought,* which appears in adolescents and adults. It is characterized by abstractness, hypothetical-deductive reasoning, and idealism. Thought is no longer limited to the real and concrete but can be applied to possibilities and to abstract propositions.

Information Processing Theory. The information processing perspective is concerned with how people process information about their world. The computer metaphor is used as an attempt to understand human cognition. One possibility is that processing speed increases with development. This change might be biological in origin, or might reflect differences in knowledge.

Key Terms

1.0 Images of Children: Piaget and Erikson as Children

2.0 Psychoanalytic Theories
unconscious
id
pleasure principle
ego
reality principle
superego
defense mechanism
displacement
projection
repression
sublimation
reaction formation
regression
erogenous zones
fixation
oral stage
anal stage
phallic stage
phallus
Oedipus complex
penis envy
latency stage
genital stage
psychosocial stages
psychosexual stages
epigenetic principle
trust versus mistrust
autonomy versus shame and doubt
initiative versus guilt
industry versus inferiority
identity versus identity confusion (diffusion)
intimacy versus isolation
generativity versus stagnation
integrity versus despair

3.0 Cognitive Theories
cognitive activity
organization
adaptation
assimilation
accommodation
sensorimotor stage
preoperational stage
operations
concrete operational stage

formal operational stage
information processing

4.0 Behavioral and Social Learning Theories
behaviorism
operants
contingent
consequences
operant (instrumental) conditioning
reinforcement
punishment
probability
social learning theory
observational learning

5.0 Phenomenological and Humanistic Theories
phenomenological theories
humanistic theories
self-concept
real versus ideal self
unconditional positive regard
empathic
genuine

6.0 Ethological Theories
ethology
imprinting
critical period
neo-ethological theory
sensitive period

7.0 Ecological Theory
ecological theory
microsystem
mesosystem
exosystem
macrosystem
culture
cross-cultural studies
chronosystem

8.0 An Eclectic Theoretical Orientation
eclectic theoretical orientation

Evaluating the Phenomenological and Humanistic Theories. The strengths of the phenomenological and humanistic theories include: (a) sensitizing us to the importance of self-perception in development, (b) reminding us to value the whole child, and (c) focusing on the child's positive nature. The weaknesses include: (a) difficulty testing the concepts empirically, (b) focusing on clinical interpretation rather than empirical research, (c) an overestimation of human freedom and rationality, and (d) being inclined to encourage self-love.

6.0 Ethological Theories

Ethologists focus on the evolutionary and biological determinants of behavior.

Lorenz's Classical Ethological Theory. Lorenz studied imprinting in greylag geese. The concept of critical periods in development indicates that there are times in development during which an organism must encounter specific experiences in order for certain behaviors to develop. Ethologists consider the development of behavior in terms of the ultimate developmental course (i.e., its evolutionary basis) and in terms of the functions of the behavior at the time it appears.

Hinde's Neo-Ethological Theory. Modern ethologists suggest that the term *sensitive period* may be more accurate in describing development than the term *critical period.* More recently, Hinde has applied an ethological approach to the study of human social behavior and personality.

Evaluating the Ethological Theories. The strengths of ethological theories include: (a) emphasis on the evolutionary basis of behavior, (b) the use of observation in naturalistic surroundings, (c) the belief that development involves some long, sensitive periods, and (d) an emphasis on the functional importance of behavior. Weaknesses include: (a) an overemphasis on sensitive periods, (b) a lack of consideration for the interaction between biology and environment, and (c) difficulty testing ideas generated by the theory.

7.0 Ecological Theory

Ecological theory is a sociocultural view of development.

Environmental Systems. Socialization involves transactions between a changing child and a changing social environment. The analysis of sociocultural influences include the microsystem (the setting in which an individual lives), mesosystem, exosystem, macrosystem, and chronosystem. These different levels help understand the various cultural contexts in which the child develops. Different societies view development differently.

Evaluating Ecological Theory. The strength of ecological theory is its comprehensive nature. Its major weakness is a lack of consideration for both biological and cognitive processes in development.

8.0 An Eclectic Theoretical Orientation

An eclectic orientation emphasizes the complexity of the developing person. This view proposes that there is no single theoretical orientation that explains all of development and advocates that one should be familiar with multiple perspectives and their most useful contribution to understanding children.

Evaluating the Cognitive Theories. Both Piaget's and the information processing approach have several strengths: (a) many of Piaget's ideas are useful, and (b) the information processing perspective provides a strong research orientation for studying children's cognition, and a precision in conceptualizing children's thought. Cognitive theories have been criticized because: (a) stages do not seem to exist empirically in the behavior of the child as they are discussed in Piaget's theory, (b) some of the concepts in Piaget's theory, while apparently powerful, are difficult to operationalize (e.g., assimilation), (c) the information processing approach has not produced an overall perspective on development, and (d) both views underestimate the role of the unconscious mind and experience in the environment.

4.0 Behavioral and Social Learning Theories

Behaviorists focus on those things that can be directly observed in the environment rather than on unconscious processes.

Skinner's Behaviorism. Skinner was a major proponent of behaviorism, the science of observable behavior and environmental causes. His theory of operant conditioning indicates that behavior (i.e., an operant response) is influenced by consequences produced by the environment. Consequences that increase the frequency of a behavior are called reinforcement, and consequences that reduce the frequency of a behavior are called punishment.

Social Learning Theory. Bandura and Mischel developed social learning theory, which proposes that learning occurs through imitation and modeling as well as through reinforcement, and that attention and memory (i.e., aspects of cognition) are important components in learning as well. Observational learning may be detected in the way in which children watch and repeat the behavior of their parents.

Evaluating the Behavioral and Social Learning Theories. Strengths of behavioral and social learning theories include: (a) an emphasis on environmental stimuli, (b) the contribution of the observational method to study development, (c) the application of a rigorous experimental approach to development, and (d) the view that children acquire the ability to control their behavior and their social world. Weaknesses include (a) being too concerned with situational influences on children's development, (b) not being focused enough on biological processes in development, (c) being too reductionistic and mechanical, and (d) in the behavioral view, a suggestion that cognitive processes are irrelevant for understanding development.

5.0 Phenomenological and Humanistic Theories

Phenomenological theories focus on the importance of children's perception of themselves and their world in understanding their development. Humanistic theories stress individual capacities for personal growth and self-determination, and comprise a positive view of people.

Roger's Humanistic Approach. Rogers proposed that individuals need to accept their own true feelings, which are innately positive. Most individuals receive only conditional regard from others, receiving love and respect only when they conform to the expectations of others. Rogers argues that the best way for a person to improve their feelings of self-worth is to receive unconditional positive regard, being valued for what one is, not for what one does. The real self and the ideal self must be congruent for the individual to be well adjusted.

Guided Review

1.0 Images of Children

1. Aside from formal training, an important influence on people's theories of child development is their _____ _____.

   life experience

2. Erikson's personal search for _____ probably influenced his psychoanalytic theory, whereas Piaget's _____ _____ probably motivated his cognitive developmental theory.

   self
   intellectual experiences

3. A _____ is a set of concepts and propositions to explain something.

   theory

2.0 Psychoanalytic Theories

1. _____ theories present a view of personality that emphasizes the unconscious aspects of a person's mind as its dominant feature.

   Psychoanalytic

2. The personality structure present at birth is a mass of sexual and aggressive instincts called the _____. Freud took the philosophical position that people are born basically _____.

   id
   selfish

3. According to Freud, the id works according to the _____ _____. It is completely _____.

   pleasure principle
   unconscious

4. The part of the personality that develops to deal with reality is the _____. Its functioning obeys the _____ _____. The ego houses the _____ mental functions.

   ego, reality principle
   higher

5. The part of the personality that deals with moral issues is the _____. It develops through interactions with _____.

   superego, parents

6. According to Freud, _____ is a dominant theme in the functioning of the personality. One way in which the ego reduces conflict is by using _____ _____.

   conflict

   defense mechanisms

7. Taking one's angry or hostile feelings out on someone or something that did not cause those feelings is called _____.

   displacement

8. Claiming that someone else has one's own undesirable characteristics is called _____.

   projection

9. According to Freud the most powerful defense mechanism is _____.

   repression

10. According to Freud, each stage of development is marked by parts of the body that give especially strong pleasure when stimulated. These are called _____ _____.

    erogenous zones

11. If the ego substitutes a socially useful activity for a distasteful one, that is called _____. If the ego makes conscious the opposite of repressed thought, that is called _____ _____. If the ego forces the person back to an earlier stage of development, that is called _____.

sublimation
reaction formation

regression

12. The part of the superego in which moral inhibitions are reflected is _____. The part that holds the image of perfect behavior is called the _____ _____. Freud believed moral behavior is largely the result of feelings of _____ wielded by the superego.

conscience
ego ideal
guilt

13. Freud's theory of personality development is a _____ theory. When conflicts are not resolved at a particular stage, _____ occurs.

stage
fixation

14. The stage during which all activity centers around pleasures of the mouth is called the _____ stage. The stage during which all pleasure comes from the control of elimination functions is called the _____ stage.

oral

anal

15. During the phallic stage the focus is on the child's _____. One of the major themes during the phallic stage is _____ with the same sex parent.

genitals
identification

16. During the phallic period boys have a sexual desire for the mother and feel rivalry with and fear of the father. This is called the _____ _____. Unresolved aspects of these feelings are repressed and this repression marks the beginning of the _____ _____.

Oedipus complex
latency stage

17. Puberty marks the beginning of the _____ _____.

genital stage

18. For Erikson, _____ was not seen as the all pervasive underlying force behind personality that Freud believed it to be. Further, Erikson _____ the importance of the first five years of life to personality formation.

sexuality

deemphasized

19. Erikson believed that the _____ _____ guides development.

epigenetic principle

20. For Erikson, the infant who develops a feeling that the world is predictable and that caregivers can be relied on develops a feeling of _____. Lacking this, a sense of _____ develops.

trust, mistrust

21. The second stage in Erikson's theory is called _____ _____ _____ _____ _____. It corresponds to Freud's _____ _____.

autonomy versus shame and doubt
anal stage

22. If children discover ways of coping with feelings of helplessness they will develop healthy feelings of being the _____ of action. Otherwise a sense of _____ may develop. This corresponds to what Freud called the _____ _____.

initiators
guilt
phallic stage

23. The feeling that children develop from positive comparisons of self with peers is called _____. If the comparison is not favorable the result is feelings of _____. This corresponds to the _____ _____ of Freud's theory.

industry
inferiority
latency stage

24. The positive resolution of a stable self-image is called _____. Failure to resolve self-image is called _____ _____.

identity
identity confusion

25. The first post-Freudian stage is _____ _____ _____. It reflects a young adult's formation of an _____ relationship.

intimacy versus isolation
intimate

26. The central issue of _____ is helping the next generation. The absence of this is called _____.

generativity
stagnation

27. Resolving each of the previous seven crises in a positive way results in satisfaction with life. Erikson calls this satisfaction _____ _____. If one or more of the previous crises has been resolved in a negative way, _____ may result.

ego integrity
despair

28. Psychoanalysis directed attention to the _____ as an important influence on an individual's current thought and behavior. Freud's interest in the stages of personality formation indicated a _____ perspective. Psychoanalysis introduced the idea that experiences can be _____ transformed. Psychoanalysis developed the concept of the _____, a part of the mind not accessible to thought. Psychoanalytic theory promoted the view that _____ is an important part of adjustment.

past

developmental
mentally
unconscious

conflict

29. A problem with psychoanalytic concepts is that they have been difficult to _____ _____. Also, evidence for the theory depends too much on patients' _____.

test scientifically
memories

3.0 Cognitive Theories

1. The father of the field of cognitive development was _____ _____.

Jean Piaget

2. For Piaget, the two basic processes underlying a child's construction of the world are _____ _____ _____. Adaptation is composed of _____, or incorporating new information into old mental structures, and _____, changing old mental structures to accept new information. Changes in thought are characterized as _____ _____.

adaptation and
organization, assimilation
accommodation

qualitatively different

3. Pretending that a cup in the bath is a boat is an example of
_____. Understanding that the thing indicated by the word *cup*
may have many different shapes is an example of _____.

assimilation
accommodation

4. According to Piaget, the newborn is in the _____ _____.
During this period the infant develops an ability to organize and
coordinate _____ _____ _____.

sensorimotor period

sensations and actions

5. The preoperational period lasts from _____ to _____
years of age. During this time _____ _____ expands but
children cannot perform _____.

two, seven
symbolic thought
operations

6. The concrete operational period lasts from _____ to _____
years of age. The child becomes able to _____ _____ a
series of actions. The concrete operational thinker is restricted to
reasoning about things that are _____.

7, 11
mentally reverse

perceivable

7. Formal operational thinking is _____. Formal operational
thinkers become interested in _____. Their thinking becomes
more systematic and they can generate _____ to test.

abstract
ideals
hypotheses

8. Those who take the information processing approach compare the
human mind to a _____.

computer

9. In the information processing approach, the physical brain is
analogous to a computer's _____, and cognition is analogous
to a computer's _____.

hardware
software

10. One developmental difference postulated in the information
processing approach is _____ _____ _____.

speed of processing

11. Piaget's theory directed research toward children's _____. The
information processing approach provided a _____ _____
atmosphere for the study of children's cognitions. In comparison
to Piaget's concepts, information processing concepts were
_____.

thoughts
research-oriented

precise

12. There is skepticism about Piaget's claim that cognition develops by
_____. Some of Piaget's concepts are _____ defined.
However, information processing theory has not produced an
overall perspective on _____. Both may have underestimated
the importance of _____ and the _____ _____ in
determining behavior.

stages, poorly

development
environment, unconscious
mind

4.0 Behavioral and Social Learning Theories

1. The behavioral perspective emphasizes the influence of the
_____. Children's behavior is said to be _____.

environment, learned

2. One of the most important figures in the development of modern behaviorism is _____ _____. He called actively emitted behaviors _____ and believed that consequences that are _____ on behavior affect the likelihood that the behavior will be repeated.

B.F. Skinner
operants
contingent

3. Skinner's type of learning is called _____ _____. Skinner believed that behavior is determined by _____ _____. A positive consequence is called _____. A negative consequence is called _____.

operant conditioning
environmental
consequences,
reinforcement
punishment

4. Bandura's view of learning is called _____ _____ _____. Bandura argues that behavior, environment, and _____ are factors in child development.

social learning theory
cognition

5. Both the behavioral and the social learning approaches have emphasized the role of _____ in determining behavior. They have emphasized use of the _____ to do research. The social learning approach has underscored the importance of _____ _____.

environment
experiment
cognitive processes

6. A criticism of the behavioral approach that does not apply to the social learning approach is failure to include _____ in explaining the children's behavior.

cognition

7. Both the behavioral and the social learning theory are said to focus too much on _____ and not enough on _____.

change, stability

8. A criticism of behavioral and social learning theories made by humanistic psychologists is that they ignore human _____ _____ _____.

spontaneity
and creativity

5.0 Phenomenological and Humanistic Theories

1. _____ theories stress the importance of the child's perception of the self in understanding child development. Phenomenological theories that stress the importance of self-perceptions, inner experiences, self-determination, and self-confidence are _____ theories.

Phenomenological

humanistic

2. What the child needs to develop self-worth is _____ _____ _____. This can be provided in a _____ _____.

unconditional positive
regard, therapeutic
relationship

3. Humanistic theories have sensitized us to the importance of _____ _____. One of their weaknesses, however, is that they are difficult to _____.

conscious experience
test

6.0 Ethological Theories

1. Ethologists stress the importance of _____ determinants of behavior. They emphasize the importance of the ____ ____ of a particular behavior in order to understand _____.

   biological
   survival value
   evolution

2. Lorenz showed that the following response of greylag goslings was determined by _____ _____ rather than _____. This phenomenon is called _____.

   early experience, instinct
   imprinting

3. A fixed time period in development during which a behavior must emerge is called a _____ _____.

   critical period

4. According to the ethological perspective, _____ must be carefully described and classified. Second, the _____ value of a behavior at its point of development must be considered.

   behaviors
   adaptive

5. The answer to the first question that ethologists ask requires _____. Ethologists prefer to work in _____ _____ rather than _____.

   description, natural
   settings
   laboratories

6. Ethologists argue that we should try to understand a behavior in terms of its _____ for the stage of development in which it is found.

   function

7. Hinde distinguished between _____ and _____ periods. He and other ethologists now believe that the former may be too rigid. The sensitive period is a time in development when a particular effect can be produced _____ _____.

   critical, sensitive

   more easily

8. Hinde's view of social behavior emphasizes that _____ with others are important parts of children's environments. Hinde also believes that we must study interactions between relationships over _____ rather than at one point in development.

   relationships

   time

9. The ethological view has emphasized the _____ basis of behavior and _____ _____. Ethologists have indicated the importance of long _____ _____ during development.

   biological
   careful description
   sensitive periods

10. Some have criticized sensitive periods as too _____ a concept, and asserted that ethological theories tilt too strongly towards _____. The theories have been _____ to develop testable ideas. The theories seem to work best _____.

    rigid

    biology, slow
    retrospectively

7.0 Ecological Theory

1. Bronfenbrenner's ecological theory is a _____ view of development that proposes that there are five _____ _____ that define the _____ of development.

   sociocultural
   environmental systems
   contexts

37

2. In ecological theory, the actual social setting in which the child lives is the _____. Microsystems include the _____, _____, _____, and _____.

microsystem, family, school, peers, neighborhood

3. According to ecological theory, individuals _____ their environments. That is, they are not _____.

construct
passive

4. The _____ is the set of relations between microsystems or contexts. The contexts in which children have no direct role but which influence children's lives are called the _____.

mesosystem

exosystem

5. The macrosystem is composed of the _____ _____ _____ of a culture.

attitudes and ideologies

6. A strength of Bronfenbrenner's ecological theory is that it _____ environmental influences on development. A major weakness of the theory is that it overlooks _____ _____ _____ determinants of development.

organizes
biological and
cognitive

7. The influence of time and sociohistorical events on development are captured in the _____.

chronosystem

8.0 An Eclectic Approach

1. An _____ _____ is a combination of the best of several other perspectives.

eclectic position

Key Terms Matching Exercise

1.0 Images of Children: Piaget and Erikson as Children (no terms)
2.0 Psychoanalytic Theories (Terms 1–34)
3.0 Cognitive Theories (Terms 35–45)
4.0 Behavioral and Social Learning Theories (Terms 46–55)
5.0 Phenomenological and Humanistic Theories (Terms 56–62)
6.0 Ethological Theories (Terms 63–67)
7.0 Ecological Theory (Terms 68–75)
8.0 An Eclectic Theoretical Orientation (Term 76)

_____

1. unconscious   *e*

2. id   *d*

3. pleasure principle   *A*

a. Involves the ego seeking to satisfy the wants and needs of the id within the bounds of reality

b. Psychoanalytic term that refers to the absence of psychological awareness, and is inferred from its effects on conscious processes

c. Freudian part of the personality that is the moral branch of personality

38

4. ego _C_ _f_

5. reality principle _D_

6. superego _C_

d. Involves always seeking pleasure and avoiding pain, regardless of the impact such behavior has on life in the real world

e. Bundle of sexual and aggressive instincts or drives that are primarily unconscious

f. Freudian element of the personality that considers the demands of reality

---

7. defense mechanism _e_

8. displacement _D_

9. projection _A_

10. repression _D_

11. sublimation _F_

12. reaction formation _C_

a. Ego defense mechanism whereby an individual shifts unacceptable feelings from one object to another more acceptable object

b. Ego defense mechanism that pushes anxiety-producing information into the unconscious

c. Ego defense mechanism in which repressed thoughts appear in the conscious part of the mind as mirror opposites of the repressed thoughts

d. Ego defense mechanism whereby an individual attributes personal shortcomings, problems and faults to others

e. Ego process for transforming the desires of the id so that they are expressed in a disguised manner; reduces conflict between the id and the ego

f. Ego defense mechanism in which a socially useful course of action replaces a socially undesirable one

---

13. regression _e_

14. erogenous zones _f_

15. fixation _D_

16. oral stage _C_

17. anal stage _B_

18. phallic stage

a. Third stage in Freud's theory, when the child focuses on the genital area and the Oedipal complex is resolved

b. Second stage in Freud's theory when the child receives pleasure from anal stimulation

c. First stage in Freud's theory, when stimulation of the mouth is the source of pleasure

d. Occurs when needs are under- or overgratified, and an individual remains at a particular stage of development

e. Ego defense mechanism that is reflected in the tendency to return to an earlier stage of development

f. Body parts in which pleasure is experienced

---

19. phallus

a. Fourth stage in Freud's theory, in which interest in sexual matters are repressed

20.	Oedipus complex	b.	Fifth and last stage in Freud's theory, in which sexual interest is reawakened; strong sexual motivation begins with puberty and lasts through adulthood
21.	penis envy	c.	Stages that span the life cycle, focusing on social development
22.	latency stage	d.	Complex that exists during the phallic stage and involves a young boy's sexual desires for his mother and his rivalrous feelings toward his father
23.	genital stage	e.	A label for the penis
24.	psychosocial stages	f.	Freudian view that women eventually recognize the anatomical superiority of having a penis that forms the basis for the Electra complex

---

25.	psychosexual stages	a.	Fourth of Erikson's stages during which the child compares self with peers, and either views self as basically competent and feels productive, or views self as incompetent and feels inferior
26.	epigenetic principle	b.	First of Erikson's stages, during which the infant comes to expect that the world will take care of its needs, or to feel fear and uncertainty
27.	trust versus mistrust	c.	The assumption that anything that grows has a plan, out of which parts arise, each in its own time, until all parts exist and form a functioning whole
28.	autonomy versus shame and doubt	d.	Stage in the life cycle that focuses on sexual development
29.	initiative versus guilt	e.	Second of Erikson's stages, during which the toddler develops a healthy attitude of being capable of independent control of own behavior, or develops an unhealthy attitude because he or she is incapable of control
30.	industry versus inferiority	f.	Third of Erikson's stages, during which the child may discover ways to overcome feelings of powerlessness by engaging in various activities or may feel guilt at being dominated by the environment

---

31.	identity versus identity confusion (diffusion)	a.	Seventh of Erikson's stages, during which the adult either feels that he or she is helping to shape the next generation or feels stagnant
32.	intimacy versus isolation	b.	Mental activities, such as thought, perception, attention, and problem solving, that influence development

33. generativity versus stagnation

    c. Fifth of Erikson's stages, centering on establishing a stable personal identity or feeling confused and troubled

34. integrity versus despair

    d. In Piaget's theory, a biologically based tendency to integrate knowledge into two interrelated cognitive structures

35. cognitive activity

    e. Sixth of Erikson's stages, or early adulthood, when the adult either forms friendships with others and a pair-bond, or feels alone

36. organization

    f. Eighth of Erikson's stages, when the person reflecting on his or her life either feels satisfied or feels doubt and despair

---

37. adaptation

    a. Second stage of Piaget's theory, from two to seven years of age, when thought is symbolic (not yet logical), egocentric, and magical

38. assimilation
39. accommodation

    b. Mental operations that are reversible

    c. Incorporating features of the environment into already existing ways of thinking about them

40. sensorimotor stage

    d. In Piaget's theory, a biologically based tendency to fit with the environment in ways that encourage survival

41. preoperational stage

    e. First stage in Piaget's theory, lasting until about two years of age, that extends from simple reflexes through the use of primitive symbols as the means of coordinating sensation and action

42. operations

    f. Incorporating new features of the environment into one's thinking by slightly modifying existing modes of thought

---

43. concrete operational stage

    a. A psychological theory that human development results primarily from conditioning and learning processes

44. formal operational stage
45. information processing
46. behaviorism

    b. Dependent on something else

    c. Responses actively emitted by an organism

    d. Third stage of Piaget's theory, from 7 to 12 years of age, when thinking is characterized by decentered and reversible thought and is restricted to concrete experience

47. operants

    e. A view concerned with how people attend, code, retrieve, and reason with information

48. contingent

    f. Final stage of Piaget's theory, when thought is characterized by abstractness, hypothetical-deductive reasoning, and idealism

49. consequences	a. A consequence to a behavior that leads to an increase in the performance of that behavior
50. operant (instrumental) conditioning	b. A reward or punishment that follows performance of a specific action
51. reinforcement	c. The presentation of consequences to behavior that decrease the frequency of that behavior
52. punishment	d. Frequency or rate of occurrence of an action or response by an individual
53. probability	e. The view that both cognitive processes and experiences determine one's personality
54. social learning theory	f. Learning that occurs as a function of the consequences that follow an organism's action; the consequences serve either to strengthen or weaken a behavior

55. observational learning	a. Refers to the perceived self as we are and would like to be
56. phenomenological theories	b. View that the individual's perception of the world is more important in understanding an individual's development than actual behavior
57. humanistic theories	c. Love and respect given to another without contingency
58. self-concept	d. A process whereby an individual learns new responses indirectly by observing the behavior of another person or model
59. real versus ideal self	e. Theories that stress self-perceptions, inner experiences, self-determination, and self-confidence
60. unconditional positive regard	f. Central aspect of humanistic theory that refers to an individual's overall perception of his or hew own abilities, behavior, or personality

61. empathic	a. The view that behavior is biologically determined, and evolution plays a key role
62. genuine	b. The belief that a fixed time period very early in development exists for the emergence of a behavior
63. ethology	c. Rogerian concept that refers to being open about one's feelings
64. imprinting	d. The ability to understand the feelings of another person
65. critical period	e. Hinde's application of ethological theory to human development that stresses sensitive periods, social development, and relationships

66.	neo-ethological theory	f.	A following response in ducks and geese to the first moving object they see after hatching

67.	sensitive period	a.	Contexts that influence the child's development even though the child does not have a role in those contexts
68.	ecological theory	b.	Refers to relations between microsystems or connections between contexts
69.	microsystem	c.	Actual social setting in which the child lives
70.	mesosystem	d.	A time in development when a given effect can be produced more easily than at times earlier or later
71.	exosystem	e.	A sociocultural view of development that consists of five systems, ranging from the fine-grained inputs of direct interactions with social agents to the broad-based inputs of culture

72.	macrosystem	a.	Research that compares or deals with two or more cultures, and identifies differences and similarities in them
73.	culture	b.	The perspective that multiple theoretical orientations are necessary for understanding child development
74.	cross-cultural studies	c.	In ecological theory, the patterning of environmental events and transitions over the life course
75.	chronosystem	d.	Attitudes and ideologies of the culture
76.	eclectic theoretical orientation	e.	Concept that refers to behavior patterns, beliefs, values, and other products that are learned and shared by a group and transmitted from one generation to another

Key Terms Matching Exercise
Answer Key

1. b	12. c	23. b	34. f	45. e	56. b	67. d
2. e	13. e	24. c	35. b	46. a	57. e	68. e
3. d	14. f	25. d	36. d	47. c	58. f	69. c
4. f	15. d	26. c	37. d	48. b	59. a	70. b
5. a	16. c	27. b	38. c	49. b	60. c	71. a
6. c	17. b	28. e	39. f	50. f	61. d	72. d
7. e	18. a	29. f	40. e	51. a	62. c	73. e
8. a	19. e	30. a	41. a	52. c	63. a	74. a
9. d	20. d	31. c	42. b	53. d	64. f	75. c
10. b	21. f	32. e	43. d	54. e	65. b	76. b
11. f	22. a	33. a	44. f	55. d	66. e	

1. According to Freud's theory, which part of the personality is responsible for interactions with reality?
   a. id
   b. ego
   c. superego
   d. Oedipus complex
2. Jimmy wants to hit his little brother, Johnny. Instead, Jimmy gives Johnny hugs and kisses. Which defense mechanism is Jimmy using?
   a. sublimation
   b. repression
   c. reaction formation
   d. regression
3. Melissa loves to bite and suck objects. She receives her primary pleasure from those activities. Freud would place Melissa in which stage of development?
   a. genital
   b. phallic
   c. anal
   d. oral
4. Which of the following is *not* a difference between Freud and Erikson?
   a. Sexuality is not seen as the underlying force behind personality in Erikson.
   b. The first five years of life in shaping personality are deemphasized by Erikson.
   c. Erikson provided concepts more easily tested than Freud did.
   d. The ego is given more strength in personality by Erikson.
5. Nabil has been comparing himself to his friends and has decided that he is good at doing things. He decides that he enjoys productive activities. Nabil has successfully completed which of Erikson's stages?
   a. autonomy versus shame and doubt
   b. initiative versus guilt
   c. industry versus inferiority
   d. identity versus identity confusion
6. Rosa has just fallen in love with a man, and is forming a very close, open relationship with him. Rosa is in which of Erikson's stages?
   a. initiative versus guilt
   b. industry versus inferiority
   c. identity versus identity confusion
   d. intimacy versus isolation
7. Which of the following is *not* a strength of the psychoanalytic position?
   a. the belief that personality develops
   b. the emphasis on an empirical data for making conclusions
   c. the belief that some behaviors are unconsciously motivated
   d. the belief that the past influences our current behavior
8. The primary focus of Piaget's theory is
   a. emotional development.
   b. social development.
   c. cognitive development.
   d. development of the self.
9. Which of the following is the purest example of assimilation?
   a. cooking a pancake on an imaginary stove
   b. building a tower of blocks
   c. riding a bicycle
   d. imitating a man shaving
10. Which of the following is the purest example of accommodation?
    a. cooking a pancake on an imaginary stove
    b. building a tower of blocks
    c. riding a bicycle
    d. imitating a man shaving
11. Which of the following is the purest example of adaptation in which assimilation and accommodation are in balance?
    a. cooking a pancake on an imaginary stove
    b. feeding a cookie to a doll at a tea party
    c. riding a bicycle
    d. imitating a man shaving

12. A very young person picks up a rattle, looks at it intently, waves it in front of his eyes, and sticks it into his mouth to chew on and explore. This person is most likely in which of Piaget's stages?
    a. sensorimotor
    b. preoperational
    c. concrete operational
    d. formal operational
13. A youngster who understands that a picture can represent an object, and who is able to use language, but who lacks operational reasoning, is in which of Piaget's stages?
    a. sensorimotor
    b. preoperational
    c. concrete operational
    d. formal operational
14. After much trial and error, a young child manages to ride down the sidewalk on a two-wheeled bicycle without falling down and skinning her knees. This is an example of what kind of learning?
    a. classical conditioning
    b. operant conditioning
    c. observational learning
    d. cognitive learning
15. After much trial and error, a young child manages to ride down the sidewalk on a two-wheeled bicycle without falling down and skinning her knees. Which is the positive reinforcer?
    a. not falling down
    b. not skinning her knees
    c. both not falling down and not skinning her knees
    d. being able to ride down the sidewalk
16. The emphasis on the role of unconditional positive regard in development is associated with which theoretical framework?
    a. phenomenological
    b. behavioral
    c. cognitive
    d. ethological
17. The concern with the evolutionary origin of behavior is the province of which theoretical perspective?
    a. psychoanalytic
    b. behavioral
    c. cognitive
    d. ethological
18. The view that the social behavior of a three-year-old child has an adaptive value in the child's life is most compatible with which theoretical perspective?
    a. psychoanalytic
    b. phenomenological
    c. ecological
    d. ethological
19. An important assumption of ecological theory is that
    a. unconscious mental processes influence human behavior.
    b. sociocultural factors are important influences on child development.
    c. the primary developmental force is biological development.
    d. personal experience is the primary influence on development.
20. A child who has a warm, affectionate relationship with her parents also develops a warm relationship with her teacher. This is an example of Bronfenbrenner's concept of
    a. microsystem.
    b. mesosystem.
    c. exosystem.
    d. macrosystem.

Self-Test Answers
Test A

1. b	4. c	7. b	10. d	13. b	16. a	19. b
2. c	5. c	8. c	11. c	14. b	17. d	20. b
3. d	6. d	9. a	12. a	15. d	18. d	

Critical Thinking Exercises

Exercise 1

Chapter 2 presents several different schools of thought about the appropriate subject matter and methods for developmental psychology. The author of the following quote was most likely a proponent of which of the following developmental perspectives:

"I never wanted to use human subjects. I hated to serve as a subject. I didn't like the stuffy, artificial instructions given to subjects. I was uncomfortable and acted unnaturally. With animals I was at home. I felt that, in studying them, I was keeping close to biology with my feet on the ground. More and more the thought presented itself: Can't I find out by watching their behavior everything that the other students are finding out by using observers?" **Circle the letter of the best answer and explain why it is the best answer and why each other answer is not as good.**

A. cognitive
B. behavioral
C. phenomenological
D. psychoanalytic
E. ecological

Exercise 2

One difficult aspect of learning about developmental psychology is that students must learn many new concepts and terms. One way to make this task easier is to identify ways in which new terms are either similar or different. Four of the following five pairs of concepts or terms have similar meanings. Your task is to identify the pair of terms that is conceptually *least alike*. **Circle the letter of the best answer and explain why it is the best answer and why each other answer is not as good.**

A. reality principle and accommodation
B. fixation and sensitive period
C. reinforcement and unconditional positive regard
D. Erikson's theory and Bronfenbrenner's ecological theory
E. social learning theory and information processing approach

Exercise 3

Read the passage about Jess and his teachers that follows. Which of the following statements is most likely to have been Graubard and Rosenberg's assumption about difficult students rather than an inference or an observation? **Circle the letter of the best answer and explain why it is the best answer and why each other answer is not as good.**

A. The students' difficult behavior was not caused by disturbed personalities or mental abnormalities.
B. The normal reactions of teachers reinforced the disruptive or harmful behavior of difficult students.
C. Students exerted control over their teachers' behavior.
D. Students changed the way that they interacted with their teachers.
E. The improved interaction between students and teachers continued for a short time after the students finished their behavior modification class.

Jess and His Teachers

Jess is an eighth grader at a junior high school in California. At 14 years old, he already weighs 185 pounds. He is the school's best athlete, but he used to get some of his biggest thrills out of fighting. Jess knocked out several fellow students with bottles and chairs and once hit the principal with a stick, for which he received a 40-day suspension from school.

Jess's teachers unanimously agreed that he was an impossible case. No one was able to control him. But one week, his teachers began to notice a complete turnabout in Jess's behavior. His math teacher was one of the first to notice the strange but improved behavior. Jess looked at her one day and said, "When you are nice, you help me learn a lot." The teacher was shocked. Not knowing what to say, she finally smiled. Jess continued, "I feel really good when you praise me." Jess continued a consistent pattern of such statements to his teachers and even came to class early or sometimes stayed late just to chat with them.

What was responsible for Jess's turnabout? Some teachers said he attended a mysterious class every day that might provide some clues to his behavior change. In that "mysterious" class, a teacher was training students in behavior modification, which emphasizes that behavior is determined by its consequences. Those consequences weaken some behaviors and strengthen others.

In an experiment, Paul Graubard and Henry Rosenberg (1974) selected seven of the most incorrigible students at a junior high school—Jess was one of them—and had a teacher give them instruction and practice in behavior modification in one 43-minute class period each day. In their daily training session, the students were taught a number of rewards to use to shape a teacher's behavior. Rewards included eye contact, smiling, sitting up straight, and being attentive. The students also practiced ways to praise the teacher, saying such things as, "I like working in this class where there is a good teacher." And they worked on ways to discourage certain teacher behaviors by saying such things as, "I just have a rough time working well when you get mad at me." Jess had the hardest time learning how to smile. He was shown a videotape of his behavior and observed that he actually leered at people when he was told to smile. Although it was somewhat hilarious, Jess practiced in front of a camera until he eventually developed a charming smile.

During the five weeks in which the students implemented their behavior-change tactics, observations indicated that teacher-student interchanges were becoming much more positive. Informal observations and comments after the program ended suggested that positive student-teacher interchanges were continuing. But what happened in the long run? In the case of this experiment, we do not know, but in many cases such behavior modification interventions do not result in long-lasting changes once the consequences for behavior are removed (Masters & others, 1988).

Research Project 1 Parent-Child Interaction

In this project you will observe a parent-child interaction and interpret it according to psychoanalytic, behavioral, and cognitive theoretical approaches. Go to a local supermarket and watch a mother or father shop with a two- to four-year-old child. Describe the interactions you observe, including demands on the part of the child, verbal exchanges between parent and child, and ways in which the parent responds to the demands of the child. Then answer the questions that follow, referring to your observations.

Age ____ Sex ____

Description:

Questions:

1. On what would a psychoanalytic theorist focus in this example? How would the sequence of observed events be explained?
2. How would a behavioral psychologist analyze the situation? What reinforcers or punishers characterized the interaction? Did specific things occur that would make a behavior more likely to occur in the future? Less likely to occur?
3. On what would a cognitive theorist focus in this situation? Why?
4. What is the child learning in this situation? What does the child already know?

Research Project 2 Autobiography and Theoretical Perspectives

This project involves writing an autobiography about one segment of your life (i.e., infancy, preschool, school years, adolescence) and interpreting your life in terms of one of the theoretical perspectives in the chapter (i.e., psychoanalytic, cognitive, behavioral and social learning, phenomenological and humanistic, ethological, or ecological). Use your memories, written records of your life (e.g., baby books, diaries, report cards, photo albums), and other persons (e.g., parents, grandparents, friends, teachers, employers, neighbors). You should write between three and eight pages of life events and another two or three pages of theoretical interpretation. Include both the broad picture of your development and some specific examples.

Which theoretical approach you apply will be influenced by the age period you choose to write about. For example, the psychoanalytic approach is most appropriate if you choose infancy or preschool years.

Questions:

1. What sources of information were helpful in developing your autobiography? What sources would have been useful but were not available to you?
2. How well did your chosen psychological theory explain your life? Which other theory would you like to have used in your paper? Which theory do you think would be least useful or applicable?
3. Do you view your life as having a high degree of continuity or discontinuity, or stability vs change? On what do you base your conclusions?

Essay and Critical Thinking Questions

Comprehension and Application Essay Questions

We recommend that you follow either our guidelines for answering essay and critical thinking questions, or those guidelines provided by your instructor in preparing your response. Your answers to these kinds of questions demonstrate an ability to comprehend and think critically about concepts and topics discussed in this chapter.

1. Compare and contrast the psychoanalytic theories of Freud and Erikson. Also indicate whether the work of Erikson changed psychoanalytic theory in a fundamental way.
2. Explain the Piagetian concepts of organization, adaptation, assimilation, and accommodation. Also indicate how these concepts help explain cognitive change during the development of the child.
3. Explain the computer metaphor for information processing in your own words. Also indicate unique kinds of questions about development raised by an information processing approach.
4. Think about your life during the past 24 hours from the perspective of behavioral and social learning theories. Provide at least two examples of how (a) rewards, (b) punishments, and (c) observational learning have influenced your behavior during this time frame.
5. Explain the extent to which each of the three major processes (biological, cognitive, and social) shapes child development according to phenomenological and humanistic theorists.
6. Explain and evaluate ethological theory by indicating its strengths, limitations, and what is missing from this approach to child development.
7. Define and distinguish the five systems in Bronfenbrenner's ecological theory. Also provide at least two examples of each system from your own life.
8. Explain what is meant by an eclectic theoretical orientation to child development. Evaluate the pros and cons of such an approach.
9. Some developmentalists argue that all other perspectives can be explained in behavioral (or social behavioral) terms. Illustrate this argument by explaining any one of the other theoretical orientations (i.e., psychoanalytic, cognitive, phenomenological and humanistic, ethological, or ecological approach) in behavioral or social behavioral terms.
10. Consider your own abilities, interests, and personal experiences, and then indicate and explain which theoretical approaches (excluding the eclectic approach) are most and least agreeable to you personally.

Critical Thinking Questions

Your answers to the following kinds of questions reflect an ability to apply your critical thinking skills to a novel problem or situation that is *not* specifically discussed in this chapter.

1. At the end of Chapter 2, Santrock concludes that no single theory is capable of explaining the rich complexity of child development. Apply your knowledge about the scientific base of child development by designing a study to determine the relative impact of the different theoretical approaches on the field of child development in the past, present, and/or future: (a) What specific problem or question do you want to study? (b) What predictions would you make and test in your study? (c) What measures would you use (i.e., observation, interviews and questionnaires, case studies, standardized tests, physiological research, or multimeasure, multisource, and multicontext approach) and how would you define each measure clearly and unambiguously? (d) What strategy would you follow—experimental or correlational, and what would be the time span of your inquiry—cross-sectional or longitudinal? (e) What ethical considerations must be addressed before you conduct your study?

2. According to Chapter 1, five issues define the nature of development: (a) biological, cognitive, and social processes, (b) periods or stages, (c) the issue of maturation (nature) versus experience (nurture), (d) the issue of continuity versus discontinuity, and (e) the issue of stability versus change. Indicate your ability to think critically by (a) perusing the alternative theoretical perspective and (b) comparing and contrasting any three of them on each of these five defining issues.

3. Chapter 2 presents six different theoretical approaches (i.e., Freudian, cognitive behavioral and social learning, phenomenological and humanistic, ethological, and ecological), but notes that no single approach explains the complexity of development. Imagine that you are a psychologist at a nearby college who has several student clients who complain of relationship problems. Indicate your ability to think critically by explaining how you would apply each theoretical perspective in analyzing and treating your clients.

4. One aspect of thinking critically is to read, listen, and observe carefully and then ask questions about what is missing from a text, discussion, or situation. For example, in Chapter 1 Santrock places considerable emphasis on sociocultural concerns. That emphasis is also apparent in a presentation of a sociocultural criticism of Freudian theory; however, no other theoretical approach receives a sociocultural criticism. Indicate your ability to think critically by
    (a) explaining why only Freudian theory is subjected to a sociocultural criticism, and
    (b) presenting your own sociocultural analysis (i.e., criticism or commendation) of each of the other theoretical approaches (i.e., cognitive, behavioral and social learning, phenomenological and humanistic, ethological, ecological, and eclectic).

5. Santrock places several quotations in the margins of this chapter. One by George Santayana says, "The tide of evolution carries everything before it, thoughts no less than bodies, and persons no less than nations." Indicate your ability to think critically by (a) learning about the author and indicating why this individual is eminently quotable (i.e., what was the individual's contribution to human knowledge and understanding), (b) interpreting and restating the quote in your own terms, and (c) explaining what concept, issue, perspective, or term in this chapter Santrock intended this quote to illuminate. In other words, about what aspect or issue in development does this quote make you pause and think reflectively?

Self-Test B

1. Chin is sleeping and has to go to the bathroom. He then dreams that he is getting up, going to the potty, and returning to his bed. According to Freud, which part of the personality is likely to be controlling Chin's dream?
   a. id
   b. ego
   c. superego
   d. pleasure principle

2. Karim is a ten-year-old boy. He is afraid of dogs. He sees a dog coming down the street and he buries his head on his mother's shoulder. This is an example of
   a. repression.
   b. sublimation.
   c. regression.
   d. reaction formation.

3. The stage in Freud's theory lasting from 18 months to three years is called
   a. oral.
   b. anal.
   c. phallic.
   d. latency.

4. Kimiko is learning how to feed and dress herself. She feels as if she is capable of controlling her actions. In which of Erikson's stages is Kimiko?
   a. trust versus mistrust
   b. autonomy versus shame and doubt
   c. initiative versus guilt
   d. industry versus inferiority

5. Each of the following has been suggested as a weakness of Freud's theory except
   a. the difficulty of testing the concepts.
   b. the lack of an empirical data base.
   c. too much emphasis on early experience.
   d. a developmental perspective on personality.

6. Piaget's theory claims that cognitive development depends greatly on
   a. emotional development.
   b. social development.
   c. biological maturation.
   d. history of reinforcement.

7. Which of the following is the purest example of assimilation?
   a. eating an imaginary hamburger
   b. bouncing a ball
   c. washing dishes
   d. imitating a dancer dancing

8. Which of the following is the purest example of accommodation?
   a. eating an imaginary hamburger
   b. bouncing a ball
   c. washing dishes
   d. imitating a dancer dancing

9. Which of the following is the purest example of adaptation, with assimilation and accommodation in balance?
   a. eating an imaginary hamburger
   b. bouncing a ball
   c. stirring in a pretend bowl, making a pretend cake
   d. imitating a dancer dancing

10. A child is given the conservation of liquid task. The child argues that the amount of liquid in the two containers is the same because one is taller but the other one is fatter. The child is in which of Piaget's stages?
    a. sensorimotor
    b. preoperational
    c. concrete operational
    d. formal operational

11. A child says to herself, "I think the way to get a good grade on a test is to study hard. Therefore, if I study hard for my next exam, I will get a good grade." This child is in which period?
    a. sensorimotor
    b. preoperational
    c. concrete operational
    d. formal operational

12. A psychologist is interested in teaching an infant to press a panel. The psychologist makes a light go on every time the infant presses a panel. This is referred to as
    a. classical conditioning.
    b. operant conditioning.
    c. observational learning.
    d. insight learning.

13. A very tired child wants to go to sleep. Her mother makes her pick up her toys and put them away before she goes to sleep. In this situation, going to sleep is
    a. a reinforcer.
    b. an adaptation.
    c. a punishment.
    d. an operant.

14. A child sees her friend turn a bowl of oatmeal upside down and spill it on the floor. The next day the child turns her own bowl of oatmeal upside down and spills it. This is an example of
    a. classical conditioning.
    b. operant conditioning
    c. behavior modification.
    d. observational learning.

15. According to humanistic theory, the concept of unconditional positive regard is a process that
    a. is used to shape acceptable behavior in children.
    b. expresses the child's view of the world.
    c. parents withdraw when children misbehave.
    d. builds a child's self-esteem.

16. According to which theory does free will play an important role in child development?
    a. psychoanalytic theory
    b. cognitive theory
    c. phenomenological theory
    d. behavioral theory

17. The concept of sensitive periods in development comes from which framework?
    a. ethological
    b. cognitive
    c. behavioral
    d. psychoanalytic

18. Hinde extended classic ethological theory to create neo-ethological theory by including a focus on
    a. human behavior.
    b. strengthening the concept of critical period.
    c. systems of human behavior.
    d. psychosexual development.

19. Ecological theory is most similar to which other theory?
    a. psychoanalytic theory
    b. behavioral theory
    c. cognitive theory
    d. ethological theory

20. To study social interactions between children, a researcher observes Tomas at home playing with his friend Jim. Which of Bronfenbrenner's systems does this most directly involve?
    a. microsystem
    b. mesosystem
    c. exosystem
    d. macrosystem

Self-Test Answers
Test B

1. a	4. b	7. a	10. c	13. a	16. c	19. b
2. c	5. d	8. d	11. d	14. d	17. a	20. a
3. b	6. c	9. b	12. b	15. d	18. a	

Chapter **3** **Biological Beginnings**

Objectives

1.0 *Images of Children: The Jim and Jim Twins*
1.1 State the basic rationale for research on fraternal and identical twins who have been reared apart.
1.2 List four criticisms of the Minnesota Study of Twins Reared Apart.

2.0 *The Evolutionary Perspective*
2.1 Define natural selection, and show how an evolutionary perspective explains human development from prehistoric times to the present.
2.2 Define and distinguish between cultural and evolutionary changes.

3.0 *Heredity*
3.1 Define and distinguish between chromosomes and genes.
3.2 Define and distinguish between gametes and zygotes, and list the steps in the process that transforms gametes into a zygote.
3.3 Define and distinguish between meiosis and reproduction.
3.4 Explain how technology might allow parents to select the sex of their child.
3.5 Explain why twins have more in common genetically with one another than with either parent.
3.6 Define and distinguish between in vitro fertilization and infertility.
3.7 Explain how an infertile couple could have a baby.
3.8 List causes of and remedies for infertility in females and males.
3.9 List treatments for infertility common to both females and males.
3.10 Evaluate adoption as an alternative to medical treatment for infertility.
3.11 Define genetic abnormality, and compare and contrast genetic abnormalities.
3.12 Describe the method and purpose for tests such as amniocentesis, ultrasound sonography, the chorionic villus test, and the maternal blood test.
3.13 Discuss what couples would learn and understand after consulting with a genetic counselor.
3.14 Define and distinguish between the dominant-recessive genes principle and polygenic inheritance.
3.15 Explain why two brown-eyed parents can have a blue-eyed child, but two blue-eyed parents cannot have a brown-eyed child.
3.16 Define and distinguish between genotype and phenotype.
3.17 Define and distinguish between reaction range and canalization.
3.18 Indicate how the concept of reaction range explains why it is hard to determine the genotype given the phenotype.
3.19 Define behavior genetics.
3.20 Define and distinguish between fraternal and identical twins.
3.21 Compare and contrast adoption studies and twin studies, and explain why these studies do not show conclusively that a behavior or trait is inherited.

4.0   *Heredity's Influence on Development*
4.1   Define intelligence.
4.2   Indicate why Jensen favors nature over nurture as an explanation of intelligence, and list criticisms of this view.
4.3   Describe the nature, purpose, and criticisms of the Repository for Germinal Choice.
4.4   Explain whether the studies of the effects of early intervention on intelligence support or refute Jensen's views.
4.5   Indicate the evidence supporting the hypotheses that (a) heredity influences intelligence and (b) environment influences intelligence.
4.6   Define temperament.
4.7   Compare and contrast Chess and Thomas's analysis with Buss and Plomin's analysis of temperament.
4.8   Describe how the influence of heredity on temperament changes as an individual ages.
4.9   Indicate the evidence supporting the hypothesis that (a) heredity influences temperament, and (b) environment influences temperament.
4.10   Compare and contrast the temperaments of European American, Chinese American, and Navaho Indian newborns.
4.11   Compare and contrast the research on the heritability of both intelligence and temperament.

5.0   *Heredity-Environment Interaction and Development*
5.1   Define the concept of heredity-environment interaction.
5.2   Indicate what researchers know and do not know about how heredity and environment interact to produce development.

Summary

1.0 Images of Children: The Jim and Jim Twins

The Minnesota Study of Twins Reared Apart investigates various aspects of the lives of identical twins and fraternal twins from all over the world. Although the study's conclusions must be evaluated in light of several methodological criticisms, the more important point is that this study illustrates a growing interest in the genetic basis of human development.

2.0 The Evolutionary Perspective

Natural selection is an evolutionary process that favors individuals within a species best adapted to survive and reproduce. Darwin believed that evolutionary change occurs at a slow pace. Biological evolution shapes humans into a culture-making species for whom cultural change can occur rapidly.

3.0 Heredity

When studying development, it is important to remember that people are biological beings.

What Are Genes? The nucleus of each human cell contain 46 chromosomes, which are composed of DNA. Chromosomes provide the blueprint for the development of an individual, and genes are the building blocks of chromosomes.

Reproduction. Genes are transmitted from parents to offspring by gametes—the ovum, or egg from the female and sperm from the male. The process of meiosis produces the gametes. In human beings each gamete has 23 chromosomes. Reproduction occurs when a sperm fertilizes an ovum, producing a zygote. Male and female sperm can be separated by a centrifuge, allowing the possibility of controlling the sex of the offspring. Approximately 10 to 15 percent of American couples are infertile, In vitro fertilization allows otherwise infertile couples to bear children; however, adoption provides an alternative choice.

Abnormalities in Genes and Chromosomes. A number of genetic problems can occur in development. PKU syndrome is a genetic problem resulting in the failure to produce an enzyme necessary for metabolism, and can cause severe mental retardation if not treated by dietary restrictions. Down syndrome is a form of mental retardation caused by the presence of an extra chromosome and is accompanied by physical abnormalities. Sickle-cell anemia is a disease of the red blood cells that causes early death; it occur primarily among blacks. Several disorders are associated with sex chromosome abnormalities. These include Klinefelter syndrome, males with an extra X chromosome; Turner syndrome, females missing an X chromosome; and XYY syndrome, males with an extra Y chromosome. Genetic counseling provides information to couples about the risks of having a genetically defective child. Four procedures can be used to determine the presence of genetic defects: amniocentesis, ultrasound sonography, the chorionic villus test, and the maternal blood test.

Some Genetic Principles. Genetic transmission is a complex process because the underlying genetic structure, or genotype, must be inferred from the actual physical characteristics of a person, the phenotype. Nonetheless, some general principles have been identified. Some genes are dominant and will always be expressed phenotypically when present, whereas other genes are recessive and will be expressed phenotypically only when paired with another recessive gene on the other chromosome. This demonstrates the principle of dominant-recessive genes. Some characteristics are determined by the interaction of many different genes, the principle of polygenic inheritance. The reaction range refers to the possible extent of phenotypes that could be expressed by a given genotype. The genetic codes set broad limits on the range of possible outcomes, which are then affected by the environment. Canalization refers to the extent to which certain genotypes might be immune to environmental influences.

Methods Used by Behavior Geneticists. The field of behavior genetics studies the nature and degree of the hereditary basis for behavior. Twin studies compare identical and fraternal twins for degree of similarity. Adoption studies compare the adopted child with both the adoptive and biological parents.

4.0 Heredity's Influence on Development

All aspects of development are influenced by heredity.

Intelligence. Jensen argues that intelligence is primarily inherited and that environment and culture play minimal roles. Jensen reviewed twin studies and claimed that the heritability of intelligence, as measured by IQ, is about 80 percent. The main criticisms of Jensen's work are that (a) IQ tests measure only a narrow range of intelligence, and (b) investigations do not include environments that differ radically. Jensen's assumption that intelligence has a strong hereditary component led to the founding of the Repository for Germinal Choice, a sperm bank. Early intervention programs try to provide favorable outcomes early in the life of children who are judged at risk for impaired intelligence.

Temperament. Temperament is another widely studied aspect of human development and is defined in terms of a person's behavioral style. Chess and Thomas identified three temperamental clusters and have labeled children as easy, difficult, and slow-to-warm-up. Buss and Plomin have identified three dimensions in which infants differ: emotionality, sociability, and activity. Temperament in newborns is conceived of as a stable characteristic shaped by later experiences. Temperament may become more malleable with experience. An important consideration is the fit between the temperament of an infant and the temperament of the parents.

5.0 Heredity-Environment Interaction and Development

Heredity and the environment interact in development. We need to know more about how they interact to allow persons to overcome potential damage during the developmental period.

Key Terms

1.0 Images of Children: The Jim and Jim Twins
fraternal twins
identical twins

2.0 The Evolutionary Perspective
natural selection
evolutionary change
cultural change

3.0 Heredity
chromosomes
DNA
genes
gametes
meiosis
reproduction
zygote
in vitro fertilization
infertility
phenylketonuria (PKU)
Down syndrome
sickle-cell anemia
Klinefelter syndrome
Turner syndrome
XYY syndrome
genetic counselor
amniocentesis
ultrasound sonography
chorionic villus test

maternal blood test
dominant-recessive genes
polygenic inheritance
genotype
phenotype
reaction range
canalization
behavior genetics
twin study
monozygotic twin
dizygotic twin
adoption study

4.0 Heredity's Influence on Development
intelligence
early intervention
temperament
easy child
difficult child
slow-to-warm-up child
emotionality
sociability
activity
imperturbability

5.0 Heredity-Environment Interaction and Development
interaction

Guided Review

1.0 Images of Children

1. Projects such as the Minnesota Study of Twins Reared Apart reflect renewed interest in the _____ determinants of _____.

   genetic, development

2. Studies of twins indicate that environmental and biological factors _____ to produce human development.

   interact

2.0 The Evolutionary Perspective

1. Human evolution is relatively _____ in Earth's history

   recent

2. _____ _____ is the evolutionary process by which organisms who are best _____ to an environment survive and _____.

   Natural selection
   adapted
   reproduce

3. The theory of evolution was published in ___ ___ ____ _____ _____ by _____ _____. Darwin noticed that reproduction rates would result in _____ were it not for the rate at which animals died. He reasoned that those which survived were _____ _____ _____ their environments and therefore passed their _____ on to the next generation. By this mechanism genetic improvement gradually _____ a species' characteristics.

   On the Origin of Species
   Charles Darwin
   overpopulation

   best adapted to
   genes
   change

4. Evolution is thought to have created human _____, which is thought to have produced human _____ of other creatures. However, no sweeping evolutionary changes have occurred in humans for the past _____ _____.

   intelligence
   dominance

   50,000 years

3.0 Heredity

1. Thread-like structures that come in structurally similar pairs and are in human cells are _____. There are _____ pairs of chromosomes in each human cell. Chromosomes are composed of _____ _____. The _____ are small parts of the chromosome which may carry the basis for individual traits.

   chromosomes, 23

   deoxyribonucleic acid
   genes

2. The cells in which the chromosomes are transmitted to offspring are called _____. They are created in the _____ of males and the _____ of females by a process of cell division called _____.

   gametes, testes
   ovaries
   meiosis

3. The process by which a _____ is formed by the union of an ovum and a sperm cell is called _____.

   zygote
   reproduction

4. A recently developed procedure for accomplishing conception outside the body is called ____ ____ ____. This method of conception is ____ ____ with any later developmental problems.

in vitro fertilization
not associated

5. From ___ to ___ percent of human couples are ____. The cause of infertility may be either ____ ____ or _____ _____ experienced by either men or women. Two medical approaches to treating infertility are ____ and _____ _____.

10, 15, infertile
biological defect
environmental harm
surgery
hormone treatments

6. A non-reproductive solution to a couple's infertility is to ____ ____ _____. Such children typically ____ ____ know their true parents. Compared to nonadopted children, adopted children experience more ____, especially at ____. Current advice is to ____ adopted children that they are adopted.

adopt a child
do not

problems, adolescence
tell

7. A number of genetic problems exist. A disorder caused by a problem in a genetic code that results in the failure of the body to produce an enzyme results in mental retardation; this is called the ____ ____. The presence of an extra chromosome that results in retardation, along with a flattened skull, short, thin body build, and a protruding tongue is called ____ ____ ____. A genetic disorder resulting in a problem with red blood cell formation is called ____ ____ ____.

PKU syndrome

Down syndrome

sickle-cell anemia

8. Some genetic disorders are related to sex chromosomes. ____ _____ is due to the presence of an extra X chromosome in males. ____ ____ can cause retardation in women, and is due to the absence of an ___ ____. ____ ____ has been thought to be related to excessive aggressiveness in males.

Klinefelter's syndrome

Turner's syndrome
X chromosome, XYY
syndrome

9. Several tests to evaluate the health of the fetus have been developed. ____ involves inserting a needle into a woman's abdomen and removing fluid, which is evaluated for genetic abnormalities. ____ ____ evaluates the fetus by obtaining a pictorial representation from aiming high-frequency sound waves at the pregnant woman's abdomen. A test that can be used as early as the end of the first trimester is the ____ _____ test. Finally, the ____ ____ ____ is used to detect neural tube defects.

Amniocentesis

Ultrasound sonography

chorionic villus
maternal blood test

10. In order to assess their likelihood of having genetically abnormal offspring, a couple may wish to seek ____ ____. Among other things, they can find out whether or not genetic disorders in themselves or their relatives are ____ or _____.

genetic counseling

hereditary
environmental

11. When George Mendel bred round and wrinkled pea plants he found that all the offspring were round. This means that the gene for round was _____ over the gene for wrinkled. The gene for wrinkled was _____. The only time the effect of a _____ gene shows is when it is carried on both chromosomes.

dominant
recessive, recessive

12. Genetic transmission that requires the interaction of many different genes is called _____ _____.

polygenic inheritance

13. The hypothetical hereditary basis of each individual is called the _____. The observable and measurable characteristics of the individual are called the _____.

genotype
phenotype

14. Given a particular genotype, _____ phenotype(s) is/are possible. The genotype may only set broad limits on the range of phenotypes, a phenomenon known as the _____ _____. When the environment has little influence on the variability of expression of a trait, the result is called _____. It is important to remember that genes _____ _____ directly cause human behavior.

many

reaction range

canalization
do not

15. Recent research on factors related to intelligence have indicated that _____ and _____ are important determinants of intelligence.

heredity, environment

16. Monozygotic and dizygotic _____ and _____ twins come from _____ and _____ ova, respectively. Two kinds of studies used by behavior geneticists are _____ and _____ studies.

identical, fraternal
one, two
twin, adoption

4.0 Heredity's Influence on Development

1. Jensen argues that intelligence is primarily _____. A fact that appears to support Jensen's view of intelligence is that there is a higher correlation between the scores of _____ twins than between scores of _____ twins.

inherited

identical
fraternal

2. The Repository for Germinal Choice represents an attempt to _____ _____ _____. _____ _____ contribute their sperm to the Repository. Whether this sperm has helped to produce children of superior intelligence is _____ _____.

breed for intelligence,
Nobel laureates
not known

3. Critics of the Repository for Germinal Choice argue that _____ is not a good measure of human worth, and in any event, claims that high IQ offspring created by its sperm are _____. However, a benefit of the Repository is that it is a source of _____ for _____ couples.

IQ

unlikely

sperm, infertile

4. Some criticize Jensen's work because his definition of intelligence is based on a _____, and environments he has sampled have been too _____.

test
similar

5. _____ is a stable characteristic of newborns that can be modified by experience. Three temperament clusters identified by Chess and Thomas are _____, _____, and _____ __ _____ _____.

Temperament

easy, difficult
slow-to-warm-up

6. Three different dimensions characterize differences between infants. The tendency to be distressed is called _____. The tendency to prefer the company of others is called _____. _____ involves the vigor of movement.

emotionality
sociability
Activity

7. Temperament becomes more _____ with experience. The _____ between the temperament of the child and the child's parents can influence the consistency of temperament.

malleable
match

8. Comparisons of Chinese American and European American newborn infants suggest that the temperamental trait of _____ has a _____ basis.

imperturbability
genetic

5.0 Heredity-Environment Interaction and Development

1. Heredity and environment operate _____ to produce development. Developmentalists say that these factors interact, which means that the influence of one _____ _____ the influence of the other.

together
depends on

2. The things we know about hereditary influences on development include knowledge of hereditary influence of _____, _____, and _____ development. Hereditary influence is usually _____, and is present during the ____ _____ ___ of individuals. Genetic influences seem to be stronger on ____ than they are on _____.

physical, intellectual,
behavioral, complicated
entire life time
intelligence
temperament

3. The things we do not know about hereditary influence include knowledge of the precise _____ of influence, how heredity and environment interact to produce _____ development, and how heredity influences development across _____ _____ _____.

mechanisms
normal
the life span

Key Terms Matching Exercise

1.0 Images of Children: The Jim and Jim Twins (Terms 1-2)
2.0 The Evolutionary Perspective (Terms 3-5)
3.0 Heredity (Term 6-36)
4.0 Heredity's Influence on Development (Terms 37-46)
5.0 Heredity-Environment Interaction and Development (Term 47)

1. fraternal twins _D_

2. identical twins _F_

3. natural selection _B_

4. evolutionary change _C_

5. cultural change _A_

6. chromosomes _C_

a. A process of potentially rapid change that involves beliefs and behavior patterns

b. An evolutionary process that favors individuals of a species that are best adapted to survive and reproduce

c. A process of slow change that involves variation in the gene pool

d. Dizygotic twins that develop from separate eggs

e. Helical structures that are paired in the cells; they are the biochemical bases of heredity, and there are 23 pairs in humans

f. Monozygotic twins that develop from a single fertilized egg that splits into two genetically identical replicas, each of which becomes a person

---

7. DNA _D_

8. genes _A_

9. gametes _E_

10. meiosis _B_

11. reproduction _f_

12. zygote _C_

a. Biochemical agents that comprise the basic building blocks of heredity; part of a chromosome

b. Process of cell division that produces cells with 23 unpaired chromosomes or gametes

c. Single-cell entity with 23 pairs of chromosomes formed by the union of a sperm cell with an ovum

d. Long molecule that runs along the length of each chromosome; the key chemical substance in an individual's genetic makeup

e. Sex cells that are created in the testes of males and ovaries of females; they each have 23 unpaired chromosomes

f. Process that occurs when a female gamete (ovum) is fertilized by a male gamete (sperm) to create a single-cell with 46 chromosomes

---

13. *In vitro* fertilization

14. infertility _C_

15. phenylketonuria (PKU) _e_

a. Caused in males with extra X chromosome, producing underdeveloped testes, and characterized by tall, thin body build, with enlarged breasts

b. Most common genetically transmitted form of mental retardation, caused by an extra chromosome

c. An inability to reproduce, typically defined by regular intercourse over a 12 month period that does not result in conception of a child

16. Down syndrome *B*

d. Genetic disorder producing disease of the red blood cells, most common among blacks

17. sickle-cell anemia *D*

e. A genetic disorder resulting in failure to produce an enzyme necessary for metabolism, resulting in severe retardation if dietary constraints are not implemented

18. Klinefelter syndrome *A*

f. When the ovum is surgically removed from the mother, fertilized in a laboratory medium with live sperm, stored in a solution that substitutes for the uterine environment, and then implanted back in the mother's uterus

---

19. Turner syndrome *B*

a. Test that detects genetic defects in the fetus; fluid is extracted through a needle inserted into the pregnant woman's abdomen, and fetal cells are grown in the laboratory for two to four weeks to be examined for abnormalities

20. XYY syndrome *e*

b. Genetic disorder in women who lack an X chromosome, may cause mental retardation

21. genetic counselor *C*

c. One who advises prospective parents about genetic disorders and how likely they are to transmit genetic defects to their children

22. amniocentesis *A*

d. Test that detects genetic defects in the fetus; a small sample of the placenta is removed between the ninth and tenth weeks

23. ultrasound sonography *f*

e. Genetic disorder in which males have an extra Y chromosome

24. chorionic villus test *D*

f. Prenatal assessment by directing high-frequency sound waves into the pregnant woman's abdomen

---

25. maternal blood test *A*

a. A prenatal technique for identifying neural tube defects by measuring the mother's blood alphaprotein level

26. dominant-recessive genes *C*

b. Range within which the environment can modify the expression of the genetic potential

27. polygenic inheritance *E*

c. Includes genes that determine the observed characteristic whenever present in the organism, and genes that determine the observed characteristic only when paired with other identical genes

28. genotype *f*

d. Observable and measurable characteristics of an individual

29. phenotype *D*

e. Phenotypic characteristic of the organism determined by the interaction of many different genes

63

30. reaction range *B*
    f. Hypothetical sum of the potential characteristics that our genetic structure makes possible

---

31. canalization *D*
32. behavior genetics *f*
33. twin study *E f*

    a. Twins that come from the same egg
    b. Twins that come from two different eggs
    c. Research design that compares the characteristics of an adopted child to those of both the biological and the adoptive parents

34. monozygotic twin *A*

    d. Narrow path or track that marks the development of some characteristics; these characteristics are those that seem immune to vast changes in environmental events

35. dizygotic twin *B*

    e. Studies that involve the comparison between identical and fraternal twins

36. adoption study *C*

    f. Field of study that is concerned with the degree and nature of the hereditary basis of behavior

---

37. intelligence *f*

    a. In this style of temperament, the child tends to react negatively and cry frequently, engages in irregular daily routines, and is slow to accept new experiences

38. early intervention *C*

    b. An individual's behavioral style and characteristic way of responding

39. temperament *B*

    c. In this style of temperament, the child is generally in a positive mood, quickly establishes regular routines in infancy, and adapts easily to new experiences

40. easy child

    d. In this style of temperament, the child has a low activity level, is somewhat negative, shows low adaptability, and displays a low intensity of mood

41. difficult child

    e. A strategy that entails a manipulation of the environment early in the life of children suspected of being at risk for impoverished intelligence

42. slow-to-warm-up child *A*

    f. Verbal ability, problem-solving skills, and the ability to learn from and adapt to the experiences of everyday life

---

43. emotionality *C*

    a. The combination of nature and nurture factors that influence human development

44. sociability *E*

    b. Involves tempo and vigor of movement

45. activity *B*

    c. Tendency to be distressed; reflects the arousal of an individual's sympathetic nervous system

46. imperturbability

47. interaction

d. A characteristic of temperament that affects the way in which adults care for infants

e. Tendency to prefer company of others to being alone

Key Terms Matching Exercise
Answer Key

1. d	8. a	15. e	22. a	29. d	36. c	43. c
2. f	9. e	16. b	23. f	30. b	37. f	44. e
3. b	10. b	17. d	24. d	31. d	38. e	45. b
4. c	11. f	18. a	25. a	32. f	39. b	46. d
5. a	12. c	19. b	26. c	33. e	40. c	47. a
6. e	13. f	20. e	27. e	34. a	41. a	
7. d	14. c	21. c	28. f	35. b	42. d	

Self-Test A

1. In evolution, a species survives by producing more offspring generation after generation than other species. This is the basic mechanism of
   a. heredity.
   b. natural selection.
   c. interaction.
   d. competition.
2. DNA makes up
   a. genes.
   b. chromosomes.
   c. gametes.
   d. both a and b.
3. Human cells consist of how many chromosomes?
   a. 23 chromosomes
   b. 23 pairs of chromosomes
   c. 46 pairs of chromosomes
   d. 47 pairs of chromosomes
4. The process of forming gametes is called
   a. meiosis.
   b. reproduction.
   c. fertilization.
   d. heredity.
5. The process of fertilization produces a(n)
   a. ovum.
   b. sperm.
   c. zygote.
   d. gamete.

6. PKU syndrome is most easily treated by
   a. dietary restrictions.
   b. hormonal injections.
   c. environmental enrichment.
   d. operation on the brain to repair damaged tissue.
7. Sickle cell anemia is most commonly found among
   a. Whites.
   b. Blacks.
   c. Asians.
   d. Latin Americans.
8. Which of the following is not associated with a sex chromosome abnormality?
   a. Turner's syndrome
   b. XYY syndrome
   c. Klinefelter's syndrome
   d. Down syndrome
9. The use of high frequency sound waves directed at a pregnant woman's abdomen is called
   a. amniocentesis.
   b. chorionic villus test.
   c. ultrasound sonography.
   d. sound scanning.
10. Eye color is an example of a trait which is controlled by
   a. polygenic inheritance.
   b. sex-linked genes.
   c. reaction range.
   d. dominant/recessive genes.

11. Genotype is to phenotype as _____ is to _____.
    a. capacity/behavior
    b. behavior/environment
    c. reality/fantasy
    d. measurement/gene
12. If a behavior appears to be immune to extensive changes in the environment, it demonstrates
    a. a large reaction range.
    b. the influence of dominant genes.
    c. canalization.
    d. low heritability.
13. Which of the following is not used by behavior geneticists?
    a. the concept of reaction range
    b. twin studies
    c. forward reference
    d. adoption studies
14. Which of the following is a twin study?
    a. Twin siblings, parents, and other siblings are compared.
    b. Fraternal and identical twins are compared.
    c. Twin siblings, parents, other siblings, aunts, uncles, and cousins are compared.
    d. Children are compared with adoptive and biological parents.
15. Jensen defines intelligence as
    a. the ability of an individual to solve problems in the real world.
    b. the score achieved on a standardized IQ test.
    c. the ability of an individual to adapt to social change.
    d. a multifaceted, complicated set of abilities not easily tapped by standard intelligence tests.

16. Chess and Thomas believe that there are _____ of temperament.
    a. dimensions
    b. facets
    c. types
    d. many varieties
17. Sociability is the tendency to
    a. be distressed when bad things happen to others.
    b. move vigorously in everyday activities.
    c. be placid even under threatening conditions.
    d. prefer the company of others to being alone.
18. According to research by Suomi and by Kagan, what trait is seen as a basic part of an individual's temperament?
    a. shyness
    b. happiness
    c. intelligence
    d. honesty
19. Jensen is at odds with behavior geneticists because he does not appear to believe that
    a. intelligence is merely a phenotype, not a genotype.
    b. heredity and environment interact to produce intelligence.
    c. intelligence is highly canalized.
    d. hereditary influences on intelligence can be controlled.
20. All but one of the following represents something we do not know about the heredity-environment interaction. Which one is the exception?
    a. whether intelligence is influenced more by heredity than is temperament
    b. how heredity and environment interact in normal development
    c. how heredity influences development at different times in life
    d. what pathways link intellectual development to heredity

Self-Test Answers
Test A

1. b	4. a	7. b	10. d	13. c	16. c	19. b
2. d	5. c	8. d	11. a	14. b	17. d	20. a
3. b	6. a	9. c	12. c	15. b	18. a	

Critical Thinking Exercises

Exercise 1

Many developmentalists believe that an important inherited determinant of personality is temperament. Researchers have attempted to identify basic dimensions of temperament and to describe the extent of their stability through individuals' lives. Which genetic principle is best illustrated by this work?
Circle the letter of the best answer and explain why it is the best answer and why each other answer is not as good.

A. dominant-recessive genes principle
B. polygenic inheritance
C. genotype/phenotype differences
D. reaction range
E. canalization

Exercise 2

Review "The Nature of Development" in Chapter 1, which describes several important issues in developmental psychology. Which of these issues receives the greatest emphasis in Chapter 3? **Circle the letter of the best answer and explain why it is the best answer and why each other answer is not as good.**

A. biological, cognitive, and social processes in development
B. continuity versus discontinuity
C. nature versus nurture
D. stability versus change
E. periods of development

Exercise 3

Focus on Education 3.1 describes two intervention studies that attempted to maintain or improve the intelligence of disadvantaged infants and children. Which of the following appears to have been an assumption rather than an inference or an observation made by the authors of one or both of these studies? **Circle the letter of the best answer and explain why it is the best answer and why each other answer is not as good.**

A. At the beginning of the study the individuals in the intervention and control groups were equally intelligent.

B. The IQs of the home-reared children in the North Carolina study declined between 12 and 18 months of age.

C. Getting families to change their children's intellectual environment is difficult if intervention does not begin early.

D. In the Texas study, mothers in the intervention group encouraged their children to talk more than did mothers in the control group.

E. In order to maintain or improve the intellectual functioning of disadvantaged infants, early intervention must involve 11 or more contacts with a family.

Research Project 1 Heritability of Height

The purpose of this project is to demonstrate the concept of heritability by using height as the characteristic. You will do a kinship study of two families (one of the families can be your own) to collect the necessary data. Record the height of all family members over 18 years of age and separate them by sex. Calculate the mean and range of heights of both sexes for both families and compare them. This exercise is intended to give you experience both with a kinship study design and with the concept of heritability for a variable with a clear operational definition. Use the following format to record heights. Then answer the questions that follow.

Person/Sex	Family 1	Family 2	Data	Family 1	Family 2
Self	_____	_____	Average female	_____	_____
Mother	_____	_____	Average male	_____	_____
Father	_____	_____	Tallest female	_____	_____
Grandmother 1	_____	_____	Tallest male	_____	_____
Grandmother 2	_____	_____	Shortest female	_____	_____
Grandfather 1	_____	_____	Shortest male	_____	_____
Grandfather 2	_____	_____			
Sibling	_____	_____			
Sibling	_____	_____			
Sibling	_____	_____			
Aunt	_____	_____			
Aunt	_____	_____			
Aunt	_____	_____			
Uncle	_____	_____			
Uncle	_____	_____			
Uncle	_____	_____			
Cousin	_____	_____			
Cousin	_____	_____			
Cousin	_____	_____			
Other	_____	_____			
Other	_____	_____			
Other	_____	_____			

Questions:

1. Which family in your sample is, on average, taller for both males and females?
2. Of the taller family, how many females are taller than the females in the shorter family? How many of the males are taller than the males in the shorter family?
3. From your data, does it appear that height is an inherited trait?
4. What is the advantage of examining the heritability of a variable like height rather than a variable such as temperament or intelligence?

Essay and Critical Thinking Questions

Comprehension and Application Essay Questions

We recommend that you follow either our guidelines for answering essay and critical thinking questions, or those guidelines provided by your instructor in preparing your response. Your answers to these kinds of questions demonstrate an ability to comprehend and think critically about concepts and topics discussed in this chapter.

1. Explain the concept of natural selection. Also explain the relationship between an evolutionary perspective and the goals and methods of behavior geneticists.
2. Explain the relationship among genes, chromosomes, and DNA. Also indicate how these entities function in reproduction.
3. What is a genotype and a phenotype? Explain how these concepts relate to the concepts of dominant and recessive genes.
4. What is infertility? What causes infertility? Explain what an infertile couple can do to have a baby.
5. List and explain at least three examples of abnormalities in genes and chromosomes.
6. Imagine that you want to start a family. Explain what you would do before attending a session with a genetic counselor and what kinds of questions you would ask during the meeting.
7. What is heritability? What kind of evidence demonstrates low and high heritability? Explain how this concept is used in discussions about intelligence and temperament.
8. Analyze your own temperament. Indicate whether your temperament is better explained by the Chess and Thomas or the Buss and Plomin approach. Also indicate how stable your temperament has been over the course of your development and what factors may have contributed to this stability or lack of stability.
9. What is the Repository for Germinal Choice? Indicate why studies of the hereditary basis of intelligence, rather than temperament, prompted its creation.
10. Indicate how you would explain to a friend that heredity and environment interact to produce development. Provide at least three examples that you would use to help your friend understand this concept.

Critical Thinking Questions

Your answers to the following kinds of questions reflect an ability to apply your critical thinking skills to a novel problem or situation that is *not* specifically discussed in this chapter.

1. Santrock discusses the role of the genetic counselor in this chapter. Apply your knowledge about the scientific base of child development by designing a study to determine whether and how prospective and expectant parents benefit from consultations with a genetic counselor: (a) What specific problem or question do you want to study? (b) What predictions would you make and test in your study? (c) What measures would you use (i.e., observation, interviews and questionnaires, case studies, standardized tests, physiological research, or a multimeasure, multisource, and multicontext approach) and how would you define each measure clearly and unambiguously? (d) What strategy would you follow—experimental or correlational, and what would be the time span of your inquiry—cross-sectional or longitudinal? (e) What ethical considerations must be addressed before you conduct your study?
2. According to Chapter 1, five issues define the nature of development: (a) biological, cognitive, and social processes, (b) periods or stages, (c) the issue of maturation (nature) versus experience (nurture), (d) the issue of continuity versus discontinuity, and (e) the issue of stability versus change. Indicate your ability to think critically by (a) analyzing the contents of this chapter for examples of each of the five defining issues, and (b) explaining which issues are most and least thoroughly discussed.
3. Chapter 1 indicates that theories help us explain data and make predictions about various aspects of development. Chapter 2 presents six different theoretical approaches (i.e., Freudian, cognitive, behavioral and social learning, phenomenological and humanistic, ethological, and ecological) but notes that no single approach explains the complexity of development. Indicate

your ability to think critically by analyzing and interpreting temperament (i.e., its causes and effects) in terms of each of the six theoretical approaches.

4. One aspect of thinking critically is to read, listen, and observe carefully, and then ask questions about what is missing from a text, discussion, or situation. For example, what is missing from this chapter's discussion of *in vitro* fertilization in light of a January 6, 1992, Associated Press article titled "America's First Test-Tube Baby Turns 10"? Indicate your ability to think critically by (a) listing as many developmental questions as you can about *in vitro* fertilization and (b) speculating why Santrock does not discuss this topic more fully.

5. Santrock places several quotations in the margins of this chapter. One by Desmond Morris says, "There are one hundred and ninety-three living species of monkeys and apes. One hundred and ninety-two of them are covered with hair. The exception is the naked ape self-named, Homo sapiens." Indicate your ability to think critically by (a) learning about the author and indicating why this individual is eminently quotable (i.e., what was the individual's contribution to human knowledge and understanding), (b) interpreting and restating the quote in your own terms, and (c) explaining what concept, issue, perspective, or term in this chapter Santrock intended this quote to illuminate. In other words, about what aspect or issue in development does this quote make you pause and think reflectively?

Self-Test B

1. A study that evaluates the extent of genetic influence on human behavior may involve
   a. twins reared apart.
   b. only identical twins.
   c. only fraternal twins.
   d. both twins and families without twins.
2. What encodes the changes in biology and behavior that result from evolution?
   a. natural selection
   b. reproduction
   c. culture
   d. genes
3. Genes are to chromosomes as _____ is to _____
   a. gametes/meiosis.
   b. DNA/heredity.
   c. chromosome/DNA.
   d. chromosome/gamete.
4. A zygote is produced by
   a. chromosomes.
   b. DNA.
   c. fertilization.
   d. meiosis.

5. Knowledge that x-carrying sperm are heavier than y-carrying sperm could be used to
   a. lower the incidence of genetic abnormalities.
   b. select the sex of offspring at conception.
   c. shape the evolution of a species.
   d. improve the process of meiosis.
6. PKU is a problem with
   a. production of an enzyme.
   b. an extra chromosome.
   c. the red blood cells.
   d. sex chromosome abnormalities.
7. Women who are missing an X chromosome, who are short in stature, and who may be mentally retarded have
   a. Klinefelter syndrome.
   b. sickle-cell anemia.
   c. Down syndrome.
   d. Turner syndrome
8. A procedure that was developed in the mid-1980s to assess prenatal risk for adverse developmental outcomes, and that is performed during the ninth or tenth week of pregnancy, is
   a. amniocentesis.
   b. ultrasound sonography.
   c. the chorionic villus test.
   d. both a and b.

9. Which treatment would not be used to treat infertility in a woman who has damaged ovaries?
   a. *in vitro* fertilization
   b. surgery
   c. antibiotics
   d. hormone therapy
10. Why do many developmentalists criticize the Repository for Germinal Choice?
    a. The evidence for hereditary influence on intelligence is controversial.
    b. We do not yet understand how hereditary factors combine to influence intelligence.
    c. The Repository is an example of unnatural selection.
    d. The goal of controlling characteristics of future offspring is repugnant to most people in our culture.
11. Intelligence is an example of a trait that is controlled by
    a. polygenic inheritance.
    b. sex-linked genes.
    c. reaction range.
    d. dominant/recessive genes.
12. The observable and measurable characteristics of an individual are
    a. the phenotype.
    b. the genotype.
    c. the reaction range.
    d. canalization.
13. If the environment has a large role in determining a characteristic of an individual, the genotype would be said to
    a. be highly canalized.
    b. have a large reaction range.
    c. be fixed by environmental factors.
    d. be not malleable.
14. Twin studies involve
    a. comparing identical and fraternal twins.
    b. doing two identical studies with two different families.
    c. comparing the offspring of siblings.
    d. comparing twins with their parents.
15. Jensen's work has been criticized because
    a. he defines intelligence in qualitative terms.
    b. investigations have not included environments that differ radically.
    c. his view of intelligence is too broad to measure readily.
    d. he did not use enough subjects in his research.
16. Twin studies demonstrate that having the identical heredity as someone else
    a. causes an individual to have similar characteristics.
    b. is associated with having similar characteristics.
    c. does not produce very much similarity to the other person.
    d. results in having an identical personality with the other person.
17. Dimensions of temperament in Plomin's work include all of the following except
    a. activity level.
    b. adaptability.
    c. sociability.
    d. distractibility.
18. Bobby generally shows little energy and has difficulty coping with new situations. According to Chess and Thomas, Bobby would be classified as
    a. difficult.
    b. easy.
    c. slow-to-warm-up.
    d. there is not enough information to tell.
19. Research on the heritability of intelligence and temperament indicates that the intelligence of identical twins should be _____ the temperament of identical twins.
    a. more similar than
    b. less similar than
    c. as similar as
    d. more variable than
20. The quote, "No genes, no organism; no environment, no organism," is used to express the concept of
    a. a natural selection.
    b. reproduction.
    c. interaction.
    d. canalization.

1. a	4. c	7. d	10. b	13. b	16. b	19. a
2. d	5. b	8. d	11. a	14. a	17. d	20. c
3. d	6. a	9. d	12. a	15. b	18. c	

Objectives

1.0 *Images of Children: Jim and Sara, An Expectant Couple*
1.1 Describe the life changes that face a couple during pregnancy.

2.0 *The Course of Prenatal Development*
2.1 Define and distinguish between (a) germination and implantation, (b) blastocyst and trophoblast, and (c) zygote and embryo.
2.2 Define and distinguish among the structures and functions of the endoderm, mesoderm, and ectoderm.
2.3 Define and distinguish between placenta and umbilical cord, and explain their roles in preventing harmful substances from being passed from mother to infant.
2.4 Explain the roles of the amnion and amniotic fluid in prenatal development.
2.5 Define organogenesis and explain its importance.
2.6 Summarize changes that take place during the fetal period.

3.0 *Miscarriage and Abortion*
3.1 Define and distinguish between miscarriage and abortion.
3.2 List some misconceptions about the cause of miscarriages.
3.3 Compare and contrast the availability and regulation of abortion in countries throughout the world.
3.4 Discuss the medical, ethical, psychological, and personal issues pertinent to the decision to have an abortion.
3.5 Indicate what researchers know and do not know about the psychological effects of an abortion on a woman.

4.0 *Teratology and Hazards to Prenatal Development*
4.1 Define teratogen and teratology, and identify the period of greatest vulnerability to teratogens.
4.2 Discuss maternal diseases and conditions that influence prenatal development such as rubella, syphilis, herpes, and AIDS.
4.3 Compare and contrast an ectopic and a normal pregnancy.
4.4 Define and distinguish the age-related risks of pregnancy for both a teenage mother an a "thirtysomething" mother.
4.5 Discuss the incidence of ectopic pregnancy as it relates to both sexually transmitted diseases (STDs) and age.
4.6 Summarize the effects of nutrition on prenatal development.
4.7 Explain how a mother's emotions and experience of stress can influence prenatal development, birth, and the newborn.
4.8 Define and distinguish how thalidomide, alcohol, cigarettes, marijuana, and cocaine affect prenatal development.
4.9 Define fetal alcohol syndrome (FAS).
4.10 Explain how alcohol use contributes to the higher risk of deformity and birth defects among younger versus older women.
4.11 List the prenatal, birth, and postnatal consequences of smoking by pregnant women.
4.12 Explain why it is difficult to know exactly how cocaine use during pregnancy influences prenatal development.
4.13 Compare and contrast the effects of various drugs on fetal development and later life.

4.14 Define toxoplasmosis.

4.15 Describe the hazards that radiation, toxic wastes, video display terminals, cats, and hot tubs pose to prenatal development.

4.16 List the legal and ethical pros and cons of attempts to protect fetuses from their mothers' potentially harmful behaviors.

4.17 Describe how surgery and therapy can be performed on a fetus.

5.0 *Expectant Parents*

5.1 Identify the early signs of pregnancy.

5.2 Explain how to calculate the due date given the fertilization date, and why the physician's method for calculating the due date for birth often confuses parents.

5.3 Discuss what a couple might learn during a parent education class on pregnancy and prenatal development.

5.4 Compare and contrast the parents' physical, psychological, and interpersonal experiences during the first, second, and third trimesters.

5.5 Describe the physical changes that occur just before birth, and define a nesting urge.

5.6 Describe nutritional changes recommended for a pregnant woman.

5.7 Summarize the exercise guidelines for expectant mothers, and distinguish between the potential risks and benefits of exercise.

5.8 Explain how a mother's view of pregnancy can influence the course of her pregnancy.

5.9 Compare and contrast the typical activities, beliefs, and intervention practices related to pregnancy among Mexican Americans, Black Americans, Native Americans, Vietnamese, and White Americans.

Summary

1.0 Images of Children: Jim and Sara, An Expectant Couple

Couples expecting their first child spend much time preparing for the birth and face many difficult questions.

2.0 The Course of Prenatal Development

Prenatal development includes conception and the germinal, embryonic , and fetal periods. Conception usually occurs when a sperm cell unites with an ovum in the female's fallopian tube.

The Germinal Period. The first two weeks of gestation is the germinal period, during which the zygote, a structure of 100 to 150 cells, forms. The inner layer is the blastocyst that later develops into the embryo. The outer layer is the trophoblast that later develops into the placenta.

The Embryonic Period. The implantation of the blastula marks the beginning of the embryonic period. During the next six weeks, the embryo differentiates into an outer layer (ectoderm), a middle layer (mesoderm), and an inner layer (endoderm). The ectoderm becomes the hair, skin, nails, nervous system, and sensory receptors. The mesoderm becomes the muscles, bones, circulatory, and excretory systems. The endoderm develops into the digestive and respiratory systems. During the embryonic period, a primitive human form takes shape, and the basic parts of the body can be identified. The placenta, umbilical cord, and amnion form and serve as a life-support system. The process of organ formation during the embryonic period is called organogenesis. The period ends at about eight weeks after conception.

The Fetal Period. The remaining seven months until birth is the fetal period. During this time, fetal size increases, the organs start functioning, reflexes appear, and there is sexual differentiation.

3.0 Miscarriage and Abortion

Miscarriages, or spontaneous abortions, are fairly common in early pregnancy. Most occur within the first trimester. Many occur without the mother's knowledge, and estimates indicate that 15 to 20 percent of pregnancies end in miscarriages. Deliberate termination of pregnancy is legal in the United States and can be done up until the end of the second trimester. The issue of deliberate abortion raises many medical, psychological, and social concerns and questions. Although abortion policies differ throughout the world, there is approximately one abortion for every two births.

4.0 Teratology and Hazards to Prenatal Development

Environmental influences can act on the developing zygote, embryo, and fetus to produce birth defects, developmental problems, or both.

Teratology. Teratogens are agents that produce birth defects and have their greatest effects during organogenesis.

Maternal Diseases and Conditions. Maternal diseases can cross the placental barrier or act at the time of birth. Maternal diseases or infections include rubella, syphilis, genital herpes, and AIDS.

The Mother's Age. Teenage mothers and mothers beyond 30 years of age are more likely to have impaired babies. Teenage mothers are twice as likely as mothers in their twenties to experience infant mortality. In an ectopic pregnancy, the embryo is implanted outside its normal location in the uterus. Ectopic pregnancies are associated with sexually transmitted diseases and with childbearing later in a woman's life. After age 30 it becomes increasingly difficult to become pregnant.

Nutrition. Mothers provide nutrition to a developing fetus, and malnourished mothers are more likely to produce malformed babies. One study of Iowa mothers documents a relationship between mother's nutrition and the well-being of their newborns.

Emotional States and Stress. The mother's emotional experiences of stress can affect both a developing fetus and the birth process. A mother's anxiety during pregnancy is reflected by the activity level and crying of her infant.

Drugs. In the early 1960s mothers who took thalidomide, a tranquilizer for morning sickness, subsequently bore many deformed babies and demonstrated the powerful effects of drugs on prenatal development. Women who consume alcohol during pregnancy increase the likelihood of producing offspring with fetal alcohol syndrome. Smoking cigarettes is associated with adverse prenatal development, birth, and postnatal development. In addition, women who smoke during pregnancy experience more fetal and neonatal deaths and have more preterm and low-birthweight infants. Other hazardous drugs include marijuana, heroin, and cocaine. Recent attention has centered on babies born to mothers who use cocaine.

Environmental Hazards. Exposure to radiation can cause chromosomal abnormalities. Pollutants and toxic wastes such as pesticides, carbon dioxide, mercury, and lead pose dangers to fetuses. A new concern is the effects of electromagnetic radiation from video display terminals. Toxoplasmosis produces coldlike symptoms in adults, but acts as a teratogen for a developing fetus. Saunas and hot tubs that raise the mother's body temperature can produce fevers that endanger the fetus. The issue of fetal rights arises from cases in which mothers have been prosecuted for prenatal use of drugs, and from cases in which companies have refused to employ women in situations where they might be exposed to substances that could harm a fetus.

Fetal Surgery and Therapy. Recent developments make it possible to surgically treat diaphragmatic hernia, hydrocephaly, sickle-cell anemia, and other diseases in a developing fetus. Possible therapies include blood transfusions and direct injections of drugs that otherwise do not pass through the placental barrier. The benefits of prenatal surgery and therapy must be weighed against the risks to the expectant mother and fetus.

5.0 Expectant Parents

Confirming the Pregnancy. One way to confirm a pregnancy is to check a woman's urine or blood for human chorionic gonadotropin (HCG), a hormone produced during pregnancy. Other signs of pregnancy include missed menstrual periods, faintness, nausea, and increased vaginal secretions.

Calculating the Due Date. Fetal life begins with fertilization; however, the first day of a woman's last menstrual period is used to calculate the length of the pregnancy. This method of dating confuses many parents.

The First Trimester. The first three months of a pregnancy encompass the period of organogenesis. Expectant mothers are often tired and experience both physical and emotional changes. Expectant parents often can benefit from parent education classes that cover topics such as self-care, fetal development, sexuality, nutrition, rest, and exercise.

The Second Trimester. Months four through six of a pregnancy typically involve less nausea and physical fatigue for the mother. Psychological concerns center around the advancing pregnancy and changing body.

The Third Trimester. The final three months of pregnancy may be accompanied by shortness of breath, indigestion, and heartburn that result from an expanding uterus. Childbirth class helps an expectant couple learn about labor, birth, and how to cope with the final stage of pregnancy.

Preparing for the Birth of the Baby. Expectant mothers' profiles change during the final two weeks of pregnancy as the fetus descends into the pelvic cavity. Pressure on the diaphragm is decreased. Noticeable contractions that prepare the uterine muscle for labor increase in frequency.

The Expectant Mother's Nutrition, Weight Gain, and Exercise. Satisfactory weight gains in the range of 25 to 35 pounds assure adequate calorie intake and are associated with favorable reproductive outcomes. Nutritional counseling may be sought when weight gains are less than 2.2 pounds per month or more than 6.6 pounds per month. The recommended daily allowance for all nutrients increases during pregnancy; however, the recommended increase varies with the nutrient in question. Uncomplicated pregnancies allow mothers to maintain normal participation in exercise; however, low impact activities are safer as a pregnancy progresses.

Cultural Beliefs about Pregnancy and Prenatal Development. Cultural beliefs govern specific actions during pregnancy. Some cultures view pregnancy as a medical condition, whereas others view it as a naturally occurring event. Health care providers need to be sensitive to the main beliefs, values, and behaviors related to pregnancy and childbearing when working with mothers from various cultural groups.

Key Terms

1.0 Images of Children: Jim and Sara, An Expectant Couple

2.0 The Course of Prenatal Development
germinal period
blastocyst
trophoblast
implantation
embryonic period
endoderm
ectoderm
mesoderm
placenta
umbilical cord
amnion
organogenesis
fetal period

3.0 Miscarriage and Abortion
miscarriage
abortion

4.0 Teratology and Hazards to Prenatal Development
teratogen
teratology
ectopic pregnancy
rubella
sexually transmitted diseases (STDs)
fetal alcohol syndrome (FAS)
environmental hazards
toxoplasmosis
fetal rights
fetal surgery

5.0 Expectant Parents
fertilization date
due data
trimester
prenatal education class

Guided Review

1.0 Images of Children: Jim and Sara, An Expectant Couple

1. A popular book about pregnancy is _____ ____ _____ _____ _____ _____.

   What to Expect When You're Expecting

2. Some of the many concerns that expectant couples face include whether both couples will continue to _____, what kinds of _____ they want to be, and _____ _____ _____ _____ _____ _____.

   work
   parents, what their child will be like

2.0 The Course of Prenatal Development

1. The reproductive cell formed in the female is called an _____. The reproductive cell formed by the male is called the _____ cell. _____ takes place when one sperm cell unites with an ovum.

   ovum
   sperm
   Conception

2. The cell formed by the union of sperm cell and ovum is called a _____. The period of time during which the zygote travels through the fallopian tube is about _____ to_____ days and is called the _____ period.

   zygote
   three, four
   zygote

3. The two weeks immediately after conception are called the
    _____ period. During this period rapid cell division results in
    the formation of a _____.

    germinal
    blastula

4. The inner layer of the blastula is called the blastocyst. The outer
    layer develops in tissues that provide nutrition and protection for
    the embryo and is called the trophoblast. During the second week
    the blastula becomes attached to the inner lining of the uterine
    wall in a process called _____.

    implantation

5. The second prenatal period of development is the _____
    period. The blastocyst differentiates into three layers: the
    _____, _____, and _____.

    embryonic
    ectoderm, mesoderm,
    endoderm

6. The _____ gives rise to the digestive and respiratory systems.
    The _____ gives rise to the nervous system, skin, and sensory
    receptors. The _____ gives rise to muscles, bones, and
    circulatory system.

    endoderm
    ectoderm
    mesoderm

7. The part of the embryo attached to the uterine wall becomes the
    _____. The _____ _____ houses the arteries and
    veins that pass very small molecules between the mother and the
    embryo. The pouch that holds the embryo suspended in a clear
    fluid is called the _____.

    placenta, umbilical cord

    amnion

8. The first two months of prenatal development have been called
    _____ because the formation of many organ systems of the
    body occurs then.

    organogenesis

9. The last part of the gestation period is called the _____
    period.

    fetal

10. By the end of three months, the length of the fetus is _____
    inch(es) and the weight is _____ ounce(s). Most physical
    features become differentiated, and gender can be identified.

    three
    one

11. By the end of the fourth month, fetal behavior involves some
    prenatal _____. The fetus is about _____ inches long and
    weighs about _____ to _____ ounces.

    reflexes, six
    six, seven

12. By the end of the fifth month, the fetus displays a preference for
    a particular _____. The fetus is _____ inches long and
    weighs about _____ ounces.

    position, 12
    16

13. By the end of the sixth month there is evidence of both _____
    movements and a _____ reflex. The fetus is _____ inches
    long and weighs _____ pounds.

    breathing
    grasping, 14
    two

14. By the end of the seventh month the fetus is _____ inches
    long and weighs _____ pounds.

    16
    three

15. The final two months are devoted mainly to overall _____.   growth
    The fetus grows to an average of _____ inches in length and   20
    a weight of _____ pounds.   seven

3.0 Miscarriage and Abortion

1. Spontaneous abortions are thought to occur for ___ to ___   15, 20
   percent of all pregnancies. Unwanted pregnancies can be
   terminated legally by _____. These can lead to _____   abortions, depression
   and _____.   guilt

2. Most women feel _____ after an abortion. Abortions are more   relief
   stressful for women who have _____ _____ _____   histories of emotional
   _____ . The upsetting effects of abortion _____ over   disturbance, diminish
   time.

3. Abortion regulations around the world are _____ . Factors   variable
   that influence regulation of abortion include _____ , ____   religion
   _____ , and _____ _____ . some countries _____   mother's needs,
   abortion.   sociomedical concerns.
                                                                            encourage

4.0 Teratology and Hazards to Prenatal Development

1. An agent that can cause a birth defect is called a _____ .   teratogen
   Sensitivity to the effects of a teratogen depends in part on the   time
   _____ during gestation when the mother is exposed. The ___   brain
   is most vulnerable 15 to 20 days after conception, the _____   eyes
   at 24 to 40 days, the _____ at 20 to 40 days, and the   heart
   _____ at 24 to 36 days.   legs

2. An outbreak of _____ caused large numbers of birth defects   rubella
   in the mid-1960s. Rubella is also called _____ _____. The   German measles
   most vulnerable time seems to be the _____ and _____   third, fourth
   weeks for the effects of rubella. _____ causes damage later   Syphilis
   in the pregnancy and after birth.

3. _____ _____ can infect the baby at _____. If it   Genital herpes, birth
   does, death or _____ _____ is possible.   brain damage

4. Mothers can transmit _____ to their offspring. The usual   AIDS
   source of the infection is use of _____ _____. Symptoms   intravenous drugs
   of the infection in the infant appear during the _____ year   first
   of life.

5. The mortality rate of infants born to adolescent mothers is ___   two
   times that of infants born to mothers over the age of 20. Much of
   this effect may be due to lack of _____ _____, but some   prenatal care
   of it may result from an immature _____ _____.   reproductive system

6. Mothers over the age of _____ are more likely to give birth   30
    to babies with _____ _____. Older women are also less   Down syndrome
    likely to _____ _____.   get pregnant

7. Pregnancies that occur outside of the uterus are called _____   ectopic, fallopian tubes,
    pregnancies. They usually occur in the _____ _____.   increased, sexually
    Recently they have _____ in frequency because of increases   transmitted diseases,
    in _____ _____ _____ and _____ _____   delays in childbearing,
    _____. Usually they are _____ to the fetus.   fatal

8. The developing fetus gets its food from its _____.   mother
    Malnutrition can cause infants to be _____ and to have less   smaller
    _____. Malnourished infants are likely to _____.   vitality, die

9. The mother's emotional state can affect the _____ of
    contractions during birth. One study found that the babies of   regularity
    anxious mothers _____ more and were more _____.   cried, active

10. In the 1960s the tranquilizer _____ was found to produce   thalidomide
    _____ _____ _____ _____ in babies when taken   missing arms and legs
    by pregnant women.

11. Consumption of _____ by the mother can adversely affect   alcohol
    fetal health. The _____ _____ _____ includes many   fetal alcohol syndrome
    defects, including microencephaly and mental retardation. Moderate
    drinking has been linked to _____ attention in infants.   lower

12. During the past decade drinking by pregnant women has _____.   decreased
    This trend has occurred entirely among _____ women.   educated

13. Cigarette smoking has been associated with _____ prematurity   higher
    rates and _____ birth weights. _____ problems are also   lower, Respiratory
    more common in the offspring of smokers.

14. Mothers who smoked marijuana while they were pregnant tend to
    have infants who have _____ _____ _____ as   tremors and startles
    newborns and poor _____ _____ _____ development   verbal and memory
    at age four.

15. Some of the consequences of mother's heroin use during pregnancy   addiction, tremors,
    to her infant are _____, _____, and _____ _____.   disturbed sleep
    _____ _____ may appear later in development.   Attention deficits

16. Use of cocaine is associated with _____ _____. These   congenital abnormalities
    may be caused by the cocaine or other _____ cocaine-using   drugs
    mothers take. Longer use of cocaine during pregnancy is
    associated with _____ _____ problems suffered by the   more severe
    infant later in life.

17. Environmental hazards to prenatal development include _____, _____, and _____ _____. Radiation appears to harm men's _____ as well as the developing _____ _____ _____.

radiation
pollutants, toxic wastes
sperm, embryo and fetus

18. Prenatal exposure to lead is associated with _____ _____. Prenatal exposure to PCBs is associated with having _____ infants who _____ _____ to stimuli.

mental retardation
premature
react slowly

19. Prenatal exposure to video display terminals is _____ associated with _____ miscarriage risk. However, working at video display terminals is associated with _____ on expectant mothers.

not
increased
stress

20. The fact that a mother's behavior can endanger her unborn child's well-being or life raises the issue of _____ _____. The fundamental issue concerns whether protecting unborn children will result in _____ _____ women.

fetal rights

discrimination against

21. _____, an infection contracted from _____ _____, produces mild symptoms in adults and _____ _____, _____ _____, and _____ _____ in human offspring.

Toxoplasmosis, cat feces
brain defects
eye defects, premature
birth

22. Hot tubs are an _____ _____ to fetuses because they cause a _____ in the mother. This interferes with _____ _____ early in pregnancy. A reasonable amount of time for a pregnant woman to spend in a hot tub is _____ _____.

environmental hazard
fever, cell division

ten minutes

23. If during prenatal development a fetus's diaphragm fails to close, an option now available is _____ _____. Other prenatal problems that can be treated prenatally include _____, _____ _____, and _____ _____ _____. A major concern about prenatal surgery is its _____ to the infant, which must be weighed against the advantage of _____ _____ _____.

fetal surgery
hydrocephaly
blocked bladder, sickle-cell anemia, risk
rapid postoperative healing

5.0 *Expectant Parents*

1. Pregnancy tests check for the presence of _____ _____ _____ in a _____ _____. _____ detection helps a mother to optimize aspects of _____ _____.

human chorionic gonadotropin, woman's blood, Early, prenatal care

2. The length of a pregnancy is calculated from the _____ day of a woman's _____ menstrual cycle. Due dates are therefore usually _____. About _____ of all babies are born within ten days of their due dates.

first
last
approximate, two-thirds

3. During the first three months, or first _____, a pregnant woman will probably be very _____ and need _____; she will often feel _____. Her breasts will _____, she may _____ more frequently, and she likely will experience ____ _____.

trimester
tired, sleep
sick, enlarge
urinate, emotional
changes

4. The first trimester is also emotionally mixed for ____ ____. Couples should _____ their feelings during this time. Although couples may find themselves in a closer relationship, their sexual activity may _____ _____ _____.

the father
share

increase or decrease

5. Classes in _____ _____ may help couples adjust to their pregnancy. Topics typically include _____ _____, _____ _____, _____, _____, and the _____ and _____ _____ _____ _____.

prenatal education,
prenatal development,
self-care, teratology,
sexuality, physical,
psychological aspects of
pregnancy

6. During the second trimester, the mother begins to feel _____. The fetus begins to fill out the _____, which expands. Physicians monitor the height of the _____ to check fetal development and estimate the _____ of the pregnancy.

better
uterus
fundus
length

7. A mother's _____ do not increase in size during the second trimester, but they may secrete _____. Mother's response to their appearance is _____.

breasts
colostrum
variable

8. During the second trimester a father may feel _____ to fetus and mother and become more _____. _____ _____ is considered to be safe.

closer
interested, Sexual
intercourse

9. During the third trimester a mother is likely to experience discomforts such as _____, _____, and _____ _____ _____, as well as varicose veins, hemorrhoids, and swollen ankles. She looks forward to birth for _____.

heartburn, indigestion
shortness of breath
relief

10. In the last three months of pregnancy couples may feel more _____ of the fetus. They must alter their _____ _____ to accommodate to mother's physical state. They need to maintain open _____.

protective, sexual
activity
communication

11. Near the end of pregnancy, a fetus _____ into the _____ _____. This creates added discomforts such as an increased need to _____. During this time mothers may also feel _____ that are not yet associated with _____. Mothers may be either especially _____ or _____.

drops, pelvic cavity

urinate
contractions, labor
fatigued, energetic

12. During pregnancy a mother should _____ weight, optimally about _____ to _____ pounds. The rate of gain should be _____ during the first trimester and _____ during the second two. Inadequate weight gain may result in _____ _____ infants.

gain
25, 35
slowest, constant
low-birthweight

84

13. Adequate nutrition involves _____ intake of all nutrients. Changes in intake are _____ across nutrients. For example, iron needs increase over _____, whereas other nutrient needs increase by _____ to _____.

    increased
    variable
    50%
    15%, 50%

14. Women's exercise needs during pregnancy are _____. A woman may _____ her normal exercise routine, but should avoid beginning _____ exercise routines. Women may be well-advised to _____ the amount of jogging they do as their pregnancy advances.

    variable
    maintain
    strenuous
    decrease

15. General rules for exercise include _____ the intensity of a workout as the pregnancy advances, avoiding _____ exercise, warming up and cooling down, and carefully monitoring the effects of exercise on the woman's own body.

    decreasing
    strenuous

16. What a woman does during her pregnancy is influenced by her _____ _____. These are _____ from culture to culture. Awareness of this is very important for _____ _____ _____.

    cultural beliefs, variable
    health care providers

17. Individuals who attend to pregnant mothers vary from culture to culture. Among Mexican-Americans they may be _____ or _____ _____ or an indigenous healer called a _____. _____ are found in Asian cultures, whereas in Black cultures the attending individuals may be _____ _____, _____ _____, or _____. A special concern to health care providers is whether the practices of these individuals _____ an unborn infant's well-being.

    mothers
    older women, curandero,
    Herbalists
    faith healers, root
    doctors, spiritualists,
    threaten

Key Terms Matching Exercise

1.0   Images of Children: Jim and Sara, An Expectant Couple (no terms)
2.0   The Course of Prenatal Development (Terms 1–13)
3.0   Miscarriage and Abortion (Terms 14–15)
4.0   Teratology and Hazards to Prenatal Development (Terms 16–25)
5.0   Expectant Parents (Terms 26–29)

---

1. germinal period   E

2. blastocyst   B

3. trophoblast   f

4. implantation   A

5. embryonic period   C

a. The blastula's firm attachment to the wall of the uterus

b. Inner layer of the blastocyst that later becomes the digestive system

c. Developmental period lasting from about two to eight weeks after conception; it begins after implantation

d. Inner layer of the blastula that will become the embryo

e. The two weeks after conception that end with completed implantation

6. endoderm _D_   f. Outer layer of cells of the blastula that will become the placenta and amniotic sac

---

7. ectoderm _e_

a. Meeting ground for the circulatory systems of the embryo and mother; oxygen and nutrients, but not blood, pass through to the embryo

8. mesoderm _f_

b. Contains the artery that transports waste material from the embryo to the placental barrier; also contains the vein that transports oxygen and nutrients from the placenta to the embryo

9. placenta _A_

c. Bag of clear fluid in which the developing embryo floats

10. umbilical cord _B_

d. First two months of prenatal development, during which time organ systems form and are sensitive to influence from environmental events

11. amnion _c_

e. Outer layer of the blastocyst that later becomes the hair, skin, and nervous system

12. organogenesis _D_

f. Middle layer of the blastocyst that later becomes the muscles and bones

---

13. fetal period _f_

a. A medical procedure that results in the deliberate termination of a pregnancy

14. miscarriage _c_

b. Field of study that focuses on birth defects

15. abortion _A_

c. A spontaneous abortion that terminates a pregnancy before the developing organism can survive outside the womb

d. Any agent that causes birth defects

16. teratogen _D_

17. teratology _B_

e. A situation in which the embryo or fetus develops outside of its normal place in the uterus

18. ectopic pregnancy _e_

f. Lasts from about eight weeks to birth

---

19. rubella

a. Agents in the environment that threaten fetal development such as chemicals and radiation

20. sexually transmitted diseases (STDs)

b. A controversy opposing an individual woman's right to privacy with obligations on the part of the government to protect individuals

21. fetal alcohol syndrome (FAS)

c. Disease conveyed through sexual contact

22. environmental hazards

d. A condition that results in minor illness in an adult, but acts as a teratogen for fetuses

23. toxoplasmosis

e. Characterized by small heads and defective limbs, joints, face, and heart; may affect the offspring of mothers who consumed alcoholic beverages during pregnancy

24. fetal rights   f. German measles

25. fetal surgery   a. A period of three months
26. fertilization date   b. The predicted day of the end of a
                                                 pregnancy, commonly determined by
                                                 physicians as 280 days after the first day of
                                                 a woman's last menstrual period
27. due date   c. Surgical intervention and treatment during
                                                 the period two months after conception until
                                                 birth
28. trimester   d. Courses in which couples may learn about
                                                 various aspects of pregnancy and fetal
                                                 development
29. prenatal education class   e. The actual date on which a child was
                                                 conceived

Key Terms Matching Exercise
Answer Key

1. e	5. c	9. a	13. f	17. b	21. e	25. c	29. d
2. d	6. b	10. b	14. c	18. e	22. a	26. e	
3. f	7. e	11. c	15. a	19. f	23. d	27. b	
4. a	8. f	12. d	16. d	20. c	24. b	28. a	

Self-Test A

1. The structure produced by the process of
   fertilization is the
   a. fetus.
   b. embryo.
   c. blastula.
   d. zygote.
2. Where does fertilization take place?
   a. in the fallopian tube
   b. in the uterus
   c. in the ovary
   d. in the vagina
3. The blastocyst is to the trophoblast as the
   _____ is to the _____
   a. blastula/embryo.
   b. endoderm/ectoderm.
   c. mesoderm/ectoderm.
   d. endoderm/mesoderm.
4. Which structure gives rise to the skin and
   nervous system?
   a. trophoblast
   b. endoderm
   c. mesoderm
   d. ectoderm

5. What event signals the end of the fetal
   period?
   a. implantation of the fetus on the uterine
      wall
   b. birth
   c. differentiation of the blastula
   d. the end of organogenesis
6. About what percent of pregnancies end in
   spontaneous abortions?
   a. 3 to 5%
   b. 10%
   c. 15 to 20%
   d. 25%
7. The Supreme Court has ruled that abortions
   can be obtained during the first
   a. six months.
   b. two months.
   c. trimester.
   d. four weeks.

8. Rubella is most likely to cause
   a. distorted limbs.
   b. blindness and deafness.
   c. damage to organs that are already formed.
   d. problems with the gastrointestinal tract after birth.

9. A child is born with a small head, defective limbs and joints, and a defective heart. She also is hyperactive and has seizures. Which substance is it most likely that her mother used during pregnancy?
   a. alcohol
   b. nicotine
   c. caffeine
   d. heroin

10. Cocaine-using mothers who stop using the drug after the first trimester are less likely to have babies who
    a. have orientation problems.
    b. show impaired motor behavior.
    c. are born preterm.
    d. spontaneously abort.

11. What risk to fetal development is associated with working at a video display terminal?
    a. miscarriage
    b. genetic mutation
    c. premature birth
    d. none

12. Prenatal surgery is performed mainly to
    a. repair damage to fetuses injured in accidents.
    b. correct congenital malformations of the infant's body or organs.
    c. deal with blood disorders.
    d. place infants in optimal positions for development.

13. The calculated due date for a baby typically
    a. is very close to the actual due date.
    b. usually agrees with parental estimates of the date of conception.
    c. errs by about two weeks.
    d. is a very rough estimate of when the pregnancy will end.

14. Bob has just found out his wife is pregnant. He is happy, but also worried about the changes this will bring about in his life. Bob's reaction is
    a. normal.
    b. unusual because most men are simply delighted to be a father.
    c. an indication that he may not be a good father.
    d. mild; most men are greatly worried about their wives' pregnancies.

15. Early prenatal classes typically include information about all of the following except
    a. birth practices.
    b. sexual activity.
    c. breast feeding.
    d. exercise.

16. During the second trimester pregnant women's feelings about their appearance
    a. improve.
    b. decline.
    c. stay the same as they were.
    d. are variable from woman to woman.

17. The time of greatest discomfort for a woman during pregnancy is probably
    a. the first trimester.
    b. the second trimester.
    c. the third trimester.
    d. variable from mother to mother.

18. All of these are signs that a pregnancy is coming to an end except
    a. frequent urination.
    b. easier breathing.
    c. weight gain.
    d. greater energy.

19. The largest source of weight gain during pregnancy is the weight of
    a. the uterus and breasts.
    b. tissue fluids.
    c. mother's stores of nutrition.
    d. the fetus and its support structures.

20. An activity believed to be good during pregnancy unique to Native American women is
    a. exercise.
    b. wearing certain clothing.
    c. using herbs.
    d. applying oils and creams.

Self-Test Answers
Test A

1. d	4. d	7. a	10. c	13. c	16. d	19. d
2. a	5. a	8. b	11. d	14. a	17. a	20. a
3. b	6. c	9. a	12. b	15. a	18. c	

Critical Thinking Exercises

Exercise 1

Chapter 4 illustrates a number of the issues discussed in "The Nature of Development" presented in Chapter 1. Which of the following topics taken from Chapter 4 correctly illustrates the Chapter 1 topic paired with it? **Circle the letter of the best answer and explain why it is the best answer and why each other answer is not as good.**

A. germinal, embryonic, and fetal periods: stability
B. embryonic development: maturation
C. teratology: biological determinants and influences
D. miscarriage/abortion: discontinuity
E. cultural beliefs: cognitive processes

Exercise 2

Chapter 4 contains several tables and figures designed to illustrate changes in both the fetus and mother during pregnancy. Which of the following statements accurately represent information contained in the table or figure with which it is paired? **Circle the letter of the best answer and explain why it is the best answer and why each other answer is not as good.**

A. Figure 4.4: Growth is most rapid during the second trimester.
B. Figure 4.5: The ear is most susceptible to damage caused by teratogens during the eighth week of pregnancy.
C. Figure 4.8: The weights of fetuses whose mothers smoke differ by nearly a constant amount from the weights of fetuses whose mothers do not smoke throughout pregnancy.
D. Figure 4.11: Mothers experience a constant rate of weight gain during pregnancy.
E. Figure 4. 12: Mothers should increase their intake of vitamin D and folacin more than other nutrients during pregnancy.

Exercise 3

In Family Issues 4.2, "Do the Unborn Have Rights?", Santrock explores two sides of the problem of protecting fetal development from hazards mothers may willingly risk. Which of the following appears to be an assumption, rather than an inference or an observation, made by people who opposed legislation to protect fetal rights? **Circle the letter of the best answer and explain why it is the best answer and why each other answer is not as good.**

A. Prenatal drug use prosecutions could open the door to punishing women for any risk to which they expose their fetuses.
B. Few drug treatment programs accept pregnant drug addicts.
C. Fertile men, but not fertile women, are allowed to risk their reproductive health when companies bar women from hazardous jobs.
D. An unborn fetus has full legal rights as a human being.
E. Barring women from jobs hazardous to reproductive health is another means to limit women's opportunities.

Research Project 1 Why Do Some Pregnant Women Drink, Smoke, or Use Drugs?

Despite the fact that the dangers of drinking alcohol, smoking, and other drug use to fetal development are now well known and widely publicized, women continue to use these substances while they are pregnant. This research activity (suggested in Salkind, S. S. (1990). *Child development.* Fort Worth: Holt, Rinehart, & Winston) attempts to find out why.

Have students invite a group of female friends who smoke or drink to talk to you about whether they will do these things when they are pregnant. Then have them ask their friends whether they know that smoking and drinking endanger prenatal development and about what they know in detail. Have them talk about the dangers (they may need to do some teaching!), and then ask again whether their friends will drink and smoke. You may want to suggest to students that they tape record the answers, but make sure they prepare an interview schedule no matter how they choose to record answers.

Research Project 2 Comparing Parenting Guides

From a library or bookstore acquire two recent parenting guides. The guides should (a) be directed toward the same age group (e.g., infancy, preschool, schoolage, adolescent) and (b) address at least one common issue in parenting. Your task is to compare the ideas in the book and critique the worth of the two guides. Include specific examples from the books, discuss the theoretical positions of the authors, and address the ways in which the authors define parenting and parent-child relationships. Write a critique of the two books in which you indicate that one book is better than the other and provide reasons for your choices. Within the context of your critique, address the following questions:

1. What kinds of parents would benefit from each of the two books? Who is the targeted audience?
2. What kinds of parenting issues do the books cover? Are the books comprehensive in approach or do they focus on just a couple of parenting concerns?
3. What is the theoretical persuasion of the authors? For example, do they use behavioristic or psychoanalytic terminology? Moreover, what is the tone of each book: sympathizing, encouraging, preaching?
4. Is each book practical? Is either book too idealistic?
5. Do the books use actual research findings to back the authors' positions? Do the authors provide useful case study examples? Do the books include practical exercises or activities for parents or for parents and children?

Essay and Critical Thinking Questions

Comprehension and Application Essay Questions

We recommend that you follow either our guidelines for answering essay and critical thinking questions, or those guidelines provided by your instructor in preparing your response. Your answers to these kinds of questions demonstrate an ability to comprehend and think critically about concepts and topics discussed in this chapter.

1. Describe development during the germinal, embryonic, and fetal periods. Also indicate and explain what factors might contribute to complications at specific times during gestation.
2. What are the placenta and umbilical cord, and what roles do they play?
3. What is organogenesis, and why is this concept important to the process of development?

4. Discuss the medical, ethical, psychological, and personal issues pertinent to the decision to have an abortion.
5. What is a teratogen? Indicate at least two examples of teratogens and their specific effects.
6. For each of the three stages of prenatal development describe when teratogens will have the most detrimental effects on the developing baby. Indicate at least two examples of those effects.
7. Compare and contrast the risks to expectant mothers who are either teenagers, twentysomething, or thirtysomething.
8. Discuss legal and ethical pros and cons of attempts to protect fetuses from their mothers' potentially harmful behaviors.
9. Explain why the physician's methods for calculating the due date of birth often confuse parents.
10. Imagine that you are an expectant parent. What would you do and learn in a parent education class on pregnancy and prenatal development?

Critical Thinking Questions

Your answers to the following kinds of questions reflect an ability to apply your critical thinking skills to a novel problem or situation that is *not* specifically discussed in this chapter.

1. According to an Associated Press article on February 20, 1992, the issue of the effects of drugs on prenatal development arose after Jeffrey Dahmer was sentenced to life imprisonment for 15 slayings. In brief, the claim was made that Dahmer's mother ingested four sedatives (meprobamate, mephobarbital, phenobarbital, and secobarbital) and the female sex hormone progestin one month after becoming pregnant. The article suggested that these drugs could have affected Dahmer and were somehow related to his slaying the victims, having sex with their corpses, and eating their flesh. Apply your knowledge about the scientific base of child development by designing a study to determine the prenatal effects of sedatives and hormones on personality development and behavior. Answer these questions: (a) What specific problem or questions do you want to study? (b) What predictions would you make and test in your study? (c) What measures would you use (i.e., observation, interviews, and questionnaires, case studies, standardized tests, physiological research, or a multimeasure, multisource, and multicontext approach) and how would you define each measure clearly and unambiguously? (d) What strategy would you follow—experimental or correlational, and what would be the time span of your inquiry—cross sectional or longitudinal? (e) What ethical considerations must be addressed before you conduct your study?
2. According to Chapter 1, five issues define the nature of development: (a) biological, cognitive, and social processes, (b) periods or stages, (c) the issue of maturation (nature) versus experience (nurture), (d) the issue of continuity versus discontinuity, and (e) the issue of stability versus change. Indicate your ability to think critically by analyzing the contents of this chapter for examples of each of the five defining issues and (b) explaining which issues are most and least thoroughly discussed.
3. Chapter 2 presents six different theoretical approaches (i.e., Freudian, cognitive, behavioral and social learning, phenomenological and humanistic, ethological, and ecological), but notes that no single approach explains the complexity of development. Imagine that you are a developmental psychologist with several clients who have considered having an abortion. In some cases, the individuals obtained an abortion, and in other cases, the individuals did not obtain an abortion. Indicate your ability to think critically by explaining how you would apply each theoretical perspective in analyzing and treating your clients.
4. One aspect of thinking critically is to read, listen, and observe carefully, and then ask questions about what is missing from a text, discussion, or situation. For example, this chapter discusses the psychological effects of abortion on the mother, but not the father. Indicate your ability to think critically by (a) speculating about why Santrock neglected to discuss the psychological

effects of abortion on fathers and (b) evaluating whether this seeming oversight represents a case of sexism in developmental research that should be avoided, according to the author's claim in Chapter 1.

5. Santrock places several quotations in the margins of this chapter. One by Lawrence Durrell says, "So the riders of the darkness pass on their circuits: the luminous island of the self trembles and waits, waits for us all my friends, where the sea's big brush recolors the dying lives, and the unborn smiles." Indicate your ability to think critically by (a) learning about the author and indicating why this individual is eminently quotable (i.e., what was the individual's contribution to human knowledge and understanding), (b) interpreting and restating the quote in your own terms, and (c) explaining what concept, issue, perspective, or term in this chapter Santrock intended this quote to illuminate. In other words, about what aspect or issue in development does this quote make you pause and think reflectively?

Self-Test B

1. The trophoblast later becomes the
   a. placenta.
   b. uterus.
   c. embryo.
   d. blastula.
2. The germinal period ends with
   a. meiosis.
   b. germination.
   c. implantation.
   d. organogenesis.
3. The muscles and skeletal system arise from which structure(s)?
   a. ectoderm
   b. mesoderm
   c. endoderm
   d. mesoderm and ectoderm, respectively
4. What does *not* appear during the embryonic period?
   a. the arms and legs
   b. the heartbeat
   c. the eyes and ears
   d. the genitalia
5. The umbilical cord allows
   a. the blood of the mother and fetus to mix.
   b. nutrition to get from the mother to the fetus.
   c. wastes to pass out of the fetus.
   d. both b and c.

6. Amniotic fluid performs all of the following functions except
   a. protection against infection.
   b. control of temperature.
   c. absorption of shock from blows to the mother's body.
   d. both a and b.
7. A likely cause of miscarriage is
   a. the mother experiencing a severe fright.
   b. the mother working at a video display terminal.
   c. a genetic abnormality in the embryo.
   d. the mother's age.
8. The most widely practiced policy on abortion in the world allows abortion
   a. on request during the first trimester.
   b. when the woman's life is in danger.
   c. on sociomedical grounds.
   d. well into the second trimester.
9. A critical period for the development of internal organs during pregnancy is
   a. germination.
   b. implantation.
   c. organogenesis.
   d. the fetal period.
10. Which of the following does *not* adversely affect the health of an infant?
    a. the age of the mother
    b. caffeine exposure during pregnancy
    c. emotional upset of the mother during pregnancy
    d. calcium pills taken by the mother during pregnancy

11. Exposure to teratogens during the germinal period typically results in
    a. prenatal death.
    b. structural abnormalities.
    c. physiological defects.
    d. premature birth.
12. The sexually transmitted disease that creates a risk of ectopic pregnancy is
    a. AIDS.
    b. syphilis.
    c. genital herpes.
    d. chlamydia.
13. Knowledge about the probable effect of drugs on prenatal development typically is based on _____ research.
    a. experimental
    b. correlational
    c. observational
    d. case study
14. Sudden infant death syndrome (SIDS) is associated with the use of _____ during pregnancy.
    a. cigarettes
    b. marijuana
    c. alcohol
    d. cocaine
15. Why did Chapter 3 not indicate that x-rays are used commonly to assess prenatal development?
    a. X-rays do not provide good views of the developing fetus.
    b. X-rays are teratogens.
    c. Other techniques are much more informative.
    d. It is not clear; x-rays are not much of a risk to unborn children.

16. What conflict has proved difficult to resolve in court cases involving fetal rights?
    a. the rights of the father versus the rights of the mother
    b. the rights of the fetus versus the rights of the mother
    c. the rights of the fetus versus the rights of the father
    d. the rights of the mother versus the rights of society
17. Which of the following is a sign of pregnancy?
    a. changes in the appearance of a woman's eyes
    b. cravings for bizarre foods
    c. dreams about babies
    d. nausea or vomiting
18. Sexual activity during pregnancy between husband and wife
    a. decreases.
    b. increases.
    c. remains constant.
    d. is variable.
19. A pregnancy commonly becomes "real" to a father during the
    a. germinal period.
    b. first trimester.
    c. second trimester.
    d. third trimester.
20. In order to supplement the amount of iron a woman gets in her diet during pregnancy, she may want to eat more
    a. dairy products.
    b. grain products.
    c. carrots and potatoes.
    d. fruits.

Self-Test Answers
Test B

1. a	4. d	7. c	10. d	13. b	16. b	19. c
2. c	5. d	8. a	11. a	14. a	17. d	20. b
3. b	6. a	9. c	12. d	15. b	18. d	

Objectives

1.0   *Images of Children: Teresa Block's Pregnancy and Her Son Robert*
1.1   Describe some problems faced by parents of premature babies.

2.0   *Stages of Birth, Delivery Complications, and the Use of Drugs during Childbirth*
2.1   Describe the three stages of birth.
2.2   List four birth complications.
2.3   Define and distinguish between precipitate and anoxia.
2.4   Explain why a breech position complicates delivery of a baby.
2.5   Define cesarean section, list factors that influence its use, and cite information that suggests cesarean sections are overused in the United States.
2.6   List reasons for administering drugs such as tranquilizers, sedatives, and analgesics to a woman giving birth to a child.
2.7   Define oxytocin, and list the pros and cons of administering drugs such as oxytocin during delivery.
2.8   Summarize what researchers know and do not know about the effects of drugs administered to a woman during childbirth.

3.0   *Childbirth Strategies*
3.1   Summarize the contemporary trends in childbirth practices.
3.2   Describe standard childbirth, the Leboyer method, and the method of prepared (natural) childbirth, and list pros and cons of each practice.
3.3   Indicate the basic philosophies underlying the standard, Leboyer, and prepared childbirth methods.
3.4   List the skills of a qualified childbirth instructor.
3.5   Describe what happens in childbirth classes and what an expectant couple might learn by taking such a class.
3.6   Explain why it is better to refer to those who support a mother through birth as a circle rather than a team.
3.7   List trends in childbirth practices in the 1990s.
3.8   Explain why many birthing practices promote relaxation by the mother.
3.9   Indicate the main emphases of today's methods of childbirth.
3.10 Summarize how the Lamaze method exemplifies prepared childbirth, and compare and contrast it with the Leboyer method.
3.11 Explain why and how fathers have become more involved in childbirth, and list the pros and cons of a father's participation in childbirth.
3.12 Explain why and how siblings have become more involved in childbirth, and list the pros and cons of a sibling's participation in childbirth.
3.13 Indicate how older children's lives change when newborns enter the family, and discuss how parents may ease problems for siblings of newborns.

4.0   *Preterm Infants and Age-Weight Considerations*
4.1   Define and distinguish between preterm and low-birthweight infants.
4.2   Discuss how to reduce the risks common to low-birthweight infants.
4.3   Discuss whether a shortened gestation period harms an infant.
4.4   Summarize recommendations about stimulation of preterm infants.

4.5   Explain how sociocultural factors contribute to developmental outcomes for preterm infants.
4.6   Explain why some countries have lower rates of low-birthweight infants than the United States.
4.7   Explain why experts argue that "preterm infant care is far too complex to be described only in terms of amount of stimulation."
4.8   Explain why experts believe that massage and exercise benefit preterm infants.
4.9   Discuss how to organize a developmental plan for a preterm infant, and explain why it is so expensive to care for preterm babies.

5.0   *Measures of Neonatal Health and Responsiveness*
5.1   Define and distinguish between the Apgar scale and Brazelton Neonatal Behavioral Assessment Scale.
5.2   Compare and contrast what you would learn about your infant from the Apgar and Brazelton scales.

6.0   *The Postpartal Period*
6.1   Explain why calling the postpartal period the "fourth trimester" might enhance our understanding of this developmental period.
6.2   Summarize the physical adjustments that women must make during the postpartum period.
6.3   Summarize the emotional and psychological adjustments that women must make during the postpartum period.
6.4   Define bonding, and evaluate the claim that bonding between infant and parent shortly after birth is crucial to the infant's development.
6.5   Describe changes in a couple's relationship that commonly occur after the birth of a child.
6.6   Explain how the advice of Eisenberg, Murkoff, and Hathaway may help a family decide whether the mother stays home or returns to work after having a baby.

Summary

1.0 Images of Children: Teresa Block's Pregnancy and Her Son Robert

Pregnancies can be relatively easy or difficult. The latter pose physical hardships for the mother and may produce low-birthweight babies. Such frail babies that survive birth often show the consequences for many years.

2.0 Stages of Birth, Delivery Complications, and the Use of Drugs during Childbirth

Stages of Birth. The birth process has been divided into three stages. In the first stage, uterine contractions dilate the woman's cervix so that the baby will be able to move from the uterus into the birth canal. The second stage begins when the baby's head starts to move through the birth canal and ends when the baby is born. The third stage, called afterbirth, involves the detachment and expulsion of the placenta.

Delivery Complications. A number of complications, such as a precipitate or breech delivery, can accompany the baby's arrival. Surgical removal of the baby from the uterus is called a cesarean section.

The Use of Drugs during Childbirth. Drugs can aid deliveries by relieving pain or anxiety. Drugs such as the hormone oxytocin can speed the process of delivery. It is difficult to make clear statements about drug effects because birthweight and social class are better predictors of problems than drugs.

Some medications are thought to have negative effects on the infant; others are thought to have no effect. However, the amount of medication given is quite an important variable.

3.0 Childbirth Strategies

Expectant parents can choose from a number of childbirth strategies.

Standard Childbirth. The expectant mother goes to a hospital where a doctor is responsible for the baby's delivery. The birth usually takes place in a space resembling an operating room, and medication is commonly administered to the mother. Critics of this method point out that other individuals important to the mother are excluded from the process, the infant is separated from the mother shortly after birth, and giving birth is treated like a disease.

The Leboyer Method. This method, often deemed "birth without violence," was developed with the intention of making the process of birth less stressful for infants.

Prepared, or Natural, Childbirth. Prepared, or natural childbirth, is a process in which the mother is informed about what will happen during the procedure and about comfort measures for childbirth. It entails little medication and involves parents in making decisions about any complications that arise. Although there are variations, they all share common concerns for making parents confident, providing self-help tools for normal childbirth, and explaining how the medical system functions. This approach endorses both the teaching and taking of childbirth classes.

New for the Nineties. The most current trend in the 1990s shifts emphases, offers new choices, and encourages understanding of obstetrical terminology.

Today's Methods. Most current methods are based on the concepts of Grantley Dick-Read. An emphasis is placed on attention and responsiveness to individual prenatal and birthing needs. One common approach, the Lamaze method, emphasizes breathing techniques.

The Father's Participation. Fathers increasingly participate in the childbirth process. Cultural change has taken place in America to encourage fathers to meet with caregivers, attend childbirth classes, and participate in the care of infants.

Siblings. Parents expecting a second or subsequent child often prepare older children for the birth of a sibling. The older child learns about pregnancy, birth, and life with a newborn in a developmentally appropriate fashion.

4.0 Preterm Infants and Age-Weight Considerations

Low-Birthweight and Preterm Infants. Normal gestation is 38 to 42 weeks from conception. Infants born earlier than 38 weeks after conception are called preterm babies. Full-term infants born after a normal gestation period but who weigh less than 5.5 pounds are called low-birthweight infants. Intervention programs now improve the developmental outcomes for low-birthweight infants. Preterm infants have a different profile than that of full-term infants.

Some Conclusions about Preterm Infants. Research has produced four important conclusions about preterm infants: (a) Advances in intensive care technology have reduced the likelihood of serious consequences for preterm infants; (b) Outcomes for infants born with an identified problem are likely to be worse than for those born without a recognizable problem; (c) More favorable outcomes for preterm infants are associated with higher socioeconomic status; and (d) Preterm infants do not generally encounter later difficulty in school.

Stimulation of Preterm Infants. Care of the preterm infant is much too complex to be described only in terms of amount of stimulation. The conceptual age, illness, and individual makeup of preterm infants affect their responses to stimulation. The appropriate stimulation changes as the preterm infant becomes less fragile and approaches full term. Intervention programs should entail individual developmental plans. National policies regarding prenatal care influence the percentage of low-birthweight infants.

5.0 Measures of Neonatal Health and Responsiveness

The Apgar scale is a quick screen of infant status that assesses heart rate, respiratory effort, muscle tone, body color, reflex irritability at one and five minutes after birth. The Brazelton Neonatal Assessment Scale is a more detailed evaluation, typically given on the third day of life. It evaluates 20 reflexes and an infant's reactions to 26 different circumstances involving both physical and social stimulation. Brazelton training involves using the Brazelton scale to show parents how their newborn responds to people. The training may be of help with high-risk infants.

6.0 The Postpartal Period

The Nature of the Postpartal Period. The postpartum period, usually lasting about six weeks after birth, comprises a time in which a woman's body adjusts both physically and psychologically to the process of childbearing. The term "fourth trimester" conveys the idea of continuity and the importance of this period for the mother.

Physical Adjustments. Physical adjustments include fatigue, involution (the process by which the uterus returns to its prepregnant size), consideration of when to resume sexual intercourse, and participation in exercises to recover former body contour and strength.

Emotional and Psychological Adjustments. Emotional fluctuations are common for recent mothers during the postpartal period. A special interest in the study of parent-infant relationship is bonding, the development of an emotional tie between parents and infant. In recent years, a critical-period hypothesis has been advanced, suggesting that bonding must occur within the first few days of life. Although the exact time period has been questioned, this view has led to a revision of hospital procedures, allowing mothers and fathers more access to their infants in hospitals than was previously permitted. New babies also change the relationship between the mother and father and raise questions about whether and when a recent mother should go back to work. Guidelines exist for making the decision to work or not to work.

Key Terms

1.0 *Images of Children: Teresa Block's Pregnancy
and Her Son Robert*

2.0 *Stages of Birth, Delivery Complications, and
the Use of Drugs during Childbirth*
dilation
birth

afterbirth
precipitate
anoxia
breech position
cesarean section
tranquilizer
sedative

analgesic
oxytocin

3.0 Childbirth Strategies
standard childbirth
Leboyer method
prepared, or natural, childbirth
childbirth instructor
health care circle
Lamaze method
sibling

4.0 Preterm Infants and Age-Weight Considerations

full-term infant
preterm infant
low-birthweight infant
stimulation

5.0 Measures of Neonatal Health and Responsiveness
Apgar Scale
Brazelton Neonatal Behavioral Assessment Scale

6.0 The Postpartal Period
postpartal period
involution
bonding

Guided Review

1.0 Images of Children: Teresa Block's Pregnancy and Her Son Robert

1. A baby that weighs 2 pounds at birth looks _____ _____.

   very tiny

2. At a birth weight of 2 pounds, Robert Block was a _____ _____ baby.

   low-birthweight

2.0 Stages of Birth, Delivery Complications, and the Use of Drugs during Childbirth

1. During the first stage of labor, uterine contractions _____ in _____ and _____. They become more regular. This phase ends when the cervix dilates to a diameter of about _____ inches.

   increase
   frequency, intensity
   4

2. The second stage of labor involves the _____ of the baby. It ends when the baby is _____ _____ _____ the mother's body.

   birth
   completely out of

3. The _____ is delivered during the third stage of labor. This is accompanied by the _____ _____ and other _____.

   placenta
   umbilical cord,
   membranes

4. A delivery that is too fast is called _____. It can disturb the normal flow of _____ in the infant. A very long delivery can result in _____, or lack of _____ in the infant. Another complication of birth involving an out-of-position baby is called a _____. Sometimes this position may require a _____ delivery.

   precipitate
   blood
   anoxia, oxygen

   breech, cesarean

5. Surgical removal of an infant from the uterus is called a _____ _____. It is _____ than a breech delivery, but entails more _____. Critics believe that cesarean sections are performed _____ _____ in the United States.

cesarean section
safer
complications
too often

6. Drugs used during delivery can cross the _____ barrier and affect the _____. A drug that has been used to speed delivery is _____. Its use is controversial because it may cause more _____.

placental
infant
oxytocin
complications

3.0 Childbirth Strategies

1. The gestation period ends with _____. Standard childbirth practices exclude individuals _____ ___ ___ _____, _____ mother and infant after birth, and treat birth as if it were a _____.

birth
related to the mother
separate
disease

2. The method that eases the transition of birth for infants is the _____ method. Leboyer characterizes standard birth practices as _____ for infants and has developed a strategy he calls "_____ _____ _____."

Leboyer
traumatic
birth without violence

3. In prepared childbirth, a woman _____ what will happen, expects little _____, and participates in _____ _____ during the birth. The strategy assumes that she will be helped by a _____ or _____.

knows
medication, making
decisions
partner, friend

4. Prepared childbirths are _____. The basic element of prepared childbirth is that mothers are _____ about procedures and _____ _____ about them. Preparing parents for childbirth now involves several _____ _____.

variable
informed
make decisions
professional disciplines

5. Current strategies of childbirth can be described as _____. For example, use of breathing methods is _____ rather than required. In general, contemporary methods seem to be designed to ensure the _____ of both mother and infant.

eclectic
flexible

comfort

6. Teachers of childbirth classes are often _____, but they do not have to be. Today they need to have _____ skills. Usually it is desirable that they be _____. In addition to having knowledge about birth and birth strategies, they need to be _____ and _____ people.

nurses
many
parents

warm, confident

7. Childbirth classes teach _____ parents birth _____. The basic aim of these classes is to _____ birth. A widely used series of photographs is the _____ _____.

both, techniques
demystify
Birth Atlas

8. One influential guide recommends that the group of individuals who help a woman give birth be called a health care _____ rather than a health care _____. This stresses the central role of the _____ during childbirth.

circle
team
mother

9. Today there are _____ childbirth methods, most of which
    appear to be based on _____ _____ concepts. Chief
    among these is the importance of _____ and _____.

    many
Grantley Dick-Read's
information, support

10. The Lamaze method of childbirth focuses on _____ and
    _____. This method has increased the involvement of _____
    in childbirth. The aim of the method is to make mothers more
    _____ in childbirth.

    breathing
    relaxation, fathers

    active

11. _____ class parents are more likely to opt for prepared
    childbirth in the United States than are _____ class parents.

    Middle
    lower

12. _____ are more involved in childbirth than they used to be.
    This seems to involve changes in cultural definitions of _____
    _____. Fathers often participate in birth as a _____.
    Professionals now support this involvement by stressing that birth
    should be an _____, _____ event for couples. However,
    there is disagreement about whether fathers are the best coaches
    during labor.

    Fathers
    gender roles
    coach

    intimate, shared

13. It is important for parents to _____ siblings for the birth of
    a baby. A good time to do this is during _____. A good
    opportunity, for example, is when a mother is feeling _____,
    or is beginning to look _____.

    prepare
    pregnancy
    sick
    fat

14. Some parents involve siblings in the birth itself. They do this to
    avoid _____ from their child and to facilitate an _____
    between the child and the baby.

    separation
    attachment

15. In order to avoid separation anxiety when an infant is born, a
    mother should _____ the child as much as possible about the
    birth. This may include a tour of the _____ as well as details
    about the _____.

    inform
    hospital
    birth

16. The birth of a sibling is _____ _____ for a child. It
    results in less _____ with parents. A common defense
    mechanism used to cope with this is _____. These reactions
    are normal, and should only cause concern if they _____.

    emotionally taxing
    time
    regression
    persist

17. To deal with the emotional upset of having a new baby
    experienced by their other children, parents basically should find
    ways to spend _____ with and pay _____ to them.

    time
    attention

4.0 Preterm Infants and Age-Weight Considerations

1. Babies born before their estimated time of delivery are now
    referred to as _____ babies. Babies who weigh less than 5.5
    pounds at birth are referred to as _____ _____ babies.

    preterm
    low-birthweight

2. In order to enhance developmental outcomes, mothers can learn to
    better understand low-birthweight infants' _____ and ____
    characteristics and cues, and how to respond _____ to them.
    In one study, low-birthweight infants whose mothers had received
    such training scored better on _____ _____ _____
    than low-birthweight infants whose mothers had not.

    behavioral, temperamental
    appropriately

    information processing
    measures

3. Low-birthweight babies that weigh less than 750 grams are likely
    _____ _____. Although the majority that weigh more than
    this survive, it is _____ to save a "_____ _____,"
    an infant who weighs 2.3 pounds or less.

    to die
    difficult, Kilogram kid

4. Preterm babies have a different _____ _____ than normal
    term infants do. For example, they are more likely to _____,
    and apparently _____ _____ differently.

    behavioral profile
    fuss
    process information

5. A problem in caring for preterm infants is that they often lack
    appropriate _____. When just born, such babies are _____
    and stimulation may upset their _____ _____. However,
    as they become healthier and more robust, stimulation may be
    guided by their _____ _____. Signs of _____ or
    _____ indicate that stimulation should be stopped. One
    beneficial sort of stimulation tested experimentally is _____.

    stimulation, fragile
    homeostatic balance

    behavioral cues, stress
    avoidance
    massage

6. The United States has a surprisingly large percentage of _____
    _____ infants. There are major discrepancies in rates for
    _____ compared to _____. Apparently, the reason is that
    pregnant women, especially Black women, in the United States do
    not receive uniform _____ _____.

    low-birthweight

    Blacks, Whites

    prenatal care

7. Interventions for preterm infants should be _____. They
    should include _____ and _____ _____. A
    developmental plan should assess parental understanding of their
    preterm infant's problems, as well as the _____ _____.

    individualized
    parents, family members

    infant's behavior

8. Improvements in _____ have reduced the incidence of serious
    consequences associated with preterm and low-birthweight births.
    Preterm infants with an identifiable problem have a poorer
    _____ than do healthy babies. _____ _____ _____
    is associated with better outcomes for the preterm infant. As a
    rule, preterm babies do not seem to be more at _____ for
    cognitive problems than do average newborns.

    technology

    prognosis, High social
    class
    risk

5.0 Measures of Neonatal Health and Responsiveness

1. The _____ Scale is a short screening procedure for evaluating
    the health of the newborn minutes after birth. It evaluates various
    _____ signs of health. A score of _____ to _____
    indicates a healthy baby; a score of _____ or lower suggests
    that the baby will _____ _____.

    Apgar

    physiological, 7, 10
    three
    not survive

2. The _____ Scale is a more complete evaluation of the newborn that includes an evaluation of the infant's reaction to _____. A low score on the Brazelton may indicate _____ _____. However, if the infant is simply _____ in reactions to people, the solution may be to _____ parents to respond to it more _____.

Brazelton

people, brain damage
sluggish
train
sensitively

6.0 The Postpartal Period

1. The period after birth is called the _____ period. It lasts about _____ weeks, and is a period of time when the mother's _____ returns to its pre-pregnant state. The speed of this adjustment depends on the _____ and _____ of delivery. During this period both _____ have to adjust to having a new baby.

postpartal
six
body
method, circumstances
parents

2. During the postpartal period most women are _____, which may _____ their self-confidence. Specific physical changes that may be related to this are _____, the uterus's return to its prepregnant size, and rapid changes in _____ _____. If the woman does not breast feed, _____ begins after _____ to _____ weeks. Physicians generally advise women to refrain from _____ _____ during this time. _____ during pregnancy helps a woman to recover faster, as does _____.

tired,
undermine
involution
hormone production
menstruation
four, eight
sexual intercourse
Exercise
relaxation

3. A common psychological problem in the postpartal period is _____ _____, possibly related to _____ adjustments. For some this may result in _____, and these women may need _____ help.

emotional fluctuation
physical
depression
professional

4. _____ is a controversial concept that implies that there is a critical period in the development of a close emotional attachment between the mother and the infant. The evidence ___ ___ support strong conclusions at this time, but the practice of bonding may enhance future _____ between parents and their infant.

Bonding

does not

interactions

5. The presence of a new baby alters mother's and father's _____ with each other. Parents have _____ time for each other and for old pursuits. They may have to _____ _____ some of their old commitments.

relationships
less
give up

6. A special concern for many mothers is whether or not to ____
after the baby is born. This choice is often _____ ____.
Some women do not have a _____. The general questions
mothers have to answer include how involved she wants to be in
_____ _____, how involvement in child care will influence
her _____, and which is more _____ to her. Mothers
must also evaluate how _____ being employed and caring for
the baby are, and whether she gets adequate _____ from her
husband and others.

work
very difficult
choice

child care
career, important
stressful
support

Key Terms Matching Exercise

1.0 Images of Children: Teresa Block's Pregnancy and Her Son Robert (no terms)
2.0 Stages of Birth, Delivery Complications, and the Use of Drugs during Childbirth (Terms 1–11)
3.0 Childbirth Strategies (Terms 12–18)
4.0 Preterm Infants and Age-Weight Considerations (Terms 19–22)
5.0 Measures of Neonatal Health and Responsiveness (Terms 23–24)
6.0 The Postpartal Period (Terms 25–27)

---

1. dilation   D

2. birth   A

3. afterbirth   F

4. precipitate   C

5. anoxia   E

6. breech position   B

a. Refers to the passage of the child from the uterus
b. Terminology describing infants born buttocks first
c. Delivery in which the baby moves too rapidly through the birth canal
d. The condition of being abnormally enlarged or stretched
e. When insufficient oxygen is available to the infant during delivery, possibly causing brain damage
f. Expelling of the placenta, umbilical cord, and other membranes

---

7. cesarean section   D

8. tranquilizer   G

9. sedative   A

10. analgesic   F

11. oxytocin   B

a. A drug that has a calming, soothing, or tranquilizing effect
b. Hormone that stimulates uterine contractions
c. Technique designed to make the birth experience less stressful for the infant; includes placing the infant on the mother's stomach immediately after birth
d. The surgical removal of a baby from the mother's uterus
e. A process for giving birth in which a woman goes to a hospital where a physician delivers the baby in a labor room that resembles an operating room

12. standard childbirth _e_

13. Leboyer method _c_

    f.   Refers to a drug that eliminates or minimizes pain

    g.   Refers to a drug used to calm or pacify

---

14. prepared, or natural, childbirth _E_

15. childbirth instructor _B_

16. health care circle _D_

17. Lamaze method _f_

18. sibling _G_

19. full-term infant _C_

20. preterm infant _A_

    a.   Term for infants born before 38 weeks in the womb

    b.   An individual, often a nurse, with a thorough understanding of birth and childbirth techniques

    c.   A baby born after spending 38 to 42 weeks in the womb between conception and delivery

    d.   A concept favored by the International Childbirth Education Association in which the prospective mother is the central figure in selecting individuals who will assist her in giving birth

    e.   A process for giving birth in which the mother is informed about what will happen during the procedure, uses little medication, and participates in decision making about any complications or problems

    f.   Form of prepared childbirth; designed to help the pregnant woman cope with the pain of childbirth and avoid medication

    g.   Refers to a brother or sister

---

21. low-birthweight infant _C_

22. stimulation _E_

23. Apgar Scale _D_

24. Brazelton Neonatal Behavioral Assessment Scale _f_

25. postpartal period _G_

26. involution _A_

27. bonding _B_

    a.   A process whereby a recent mother's uterus returns to its prepregnant state about 5 to 6 weeks after birth

    b.   Occurrence of an emotional tie between neonate and mother

    c.   An infant weighing less that 5.5 pounds at birth with a normal length gestation period

    d.   Method used to assess the health of the newborn that measures heart rate, respiratory effort, muscle tone, body color, and reflex irritability

    e.   Refers to various methods for treating preterm infants such as exercise and massage

    f.   Assessment of a newborn's neurological integrity; it measures 20 reflexes, and reactions to 26 circumstances such as physical and social stimulation

    g.   The period of time shortly after birth during which time the mother's body returns to a prepregnancy state

Key Terms Matching Exercise
Answer Key

1. d	5. e	9. a	13. c	17. f	21. c	25. g
2. a	6. b	10. f	14. e	18. g	22. e	26. a
3. f	7. d	11. b	15. b	19. c	23. d	27. b
4. c	8. g	12. e	16. d	20. a	24. f	

Self-Test A

1. Which stage of birth begins when the baby's head begins to move through the cervix?
   a. first
   b. second
   c. third
   d. fourth

2. A birth complication that threatens an infant's blood flow is
   a. a cesarean section.
   b. breech position.
   c. anoxia.
   d. precipitate birth.

3. Why would a physician administer a risk-producing drug such as oxytocin?
   a. to tranquilize the mother
   b. to avoid anoxia
   c. to reduce the mother's pain
   d. to slow a birth

4. All but one of the following is a standard criticism of standard childbirth practices. Which one is the exception?
   a. Important people are excluded from the birth.
   b. The mother and newborn are separated for too long a time.
   c. Birth is treated as a disease.
   d. The newborn is severely traumatized.

5. The core idea of prepared childbirth is that
   a. parents learn how to give birth to a baby.
   b. parents learn about birth and participate in decisions about it.
   c. parents anticipate the birth and make preparations for the new baby.
   d. parents plan their pregnancy and the time of birth.

6. A unique focus of the Leboyer method of childbirth is concern about
   a. breathing.
   b. the newborn's experience of birth.
   c. the influence of the birth environment on mother and newborn.
   d. preparing parents for the birth of their baby.

7. The birth method designed to teach the pregnant mother to cope with the pain of childbirth in an active way and to reduce the medication is
   a. Leboyer.
   b. cesarean.
   c. Lamaze.
   d. standard childbirth.

8. Which practice emphasized by the Lamaze is receiving less emphasis in birth practices of the '90s?
   a. breathing methods
   b. use of imagery to relax
   c. providing warm water for comfort
   d. making the atmosphere homelike

9. Good childbirth instructors have
   a. warm hands.
   b. nursing degrees.
   c. a clinical approach to childbirth.
   d. knowledge about psychology.

10. More fathers are participating in the birth of their children because
    a. they want to share an important moment with their wives.
    b. men are assuming feminine roles.
    c. they are the best support for their wives at this time.
    d. new birth methods require that they do so.

11. Children may participate in the births of their siblings because
    a. they are a good source of support for their mothers.
    b. this helps them to deal with separation from their parents.
    c. it is an optimal way to prepare them for life with a new baby.
    d. doing so helps to avoid behavior problems later.

12. A special concern about short-term infants is that
    a. their mothers may not know how to interact with them.
    b. their development may be retarded.
    c. they tend to be low-birthweight babies.
    d. development may stop prematurely.

13. Which high-risk infant has the greatest chance of a good outcome?
    a. upper social class, no identified problem
    b. lower social class, no identified problem
    c. upper social class, lung problem
    d. lower social class, lung problem

14. All but one of the following is an important concern for a plan to stimulate a preterm infant. Which one is the exception?
    a. infant's age
    b. including family members
    c. mother's ability to "read" her baby's signs
    d. conformity to a fixed, regular plan

15. The percentage of low-birthweight infants in the United States is greater than the percentage born in
    a. India.
    b. Iran.
    c. Israel.
    d. China.

16. The Brazelton Neonatal Assessment Scale measures all of the following except
    a. body color.
    b. social responsiveness.
    c. cuddliness.
    d. defensive movements.

17. A physician declares that the newborn baby is in excellent health. She has just administered the
    a. Apgar scale.
    b. Brazelton scale.
    c. Leboyer scale.
    d. Lamaze scale.

18. Involution is a(n) _____ adjustment to birth.
    a. emotional
    b. physical
    c. psychological
    d. sexual

19. The arrival of a new baby is likely to produce which change in parents' relationship with each other?
    a. more intense and satisfying time together
    b. less love
    c. less time together
    d. increased joy in their companionship

20. What is the status of the critical period argument for bonding?
    a. It is widely accepted.
    b. It has been disproved.
    c. It is a controversial issue.
    d. The infant should be kept in a newborn nursery so the mother doesn't expose it to germs.

Self-Test Answers
Test A

1. b	4. d	7. c	10. a	13. a	16. a	19. c
2. d	5. b	8. a	11. b	14. d	17. a	20. c
3. b	6. b	9. d	12. a	15. d	18. b	

Critical Thinking Exercises

Exercise 1

Chapter 5 contains a broad range of topics concerning childbirth. A special feature of this chapter is that it contains much advice to parents about how to prepare for childbirth, deal with difficulties such as a prematurely born baby, and adjust to their changed lives with a new infant. Interestingly, some of the advice is given with clearly described research backing and some is not. Which of the following topics is best documented with research? **Circle the letter of the best answer and explain why it is the best answer and why each other answer is not as good.**

A. use of drugs during childbirth
B. methods of childbirth
C. participation of fathers and siblings in childbirth
D. stimulation of preterm infants
E. bonding

Exercise 2

The material on preterm infants and age-weight considerations in your text describes two intervention studies done with low-birthweight and preterm infants. These studies are important because they evaluate ways to improve the care of infants. An important aspect of evaluating these studies, however, is identifying the research techniques used in them. Which of the following pairs of terms best represents this intervention research? **Circle the letter of the best answer and explain why it is the best answer and why each other answer is not as good.**

A. correlational, cross-sectional
B. correlational, longitudinal
C. experimental, cross-sectional
D. experimental, longitudinal
E. both correlational and experimental, and cross-sectional and longitudinal

Exercise 3

Methods for supervising and assisting childbirth have changed considerably in the past two decades. Your text describes the basics of today's methods as well as a number of new and experimental practices. An interesting feature of current practices is that they represent a renewed assumption about the process of childbirth that did not get much emphasis in the more physician-controlled practices of previous years. Which of the following is a statement of assumption, rather than an inference or an observation? **Circle the letter of the best answer and explain why it is the best answer and why each other answer is not as good.**

A. Most current methods are based on Grantley Dick-Read's concepts.
B. The father may not be the best coach during labor.
C. Active breathing is associated with less pain during delivery.
D. Women know how to give birth.
E. Including siblings in the birth presents sibling rivalry.

Research Project 1 Child Delivery Practices

This project is designed to look at generational differences in child delivery practices. Work in groups of four and give the following questions to your mother and to a woman who has an infant under two years of age. Pool your data with your group members to answer the questions.

		Parent	Other
1.	Was the delivery cesarean or vaginal?	C/V	C/V
2.	Were medications used?	Y/N	Y/N
3.	Was the father present in the delivery room?	Y/N	Y/N
4.	Did the pregnant woman attend childbirth classes?	Y/N	Y/N

Questions:

1. Has the percent of medication-free deliveries changed in the past 2 decades? If so, how?
2. Has the percent of cesarean deliveries relative to vaginal deliveries changed in the past decades? If so, how?
3. What percent of fathers were present in previous decades compared to now?
4. What percent of women attended childbirth classes in previous decades compared to now?
5. How do your data compare with the historical trends in delivery practices described in the text?

Research Project 2 Fatherhood

How actively are fathers participating in the births of their children these days? Find out by carrying out an interview project suggested in a child development text by Neil Salkind (Salkind, N. (1990). *Child Development.* Fort Worth: Holt, Rinehart, & Winston).

Invite two first-time, expectant fathers and two fathers of children under the age of two. Interview these men using the following sets of questions:

Expectant fathers:

1. What are your feelings about becoming a father?
2. How have you been involved in your wife's pregnancy?
3. What part will you play in your child's birth? What part would you like to play?
4. What do you think being a "good father" means?
5. How will having a child change your life?

Fathers:

1. What part did you play in the birth(s) of your child (children)? What were your feelings about this experience?
2. What are the three biggest challenges you face as a father?
3. What do you think a "good father" is?
4. How has having a child changed your life?
5. What advice would you give a new father?

Write a brief report indicating what you were trying to find out, describe your sample and how you interviewed the fathers and soon-to-be fathers, and then summarize similarities and differences between the two pairs of men. Relate what you learn to material on fathers' participation in childbirth that is in the text.

Essay and Critical Thinking Questions

Comprehension and Application Essay Questions

We recommend that you follow either our guidelines for answering essay and critical thinking questions, or those guidelines provided by your instructor in preparing your response. Your answers to these kinds of questions demonstrate an ability to comprehend and think critically about concepts and topics discussed in this chapter.

1. Describe the stages of birth, and explain three birth complications.
2. What is a cesarean section? What factors determine its use? Evaluate whether cesarean sections are overused in the United States.
3. Imagine that you are about to give birth. What questions about the use of drugs during delivery would be important to you? What reasons would lead you to accept or reject drugs such as tranquilizers, sedatives, and analgesics prior to delivering your child?
4. Imagine that you are a member of an expectant couple. What would you learn and do in childbirth classes?
5. Explain why many birthing practices promote relaxation by the mother.
6. Why and how have fathers become more involved in childbirth? Also discuss the pros and cons of this involvement.
7. How do preterm and low-birthweight infants differ?
8. What would you learn about your newborn from the Apgar and Brazelton Neonatal Behavioral Assessment scales?
9. What is bonding? What is the evidence for and against the claim that bonding between infant and parent shortly after birth is crucial to the infant's development?
10. Having a newborn baby often raises a question as to whether the mother will return to work outside the home or stay home with the baby. Explain how the advice of Eisenberg, Murkoff, and Hathaway would help you make this decision.

Critical Thinking Questions

Your answers to the following kinds of questions reflect an ability to apply your critical thinking skills to a novel problem or situation that is *not* specifically discussed in this chapter.

1. This chapter describes a change from standard childbirth practices to alternative strategies; however, it is not clear whether the selection of a childbirth strategy rests more on common sense or scientific research. Apply your knowledge about the scientific base of child development by designing a study to determine how the method of birth influences children's development: (a) What specific problem or question do you want to study? (b) What predictions would you make and test in your study? (c) What measures would you use (i.e., observation, interviews, and questionnaires, case studies, standardized tests, physiological research, or a multimeasure, multisource, and multicontext approach) and how would you define each measure clearly and unambiguously? (d) What strategy would you follow—experimental or correlational, and what would be the time span of your inquiry—cross sectional or longitudinal? (e) What ethical considerations must be addressed before you conduct your study?
2. According to Chapter 1, five issues define the nature of development: (a) biological, cognitive, and social processes, (b) periods or stages, (c) the issue of maturation (nature) versus experience (nurture), (d) the issue of continuity versus discontinuity, and (e) the issue of stability versus change. Indicate your ability to think critically by (a) perusing this chapter for two examples of

each of the five defining issues and (b) explaining how and why each of your examples illustrates one of the five defining issues.

3. Chapter 1 indicates that theories help us explain data and make predictions about various aspects of children. Chapter 2 then presents six different theoretical approaches (i.e., Freudian, cognitive, behavioral and social learning, phenomenological and humanistic, ethological, and ecological), but notes that no single approach explains the complexity of development. Indicate your ability to think critically by (a) perusing this chapter for topics influenced by at least one of the six theoretical approaches and (b) explaining which theoretical approach dominates the topic in question. If the presentation is entirely atheoretical, identify and explain how one of the theoretical approaches could be used to guide the analysis of the topic in question.

4. One aspect of thinking critically is to read, listen, and observe carefully, and then ask questions about what is missing from a text, discussion, or situation. For example, this chapter ends with a discussion of the difficult question about whether recent mothers should stay home with the baby or return to a job outside the home. Indicate your ability to think critically by (a) speculating about why Santrock does not give equal attention to the question of whether recent fathers should stay home with the baby or return to a job outside the home and (b) evaluating whether the treatment of this issue represents a case of sexism in developmental research that should be avoided, according to claims in Chapter 1.

5. Santrock places several quotations in the margins of this chapter. One by Francis Bacon says, "Children sweeten labors . . .," and another by Frederick Leboyer says, "We must respect this instant of birth, this fragile moment. The baby is between two worlds, on a threshold, hesitating . . . ." Indicate your ability to think critically by (a) learning about the author and indicating why this individual is eminently quotable (i.e., what was the individual's contribution to human knowledge and understanding), (b) interpreting and restating the quote in your own terms, and (c) explaining what concept, issue, perspective, or term in this chapter Santrock intended this quote to illuminate. In other words, about what aspect or issue in development does this quote make you pause and think reflectively?

Self-Test B

1. The second stage of birth begins when
   a. contractions begin.
   b. the cervix begins to dilate.
   c. the baby's head moves through the cervix.
   d. placenta and umbilical cord are expelled.

2. When the baby moves too rapidly through the birth canal, the birth is termed
   a. precipitate.
   b. anoxic.
   c. breech.
   d. a stage three delivery.

3. When a delivery is proceeding too slowly a physician may administer _____ to the mother
   a. a tranquilizer
   b. oxytocin
   c. relaxation procedures
   d. pain killers

4. A characteristic of the Leboyer method of childbirth is that
   a. midwives are usually present.
   b. the infant is placed on its mother's stomach immediately after birth.
   c. infants are separated from their mothers immediately after birth.
   d. women are coached by their husbands to cope with the pain of childbirth.

5. The method of birth that seeks to reduce the physical and psychological distress that babies experience is called the
   a. standard childbirth.
   b. Lamaze method.
   c. Leboyer method.
   d. prepared birth.

6. A key element of prepared childbirth is
   a. use of special breathing techniques.
   b. not using surgical or other invasive medical interventions.
   c. inclusion of the woman's husband at birth.
   d. presence of a supportive companion at birth.

7. All but one of the following is "new for the nineties" in childbirth. Which one is the exception?
   a. using warm water for comfort
   b. inclusion of siblings as supportive companions during the birth
   c. allowing birthing mothers more freedom to move about during birth
   d. use of diverse, non-drug relaxation techniques.

8. An important assumption of modern birth methods is that
   a. women know how to have babies.
   b. birth is not a painful experience.
   c. medical supervision is unnecessary.
   d. the key element of a successful birth is controlled breathing.

9. Who is the best companion for a woman during labor?
   a. her husband
   b. a close, female friend who has been through childbirth
   c. a midwife
   d. the individual the woman chooses to have present

10. All but one of the following are ways to help a child cope with the birth of a sibling. Which one is the exception?
   a. Give the child attention when the newborn is asleep.
   b. Let the child overhear you explain to the new baby that she has a very special brother or sister.
   c. Allow the child to express anger by acting it out away from the baby.
   d. Teach the child about living with a new baby.

11. A preterm infant is to a low-birthweight infant as _____ is to _____.
   a. 39 weeks/6 pounds
   b. 35 weeks/4 pounds
   c. 6 pounds/32 weeks
   d. 4 pounds/37 weeks

12. Which of the following statements is true about recent studies of preterm infants?
   a. There are as many serious consequences now for preterm infants as there were 15 years ago.
   b. Social class is not related to the outcome for the infant.
   c. Outcomes are worse for infants born with identified problems than for others.
   d. Preterm infants generally have difficulty later in school.

13. All but one of the following are factors that must be assessed in planning interventions to stimulate preterm infants. Which one is the exception?
   a. caregivers' abilities to "read" infants' responses
   b. the degree of prematurity
   c. the structure of the infants' families
   d. the degree of developmental retardation suffered by the baby

14. Countries that enjoy a lower incidence of low-birthweight babies than the United States does also provide
   a. more advanced medical care to pregnant women.
   b. low or no cost prenatal care to women.
   c. low or no cost postnatal care to infants.
   d. supplementary incomes to new parents.

15. When is the Apgar Scale used?
   a. the third day after birth
   b. 1 minute and 5 minutes after birth
   c. every month for the first six months after birth
   d. while the infant moves down the birth canal

16. In contrast to the Brazelton, the Apgar scale assesses an infant's
   a. health
   b. neurological development.
   c. reflexes.
   d. reactions to people.

17. In order to stress the continuity between life after birth and life before birth, some experts call this time the
   a. postpartum.
   b. involution.
   c. bonding period.
   d. fourth trimester.

18. All of the following are symptoms of postpartal depression except
   a. inability to sleep.
   b. disinterest in sex.
   c. large changes in appetite.
   d. crying spells.
19. What time period is thought by some to be the critical period for bonding between mother and child?
   a. the week before birth
   b. the initial days of the neonate's life
   c. the first six months
   d. all of the first year

20. Which of the following is a question that Eisenberg, Murkoff, and Hathaway suggest that mothers ask themselves about going back to work after having a baby?
   a. What is important to me?
   b. Is it moral to work and be a mother?
   c. Does my baby need me more than anyone else?
   d. Will my family and neighbors think well of me?

Self-Test Answers
Test B

1. c	4. b	7. b	10. c	13. d	16. a	19. b
2. a	5. c	8. a	11. b	14. b	17. d	20. a
3. b	6. d	9. d	12. c	15. b	18. b	

Chapter **6** Physical Development in Infancy

Objectives

1.0 *Images of Children: Studying Newborns*
1.1 Explain how it is possible to study newborns.
1.2 Discuss why contemporary researchers have changed their assumptions about the perceptual abilities of infants.

2.0 *Physical Growth and Development in Infancy*
2.1 Define infancy, and contrast it with the stages of development that precede and follow it.
2.2 Explain the role of natural selection in the development of reflexes.
2.3 Define and distinguish between the sucking and rooting reflexes and between the Moro and grasping reflexes.
2.4 Explain why some reflexes disappear during infancy whereas others persist throughout life.
2.5 Compare and contrast any three reflexes with regard to the nature of the eliciting stimulus, an infant's behavior, and the course of development.
2.6 Define and distinguish between nutritive and nonnutritive sucking, and identify the one developmentalists have found more useful for purposes of research.
2.7 Discuss the variation in the ability of infants to suck.
2.8 Distinguish what crying by newborns and 9 to 10 month-old infants can reveal to parents and developmental researchers.
2.9 Explain how behaviorists' and ethologists' views on the pros and cons of responding to infant crying can both be right.
2.10 Define and distinguish between reflexive and social smiles, and indicate what each can reveal to parents and developmental researchers.
2.11 Define and distinguish between cephalocaudal and proximodistal growth patterns, and explain how the development of gross and fine motor skills during infancy follows both of these patterns of growth.
2.12 Describe the course of height and weight increases during infancy.
2.13 Define and distinguish between fine and gross motor skills, and describe how each changes during infancy.
2.14 Discuss the relationship between gross motor development and an infant's independence.
2.15 Explain why infants do not need exercise classes.
2.16 Describe the sequence of activities appropriate to optimal physical development during the first year of life.
2.17 Describe how the brain changes during infancy.
2.18 Define infant state, and distinguish among Brown's seven infant states.
2.19 Define sleep-wake cycle, and describe the development of sleep patterns during the first year.
2.20 Define REM sleep, and explain why infants spend so much time in REM sleep.
2.21 Define sudden infant death syndrome (SIDS), and list factors related to an infant's heightened or diminished susceptibility to SIDS.
2.22 Explain the recommendation that infants eat infant cereal as their first solid food.
2.23 Explain how changes in eating patterns are made possible by motor development during infancy.

2.24 Indicate what considerations determine whether parents elect to feed their baby on a demand or parent-regulated schedule.

2.25 Explain how health-conscious parents can malnourish their infants.

2.26 Discuss the pros and cons of breast- versus bottle-feeding, and indicate sociocultural factors that encourage bottle-feeding rather than breast-feeding.

2.27 Define marasmus and describe the feeding practices associated with that condition.

2.28 Describe evidence for the claim that malnutrition limits cognitive and social development during infancy.

2.29 Explain why the incidence of infant malnutrition and associated infant mortality in the United States may be underestimated.

2.30 Summarize the advice developmentalists offer about toilet training 20-month-old infants.

2.31 Explain whether toilet training entails a fine or gross motor skill.

2.32 Indicate the infectious disease immunization schedule appropriate for infants and children.

2.33 List the types of accidents accounting for the greatest number of deaths and injuries in infancy.

2.34 Explain how motor development influences the accident risks faced by infants, and describe measures to prevent infants from having accidents.

3.0 *Sensory and Perceptual Development*

3.1 Define and distinguish between sensation and perception.

3.2 Discuss whether what humans see resembles or differs from a photograph.

3.3 Explain why William James's ideas about the infants' perceptual world were wrong.

3.4 List aspects of visual perception present at birth and those that develop after birth.

3.5 Compare the visual acuity of infants and adults.

3.6 Describe the kinds of visual stimuli that newborn infants prefer to view.

3.7 Describe the development of face perception.

3.8 Explain how scientists learn about infants' sensory and perceptual capacities even though infants cannot communicate directly what they experience.

3.9 List appropriate ways to stimulate an infant's visual perception.

3.10 Explain how we know that infants can hear before birth.

3.11 List appropriate ways to stimulate an infant's hearing and sense of touch.

3.12 Discuss the evidence that challenges the long-standing practice of not administering anesthesia to infants having operations.

3.13 Identify odors and tastes discriminable by newborns.

Summary

1.0 Images of Children: Studying Newborns

Studying newborns is challenging and has prompted researchers to devise various methods to examine their subtle, but complex, perceptual motor skills.

2.0 Physical Growth and Development in Infancy

Reflexes. The neonate is not passive. The neonate is born with reflexes and skills that are needed to sustain life functions such as sucking, swallowing, and elimination, and perceptual abilities such as seeing, hearing, and smelling. Other reflexes such as the Moro reflex, grasping, and rooting reflexes are also present. Sucking obtains nourishment, but also can provide researchers with a means to evaluate an infant's attention. Neonates communicate primarily through crying. Adults can differentiate between distressful crying and intentional crying and should always respond to an infant's cries early in development. Smiling changes from reflexive smiling to social smiling after two to three months.

Cephalocaudal and Proximodistal Sequences. Muscular control develops during the first year. Development follows a cephalocaudal pattern (from the head down) and a proximodistal pattern (from the center of the body toward the extremities).

Height and Weight. The average North American newborn is 20 inches long and weighs 7.5 pounds. Infants grow about 1 inch per month during the first year, and nearly triple their weight by the end of their first year. Rate of growth is slower during the second year of life.

Gross and Fine Motor Skills. Gross motor skills involve large muscle activities whereas fine motor skills such as finger dexterity entail more precision. A milestone in gross motor activity that typically first occurs at an average age of 12–13 months is walking. The idea of trying to accelerate an infant's physical skills through an exercise class is unwise; however, there are developmentally appropriate exercise activities and toys for infants. A milestone in fine motor activity entails the development of reaching and grasping skills.

The Brain. Changes in the brain occur during infancy. Although infants probably have all of the neurons they are going to have in life by birth, the interconnections between neurons increase dramatically during infancy.

Infant States. Infants show a variety of states of consciousness, including deep sleep, regular sleep, disturbed sleep, drowsy, alert activity, alert and focused attention, and inflexibly focused. The sleep-wake cycle of infants differs from that of adults. Younger infants spend about 50 percent of their sleep in REM sleep, in contrast to 20 percent for adults. REM sleep may provide self-stimulation or promote brain development. Sudden infant death syndrome (SIDS) is a condition that occurs when an infant stops breathing and suddenly dies without any apparent cause. SIDS is associated with biological vulnerabilities early in development.

Nutrition. Infants need to consume about 50 calories per day for each pound of their body weight. A major change during the second half of the first year is the introduction of solid foods. The newborn's main source of nutrition is human milk or formula. Weaning usually refers to relinquishing the breast or bottle for a cup. Food that is low in fat and calories is good for adults, but not infants. Demand feeding is more popular than scheduled feeding. Breast-feeding is thought to be better for an infant's health than bottle-feeding, especially in Third World countries. Marasmus can develop under conditions of severe protein-calorie malnutrition. Malnourished infants are shorter in stature and slower in cognitive growth in middle and late childhood than their better nourished peers.

Toilet Training. Toilet training entails a motor skill that is expected to be achieved in North American culture by three years of age. The recent trend is towards beginning toilet training later than in the past (e.g., at 20 to 24 months of age).

Health. Two important aspects of infant health are immunization and accidents. Widespread immunizations have reduced infectious diseases over the last 40 years. Accidents, especially in the 6–12 month range, are a major cause of death for infants, and accident prevention is a major concern for caregivers.

3.0 Sensory and Perceptual Development

What Are Sensation and Perception? Sensation occurs when physical energy contacts the sensory receptors, whereas perception occurs when our brain interprets what is sensed.

Visual Perception. Visual perception is one of the most explored areas of infant perception. Robert Fantz used infants' gazes to determine that they have visual preferences for patterns over colors or brightnesses. Visual acuity in the neonate is about 20/200, but become 20/100 by six months of age. Perception of the human face develops over the first five months of life. Depth perception demonstrated by using a visual cliff has been shown to be a natural response in infants six months of age. Infants two to four months old can discriminate visually between the shallow and deep sides of a visual cliff, but it remains controversial as to whether depth perception is innate. There are developmentally appropriate activities for the visual stimulation of infants.

Hearing. Research on hearing suggests that the ability to hear might exist before birth. There are developmentally appropriate activities for the auditory stimulation of infants.

Touch and Pain. Newborns clearly respond to touch because many reflexes are easily elicited by mild tactile stimulation. There are developmentally appropriate activities for the tactile stimulation of infants. Studies of circumcision indicate that neonates feel pain and that they can cope with it. This finding challenges the medical practice of operating on newborns without providing anesthesia.

Smell. Newborns are sensitive to unpleasant odors such as rotten eggs. Infants 2 to 7 days old can recognize the smell of their mother's milk on a breast pad compared with a breast pad with no milk.

Taste. Sensitivity to taste may be present before birth because increased swallowing has been observed when saccharin was added to the amniotic fluid of a near-term fetus. The facial expressions of newborns differ when they are sucking a sweet or sour substance.

Key Terms

1.0 Images of Children: Studying Newborns
perceptual motor system

2.0 Physical Growth and Development in Infancy
sucking reflex
rooting reflex
Moro reflex
grasping reflex
nutritive sucking
nonnutritive sucking
crying
reflexive smile
social smile
cephalocaudal pattern
proximodistal pattern
gross motor skills
fine motor skills
infant states

REM (rapid eye movement) sleep
sudden infant death syndrome (SIDS)
nutrition
weaning
scheduled feeding
demand feeding
marasmus
immunization

3.0 Sensory and Perceptual Development
sensation
perception
pattern perception
depth perception
visual stimulation
auditory stimulation
tactile stimulation
circumcision

Guided Review

1.0 Images of Children: Studying Newborns

1. A problem researchers who study infants have is finding ways to _____ with infants. They typically do this by observing infant's _____, something which often involves sophisticated _____.

communicate
behavior
equipment

2. Until recently it was widely believed that infants were _____. Now we believe that infants possess highly developed _____ _____ _____.

blind
perceptual motor systems

2.0 Physical Growth and Development in Infancy

1. The movements that govern the newborn are called _____. They are genetically carried _____ mechanisms beyond the infant's control.

reflexes ✓
survival

2. The food-getting reflex of neonates is _____. The reflex that allows neonates to find where to suck is the _____ reflex.

sucking ✓
rooting ✓

3. One reflex that can be thought of as a vestige of our evolutionary past is called the _____ reflex. A reflex that becomes incorporated into more complex, voluntary behavior is the _____ reflex.

Moro ✓
grasping ✓

4. The abilities of infants to suck effectively and successfully during feeding are _____. It may take them _____ weeks to learn to suck in a way that is _____ with how their mothers are feeding them.

variable, several
coordinated

5. Infants often suck _____ _____ or other objects. This may continue for some time; _____ of children suck their _____ after they have started school. The cause of this is _____ _____, but most developmentalists do not consider it important.

their fingers
40%
thumbs
not known

6. Infants engage in considerable nonnutritive sucking until about _____ year(s) of age. It is a measure that can be used to study infants' _____ and _____.

one
attention, learning

7. Crying is the infant's first _____ behavior. It first appears as a _____ response to discomfort.

emotional
reflexive

8. Adults can distinguish the cries associated with _____ from those associated with _____.

arousal
hunger

122

9. Watson argued that the parent should not _____ to a crying neonate. He thought that the attention would act as a _____ and increase the incidence of crying.

respond
reinforcer

10. Ainsworth and others with an _____ background argue the _____ position. They believe that attention of the care giver contributes to a _____ _____ between the infant and the care giver.

ethological
opposite
secure attachment

11. When an infant is about _____ year(s) old, adults should respond to infant's _____ cries, but not to cries caused by _____ if they want to get a full night's sleep themselves.

one
distress
boredom

12. A _____ smile, which does not appear in response to social stimulation, occurs _____ in development than a _____ smile. Social smiles do not usually occur until ____ to ____ months of age.

reflexive
earlier, social
two, three

13. The principle that describes the pattern of growth as being from the head down is the _____ pattern. A second principle that describes this period of early growth is the _____ pattern.

cephalocaudal
proximodistal

14. The average North American newborn is _____ inches long and weighs _____ pounds. Just after birth infants _____ weight. Soon after they begin to grow _____. During the first year they grow an average of _____ inch(es) per month. They _____ their weight during the year.

20
7.5, lose
rapidly
1
triple

15. Growth _____ during the second year. By the end of the second year they have achieved about _____ of their adult weight and _____ of their adult height.

slows
1/5
1/2

16. The infant's ability to hold the chest up while prone and to reach for seen objects develops by about _____ months of age. Sitting with help appears by _____ months and rolling over by _____ months.

two
five
six

17. Standing alone and perhaps pulling up to a standing position appears at about _____ months and walking by about ____ months. However, there is a great deal of _____ in the onset of motor milestones.

eight, 11
variability

18. During the second year infants want to move ____ ____ _____ _____. By 13 to 18 months they can climb _____; by _____ years they can walk or run stiffly for a short distance. Experts believe that such activity is _____ for development and that infants should ____ ____ ____ except to ensure _____.

all over the place
steps
two
vital
not be restricted
safety

19. The skills described in the previous three items are _____ motor skills.

gross

20. Infants have _____ control of fine motor skills at birth. The development of reaching and grasping takes _____ years, as does _____ _____ _____. Early on infants show only crude _____ and _____ movements.

little
two
eye-hand coordination
shoulder, elbow

21. Experts believe that babies do not need special _____ for motor development. In fact, exercise may _____ infants. For example, swimming may lead to _____ _____ because infants swallow too much water. _____ activity stimulated by touch, face-to-face encounters, and toys should be enough for optimal motor development.

exercise
hurt
brain swelling
Normal

22. The number of brain _____ does not increase after birth, but the number of _____ does. At birth the brain weighs about _____ of its adult weight; at two years of age it weighs _____ of its adult weight.

cells
connections
25%
75%

23. Brown described three states of sleep. _____ _____ exists when the infant lies motionless with eyes closed and does not respond to stimulation. In _____ _____ there is little movement, but respiration may be irregular. During _____ _____ there may be movement and eyelids may flutter. Breathing is _____ and there may be _____.

Deep sleep

regular sleep
disturbed sleep

irregular, vocalizations

24. Brown also described four waking states. _____ is displayed by an infant with partially opened and glassy eyes, with little movement but more _____ than occur in disturbed sleep. When the infant is awake with open and bright eyes, shows a variety of movements, frets, has reddish skin, and shows _____ changes when upset, she is displaying alert activity. The _____ and _____ states are more characteristic of older infants. This is much the same as alert activity except that _____ are integrated around a specific activity. The _____ _____ infant is awake but nonresponsive because attention is centered on some activity such as _____ or _____.

Drowsy

vocalizations

respiration
alert
focussed
movements
inflexibly focussed

sucking, crying

25. Sleep occupies up to _____ or _____ hours of neonates' days. By _____ month of age infants begin to sleep longer at night. By _____ months their sleep patterns are more like adults'.

16, 17
one
four

26. About _____ of neonates' sleep is _____ sleep. This form of sleep is correlated with _____ in adults and occupies about _____ of the adult sleep period. By _____ months of age the proportion of REM sleep falls to _____.

50%, REM
dreams
25%, three
40%

27. A special concern about infant sleep is _____, which occurs when an infant stops _____ during sleep and dies. This is the leading _____ of infants during the first year. Its cause is _____, but seems to be related to biological _____.

SIDS
breathing
killer
unknown, vulnerabilities

28. Defining infants' nutrition needs is _____ because they are so _____. A general rule is to feed them _____ calories for _____ pound they weigh per day.

difficult
variable, 50
each

29. During the first year of life infants' primary food should be _____ _____ or _____. However, solid foods may be introduced during the year. The one rule about this is to feed infants _____ _____ because it contains much needed _____. Addition of other foods is _____.

human milk, formula

infant cereal
iron, arbitrary

30. Giving up one method of feeding for another is called _____. The best time for this is different for every infant, but most are ready during the _____ _____ of the first year. Weaning should be _____.

weaning

second half
gradual

31. Infants have _____ nutritional needs from adults. For example, they need more _____. Ironically, this seems to be something overlooked by _____ and _____ _____ parents.

different
fat
affluent, well-educated

32. There is much controversy about the benefits of _____ versus _____ feeding and whether feeding should be on a _____ or by _____.

breast
bottle, schedule
demand

33. It is generally believed that _____ feeding is healthier than _____ feeding. The proportion of mothers that nurse their babies is about _____.

breast
bottle
50%

34. Watson argued for feeding by _____. He thought it would teach _____. Recently there has been a trend toward _____ feeding.

schedule
control
demand

35. Severe _____ is a major problem in many parts of the world. Protein-calorie deficiency can cause _____. In Third World countries, infants fed by _____ have a higher death rate than infants fed by _____.

malnutrition
marasmus
bottle
breast

36. Malnutrition is detrimental to _____, _____, and _____ _____. In one study, South African infants who received adequate nourishment had higher _____ _____ than did malnourished counterparts.

physical, cognitive
social development
intelligence scores

37. The incidence of malnourishment is _____ in the United States. This is because poor parents typically do not _____ their babies' deaths.

underestimated
report

38. North American parents expect their children to be toilet trained by _____ years of age, and _____ of their children are. Ability to control elimination depends on _____ _____ and _____, as well as _____ _____. This means that toilet training possibly should begin later than at _____ years, the age it typically begins.

three, 84%
muscular maturation
motivation, cognitive
maturity, two

39. Over the past four decades a dramatic improvement in infant
health has been the decline in _____ _____. This has
been due to _____.

infectious diseases
immunization

40. Between _____ and _____ _____ of age infants are
especially prone to accidents, a major cause of infant _____.
Therefore parents need to _____ motor activity, and take
special care about what infants put into their _____.
Especially dangerous toys are _____, which cause more deaths
than any other object.

6, 12 months
death
monitor
mouths
balloons

41. Blankets, plastic bags, strings, and sleeping with care givers can
cause _____. Parents should not leave infants unsupervised
near _____.

suffocation
water

42. After _____ months of age, falls begin to injure infants, who
are beginning to learn to _____ _____. Infants should
not be left unattended on high objects that do not have _____
_____.

four
roll over
guard rails

43. The main cause of death in children under five is _____, with
the highest incidence occurring in children aged _____ years.
This is related to the infant's ability to _____. An especially
dangerous source of poisons is the _____.

poisoning
two
move
kitchen

44. The leading cause of accidental infant death during the first year
is _____ _____. To avoid this parents should use special
_____ _____.

automobile accidents
car restraints

3.0 Sensory and Perceptual Development

1. One of the challenges of studying perception in infants and young
children is that these individuals do not possess adequate _____
to describe their perceptual world. However, one can assess an
infant's perception by presenting two or more stimuli and
measuring the infant's _____ for one or the other.

language

preference

2. Human vision is not much like _____. For example, it conveys
a richer sense of _____, _____, and _____. Human
vision and its development are _____.

photographs
depth, color, texture
complex

3. The influential William James thought that neonate vision was very
_____. Modern research suggests that he was _____.

disorganized, wrong

4. A pioneering device for studying infants' vision was Fantz's
_____ _____. Using this, researchers could document
whether infants _____ on one of _____ stimuli thus
describe what infants _____ to see. Research with this device
suggests that _____ perception has an innate basis.

looking chamber
fixated, two
preferred
pattern

126

5. An infant's visual acuity is about _____. This improves to _____ by 6 months of age.

20/200
20/100

6. Face perception focusses on _____ at one to two months and on the _____ at 3½ months. An infant can recognize _____ faces by six months.

contour
eyes, familiar

7. The purpose of the _____ _____ designed by Gibson and Walk was to simulate a dangerous chasm without the danger of a chasm. Infants in the age range of _____ to _____ months are less likely to crawl on the deep side than on the shallow side. It is not clear whether depth perception occurs earlier than six months of age, but some research suggests it is present as early as _____ months.

visual cliff

6, 14

two

8. Whaley and Wong (1989) make many suggestions for visual stimulation of infants. For example, they suggest parents hang bright, shiny objects about 8-10 inches from infants faces from _____ to _____ _____ of age. When infants reach one year, show them _____ _____ _____ _____.

birth, one month
large pictures in books

9. Some studies have indicated that a _____ can hear sounds. For example, one study showed that infants _____ a story read to them before they were born. Immediately after birth the neonate _____ hear. A neonate's sensor thresholds is _____ than an adult's.

fetus
preferred

can, higher

10. Whaley and Wong (1989) make many suggestions for the auditory stimulation of infants. For example at two to three months of age they recommend that parents _____ to infants. At six to nine months they recommend that parents name _____ _____.

talk
body parts

11. A touch to the cheek of an infant results in a _____ _____ response. Interestingly, at 6 months infants can _____ touch and vision.

head-turning
coordinate

12. Whaley and Wong (1989) make many suggestions for tactile stimulation of infants. For example, at four to six months they urge parents to allow their babies to _____ in the bath. At 9-12 months they recommend that parents give their children _____ _____ to eat.

splash

finger foods

13. _____ are good for stimulating vision during the first six months; _____ are good for stimulating hearing in the second six months; _____ _____ are good for stimulating touch during the first six months.

Mirrors
rattles
soft clothes

14. Male infants do react to the _____ of circumcision. Research indicates that infants cope _____ with this procedure.

pain
well

15. Neonates apparently have a sense of _____ because they respond to asafetida in the air. Very young infants can seem to _____ the smell of a mother's breast but not necessarily their own mother's.

smell

recognize

16. When the sucking of a newborn is rewarded with a sweetened solution the amount of sucking _____. One study found that a sweet taste resulted in a _____ from the neonate while a sour taste resulted in a _____ _____ _____ _____.

increases
smile
pursing of the lips

Key Terms Matching Exercise

1.0   Images of Children: Studying Newborns (Term 1)
2.0   Physical Growth and Development in Infancy (Terms 2–23)
3.0   Sensory and Perceptual Development (Terms 24–31)

---

1. perceptual motor system   E

2. sucking reflex   A

3. rooting reflex   D

4. Moro reflex   F

5. grasping reflex   C

6. nutritive sucking   B

a. Response in the newborn that allows them to get nourishment prior to associating the nipple with food

b. Sucking that provides nourishment to a newborn

c. Infant's hand closes tightly when something touches the palm

d. Head-turning response to the side of a touch on the cheek in a newborn

e. A system that allows individuals to perceive the world and then respond to it

f. Startle response of the neonate that involves arching the back, throwing the head back, flinging out the arms and legs, and then rapidly closing them to the center of the body; triggered by the sudden loss of support, bright light, or loud noise

---

7. nonnutritive sucking   D

8. crying   C

9. reflexive smile   F

10. social smile   A

11. cephalocaudal pattern   E

12. proximodistal pattern   B

a. Smiling by an infant that occurs in response to a face

b. Pattern of growth starting at the center of the body and moving toward the extremities

c. Inarticulate sounds that often express a demand or require immediate action

d. Sucking behavior by the infant that is unrelated to the infant's feeding

e. Pattern of growth occurring first at the top (or head) and gradually working its way down from top to bottom

f. Smiling by a neonate that does not occur in response to external stimuli

13. gross motor skills _C_
14. fine motor skills _A_
15. infant states _E_
16. REM (rapid eye movement) sleep _D_
17. sudden infant death syndrome (SIDS) _F_
18. nutrition _B_

a. Motor behaviors involving small muscle groups such as scribbling with a pencil
b. Process whereby an individual assimilates foods and uses it for growth and tissue replacement
c. Motor behaviors involving large muscle groups such as walking and climbing
d. Sleep state characterized by rapid eye movements, and during which dreams are often reported
e. Term that refers to the levels of awareness experienced by infants
f. Unusual death of an apparently healthy infant who stops breathing, which often occurs between 2 and 4 months of age; the cause is unknown

19. weaning _C_
20. scheduled feeding _E_
21. demand feeding _F_
22. marasmus _B_
23. immunization _A_
24. sensation _D_

a. Medical treatment that protects an individual from a disease
b. A wasting away of body tissues caused by severe protein-calorie deficiency
c. The process by which an infant is shifted from mother's milk to other forms of nourishment
d. Detection of the environment through stimulation of receptors in the sense organs
e. A procedure whereby infants are fed at regular intervals of time determined by the parents
f. A procedure whereby infants are fed at times determined by the infant

25. perception _C_
26. pattern perception _G_
27. depth perception _B_
28. visual stimulation _F_
29. auditory stimulation _E_
30. tactile stimulation _A_
31. circumcision _D_

a. Touching the skin or surface of the body
b. An ability to recognize height that is tested through use of a visual cliff apparatus
c. The interpretation of what is sensed
d. Medical treatment in which a physician surgically removes the prepuce of a male
e. Activities designed to engage the listening skills of infants and presumably make them better
f. Activities designed to engage the visual skills of infants and presumably facilitate them
g. An ability to recognize visual patterns such as faces that seems to be innate or requires minimal environmental experience

Key Terms Matching Exercise
Answer Key

1. e	6. b	11. e	16. d	21. f	26. g	31. d
2. a	7. d	12. b	17. f	22. b	27. b	
3. d	8. c	13. c	18. b	23. a	28. f	
4. f	9. f	14. a	19. c	24. d	29. e	
5. c	10. a	15. e	20. e	25. c	30. a	

Self-Test A

1. As Charlie's cheek is stroked, he turns his head in the direction of the touch. He is demonstrating which reflex?
   a. sucking
   b. rooting
   c. Moro
   d. Babinski

2. Which reflexes are most important in eating?
   a. grasping and sucking
   b. grasping and rooting
   c. Moro and rooting
   d. sucking and rooting

3. The first effective communication behavior of the newborn infant is
   a. smiling.
   b. cooing.
   c. babbling.
   d. crying.

4. Infants gain control of their shoulders before they gain control of their legs. This illustrates the principle of
   a. proximodistal development.
   b. cephalocaudal development.
   c. reflex development.
   d. differentiation.

5. Infants can sit with support at
   a. three months.
   b. four months.
   c. five months.
   d. six months.

6. An activity that is appropriate for a six-month-old infant is
   a. helping an infant to roll over.
   b. swimming classes.
   c. placing furniture in a circle to encourage "cruising."
   d. playing with large push-pull toys.

7. Which list accurately represents the sequence of fine motor skill acquisition during infancy?
   a. pulls string to get an object; transfers object from hand to hand; zips and unzips a zipper
   b. grasps with thumb and forefinger; carries an object to mouth; places pegs in a pegboard
   c. transfers objects from hand to hand; uses a pincer grasp; places large pegs in a pegboard
   d. bangs in play; puts three objects in a container; glances from one object to another

8. Brown termed the state in infants characterized by open but glassy eyes, little movement, and some vocalizations
   a. drowsy.
   b. regular sleep.
   c. disturbed sleep.
   d. alert activity.

9. Sudden infant death syndrome (SIDS) appears to be related to
   a. abnormal patterns of brain development.
   b. irregular sleep patterns.
   c. experiencing anoxia at birth.
   d. premature birth with respiratory problems.

10. Which nutrient do infants appear to need more than adults?
    a. sugar
    b. protein
    c. carbohydrate
    d. fat

11. All but one of the following is a reason breast-feeding is superior to bottle feeding. Which one is the exception?
    a. Breast-fed babies gain weight more rapidly.
    b. Breast-fed babies are immunized by mother's milk.
    c. More nutrients are available to breast-fed babies.
    d. Breast-fed babies are more strongly attached to their mothers.
12. What are the names of the processes used to gather and interpret information about the world?
    a. sensation and perception
    b. vision and touch
    c. sight and hearing
    d. sensation and memory
13. Face perception is focussed on contour at about what age?
    a. 3½ weeks
    b. one to two months
    c. three months
    d. five months
14. Infants can visually discriminate the deep and shallow sides of the visual cliff at what age?
    a. 12 months
    b. eight months
    c. six months
    d. two to four months
15. A good way to stimulate vision in a four-to six-month-old baby is to
    a. look at the baby at close range.
    b. give the baby bright objects.
    c. let the baby look in a mirror.
    d. show the baby pictures in books.

16. Some researchers believe that hearing occurs
    a. by the end of the second trimester.
    b. late in the third trimester.
    c. at birth.
    d. by two months after birth.
17. What type of behavior provided evidence for the answer in question 15?
    a. sucking
    b. habituation
    c. control of gaze
    d. reflexes
18. Newborn males appear to suffer pain when they are circumcised. Research indicates that this experience
    a. is probably traumatic and damaging.
    b. activates effective stress coping mechanisms.
    c. should not worry parents at all, because the pain is only brief.
    d. is highly variable from infant to infant.
19. Research has demonstrated that the sense of smell is working by the age of
    a. three months.
    b. three weeks.
    c. three days.
    d. less than 24 hours.
20. All but one of the following capacities is present at birth. Which one is the exception?
    a. sensitivity to sweet tastes
    b. preference for the smell of mother's breasts
    c. sensitivity to sour tastes
    d. ability to discriminate sound patterns.

Self-Test Answers
Test A

1. b	4. b	7. c	10. d	13. b	16. b	19. d
2. d	5. c	8. a	11. d	14. d	17. a	20. b
3. d	6. d	9. d	12. a	15. b	18. b	

Critical Thinking Exercises

Exercise 1

Chapter 6 contains a number of tables and figures that illustrate various topics. Some of these are listed below, paired with an interpretation of the information they present. Which interpretation is most accurate? **Circle the letter of the best answer and explain why it is the best answer and why each other answer is not as good.**

A. Figure 6.1: Reflexes that disappear involve patterns of gross motor behavior.
B. Figure 6.2: Growth in height and weight slows down during the first two years of life.
C. Figure 6.3: Most infants can walk by themselves before they are one year old.
D. Figure 6.4: The number of brain cells increases dramatically during the first two years of life.
E. Figure 6.5: There is no evidence that two-month-old infants can discriminate between colors.

Exercise 2

In this chapter, Santrock distinguishes between the concepts of sensation and perception, and then takes the reader on a tour of the sensory and perceptual capacities of human infants. For which sense do we appear to know the most about the perceptual capabilities of infants? **Circle the letter of the best answer and explain why it is the best answer and why each other answer is not as good.**

A. vision
B. hearing
C. smell
D. taste
E. touch

Exercise 3

Family Issues 6.1 makes a case against having infants participate in exercise classes. Which of the following is an assumption underlying this advice, rather than an inference or an observation? **Circle the letter of the best answer and explain why it is the best answer and why each other answer is not as good.**

A. More infants are suffering bone fractures and other injuries today than in the past.
B. Adults do not usually know babies' physical limits.
C. Infants achieve no aerobic benefits from exercise.
D. There is a variety of infant exercise programs.
E. Today's parents regularly touch and play with their infants.

Research Project 1 Gross Motor Activity

This project provides an observational exercise for examining the gross motor activity of children. Pair up with another student in the class and go to a local playground. Observe two children, one about four years old and the other about eight years old. For each child, describe five gross motor behaviors the child performs while you are observing. These can include running, climbing, skipping, jumping, hopping, walking, throwing, catching, etc. Describe the same five behaviors for each child, noting differences in the way they perform the behaviors. Use the data sheet below for recording your observations. Then answer the questions that follow.

Child 1

Sex ___ Age ___

Behavior 1 (   ):
Behavior 2 (   ):
Behavior 3 (   ):
Behavior 4 (   ):
Behavior 5 (   ):

Child 2

Sex ___ Age ___

Behavior 1 (   ):
Behavior 2 (   ):
Behavior 3 (   ):
Behavior 4 (   ):
Behavior 5 (   ):

Questions:

1. What were the five behaviors you observed?
2. In general how can these behaviors be characterized or described for the four-year-old? For the eight-year-old?
3. How did the children differ in the way they performed the behaviors?
4. From your observations of the two children and five behaviors, what do you see as the course of development of gross motor behavior between four and eight years? How do your specific findings compare with the general descriptions reported in the text?

Research Project 2 Reflexes

For this research project, you will need the permission of parents of a young infant (one to four months old) and an older infant (six to twelve months old) to examine their infant's reflex repertoire. In order to test the two infants, you will need to clear this project through the human subjects review board at your school and get a signed informed consent form from the baby's parents. You may work in groups of 2 to 4 to make it easier to locate and gain access to the appropriately aged infants. Be certain to indicate age by months because your results will vary if you use a 2-month vs a 4-month baby or a 6-month vs an 11-month baby.

For each infant, perform the stimulation necessary to elicit the reflexive behavior. Note which of the reflexes are present (P) or absent (A) for each infant. You may mark these responses in the chart below. After performing the demonstration with each infant, answer the questions.

Infant 1	Infant 2		
Sex ___ Age ___	Sex ___ Age ___		
Reflex	Stimulation and reflex		
Placing	Backs of infant's feet are drawn against a flat surface's edge: Baby withdraws foot	P/A	P/A
Walking	Hold baby under arms with bare feet touching flat surface: Baby makes steplike motions that appears like coordinated walking	P/A	P/A
Darwinian (grasping)	Stroke palm of infant's hand: Baby makes strong fist; if both fists are closed around a stick, the infant could be raised to standing position.	P/A	P/A
Tonic neck	Baby is laid down on back: Infant turns head to one side and extends arms and legs on preferred side and flexes opposite limbs	P/A	P/A
Moro (startle)	Make a sudden, loud noise near infant: Infant extends legs, arms, and fingers, arches back, and draws back head.	P/A	P/A
Babinski	Stroke sole of baby's foot: Infant's toes fan out and foot twists in.	P/A	P/A
Rooting	Stroke baby's cheek with one's finger: Baby's head turns, mouth opens, and sucking movements begin.	P/A	P/A

Questions:

1. How many of the reflexive behaviors were exhibited by the younger infants? By the older infants?
2. Which reflexes dropped out early?
3. What responses seem to replace each of the reflexive behaviors in the older infants?
4. What might be the adaptive value of each reflex in the newborn's repertoire?

Essay and Critical Thinking Questions

Comprehension and Application Essay Questions

We recommend that you follow either our guidelines for answering essay and critical thinking questions, or those guidelines provided by your instructor in preparing your response. Your answers to these kinds of questions demonstrate an ability to comprehend and think critically about concepts and topics discussed in this chapter.

1. Increasingly, developmentalists have been surprised by the early competencies of newborns and young infants. Explain how it is possible for them to study newborns.
2. How would you explain the importance of reflexes, and their development, to a friend?
3. Identify and describe the general patterns in the development of infant motor capabilities during the first year.
4. Describe the various states of infant consciousness. Also explain their relationship to sleep and waking.
5. Compare and contrast the development of gross and fine motor skills during infancy.
6. Discuss the pros and cons of breast- versus bottle-feeding.
7. What are sensation and perception, and why do they make interesting problems for study by developmentalists? What practical problems might their study solve?
8. Apparently infants can imitate facial expression nearly at birth, but have only 20/200 to 20/400 vision at birth. Provide a rationale for understanding this apparent inconsistency.
9. Explain what is known about the ability of infants to hear.
10. Do infants feel pain? Also indicate evidence that challenges the traditional practice of not administering anesthetics to infants undergoing surgery.

Critical Thinking Questions

Your answers to the following kinds of questions reflect an ability to apply your critical thinking skills to a novel problem or situation that is *not* specifically discussed in this chapter.

1. At the 1992 meeting of the American Association for the Advancement of Science, Michelle Lampl (University of Pennsylvania) reported that, contrary to the belief that growth is gradual, babies between the ages of 3 and 15 months literally grew overnight, up to three-quarters of an inch. Carl Fackler, an orthopedic surgeon, said that he was intrigued by the report, but felt a larger study was needed to determine its factual correctness. Apply your knowledge about the scientific base of child development by designing a study to determine whether tiny tots grow gradually or in spurts: (a) What specific problem or question do you want to study? (b) What predictions would you make and test in your study? (c) What measures would you use (i.e., observation, interviews, and questionnaires, case studies, standardized tests, physiological research, or a multimeasure, multisource, and multicontext approach) and how would you define

each measure clearly and unambiguously? (d) What strategy would you follow—experimental or correlational, and what would be the time span of your inquiry—cross sectional or longitudinal? (e) What ethical considerations must be addressed before you conduct your study?

2. According to Chapter 1, five issues define the nature of development: (a) biological, cognitive, and social processes, (b) periods or stages, (c) the issue of maturation (nature) versus experience (nurture), (d) the issue of continuity versus discontinuity, and (e) the issue of stability versus change. Indicate your ability to think critically by (a) analyzing the contents of this chapter for two examples of each of the five defining issues and (b) explaining which issues are most and least thoroughly discussed.

3. Chapter 2 presents six different theoretical approaches (i.e., Freudian, cognitive, behavioral and social learning, phenomenological and humanistic, ethological, and ecological), but notes that no single approach explains the complexity of development. Indicate your ability to think critically by explaining how any two of the approaches would regard the relationship between weaning and the development of infants.

4. One aspect of thinking critically is to read, listen, and observe carefully, and then ask questions about what is missing from a text, discussion, or situation. Indicate your ability to think critically by (a) perusing this chapter for topics influenced by at least one of the six theoretical approaches and (b) explaining which theoretical approach dominated the topic in question. If the presentation is entirely atheoretical, identify and explain how one of the theoretical approaches could be used to guide the analysis of the topic in question.

5. Santrock places several quotations in the margins of this chapter. One by Selma Fraiberg says, "The experiences of the first three years of life are almost entirely lost to us, and when we attempt to enter into a small child's world, we come as foreigners who have forgotten the landscape and no longer speak the native tongue." Indicate your ability to think critically by (a) learning about the author and indicating why this individual is eminently quotable (i.e., what was the individual's contribution to human knowledge and understanding), (b) interpreting and restating the quote in your own terms, and (c) explaining what concept, issue, perspective, or term in this chapter Santrock intended this quote to illuminate. In other words, about what aspect or issue in development does this quote make you pause and think reflectively?

Self-Test B

1. When she feels a sudden change in posture, Maria startles, arches her back, throws her head back, flings her arms out to the sides, and then brings them back over her body. What reflex is this?
   a. Babinski
   b. rooting
   c. Moro
   d. tonic neck

2. An experimenter puts a pacifier into a baby's mouth. When the baby sucks on the pacifier at a certain rate, a picture comes into focus. The experimenter is using which technique?
   a. habituation
   b. preference
   c. natural response
   d. nonnutritive sucking

3. Those who argue that responding quickly to an infant's cry will reward crying and increase its frequency represent which theoretical perspective?
   a. psychodynamic
   b. behavioral
   c. ethological
   d. cognitive

4. Infants gain control of the trunk before they gain control of the fingers. This illustrates the principle of
   a. proximodistal development.
   b. cephalocaudal development.
   c. reflexive behavior.
   d. differentiation.

138

5. During the first year of life, after an initial weight loss, infants appear to grow at a(n)
   a. constant rate.
   b. accelerating rate.
   c. decelerating rate.
   d. variable rate.
6. Infants can walk unaided by about
   a. five months.
   b. eight months.
   c. 11 months.
   d. 15 months.
7. Pedro is lying motionless with his eyes closed, shows regular breathing and no vocalizations, and does not respond to stimulation. According to Brown's classification, Pedro is in which state?
   a. drowsy
   b. disturbed sleep
   c. regular sleep
   d. deep sleep
8. The goal of scheduled feeding was to produce children who were
   a. autonomous.
   b. orderly and controlled.
   c. independent.
   d. goal directed.
9. Malnutrition has been found to produce individuals who are _____ than better nourished peers.
   a. shorter
   b. slower in cognitive growth
   c. less helpful to peers
   d. all of the above
10. All but one of the following is necessary for successful toilet training. Which is the exception?
    a. fine motor coordination
    b. motivation
    c. muscular maturation
    d. cognitive maturity
11. Why is the incidence of death due to disease and malnutrition among the poor underestimated in the United States?
    a. The government deliberately falsifies the statistics.
    b. Hospitals do not keep good records on the health of poor people.
    c. The poor often do not report the death of infants.
    d. The poor try to conceal the death of babies.

12. When is the risk of poisoning the highest in the life of an infant or young child?
    a. six months
    b. one year
    c. two years
    d. four years
13. When light is focussed on the retina, what is the immediate effect?
    a. sensation
    b. perception
    c. vision
    d. sensation and perception
14. If an infant looks longer at one of two concurrent displays, the infant is showing
    a. generalization.
    b. discrimination.
    c. dishabituation.
    d. habituation.
15. Research on the visual cliff with infants has found that
    a. six-month-old infants do not avoid the deep side, while 12-month-old infants do.
    b. both six- and 12-month-old infants avoid the deep side.
    c. neither six- nor 12-month-old infants avoid the deep side.
    d. six-month-old infants avoided the deep side, but 12-month-old infants had learned not to.
16. Which visual capacity occurs first in infancy?
    a. pattern discrimination
    b. face perception
    c. depth perception
    d. 20/100 vision
17. Before birth infants appear to be capable of learning to discriminate
    a. their mother's voice from other voices.
    b. rhyme patterns.
    c. musical intervals.
    d. speech from nonspeech.
18. An appropriate form of auditory stimulation for a six- to nine-month-old infant is to
    a. play a music box.
    b. expose the infant to rattles and wind chimes.
    c. laugh when the infant laughs.
    d. call the infant by name.

19. Are infants born with a preference for the smell of their mother's breasts?
    a. Yes, they show the preference as early as two days.
    b. No, they need experience before they recognize this odor.
    c. No, because infants cannot discriminate odors at an early age.
    d. Research has not answered this question.

20. Sensitivity to taste has been observed
    a. three months after birth.
    b. two months after birth.
    c. one month after birth.
    d. prior to birth.

Self-Test Answers
Test B

1. c	4. a	7. d	10. a	13. a	16. a	19. b
2. d	5. a	8. b	11. c	14. b	17. b	20. d
3. b	6. c	9. d	12. c	15. b	18. c	

Objectives

1.0 *Images of Children: The Doman Better Baby Institute and What Is Wrong with It*
1.1 List concerns about the Doman Better Baby Institute.
1.2 Indicate why developmentalists have been excited about infant cognition.

2.0 *Piaget's Theory of Infant Development*
2.1 Describe Piaget's method for studying infant cognition.
2.2 Compare and contrast quantitative and qualitative approaches to cognitive development.
2.3 Explain why Piaget identified the initial period of cognitive development as the sensorimotor period.
2.4 Define and distinguish among scheme, reflex, and habit.
2.5 Explain what Piaget meant by saying that a child constructs knowledge of the world.
2.6 Define and distinguish the features of each of the six substages in the sensorimotor period.
2.7 Explain what Piaget thought was happening when a one-month-old sucked merely at the sight of a bottle.
2.8 Distinguish infant imitation during the substage of secondary circular reactions from true imitation later in life.
2.9 Define and distinguish among the concepts of intentionality, novelty, and curiosity, and describe observations that indicate their presence in infants.
2.10 Define and distinguish between symbol and scheme, and describe observations that indicate their presence in infants.
2.11 Indicate how LaVisa Wilson's day-care curriculum constitutes an application of Piaget's theory.
2.12 Indicate whether Piaget accepts or rejects William James's claim that the newborn's world is a "blooming, buzzing confusion."
2.13 Define object permanence, and describe observations that indicate its presence in infants.
2.14 List criticisms of Piaget's view of infant cognitive development.

3.0 *Information Processing*
3.1 Compare and contrast the Piagetian and the information processing approaches to infant cognitive development.
3.2 Define and distinguish between habituation and dishabituation, and describe observations that indicate their presence in infants, and indicate their value to parents.
3.3 Define and distinguish between memory and conscious memory, and describe observations that indicate their presence in infants.
3.4 Discuss why developmentalists think that conscious memory is not present in infants prior to six months of age.
3.5 Define infantile amnesia and describe what observations indicate its presence in adults.
3.6 Define and distinguish between imitation and deferred imitation, and describe observations that show newborns really can imitate facial expressions.
3.7 Explain why Meltzoff believes that newborn imitation is not a simple biologically-based reflex.
3.8 List the ways that information processing discoveries either support or refute Piaget's findings.

4.0 *Individual Differences in Intelligence*
4.1 Compare and contrast the Piagetian, information processing, and individual differences approaches to infant cognitive development.
4.2 Define developmental quotient (DQ).

4.3   Compare and contrast the Gesell and Bayley approaches to testing individual differences in infant intelligence.

4.4   Discuss applied and scientific uses of scales for infant mental development.

4.5   List the kinds of items used on the Bayley Scales of Infant Development to measure mental development.

4.6   Explain why researchers believe that measures of habituation and dishabituation predict children's intelligence.

4.7   Compare and contrast the measures of cognitive development such as habituation and imitation with those on the Gesell and Bayley scales.

5.0   *Language Development*

5.1   List language development issues prompted by children such as the Wild Boy of Aveyron.

5.2   Define and distinguish among language, infinite generativity, and the five-rule systems of language.

5.3   Define and distinguish between phonemes and morphemes, grammar and syntax, deep and surface structure, and semantics and pragmatics.

5.4   Explain how the context of language influences the appropriateness of utterances.

5.5   Describe evidence that supports the hypothesis that language is the result of biological evolution.

5.6   Define language acquisition device (LAD) and indicate its presumed role in language development.

5.7   Describe attempts to teach language to chimpanzees, and evaluate whether the evidence supports any claim that a nonhuman species has been able to learn a language.

5.8   Compare and contrast the acquisition of language in chimpanzees, Genie, and human infants.

5.9   Indicate how behaviorists explain language acquisition.

5.10   Describe evidence that indicates that environment influences language development.

5.11   Explain how living in poverty may impair language development.

5.12   Define and distinguish among motherese, recasting, echoing, expanding, and labeling.

5.13   Describe the forms of language that appear during the first year of life.

5.14   Describe evidence for the claim that the onset of babbling is determined by biological maturation, not an environmental factor.

5.15   Summarize Burton White's views on language development, and discuss whether White's recommendations accurately encompass theories and observations about language development.

5.16   Define and distinguish between receptive vocabulary and spoken vocabulary.

5.17   Define the holophrase hypothesis, and explain how infants and toddlers can communicate using only one- and two-word utterances and telegraphic speech.

5.18   Define mean length of utterance (MLU), and explain how it is used to measure language maturity.

5.19   Explain why developmentalists believe that all languages develop in the same way.

Summary

1.0 Images of Children: The Doman Better Baby Institute and What Is Wrong with It

Glenn Doman's Better Baby Institute endeavors to accelerate the learning of infants and thereby illustrates what Piaget meant by the American question. Developmentalists question the scientific basis of Doman's approach and suggest that the most appropriate action entails providing a rich and emotionally supportive atmosphere for learning by infants. A controversial issue in development is whether infants construct their knowledge of the world or whether they experience it directly.

2.0 Piaget's Theory of Infant Development

Piaget's theory of cognitive development includes four stages: sensorimotor, preoperational, concrete operational, and formal operational.

The Stage of Sensorimotor Development. The sensorimotor stage lasts from birth to about two years. During this stage, infants progress in their ability to organize and coordinate sensations with physical movement. By the end of this stage, the ability to use simple symbols develops.

Piaget described six substages of the sensorimotor period. A scheme is the basic unit for an organized pattern of sensorimotor functioning. In the first stage, knowledge is gained through simple reflexive behaviors, the only action of which the infant is capable. In the second substage, the child becomes capable of primary circular reactions, actions in which an infant attempts to repeat an action that initially occurred by chance. The third substage is characterized by secondary circular reactions, in which infants repeat actions because they caused an interesting event to occur in the environment. Despite an object orientation, there is a lack of goal-directed activity. The fourth substage involves the coordination of secondary reactions and also the appearance of intentionality. The infant can use one action to be able to perform another. The fifth substage is characterized by tertiary circular reactions. The infant systematically explores the effects of a variety of actions on an object. This is the developmental starting point for curiosity and an interest in novelty. The final substage is the internalization of schemes. The child becomes able to use primitive symbols, and mental representation appears. LaVisa Wilson has proposed a day-care curriculum based on Piaget's substages of sensorimotor development.

Object permanence. The development of object permanence is an important achievement of the sensorimotor stage. The child develops the ability to understand that objects and events continue to exist even though the child is not in direct contact with them. This ability is the end product of the six substages of sensorimotor development.

3.0 Information Processing

The Information Processing Perspective and Infant Development. Unlike Piaget, information processing psychologists do not describe infancy as a series of substages of sensorimotor development. They do, however, emphasize the importance of cognitive processes such as attention, memory, and thinking. This view assumes a much greater level of competence than does Piaget.

Habituation and Dishabituation. Infants habituate to repeated presentations of the same stimulus and dishabituate to a new stimulus, demonstrating the ability to discriminate between two different stimuli. Habituation allows researchers to study exactly what kinds of things infants can tell from other things. An understanding of these learning principles can benefit parent-infant interactions.

Memory. Mobile objects that an infant can move provides a technique to study memory in infants. Using this technique, infants as young as 6 weeks old have demonstrated memory over as long as two weeks. A distinction is made between conscious memory and the type of memory that infants show in the mobile studies. In contrast to recognition memory, conscious memory involves feelings of having experienced something before. Infantile amnesia exists for events that occur prior to 3 years of age and may indicate that memory, in the strict sense, does not occur until then.

Imitation. Research suggests that infants as young as 1 day old can imitate some facial expressions. In addition, Meltzoff has observed deferred imitation, imitation that occurs after a delay of hours or days, by infants about 9 months old. The latter finding contradicts the belief of Piaget that deferred imitation does not occur before the age of 18 months.

143

4.0 Individual Differences in Intelligence

Infant intelligence tests are called developmental scales and are oriented toward motor development, in contrast to the heavy verbal orientation of intelligence tests for older children and adults. The developmental quotient is an overall developmental score on the Arnold Gesell test of motor, language, adaptive, and personal-social behavior. A commonly used measure is the Bayley Scales of Infant Development. Although infant intelligence tests do not predict later intelligence well, recent research on information processing skills such as attention, and habituation and dishabituation better predict intelligence in childhood. There is both continuity and discontinuity between cognitive development in infancy and later in childhood.

5.0 Language Development

What Is Language? Language involves a system of symbols that we use to communicate with one another. Language is characterized by infinite generativity and a complex set of rules. The five most prominent rule systems are: (a) phonology, the sound system of a language, (b) morphology, the smallest units of language that carry meaning, (c) syntax, the rules governing how words are combined into sequences, (d) semantics, the meaning of words and sentences, and (e) pragmatics, rules about the social context of language.

Biological Influences. The nativist theory assumes a biological component to language development. One proposal is that a language acquisition device is wired into the brain and is sensitive to the grammaticality of language. One question is whether animals have language, and a second question is whether there is a critical period for learning a language, an issue raised by the discovery of Genie—a modern-day wild child. Language appears to be a species-specific behavior because communication systems in nonhuman species are not like language. Puberty appears to close the critical period for fully acquiring phonological rules of different languages.

Behavioral and Environmental Influences. The behavioral view sees language as verbal behavior and explains language acquisition through the processes of shaping, reinforcement, and imitation. There are various criticisms of this approach to language. Brown found that mothers did not just reinforce grammatically correct utterances. The behavioral view also does not explain the orderliness of language, and imitation cannot totally explain language learning. All children master language despite large individual differences between children in imitation. A further argument against the behavioral position is that it is difficult to explain infinite generativity based on learning principle alone. Children appear to generalize complex rules in mastering language. However, a number of environmental factors may contribute to the acquisition of language. These include motherese, reacting, echoing, expanding, and recasting. Another experience that may facilitate language development is the labeling game that children play with their parents.

How Language Develops. Language development occurs in a number of different stages. In the preverbal stage, infants begin to babble, which may be necessary for the development of articulatory skills. Preverbal infants also develop pragmatic skills for communicating. These include eye contact and pointing in conjunction with vocalizing. Receptive vocabulary develops prior to spoken vocabulary. In the one-word stage, infants use single words that can belong to complete sentences, with limitations on production. The two-word stage allows different meanings to be captured. A semantic analysis of the two-word stage gives a promising view of the richness of children's language ability. During the two-word stage, language has been described as telegraphic because articles, auxiliary verbs, and other connectives are left out. The mean length of utterance is a measure of the child's language maturity.

144

Key Terms

1.0 Images of Children: The Doman Better Baby Institute and What Is Wrong with It
constructed knowledge
direct knowledge

2.0 Piaget's Theory of Infant Development
qualitative difference
sensorimotor stage of development
scheme (schema)
simple reflexes
first habits and primary circular reactions
habit
primary circular reaction
secondary circular reactions
coordination of secondary circular reactions
intentionality
tertiary circular reactions, novelty, and curiosity
tertiary circular reactions
internalization of schemes
symbol
object permanence

3.0 Information Processing
information processing perspective
habituation
dishabituation
memory
conscious memory
infantile amnesia
imitation
deferred imitation

4.0 Individual Differences in Intelligence
individual differences
developmental quotient
Bayley Scales of Infant Development

5.0 Language Development
language
infinite generativity
language rule systems
phonemes
phonology
morpheme
morphology
syntax
grammar
surface structure
deep structure
semantics
pragmatics
language acquisition device (LAD)
critical period
motherese
recasting
echoing
expanding
labeling
receptive vocabulary
spoken vocabulary
holophrase hypothesis
telegraphic speech
mean length of utterance (MLU)

Guided Review

1.0   Images of Children: The Doman Better Baby Institute and What Is Wrong with It

1. Institutions such as the Doman Better Baby Institute attempt to
    _____ infant cognitive development. One of its techniques is   accelerate
    to use flash cards to imprint words in infants _____.   memories

2. Critics claim that the techniques of the Doman Institute are not
    based on _____ _____. They argue that infants should   scientific evidence
    _____ and _____ their knowledge, and worry that infants   explore, construct
    exposed to Doman's techniques will _____ _____ on   burn out
    learning.

2.0 Piaget's Theory of Infant Development

1. In Piaget's theory, development occurs because of biological pressure to _____ to the environment. Thinking changes in _____ ways from one developmental stage to the next.

   adapt
   qualitative

2. The newborn is in the _____ stage. During the sensorimotor period the infant develops the ability to organize and coordinate _____ and _____.

   sensorimotor
   sensations, actions

3. The _____ is the basic unit for an organized pattern of sensorimotor functioning. It is the entity that _____ during the sensorimotor period.

   scheme
   develops

4. The first substage of the sensorimotor period is simple _____. During this substage the infant develops the ability to produce simple _____ in the absence of a triggering stimulus.

   reflexes
   reflexes

5. A scheme based on a reflex divorced from its eliciting stimulus is called a _____. A primary circular reaction is a _____ based on an infant's attempt to reproduce an interesting or pleasurable event that happened accidentally. These schemes are _____ oriented and _____ during this substage.

   habit, scheme
   body-, stereotyped

6. The infant becomes _____ oriented during the substage of secondary circular reactions. According to Piaget, simple _____ is observed, limited to behavior already in the infant's repertoire. In addition, schemes are not _____ directed.

   object-
   imitation
   goal-

7. The coordinated combination of schemes is a development of the _____ substage. During this substage the quality of _____ develops. This involves the separation of _____ and _____ in doing simple acts.

   fourth, intentionality
   means, goals

8. During the substage of tertiary circular reactions, the infant _____ new possibilities with objects. All such exploration is physical.

   explores

9. During the final substage of the sensorimotor period, the infant _____ the actions of the previous substage. For Piaget, a symbol is a sensory image or word that has been internalized and that represents an event.

   internalizes

10. LaVisa Wilson has suggested many ways that day care curricula could be made _____ _____ by being based on Piaget's theory. For example, caregivers should place objects near infants in substage four of the sensorimotor period, but _____ objects for infants in substage five.

    developmentally
    appropriate
    hide

11. The understanding that objects do not cease to exist when out of perceptual contact is called _____ _____. One meaning of the concept of object permanence is the understanding of self-world _____.

object permanence

differentiation

12. If an infant shows no reaction when an interesting toy is hidden, the inference is that she _____ _____ developed object permanence. The substage during which strong active search for a hidden toy appears is _____ _____ _____ _____ _____.

has not

coordination of secondary circular reactions

3.0 Information Processing

1. Information processing psychologists do not describe infant cognitive development as a series of _____. Instead they emphasize cognitive _____. While Piaget believed that infants only begin to understand the world after about _____ years, information processing psychologists believe that abilities needed to understand the world develop _____.

stages
processes
two

earlier

2. An infant will attend to _____ stimuli. As stimulation is _____ or _____, response decreases. This decrease is called _____.

new
continued, repeated
habituation

3. A new stimulus presented after habituation causes _____ if the individual detects a _____ between the new stimulus and the old one.

dishabituation
difference

4. _____ pertains to retaining information over time. Using mobiles that infants can learn to move has demonstrated a kind of memory in infants as young as _____ _____ old.

Memory

6 weeks

5. _____ memory of a stimulus involves feelings of having seen the stimulus before. Neonates _____ _____ _____ conscious memory. Conscious memory seems to appear after ___ months.

Conscious
do not have
6

6. Adults' lack of memories for events from before about 3 years of age is referred to as _____ _____.

infantile amnesia

7. Recent research has apparently demonstrated _____ of facial expression in _____. Meltzoff argues this means that imitation is _____ _____. He also believes that the ability to imitate is _____ and adaptive. For example, the imitation of facial expressions _____ over a period of days.

imitation
neonates
biologically based
flexible
improves

8. Unlike Piaget, Meltzoff has observed _____ _____ in infants at _____ months of age. This means that imitation occurred after a delay of _____ or _____.

deferred imitation
9
hours, days

4.0 Individual Differences in Intelligence

1. Intelligence tests given to infants are usually called _____ _____. They investigate _____ _____ among infants.

    developmental scales
    individual differences

2. One of the early contributors to this testing effort was _____. The scores from his scale include _____, _____, _____, and _____ _____. They can be combined to yield an overall _____ _____.

    Gesell
    motor, language,
    adaptive, personal-social
    developmental quotient

3. Today's most often used developmental scale was developed by _____. It includes a _____ scale, a _____ scale, and an _____ _____ _____.

    Bayley, mental, motor
    infant behavior profile

4. For normal children, infant developmental scales do not predict later measures of _____. One way to get continuity with measures of intelligence is to use measures of _____ and _____. In particular, measures of habituation called _____ _____ _____ and measures of dishabituation called _____ _____ _____ can be used to develop better predictors of standard intelligence test performance than the usual developmental scales.

    intelligence
    habituation
    dishabituation
    decrement of attention
    recovery of attention

5. Researchers are now suggesting that we should think of infant intelligence as being both _____ and _____ with later intelligence.

    continuous, discontinuous

5.0 Language Development

1. Language is a system of _____ used to communicate. In humans language possesses a creative aspect called _____ _____. Language's power to communicate knowledge across both space and time is called _____.

    symbols
    infinite generativity

    displacement

2. The basic speech sounds are _____ and the study of these sounds is _____.

    phonemes
    phonology

3. The smallest unit of meaning in a language is the _____. _____ is the study of rules that govern the combining and sequencing of morphemes.

    morpheme
    Morphology

4. _____ refers to the rules for combining words into acceptable phrases and sentences. The formal description of a language's syntactic rules is called _____.

    Syntax

    grammar

5. Many contemporary linguists refer to the order of words in a sentence as the _____ structure. The syntactic relations among the words in a sentence is referred to as the _____ structure. If a sentence has two different deep structures its meaning is _____.

    surface
    deep

    ambiguous

6. Semantic rules are those that pertain to the _____ of words. The sentence "The car looked at the mechanic" does not make _____ sense.

    meaning

    semantic

7. Pragmatics deal with rules for the _____ of language. Of particular interest is the _____ _____ in which language is used.

    use

    social context

8. Experts such as Chomsky stress the _____ basis of language. They point out that the physical apparatus for human language _____ over hundreds of thousands of years. Estimates suggest that language evolved in the past _____ to _____ years.

    biological

    evolved

    20,000, 70,000

9. Human infants might be born with an _____ mechanism that helps them to acquire language. Chomsky calls this a _____ _____ _____.

    innate

    language acquisition device

10. The idea that language has evolved has led researchers to study language in _____. In particular, researchers have attempted to teach language to _____ because they are _____ related to humans. One chimp named Washoe was able to learn 138 signs in _____ years.

    animals

    chimpanzees, biologically

    two

11. There are two issues that cause debate about whether chimpanzees have learned language. They concern whether chimps _____ the symbols they are taught to use, and whether their use of the symbols has _____. There is strong evidence for _____, but no strong evidence for _____.

    understand

    syntax, understanding

    syntax

12. The sad case of Genie illustrates the concept of a _____ or _____ period for language acquisition. _____ appears to mark the end of the period for language acquisition. Individuals who learn a new language after puberty are not likely to eliminate the _____ of their first language, but those who learn a new language before puberty can. This is also evidence for a _____ period.

    critical

    sensitive, Puberty

    accents

    critical

13. Supporters of the _____ view of language acquisition argue that language is learned. A major proponent of this view has been _____. The three principles of learning that have been invoked to explain language acquisition are _____, _____, and _____.

    behavioral

    Skinner

    shaping, reinforcement, imitation

14. Roger Brown and his associates have found that mothers respond to their children's _____ utterances in a reinforcing way. Brown concluded that evidence does not support the claim that language is learned through _____.

    ungrammatical

    reinforcement

15. The behavioral approach also fails to explain the _____ of language. It predicts large _____ _____ in language that do not appear to exist.

    imitation

    individual differences

16. Recent evidence suggests that reinforcement and imitation may   facilitate
    _____ language development, but that neither are necessary
    for it.

17. Children living in inner city housing projects have few _____   language
    interactions with their mothers. This may impede these children's
    _____ and _____ development.   cognitive, social

18. If you speak in short sentences with exaggerated intonation
    contours, long pauses between utterances, stress important words,
    and repeat yourself frequently, you are speaking _____. This   motherese
    dialect is used with _____ language users.   immature

19. _____ is phrasing the same meaning of a sentence in a   Recasting
    different way. Repeating what the child has said to you is called
    _____. Restating a child's utterance in another, more   echoing
    sophisticated form is called _____.   expanding

20. The process of labeling via the _____ _____ _____   great word game
    may account for a large part of a child's early vocabulary.

21. Burton White urges parents to talk to their babies from ____.   birth
    They should talk about the _____ _____ _____, and   here-and-now
    provide infants with as many experiences of _____ language   live
    as possible. Parents should also _____ to understand what   pretend
    their toddlers are telling them, even if they cannot.

22. An early preverbal linguistic behavior that first appears between
    3 and 6 months of age is _____. The infant's earliest   babbling
    communications are directed at _____ _____. The shifting   attracting attention
    of eye contact between an adult and a toy involves _____.   pragmatics

23. Between 6 to 9 months infants begin to understand words even
    though they do not speak. This means they have a _____   receptive vocabulary
    _____. This capacity grows to about _____ words by the   300
    second year of age.

24. Infants utter their first words between _____ and _____   10, 15
    months. However, several language _____ have already been   milestones
    passed. By 2 years of age spoken vocabulary reaches _____ to   200
    _____ words.   275

25. The possibility that the single word utterance of the one-word
    stage really represents a complete sentence which the baby has in
    her mind is called the _____ hypothesis.   holophrase

26. The two-word utterance makes its appearance between _____ and _____ months of age. The use of speech at this time has been referred to as _____ because small words are left out. Brown describes the _____ _____ _____ _____ as a better measure of language than age. Brown also has described _____ stages of language based on MLU. The first of Brown's stages involves utterance of _____ words; the fifth stage involves utterances of _____ words.

18
24
telegraphic
mean length of utterance

five
one +
four

Key Terms Matching Exercise

1.0 Images of Children: The Doman Better Baby Institute and What Is Wrong with It (Terms 1–2)
2.0 Piaget's Theory of Infant Development (Terms 3–17)
3.0 Information Processing (Terms 18–25)
4.0 Individual Differences in Intelligence (Terms 26–28)
5.0 Language Development (Terms 29–53)

---

1. constructed knowledge

2. direct knowledge

3. qualitative difference

4. sensorimotor stage of development

5. scheme (schema)

6. simple reflexes

a. Piagetian stage lasting from birth to about 2 years of age

b. Piagetian view that a child builds his or her own understanding of the world by coordinating sensory experiences with physical motor actions

c. Basic unit for an organized pattern of sensorimotor functioning

d. First substage in Piaget's sensorimotor period; reflexes are the basic means of coordinating action

e. Firsthand or immediate experience of an object or event

f. Variations in the characteristics rather than the amount or quantity of such things as abilities, objects, and events

---

7. first habits and primary circular reactions

8. habit

9. primary circular reaction

10. secondary circular reactions

11. coordination of secondary circular reactions

a. The separation of means and goals in accomplishing simple feats

b. Second substage in Piaget's sensorimotor period, when the infant learns to coordinate sensation and type of schemes or structures

c. Scheme based on the infant's attempt to reproduce an interesting event concerning his body that initially occurred by chance

d. Scheme based on a simple reflex that is completely divorced from its eliciting stimulus

e. Scheme based on the infant's attempt to reproduce an interesting event that followed the infant's chance action on an object

12. intentionality

f. When the infant readily combines and recombines previously learned schemes in an organized way

---

13. tertiary circular reactions, novelty, and curiosity

a. Schemes in which an infant purposely explores new possibilities with objects, continually changing what is done to them and exploring the results

14. tertiary circular reactions

b. Internalized sensory image or word that represents an event

15. internalization of schemes

c. The knowledge that objects and events continue to exist even when one is not in direct perceptual contact with them

16. symbol

d. Theory of cognition that is concerned with the processing of information; involves such processes as attention, perception, memory, and problem-solving

17. object permanence

e. When the infant's mental functioning shifts from a purely sensorimotor plane to the ability to use primitive symbols

18. information processing perspective

f. Schemes in which the infant purposefully investigates new possibilities with objects by changing what is done to them and exploring the results

---

19. habituation

a. The finding that, as children and adults, we have little or no memory for events experienced before 3 years of age

20. dishabituation

b. Renewed interest shown to a different stimulus presented after habituation has occurred to an original stimulus

21. memory

c. An observer's behavior that results from and is similar to the behavior of a model

22. conscious memory

d. Feature of cognition that involves retaining information over time

23. infantile amnesia

e. Retention of information over time

24. imitation

f. Reduced attention after repeated presentations of the same stimulus

---

25. deferred imitation

a. Variation in the characteristics or traits of persons that are commonly assumed to be normally distributed

26. individual differences

b. Overall developmental score for the infant, based on her performance on Gesell's scale

27. developmental quotient

c. The currently most widely used developmental scale; composed of a Mental scale, a Motor scale, and an Infant Behavior Profile

28. **Bayley Scales of Infant Development**

d. Ability to combine a finite number of individual words into an infinite number of sentences

29. language

e. A type of imitation that occurs after a time delay of hours or days

30. infinite generativity

f. Defined as a sequence of words; also shows properties such as infinite generativity and displacement

---

31. language rule systems

a. The rules of a language involved in combining words into acceptable phrases and sentences

32. phonemes

b. Smallest unit of language that carries meaning

33. phonology

c. Speech sound that marks the minimal difference between it and another sound in a language

34. morpheme

d. One of the defining characteristics of language along with infinite generativity

35. morphology

e. Study of rules that govern the sequencing of phonemes in a language

36. syntax

f. The study of the rules involved in the combining and sequencing of morphemes

---

37. grammar

a. Set of language rules that pertains to the meaning of words and sentences

38. surface structure

b. Actual order of words in spoken sentence

39. deep structure

c. Rules that pertain to the social context of language and how people use language in conversation

40. semantics

d. Syntactical relations among words in a sentence

41. pragmatics

e. Hypothetical ability of the young child to detect certain language categories

42. language acquisition device (LAD)

f. A formal description of syntactical rules

---

43. critical period

a. Characteristic way in which adults talk to young language learners; involves simple, short sentences, exaggerated intonation contours, long pauses between sentences, and great stress on important words

44. motherese

b. A restatement in a more sophisticated form of what a language learner has already said

45. recasting

c. Rephrasing the same or similar meaning in a different way

46. echoing

d. Repeating what is said by an immature language speaker

153

47. expanding
48. labeling

e. Providing a name for a specified object
f. The belief that a fixed time period very early in development exists for the emergence of a behavior

---

49. receptive vocabulary

a. Tendency of children to misuse a word by not applying a word's meaning to other appropriate contexts for the word

50. spoken vocabulary

b. The number of words that an individual can use in regular speech; usually smaller than receptive vocabulary

51. holophrase hypothesis

c. Use of mainly nouns and verbs in children's sentences, and the omission of articles, auxiliary verbs, and other connectives

52. telegraphic speech

d. View of the one-word stage that the single word stands for a complete sentence in the young child's mind

53. mean length of utterance (MLU)

e. The number of words that an individual can understand; usually larger than the spoken vocabulary

Key Terms Matching Exercise
Answer Key

1. b	9. c	17. c	25. e	33. e	41. c	49. e
2. e	10. e	18. d	26. a	34. b	42. e	50. b
3. f	11. f	19. f	27. b	35. f	43. f	51. d
4. a	12. a	20. b	28. c	36. a	44. a	52. c
5. c	13. f	21. e	29. f	37. f	45. c	53. a
6. d	14. a	22. d	30. d	38. b	46. d	
7. b	15. e	23. a	31. d	39. d	47. b	
8. d	16. b	24. c	32. c	40. a	48. e	

Self-Test A

1. How did Piaget study infant cognitive development?
   a. experimental method
   b. correlational method
   c. observational method
   d. case method

2. In Piagetian theory, the two processes central to adaptation are
   a. reinforcement and imitation.
   b. assimilation and accommodation.
   c. adaptation and organization.
   d. action and perception.

3. In Piagetian theory, the term for the basic unit of an organized pattern is
   a. assimilation.
   b. accommodation.
   c. learning.
   d. scheme.

4. A scheme based on a reflex that is independent of its eliciting stimulus is a
   a. schema.
   b. complex reflex.
   c. habit.
   d. primary circular action.

5. An infant hits the palm of one hand with a finger of the other and triggers a reflexive grasp. He attempts to repeat this sequence. Which of the following most closely resembles the behavior?
   a. reflexes
   b. primary circular reactions
   c. secondary circular reactions
   d. tertiary circular reactions

6. An infant sees his mother go out the door. He briefly looks at the spot where she disappeared, as if expecting her to reappear. He soon stops looking for her and plays with his toes. The infant is most likely in which of Piaget's stages of sensorimotor development?
   a. substage 1
   b. substage 2
   c. substage 3
   d. substage 4

7. How does the information processing approach differ from Piaget's approach?
   a. The information processing approach seeks to measure infant intelligence.
   b. Piaget's approach is quantitative, whereas the information processing approach is qualitative.
   c. The information processing approach tends to underestimate infants' mental capacities.
   d. Information processing researchers study separate mental processes.

8. Habituation and dishabituation are important responses in evaluating
   a. discrimination.
   b. object permanence.
   c. sucking ability.
   d. reflexes.

9. Beth, age 10, cannot remember the birth of her younger sister, who is 8. This demonstrates
   a. memory.
   b. conscious memory.
   c. repression.
   d. infantile amnesia.

10. Infants have been observed to imitate surprise on adults' faces by widely opening their mouths at age
    a. 36 hours.
    b. 3 weeks.
    c. 3 months.
    d. 6 months.

11. What did Nancy Bayley attempt to do with her scales of infant development that differed from what Gesell attempted with his developmental quotient?
    a. assess motor development
    b. predict later development
    c. assess mental functions
    d. identify abnormal infants

12. Results from individual differences research suggest that cognitive development from infancy to childhood is
    a. highly stable.
    b. stage-like.
    c. caused by both biological and environmental factors.
    d. both continuous and discontinuous.

13. During the first year of life the sounds infants make become increasingly restricted to those that occur in the language they regularly hear. This represents development in the language system called
    a. phonology.
    b. semantics.
    c. syntax.
    d. pragmatics.

14. Miriam had a blow to the head and now has difficulty understanding what someone means when they speak to her. Miriam's problem would support which of the following views?
    a. Language is learned through reinforcement.
    b. Language has a biological base.
    c. Language is based on general cognitive principles.
    d. There are universal properties to language.

15. The finding that children are unable to use such terms as *more* or *all-gone* until they acquire object permanence, in spite of frequent reinforcement, would refute which view of language development?
    a. nativist
    b. critical period hypothesis
    c. behaviorist
    d. cognitive theorist

16. Why do researchers doubt that animals can learn language?
    a. No animal has acquired syntax.
    b. Animals cannot acquire semantics.
    c. Animals cannot learn a communication system not natural to them.
    d. Animal communication does not seem to have all the characteristics of human language.

17. The case study of Genie reported in your text suggests that there is a sensitive period for acquisition of
    a. phonology.
    b. semantics.
    c. syntax.
    d. pragmatics.

18. A child says to her father, "more milk, Daddy." The father replies, "Shall I get you more milk?" This is an example of
    a. labeling
    b. echoing.
    c. expanding
    d. recasting.

19. What is thought to cause the onset of babbling?
    a. maturation
    b. imitation
    c. reinforcement
    d. secondary circular reactions

20. An average toddler can do all of the following by age 2 years except
    a. repeat two consecutive numbers.
    b. use past tenses of verbs.
    c. use the word no.
    d. make requests.

Self-Test Answers
Test A

1. c	4. c	7. d	10. a	13. a	16. d	19. a
2. b	5. d	8. a	11. b	14. b	17. c	20. b
3. d	6. b	9. d	12. d	15. c	18. c	

Critical Thinking Exercises

Exercise 1

In this chapter Santrock presents findings about infant cognitive development from the Piagetian, information processing, and individual differences perspectives. The Piagetian perspective is the oldest and most influential of the three; however, both the information processing and individual differences perspectives have challenged basic claims of Piaget. Which of the following statements from either information processing or individual differences research does *not* contradict one of Piaget's observations? **Circle the letter of the best answer and explain why it is the best answer and why each other answer is not as good.**

A. In Rovee-Collier's study, 6-week-old infants moved a leg or an arm to rotate a mobile. They "remembered" to do so again two weeks later.
B. Tiffany Field watched 3-day-old babies imitate facial expressions.
C. Ashmead and Perlmutter found that 5- to 11-month-old infants would search for a ribbon in the place they remembered leaving it.
D. Tested on the Bayley Scales, an average 6-month-old infant will search persistently for objects just out of reach.
E. By seven months of age infants' behavior shows evidence of conscious memory.

Exercise 2

Santrock's treatment of early language development uses many of the organizing concerns and questions that developmentalists employ to study other aspects of human development. Which one of the following developmental concepts, issues, or themes receives the *least* coverage during Santrock's discussion of early language development? **Circle the letter of the best answer and explain why it is the best answer and why each other answer is not as good.**

A. Development is a product of biological, cognitive, and social processes
B. The nature versus nurture issue
C. The continuity versus discontinuity issue
D. The issue of qualitative versus quantitative change
E. The concept of sensitive periods

Exercise 3

Read the following passage—"Ape Talk—From Gua to Nim Chimpsky"—that outlines the history of attempts to teach apes to talk and sketches the controversy resulting from these attempts. Which of the following statements represents an assumption shared by individuals on each side of the argument, rather than an inference or an observation? **Circle the letter of the best answer and explain why it is the best answer and why each other answer is not as good.**

A. Communication cannot be called language unless it has phonology, morphology, syntax, semantics, and pragmatics.
B. Washoe put signs together in ways that her trainer had not taught her.
C. Apes do not understand language; rather, they learn to imitate their trainers.
D. Sarah used a symbol that meant "same as" when she asked whether "banana is yellow" was the same as "yellow color of bananas."
E. Chimps use signs to communicate meaning.

Ape Talk—From Gua to Min Chimpsky

It is the early 1930s. A 7-month-old chimpanzee named Gua has been adopted by humans (Kellogg & Kellogg, 1933). Gua's adopters want to rear her alongside their 10-month-old son, Donald. Gua was treated much the way we rear human infants today—her adopters dressed her, talked with her, and played with her. Nine months after she was adopted, the project was discontinued because the parents feared that Gua was slowing down Donald's progress.

About 20 years later, another chimpanzee was adopted by human beings (Hayes & Hayes, 1951). Viki, as the chimp was called, was only a few days old at the time. The goal was straightforward: teach Viki to speak. Eventually she was taught to say "Mama," but only with painstaking effort. Day after day, week after week, the parents sat with Viki and shaped her mouth to make the desired sounds. She ultimately learned three other words—Papa, cup, and up—but she never learned the meanings of these words and her speech was not clear.

Approximately 20 years later, another chimpanzee named Washoe was adopted when she was about 10 months old (Gardner & Gardner, 1971). Recognizing that the earlier experiments with chimps had not demonstrated that apes have language, the trainers tried to teach Washoe the American sign language, which is the sign language of the deaf. Daily routine events, such as meals and washing, household chores, play with toys, and car rides to interesting places provided many opportunities for the use of sign language. In two years Washoe learned 38 different signs and by the age of 5 she had a vocabulary of 160 signs. Washoe learned how to put signs together in novel ways, such as "you drink" and "you me tickle."

Yet another way to teach language to chimpanzees exists. The Premacks (Premack & Premack, 1972) constructed a set of plastic shapes that symbolized different objects and were able to teach the meanings of the shapes to a 6-year-old chimpanzee, Sarah. Sarah was able to respond correctly using such abstract symbols as "same as" or "different from." For example, she could tell you that "banana is yellow" is the same as "yellow color of banana." Sarah eventually was able to "name" objects, respond "yes," "no," "same as," and "different from" and tell you about certain events by using symbols (such as putting a banana on a tray). Did Sarah learn a generative language capable of productivity? Did the signs Washoe learned have an underlying system of language rules?

Herbert Terrace (1979) doubts that these apes have been taught language. Terrace was part of a research project designed to teach language to an ape by the name of Nim Chimpsky (named after famous linguist Noam Chomsky). Initially, Terrace was optimistic about Nim's ability to use language as human beings use it, but after further evaluation he concluded that Nim really did not have language in the sense that human beings do. Terrace says that apes do not spontaneously expand on a trainer's statements as people do; instead, the apes just imitate their trainer. Terrace also believes that apes do not understand what they are saying when they speak; rather they are responding to cues from the trainer that they are not aware of.

The Gardners take exception to Terrace's conclusions (Gardner & Gardner, 1986). They point out that chimpanzees use inflections in sign language to refer to various actions, people, and places. They also cite recent evidence that the infant chimp Loulis learned over 50 signs from his adopted mother Washoe and other chimpanzees who used sign language.

The ape language controversy goes on. It does seem that chimpanzees can learn to use signs to communicate meanings, which has been the boundary for language. Whether the language of chimpanzees possesses all of the characteristics of human language such as phonology, morphology, syntax, semantics, and pragmatics is still being argued (Maratsos, 1983; Rumbaugh, 1988).

Research Project 1 Object Permanence

For this project, in which you may work in groups of two to four, you will need an infant from two of the following four age groups: 4 to 8 months, 8 to 12 months, 12 to 18 months, and 18 to 24 months. In order to do the object permanence task with these two infants, you need to clear your project through the human subjects review board at your school and get a signed informed consent form from the infants' parents. With each infant, perform each of the following three tasks and record the infants' responses:

Infant Responses:

	Infant 1		Infant 2	
Task Description	Sex ___	Age ___	Sex ___	Age ___

1. Show each infant an interesting object (e.g., ball or rattle). Then cover it with a piece of cloth. Note the response.

   Now move the cloth so that part of the rattle is exposed. Note the response.

2. Show the child the rattle again. Now move it so that it disappears behind a screen. Note the response.

   Now do the task again, but this time have the toy go behind one screen and then another one located close by. Note the response.

3. Show the infant the rattle, then cover it with a small box. Move the box behind the screen. Let the rattle remain behind the screen, but bring the box back into view. Note the response.

Questions:

1. How do the younger and older infants respond in task one? Do both seem to understand that the rattle is under the cloth? When part of the rattle is exposed, does the baby exhibit surprise? Reach out for the rattle?
2. In the second task, which infants realize the rattle is behind the screen? Can either baby follow the action when the rattle is moved to a second screen?

3. How do each of the infants respond when the rattle is in the box? When the box no longer contains a rattle, does either of the infants look behind the screen?
4. How does object permanence change as infants get older? Do your observations agree with Piaget's findings about object permanence?

Research Project 2 Mother-Infant Language

In this project, you will examine recasting, echoing, and expanding using naturalistic observation. Go to a local shopping mall and observe a mother with an infant 18 to 24 months old. Observe them for 15 minutes. Record three instances of speech by the mother to the infant, and classify each instance as recasting, echoing, or expanding. Note on the data sheet the mother's statements and then the infant's response to each statement. Then answer the questions that follow.

DATA SHEET

Speech	Response of Infant	Age ___ Sex ___
Statement 1		
Statement 2		
Statement 3		

Questions:

1. What types of techniques did the mother use with the infant you observed?
2. How did the infant respond to the statement made by the mother?
3. From your observations, do you think recasting, echoing, and expanding are effective techniques in aiding infants to learn language? Why or why not? What variables might have affected the quality of data you collected? Might your conclusions have been different if you had observed a different mother-infant pair? How?

Essay and Critical Thinking Questions

Comprehension and Application Essay Questions

We recommend that you follow either our guidelines for answering essay and critical thinking questions, or those guidelines provided by your instructor, in preparing your response. Your answers to these kinds of questions demonstrate an ability to comprehend and think critically about concepts and topics discussed in this chapter.

1. Compare and contrast the methods of Piaget and information processing researchers to study infant cognition.
2. Explain why Piaget referred to the initial stage of cognitive development as the sensorimotor period.
3. What is the relationship between each of the substages in Piaget's theory of the sensorimotor period? How does the infant get from one stage to the next?
4. According to Piaget, the development of object permanence is a major accomplishment of the sensorimotor period. There is, however, no longer complete agreement on what it means or how it develops in the infant. Compare and contrast Piaget's view and one of the two alternative views about the development of object permanence.
5. What is an information processing approach to development? How would you convince a friend that imitation and deferred imitation demonstrate information processing by infants?
6. Explain the similarities and differences among memory, conscious memory, and infantile amnesia.
7. If you were a parent of an infant, what would you learn about your infant from the Gesell test and the Bayley Scales of Infant Development?
8. Explain infinite generativity and the five rule systems of language.
9. Discuss evidence regarding the nature and nurture bases for language development.
10. For a period of time, the child speaks in utterances of approximately one word. Explain whether these utterances accurately reflect the level of thinking of a child.

Critical Thinking Questions

Your answers to the following kinds of questions reflect an ability to apply your critical thinking skills to a novel problem or situation that is *not* specifically discussed in this chapter.

1. At the beginning of Chapter 7, Santrock discussed the Doman Better Baby Institute. Apply your knowledge about the scientific base of child development by designing a study to evaluate whether Doman's claim that memory for a large number of words encourages infants to read: (a) What specific problem or questions do you want to study? (b) What predictions would you make and test in your study? (c) What measures would you use (i.e., observation, interviews and questionnaires, case studies, standardized tests, physiological research, or a multimeasure, multisource, and multicontext approach) and how would you define each measure clearly and unambiguously? (d) What strategy would you follow—experimental or correlational, and what would be the time span of your inquiry—cross-sectional or longitudinal? (e) What ethical considerations must be addressed before you conduct your study?
2. According to Chapter 1, five issues define the nature of development: (a) biological, cognitive, and social processes, (b) periods or stages, (c) the issue of maturation (nature) versus experience (nurture), (d) the issue of continuity versus discontinuity, and (e) the issue of stability versus change. Indicate your ability to think critically by (a) perusing this chapter for two examples of each of the five defining issues and (b) explaining how and why each of your examples illustrates one of the five defining issues.

3. Chapter 2 presents six different theoretical approaches (i.e., Freudian, cognitive, behavioral and social learning, phenomenological and humanistic, ethological, and ecological), but notes that no single approach explains the complexity of development. Indicate your ability to think critically by explaining how any two of the approaches would analyze and explain individual differences among infants.

4. One aspect of thinking critically is to read, listen, and observe carefully, and then ask questions about what is missing from a text, discussion, or situation. For example, this chapter discusses several aspects of language development and makes a critique of one approach to language. Indicate your ability to think critically by (a) explaining why the behavioral and biological views of language development do not receive comparable kinds of evaluation and criticism and (b) balancing the textbook's presentation by making your own critique of the neglected view.

5. Santrock places several quotations in the margins of this chapter. One by Lord Chesterfield says, "We are, in truth, more than half what we are by imitation," and another by Erick Fromm says, "Man is the only animal that can be bored." Indicate your ability to think critically by (a) learning about the author and indicating why this individual is eminently quotable (i.e., what was the individual's contribution to human knowledge and understanding), (b) interpreting and restating the quote in your own terms, and (c) explaining what concept, issue, perspective, or term in this chapter Santrock intended this quote to illuminate. In other words, about what aspect or issue in development does this quote make you pause and think reflectively?

Self-Test B

1. In Piaget's view, thinking in different stages is different in what way?
   a. qualitatively
   b. quantitatively
   c. Later stages had fewer schemes than earlier stages.
   d. Assimilation and accommodation appeared in later stages, but were absent in earlier stages.

2. In infancy, Piaget characterized thought as dependent on
   a. operations
   b. action and sensation.
   c. assimilation.
   d. representation.

3. An infant bangs a spoon on a tray, hears the sound, and continues banging the spoon on the tray to hear the sound. This illustrates
   a. simple reflexes.
   b. habits.
   c. primary circular reactions.
   d. secondary circular reactions.

4. An infant hits her father's hand away to get a ball that she sees, but that her father's hand blocks her from getting. This is an example of which behavior?
   a. habit
   b. primary circular reactions
   c. secondary circular reactions
   d. coordination of secondary reactions

5. An infant recovers an object under a cup on his right. The object is next hidden under a cloth on his left. He lifts up the cup on his right again to search for the object. This child is in which of Piaget's stages of sensorimotor development?
   a. stage 3
   b. stage 4
   c. stage 5
   d. stage 6

6. Michelle is presented with a bell ringing over and over again. At first she looks to the sound, but eventually she ignores it. This behavior is called
   a. memory.
   b. attention.
   c. dishabituation.
   d. habituation.

7. The brain structure that may be involved in the development of conscious memory is the
   a. hippocampus.
   b. parietal lobe.
   c. prefrontal region.
   d. amygdala.

8. What behavior do infants show at the highest frequency when they are presented with a sad face?
   a. widely open their mouths
   b. widen their lips
   c. pout their lips
   d. start to cry

9. Information processing research on infant mental processes suggests that Piaget
   a. accurately anticipated the findings of more detailed research.
   b. did not focus on important elements of cognitive development.
   c. correctly identified stages of infant cognitive development.
   d. underestimated infants' mental capacities.

10. Infant intelligence tests focus more heavily on _____ abilities than do tests for older children and adults.
    a. motor
    b. memory
    c. verbal
    d. attention

11. What aspect of infant behavior seems most related to later IQ scores on standard intelligence tests?
    a. motor ability
    b. memory
    c. attention
    d. onset of babbling

12. The creative aspect of language is called
    a. infinite generativity.
    b. displacement.
    c. syntax.
    d. semantics.

13. In Chapter 8 you will learn about a form of caregiver-infant interaction called scaffolding. Which aspect of language development does scaffolding promote?
    a. phonology
    b. semantics
    c. syntax
    d. pragmatics

14. Which of the following arguments or data best support claims about the biological basis of language?
    a. Parents reinforce the truth of statement rather than correct grammar.
    b. Children create and generalize rules.
    c. Language is infinitely productive.
    d. There is a critical period for acquiring phonological rules.

15. Genie was a child isolated from language by her family. Discovered at 13½, she has since learned vocabulary and the ability to produce up to three-word utterances. However, her language skills lag far behind her cognitive skills. This evidence is used to argue in favor of which of the following?
    a. linguistic universals
    b. lateralization of language and cognitive functions
    c. critical period
    d. infinite generativity

16. In an observation of mothers and children, it was discovered that a child made the following utterances: "Him give me candy," "The 'Cosby Show' is on TV on Monday." The first response was greeted with, "Yes, he did, didn't he?" The second response was, "No, it is on Thursdays." These observations argue against which behavioral process as an explanation for the development of syntax?
    a. imitation
    b. shaping
    c. reinforcement
    d. classical conditioning

17. A behavioral process that appears to make important contributions to language development is
    a. operant conditioning.
    b. imitation.
    c. reinforcement.
    d. none—language acquisition does not use behavioral processes.

18. Angie says, "Milk dog." Her father doesn't understand what she means, and says, "Milk dog." This illustrates which process?
    a. labeling
    b. echoing
    c. expanding
    d. recasting

19. The sentence "Baby throw ball" is an example of
    a. the mean length of utterance.
    b. the holophrase hypothesis.
    c. two-word utterance.
    d. telegraphic speech.

20. Mean length of utterance is a better measure of langauge maturity than
    a. telegraphic speech.
    b. two-word utterances.
    c. age.
    d. holophrases.

Self-Test Answers
Test B

1. a	4. d	7. a	10. a	13. d	16. c	19. d
2. b	5. b	8. c	11. c	14. d	17. c	20. c
3. d	6. d	9. d	12. a	15. c	18. b	

Chapter 8 Social Development in Infancy

Objectives

1.0 *Images of Children: The Newborn Opossum, Wildebeest, and Human*
1.1 Compare and contrast the developmental status of newborn opossums, wildebeests, and human infants.

2.0 *Family Processes*
2.1 Compare and contrast the adaptations of fathers and mothers to life with a newborn.
2.2 Define postpartum depression.
2.3 Explain how a newborn can both unite and separate parents emotionally.
2.4 Define and distinguish between reciprocal socialization and scaffolding, and indicate what observations support inferences about both.
2.5 Explain how infants socialize their parents.
2.6 Define and distinguish direct and indirect effects in a family system, and explain how the family is a system of interacting individuals.
2.7 Define and distinguish between dyadic and polyadic family subsystems.

3.0 *Attachment*
3.1 Define attachment, and describe observations that indicate its presence in an infant.
3.2 Compare and contrast the explanations for attachment proposed by Freud, Harlow, Lorenz, Erikson, and Bowlby.
3.3 Explain why researchers believe that contact comfort is more important than feeding to attachment, and explain which theories are best supported by research.
3.4 Identify theories that describe attachment as a system of behaviors involving a dyad.
3.5 Define and distinguish between secure and insecure attachment.
3.6 Define and distinguish types A, B, and C attachment, and describe the observations that indicate the presence of each in an infant.
3.7 Discuss possible causes of individual differences in attachment.
3.8 Indicate how the quality of attachment relates to later social adjustment.
3.9 Compare and contrast Kagan's views of individual differences in infants' adaptations to the social world with those of attachment theorists.
3.10 List criticisms of attachment theory.

4.0 *The Father's Role*
4.1 Describe recent changes in fathers' involvements with their children.
4.2 Compare and contrast fathers' and mothers' ability to care for infants, and identify their typical caregiving practices.
4.3 Explain how we can tell to which parent an infant is more strongly attached.
4.4 Compare and contrast parenting practices in families that adopt traditional and nontraditional gender roles.
4.5 Describe child-care practices in Sweden and other countries that offer both maternity and paternity leave.

5.0 *Day Care*
5.1 Evaluate the day-care experience of Ellen Smith and Barbara Jones.
5.2 Describe the variety of day-care services offered in the United States today.
5.3 Evaluate the claim that day care is harmful to infant social development.

5.4 State Belsky's point about day care in the United States and describe evidence to support it.
5.5 Explain why it is hard to reach firm conclusions about day-care's effect on child development.
5.6 List criteria for high quality day care, and describe evidence that supports these criteria.
5.7 Compare and contrast Kagan's criteria for high quality day care with those provided by the National Association for the Education of Young Children.
5.8 Discuss Zigler's solution to America's day-care needs.

6.0 *Emotional and Personality Development*
6.1 Explain how emotions may contribute to an infant's survival.
6.2 Describe observations that indicate the presence of emotion in infants.
6.3 Describe the Maximally Discriminative Facial Movement Coding System (MAX), and indicate the developmental sequence for the expression of emotions.
6.4 Compare and contrast Erikson's concept of trust versus mistrust and Ainsworth's concept of secure versus insecure attachment.
6.5 Discuss whether trust must be established in infancy.
6.6 Describe observations that indicate an infant has a sense of self and independence.
6.7 Compare and contrast Mahler's and Erikson's explanations for the development of independence and the self during infancy.
6.8 Describe the negativism often displayed by 2-year-olds, and indicate useful strategies for parents in coping with it.

7.0 *Adapting Caregiving to the Developmental Status of the Infant and Toddler, and the Goals of Caregiving*
7.1 Summarize LaVisa Wilson's recommendations for developmentally appropriate caregiving.
7.2 List the personal characteristics of competent caregivers according to LaVisa Wilson, and explain why these are important to providing high quality day care.
7.3 List goals for caregiving to infants according to Burton White.
7.4 Identify the concepts or research findings applied by Wilson and White in their respective caregiving recommendations.
7.5 Compare and contrast the Japanese and American views of child development and parenting.

Summary

1.0 Images of Children: The Newborn Opossum, Wildebeest, and Human

Newborns of different species vary in their ability to enter the world and function on their own. The newborn wildebeest is relatively independent, whereas the newborn opossum is quite dependent on others. The human newborn falls between these two extremes.

2.0 Family Processes

Most children grow up in a family. Hence, families are important agents of socialization for children.

Transition to Parenthood. The transition to parenthood can be both stressful and exciting for parents. Women may experience postpartum depression for up to nine months. Fathers generally are insensitive to the extreme demands placed on mothers. Work and family roles must be juggled differently with the arrival of an infant, and the couple has less time and money to spend on their relationship with one another.

Reciprocal Socialization. The current view is that socialization is reciprocal: Parents socialize children and in turn are socialized by them. When the infant is very young, the mother carries the load in facilitating the interaction through scaffolding. Scaffolding may help children learn social rules.

The Family as a System. The family is composed of various subsystems. Mother-infant and mother-father exemplify dyadic interactions; however, polyadic interactions are also common. Families are characterized by direct and indirect effects among marital relations, parenting, and infant behavior.

3.0 Attachment

What Is Attachment? Attachment is an affectional tie that one individual has for another as illustrated by the bond between infant and caregiver. There are alternative theoretical explanations for attachment. Freud's view was that oral gratification provided the mechanism for attachment, and as a result, infants became attached to the individual who fed him or her. Harlow's work suggests that attachment results from contact comfort rather than nourishment. Lorenz viewed familiarity as critical for attachment, whereas Erikson nominated trust for that role. The ethological perspective proposed by Bowlby argues that the infant and mother instinctively trigger each other's behavior to form an attachment bond. Attachment to the caregiver intensifies at about 6 to 7 months.

Individual Differences. Ainsworth describes secure attachment, in which infants (type B babies) use mothers as a secure base for exploration, respond positively to being picked up, and move away freely to play when put down. Insecure attachment can be either anxious-avoidant (type A babies) or anxious-resistant (type C babies). According to Bowlby, attachment security relates to the sensitivity and responsivity of the caretaker to signals from the infant. Attachment relationships carry forward into other relationships.

Attachment, Temperament, and the Wider Social World. Some developmentalists believe that the role of attachment is overemphasized and that genetics, temperament, and diverse social agents and contexts are more important to understanding a child's social competence than attachment theorists acknowledge.

4.0 The Father's Role

Over time, the father's role has changed. Contemporary fathers may be active, nurturant caregivers. Attachment between father and infant occurs at the same time as attachment between mother and infant. Fathers can be just as sensitive to infants as mothers; however, mothers operate more in a caregiving role than do fathers, and fathers act more as playmates than do mothers.

5.0 Day Care

More children are in day care today than at any other time in history. Infants may begin receiving day care at 1 or 2 years of age or earlier. For some infants, these are positive experiences, for others negative experiences. In day-care centers that are university based or staffed, the programs for infants and young children are good, and the infants are not different in attachment behavior from infants reared at home by their mothers. According to Belsky, poor quality day care may have negative developmental outcomes for children, such as insecure attachment, increased aggression, and noncompliance. For some infants, there may be positive benefits in social development from day-care experience. Quality day care does not have any negative effects on the social or cognitive development of an infant. Zigler believes schools should provide quality day care within the school

building, along with after-school care for school-aged children requiring such services. Guidelines exist for judging what constitutes quality day care.

6.0 Emotional and Personality Development

Emotional Development. Emotions begin to develop during infancy and function in adaptive, survival-promoting ways. Emotions serve both communicative and regulative functions. Infants display a wide range of emotional expressions, including joy, interest, anger, surprise, and fear. Carroll Izard developed a coding system for scoring facial expressions of infants and observed a reliable pattern for emotional development.

Personality Development. Several facets of personality develop during infancy. According to Erikson, trust or mistrust, a basic personality orientation to the world, is the outcome of infancy. Infants also develop a sense of self and the beginnings of independence. A mirror technique, observing infants' response to their reflections in a mirror, is often used as a measure of self-recognition. Margaret Mahler describes the process of separation-individuation as a critical development of the first three years, when the child acquires individual characteristics. A sense of trust and a sense of the self are both needed for separation-individuation to develop. Independence is also the theme of Erikson's stage of autonomy versus shame and doubt. Erikson believes that the resolution of this issue paves the way for identity development in adolescence. A special concern in toddler's development is their negativism. Dealing with toddlers in a loving, but firm manner generally makes it easier to live with the "terrible twos" and reduces the chances of spoiled children.

7.0 Adapting Caregiving to the Developmental Status of the Infant and Toddler, and the Goals of Caregiving

Adapting Caregiving to the Developmental Status of the Infant and Toddler. Caregivers should behave differently toward an infant at different ages. For example, up to four months of age, caregivers should respond quickly to an infant's needs with love, affection, and care. At 18 to 24 months of age, caregivers can encourage the toddler's development of self, monitoring their negativism, and give them much affection.

Goals of Caregiving. LaVisa Wilson has delineated the personal characteristics of competent caregivers. Burton White has specified three basic goals for caregiving to infants: (a) giving an infant a sense of being loved and cared for, (b) helping an infant to develop specific skills, and (c) encouraging an infant's interest in the outside world. American and Japanese cultures share striking similarities and display conspicuous differences in their views of child development.

Key Terms

1.0 Images of Children: The Newborn Opossum, Wildebeest, and Human

2.0 Family Processes
postpartum depression
reciprocal socialization
mutual gaze
synchronization
mutual regulation

scaffolding
social rules
dyadic family subsystem
polyadic family subsystem
direct and indirect effects

3.0 Attachment
attachment
secure attachment

anxious-avoidant attachment
anxious-resistant attachment
type A babies
type B babies
type C babies
temperament

4.0 The Father's Role
child-care policy
nontraditional gender role

5.0 Day Care
day care

6.0 Emotional and Personality Development
emotions
maximally discriminative facial movement coding system (MAX)
independence
trust versus mistrust
self
negativism

7.0 Adapting Caregiving to the Developmental Status of the Infant and Toddler, and the Goals of Caregiving
developmentally appropriate caregiving
competent caregiver

Guided Review

1.0 Images of Children: The Newborn Opossum, Wildebeest, and Human

1. Species differ in how _____ their offspring are. The independence of a human newborn lies somewhere between that of an _____ and a _____.

independent

opossum, wildebeest

2. A human infant must _____ and _____ a great deal. It cannot feed itself and requires extensive _____.

learn, develop
care

2.0 Family Processes

1. A new infant is likely to result in parents' having less free _____ and less extra _____. For two working parents, there will be concerns about the effects of day care.

time, money

2. Mothers may develop _____ _____, a kind of depression that may last as long as _____ months.

postpartum blues
nine

3. Many fathers are not _____ to the demands a new child places on the mother. Success of a marriage during this time depends on fathers' abilities to sense and _____ to this stress.

sensitive

adapt

4. The birth of a baby leads to _____ _____ marital relations, but about _____ of couples report _____ marital satisfaction. Having babies makes couples move both _____ and _____ _____.

less positive
1/3, increased

closer, farther apart

5. The current view is that the socialization process is a _____ one. One of the most studied examples of reciprocal socialization in infancy involves mutual _____.

reciprocal

gazing

170

6. _____ occurs when parents provide a framework for their interaction with their infants. This process facilitates _____ _____ with peers.

Scaffolding
turn-taking

7. The family can be thought of as a _____ defined in terms of generation, gender, and role. Interactions in one subsystem can have both _____ and _____ influences on interactions in other subsystems in the family.

system

direct, indirect

3.0 Attachment

1. _____ refers to a relation between particular social figures in which at least one acts to maintain the relationship.

Attachment

2. According to Freud, the infant becomes attached to a person who provides _____ satisfaction. The infant is most likely to attach to the _____ because of the _____ experience. Erikson believed that _____ on the part of the infant is essential for the formation of attachment.

oral
mother, feeding
trust

3. In a classic study by Harlow and Zimmerman, infant monkeys were raised on _____ mothers. They were _____ either on a soft cloth mother or on a hard wire one. Regardless of where the monkeys nursed, they spent more time on the _____ surrogate.

surrogate, fed

cloth

4. Lorenz postulated that _____ was responsible for attachment. For goslings, familiarity is important in the first _____ hours after hatching.

familiarity
36

5. The basis of Bowlby's ethological theory of attachment is that the infant and the mother have _____ that trigger each other's behavior to form an attachment bond. The initial goal for the infant is to keep _____ the mother.

instincts
near

6. According to Ainsworth, an infant who uses the caretaker as a "safe" base from which to explore is said to have a secure attachment. Some insecurely attached infants avoid the mother by ignoring her or failing to meet her gaze. This is called a Type ___ baby. Other insecurely attached infants kick the mother as she picks them up. This is called a Type ___ baby.

A
C

7. Currently an argument has been made that genetic and _____ characteristics are more important in social competence than attachment theorists have acknowledged. Attachment theory has also been criticized for ignoring the diversity of social _____ and social _____ in the infant's environment.

temperamental

agents
contexts

4.0 The Father's Role

1. During the colonial period the father's role was that of a teacher of _____. With the Industrial Revolution came the father's role as the _____. By the end of World War II, the father was expected to provide a _____ _____ model. Since the 1970s, fathers are evaluated to the extent that they are involved with their children in an _____ and _____ way.

    morals
    breadwinner
    sex-role

    active, nurturing

2. In families in which the mother is a homemaker, the father spends about _____ as much time as the mother interacting with a child. This rises _____ when the mother works.

    1/3
    slightly

3. At about the same time infants form attachments to their mothers, they bond to their _____. Infants seem to prefer fathers for _____ and mothers for _____.

    fathers
    play, comfort

4. In a study of nontraditional Swedish couples in which the _____ took parental leave to care for their infants, fathers were _____ likely than mothers to discipline, vocalize, soothe, hold, and kiss their infants.

    fathers
    less

5. In Sweden and other countries _____ _____ _____ can have paid child care leave for up to _____ months. This contrasts with the United States, which _____ _____ have a policy of paid leave for child care.

    fathers and mothers
    9
    does not

6. More than _____ countries have effective child-care policies, which are policies designed to get a child off to a _____ start in life and to _____ maternal health.

    100
    competent
    protect

7. Since the 1960s maternity policies have been linked strongly with _____. A second aspect of policies such as Sweden's is the _____ is also important and allows _____ to participate in parenting _____. About _____ of Swedish fathers take this leave.

    employment
    parenting, fathers
    leave, 1/4

8. All industrialized countries except _____ _____ _____ recognize the importance of parenting leave. These policies allow parents to take such leave without losing _____.

    the United States

    employment

5.0 Day Care

1. In the 1990s about _____ million children are in formal, licensed day care, and another _____ million attend kindergarten. The number in _____ day care can only be estimated.

    2
    5
    unlicensed

2. The quality of day care received by most children in the United States is _____ and can have _____ developmental outcomes for the children. In one study, children who began day care as infants were rated as less _____ and had poorer _____ relationships. However, day care per se is not the problem; rather, it is the _____ of the day care that is important.

poor, negative

compliant

peer

quality

3. Zigler argues that _____ should take over housing and providing day care for children.

schools

6.0 Emotional and Personality Development

1. Emotions such as _____, _____, and _____ are present early in infancy. Before infants can talk they add the emotions of _____, _____, _____, _____ and _____ to their capabilities.

interest, distress, disgust

joy, anger, surprise, shyness, fear

2. Most views of emotion claim that it has _____ and survival-promoting functions, serves as a form of _____, and has _____ functions. For example, _____ serves as a linkage between certain events and possible danger. The _____ expresses pleasure whereas the cry expresses _____. The infant can display emotions to regulate the distance to others.

adaptive
communication
regulative, fear
smile
distress

3. Izard and others developed the _____, a coding system for evaluating _____ _____.

MAX
facial expressions

4. If an infant develops a feeling that the world is predictable and that she can depend on her mother, she will develop feelings of _____. This is actually an expectancy that develops as a result of care that is _____ and _____.

trust
consistent, warm

5. The sense of _____ that develops from inconsistent care produces a _____ _____ of new experiences.

mistrust
fearful apprehension

6. Erikson's views are very compatible with _____ views on attachment.

Ainsworth's

7. Children recognize their reflection in a mirror by about the age of _____ months. Among the animals, only humans and the _____ _____ have this ability. It seems to be tied to the ability to form a _____ _____ of one's own face. This accomplishment indicates the presence of a sense of _____.

18
great apes
mental image
self

8. Mahler believes that toddlers develop independence by a process of _____ _____.

separation-individuation

9. According to Erikson, a necessary precursor to the development of independence is the development of a sense of _____. Major changes in competencies can result in the dependent child beginning to experience a sense of _____. If the child does not develop a sense of autonomy, she or he may develop lasting _____ and _____.

trust

autonomy

shame, doubt

10. Two-year-olds are very _____ because they cannot _____ the adult world. Nevertheless they want to _____ every situation, which is very trying for parents.

frustrated, control
dominate

11. Developmentalists believe it is better to be _____ with toddlers and to set _____ on their behavior rather than to make _____ for negativism. This makes toddlers _____ to live with during their period of negativism.

firm
limits
allowances, easier

7.0 Adapting Caregiving to the Developmental Status of the Infant and Toddler, and the Goals of Caregiving

1. From birth to 4 months, infant caregivers should respond _____ to infants' needs and _____ social interaction. Caregivers must become _____ _____ with infants.

quickly
initiate
emotionally involved

2. Between 4 and 8 months infants develop a focussed _____ to a primary caretaker. This means that in a day care a _____ caregiver should be assigned to each infant. During this time some infants also develop _____ _____. This means strangers should be introduced to infants _____.

attachment
consistent

stranger anxiety
carefully

3. From 8 to 12 months infants _____ social interaction with others. Caregivers should _____ with infants, allow access to _____ _____. This is a good time for _____ _____ games. During this time infants may be very _____ of their caregivers.

increase
talk
other people, turn-taking
possessive

4. Between 8 and 12 months caregivers may have to say _____ to control an infant's behavior, which they should follow with an _____. If infants stop negative behavior on their own caregivers should _____ them. _____ should be ignored.

"No"

explanation
praise, Tantrums

5. From 12 to 18 months toddlers are both _____ and _____. Thus they may need _____ _____ at the same time that they are very _____. Caregivers should not _____ _____ when a toddler can do something on his own. Toddlers should be allowed to interact with people they _____ to interact with.

independent, dependent
emotional support
defiant, take over

choose

6. An important event between 18 and 24 months is development of the _____. Caregivers should reinforce toddlers' use of _____ referring to the self.

self
pronouns

174

7. From 18 to 24 months toddlers expand their _____ _____. Their behavior varies from _____ to _____ and _____. Caregivers must accept them as _____ and show love even when toddlers _____ them.

social relationships
lovable, demanding,
stubborn, persons
reject

8. LaVisa Wilson has suggested _____ characteristics of competent caregivers. Competent caregivers are _____ and _____ healthy, have a _____ _____ _____, are _____, are _____, are positive _____ for infants, are _____ _____ _____, and enjoy _____.

eight, mentally,
physically, positive self-
image, flexible, patient,
models, open to learning
caregiving

9. Burton White believes that the three goals of caregiving should be giving an infant a sense of being _____, helping an infant to develop _____, and encouraging an infant's _____ in the world.

loved
skills, interest

10. Both Japanese and American cultures are _____ _____. However, Japanese mothers emphasize the _____ to their infants and encourage _____, whereas American mothers emphasize _____ from their infants and encourage _____.

child-centered
connection
dependence
separation, autonomy

11. Whereas Japanese mothers encourage traits of _____, _____, and _____, American mothers encourage _____, _____, and _____ _____. Japanese and American parents have the same _____ for their children, but _____ their children in very different ways.

patience, persistence,
conformity, originality,
exploration, self-assertion
goals, rear

Key Terms Matching Exercise

1.0 Images of Children: The Newborn Opossum, Wildebeest, and Human (no terms)
2.0 Family Processes (Terms 1–10)
3.0 Attachment (Terms 11–18)
4.0 The Father's Role (Terms 19–20)
5.0 Day Care (Term 21)
6.0 Emotional and Personality Development (Terms 22–27)
7.0 Adapting Caregiving to the Developmental Status of the Infant and Toddler, and the Goals of Caregiving (Terms 28–29)

---

1. postpartum depression _e_

a. A component of infant-mother interaction thought to be important to the process of socialization

2. reciprocal socialization _d_

b. One individual's behavior depends on another individual's behavior

3. mutual gaze _A_

c. Individual provides a framework for interaction with another that allows the other to learn ways of interacting

4. synchronization _b_

d. The view that socialization is bidirectional; children socialize parents just as parents socialize children

175

5. mutual regulation *A*

    e. A period of depression for a woman extending up to nine months after giving birth

6. scaffolding *C*

    f. Eye contact by two individuals such as a mother and infant

---

7. social rules *d*

    a. Relationship between two individuals, in which each person feels strongly about the other and does things to ensure the continuation of the relationship

8. dyadic family subsystem *e*

    b. Refers to influences on another, such as a parenting practice which directly affects a child or the marital relationship of parents that indirectly affects a child

9. polyadic family subsystem *f*

    c. Relationship in which the infant uses the mother as a base from which to explore the environment; infants respond positively to being picked up and, when put down, move away freely to play

10. direct and indirect effects *b*

    d. Rules for interacting with others such as learning to take turns

11. attachment *a*

    e. A family unit composed of two individuals such as a mother and a father, or a child and a parent

12. secure attachment *c*

    f. An interacting family unit composed of three or more individuals

---

13. anxious-avoidant attachment *C*

    a. Infants who exhibit insecure attachment by resisting the mother

14. anxious-resistant attachment *d*

    b. Infants who exhibit insecure attachment by avoiding the mother

15. type A babies *b*

    c. An insecurely attached child commonly called a type A baby

16. type B babies *f*

    d. An insecurely attached child commonly called a type C baby

17. type C babies *A*

    e. An individual's behavior style and characteristic way of responding

18. temperament *C*

    f. Infants who are securely attached to the mother

---

19. child-care policy *A*

    a. An aspect of social policy that specifically addresses the welfare of children such as maternity and paternity leaves for parents

20. nontraditional gender role *E*

    b. System for coding emotions on infant's faces

21. day care *D*

    c. A complex and often strong subjective reaction

22. emotions *c*

    d. An institution or facility that substitutes for parents by providing attention and care to children

176

23. maximally discriminative facial movement coding system (MAX) *D*

    e. Exemplified by active care-taking of infants by fathers

24. independence *f*

    f. Refers to a child's progress self-reliance

---

25. trust versus mistrust

    a. An individual's overall perception of personal abilities, behavior, and personality

26. self

    b. An individual who is adept at promoting the social and emotional development of infants

27. negativism

    c. A period during development in which children actively employ the term "no" and regularly test parental authority

28. developmentally appropriate caregiving

    d. Erikson's first psychosocial stage is experienced during the first year; a sense of trust requires a feeling of physical comfort and a minimal amount of fear and apprehension

29. competent caregiver

    e. Strategies for developing the social and emotional abilities of infants that change as the infant matures

Key Terms Matching Exercise
Answer Key

1. e	5. a	9. f	13. c	17. a	21. d	25. d	29. b
2. d	6. c	10. b	14. d	18. e	22. c	26. a	
3. f	7. d	11. a	15. b	19. a	23. b	27. c	
4. b	8. e	12. c	16. f	20. e	24. f	28. e	

Self-Test A

1. When contrasted with the infant opossum, the human infant is relatively
   a. immature at birth.
   b. fetal in behavior.
   c. mature at birth.
   d. protected in the months following birth.

2. The period of depression that may come after the birth of a baby
   a. is called "postpartum blues."
   b. can have disastrous consequences for bonding.
   c. predicts child abuse.
   d. is found more in fathers than in mothers.

3. The view that children socialize parents as well as being socialized by them
   a. is referred to as social mold theory.
   b. supports social mold theory.
   c. refutes the concept of reciprocal socialization.
   d. illustrates the concept of reciprocal socialization.

4. A polyadic family subsystem is defined as
   a. the interactions of two people.
   b. the process of reciprocal socialization.
   c. the combined interactions of three or more people.
   d. the indirect effects family members have on each other.

5. What kind of experience is most likely to facilitate turn-taking in infants interacting with peers?
   a. reciprocal socialization
   b. mutual gaze with mother
   c. scaffolding
   d. imitating father

6. Sally is playing with a toy, sees her mother leave the room, drops the toy, and begins to cry. This illustrates
   a. separation anxiety.
   b. stranger anxiety.
   c. insecure attachment.
   d. type C behavior.

7. Defining attachment as the goal of the infant to keep the mother nearby is attributed to which theory of attachment?
   a. ethological
   b. psychoanalytic
   c. behavioral
   d. cognitive

8. According to Ainsworth, an infant who moves away freely from the mother to explore the environment, but looks at her occasionally, would be classified as
   a. securely attached.
   b. insecure-avoidant.
   c. insecure-resistant.
   d. unattached.

9. One application of Kagan's critique of attachment theory is that securely attached babies are babies that
   a. are easy to care for.
   b. receive support from many social agents.
   c. do not need parenting.
   d. socialize their parents to be good parents.

10. By the end of World War II, which role of fathers became important?
   a. breadwinner
   b. moral teacher
   c. caregiver
   d. sex-role model

11. Male primates who are forced to live with motherless infants
   a. ignore the infants.
   b. abuse the infants.
   c. competently raise the infants.
   d. sexually mount the infants.

12. According to research on infants in day-care programs, infants who are in high quality day care
   a. are more aggressive than home-reared infants.
   b. are more compliant than home-reared infants.
   c. are less attached to their mothers than home-reared infants.
   d. show few differences in cognitive or social development from home-reared infants.

13. Current research on the effects of day care on infants is mainly
   a. observational.
   b. correlational.
   c. experimental.
   d. based on case studies.

14. A characteristic of high quality day-care centers is that
   a. parents occasionally work at them.
   b. day-care staff do not spoil the children with too much affection.
   c. infants and children are exposed to a continuously changing variety of adults.
   d. there are many kinds of activities for infants and children.

15. Emotions serve all of the following functions for infants except
   a. communication.
   b. regulating distance from others.
   c. deception.
   d. influencing information selected from the world.

16. An emotion that infants display earliest in life is
   a. interest.
   b. disgust.
   c. anger.
   d. fear.

17. According to Erikson, the developmental task of infancy is
   a. developing self-control.
   b. developing trust.
   c. separation/individuation.
   d. becoming attached to the mother.

18. The process of emerging from the symbiotic relationship with the mother and acquiring individual characteristics is called
    a. developing self-control.
    b. developing trust.
    c. separation/individuation.
    d. becoming attached to the mother.
19. According to LaVisa Wilson, infant caregivers should be especially careful about introducing infants to strangers during the age range of
    a. 0 to 4 months.
    b. 4 to 8 months.
    c. 8 to 12 months.
    d. 12 to 18 months.
20. Burton White recommends that infant caregivers adopt the goal of
    a. accelerating infants' cognitive development.
    b. helping infants to regulate their emotions.
    c. allaying infants' fear of strangers.
    d. helping infants to acquire language and other skills.

Self-Test Answers
Test A

1. c	4. c	7. a	10. d	13. b	16. a	19. b
2. a	5. c	8. a	11. c	14. d	17. b	20. d
3. d	6. a	9. a	12. d	15. c	18. c	

Critical Thinking Exercises

Exercise 1

In Chapter 8 Santrock describes many claims about social development during infancy. The quality of the evidence that supports each claim is quite varied. Which of the following claims is *least* supported? This is, which evidence is least convincing according to scientific criteria? **Circle the letter of the best answer and explain why it is the best answer and why each other answer is not as good.**

A. Secure attachment is related to social competence.
B. Under stress, infants show stronger attachment to their mothers than their fathers.
C. Extensive day care during the first year of an infant's life is associated with negative outcomes later in life.
D. The expression of emotions by infants follows a predictable developmental course.
E. During the second year of life, an infant experiences conflict between autonomy versus shame and doubt.

Exercise 2

In previous chapters of *Children* there has been little opportunity to apply the various theories of development that were outlined in Chapter 2. Chapter 8, however, presents research and theorizing motivated by several of these theories. Santrock directly identifies some of these, but does not do so for all topics. Listed below are topics from Chapter 8 paired with theoretical perspectives. Decide which of these pairs is accurate. **Circle the letter of the best answer and explain why it is the best answer and why each other answer is not as good.**

A. reciprocal socialization: psychoanalytic theory
B. attachment: humanistic theory
C. temperament: ethological theory
D. the father's role: behavioral theory
E. day care: ecological theory

Exercise 3

Attachment is a major topic in the study of infant social development. One reason why it is given emphasis is because that attachment represents a centerpiece for several different theoretical accounts of early social relationships. Which of the following statements best represents an assumption by attachment researchers, rather than an inference or an observation? **Circle the letter of the best answer and explain why it is the best answer and why each other answer is not as good.**

A. An infant cries when separated from its mother because she is attached to her mother.
B. The most important relationship in an infant's life involves attachment to a primary caretaker.
C. Eighteen-month-old infants who are insecurely attached to their mothers exhibit more frustration behavior than securely attached infants.
D. Providing an infant with a comfortable, safe environment creates an attachment bond between an infant and caretaker.
E. Some babies do not look at their mothers or try to be near them.

Research Project 1 Attachment Behaviors

In this exercise you will examine attachment behavior using naturalistic observation. Go to a local shopping mall and observe a mother with an infant 12 to 18 months old. Observe for a period of 15 minutes. Describe the behaviors you see occurring using the following data sheet. Then answer the questions that follow.

Behaviors   Child Age ___ Sex ___

Talking
Laughing
Tickling
Clinging
Crying
Escaping
Retrieving
Mutual gaze
Hitting
Smiling
Yelling
Generally positive
    interaction
Generally negative
    interaction

Questions:

1. What kinds of behaviors did your mother-infant engage in? Did the infant use the mother as the base for exploration? Was the infant allowed to explore?
2. According to the categories secure and insecure, how did this pair seem? Were interactions generally positive or generally negative? Did the relationship seem warm and affectionate or hostile?
3. What kind of parenting style seemed to characterize this pair: authoritarian, authoritative, permissive indulgent, or permissive indifferent? Do you think the style is partially determined by the age of the infant? How?

Research Project 2 Development of Self in Infants

This project examines the development of the self in infants. You will test an 8-month-old infant and an 18-month-old infant with a mirror recognition task. Two tasks will test for mirror recognition of the self and of an object near the infant. Then answer the questions about your observations. The task descriptions, worksheet, and questions follow.

Task 1: Have the mother stand behind the infant and hold an attractive toy above and slightly behind the infant's head, so that the infant can see the toy in the mirror but cannot see the toy itself. Record whether the infant reaches for the reflection of the toy in the mirror or turns around and reaches for the toy itself.

Task 2: For one minute, count the number of times the infant touches his or her nose while looking in the mirror. Then have the mother put a dab of rouge on the infant's nose, and turn the infant back toward the mirror. For the next minute count the number of times the infant touches its nose and the number of times it touches the reflection of its nose. Use the following worksheet for your data.

	Child 1 Sex ___ Age ___	Child 2 Sex ___ Age ___
Task 1		
Reaches to mirror		
Reaches to toy		
Task 2		
Touches mirror		
Touches nose		

Questions:

1. Does the 8-month-old infant reach for the object? Does the 18-month-old reach for the object? Does either infant reach for the reflection of the toy in the mirror? If so, which infant?
2. How does the 8-month-old infant react to his or her image in the mirror with the rouge on his or her nose? How does the 18-month-old infant react to the image in the mirror with the rouge on the nose? Do the infants of different ages react differently? Explain this difference.
3. Is there a difference in the development of the ability to recognize the self and the ability to recognize an object in a mirror? If so, why would this be?

Essay and Critical Thinking Questions

Comprehension and Application Essay Questions

We recommend that you follow either our guidelines for answering essay and critical thinking questions, or those guidelines provided by your instructor in preparing your response. Your answers to these kinds of questions demonstrate an ability to comprehend and think critically about concepts and topics discussed in this chapter.

1. Explain reciprocal socialization. Provide at least two examples of how parents socialize their children and two examples of how children socialize their parents in your response.
2. Define attachment, and compare and contrast the psychoanalytic, social learning, cognitive, and ethological explanations for its development.
3. The father's role has changed considerably in the twentieth century. Characterize those changes, and speculate about what role fathers will play in child development in the twenty-first century.
4. Compare and contrast fathers' and mothers' ability to care for infants, and the typical caregiving practices of each parent.
5. If you were a parent who could stay home with your children or place them in day care, what factors would you consider in making this decision?
6. Explain how developmentalists have studied emotions in infants, and summarize their findings about infant emotions.

7. Explain Erikson's concept of trust versus mistrust.
8. Compare and contrast Mahler's and Erikson's explanations for the development of independence and the self during infancy.
9. Explain what is meant by developmentally appropriate caregiving.
10. Compare and contrast the Japanese and American views of child development and parenting.

Critical Thinking Questions

Your answers to the following kinds of questions reflect an ability to apply your critical thinking skills to a novel problem or situation that is *not* specifically discussed in this chapter.

1. In this chapter Santrock briefly discusses how policies regarding maternity/paternity leave differ throughout the world. Apply your knowledge about the scientific base of child development by designing a study to determine whether paid maternity/paternity leaves affect children's development: (a) What specific problem or question do you want to study? (b) What predictions would you make and test in your study? (c) What measures would you use (i.e., observation, interviews, and questionnaires, case studies, standardized tests, physiological research, or a multimeasure, multisource, and multicontext approach) and how would you define each measure clearly and unambiguously? (d) What strategy would you follow—experimental or correlational, and what would be the time span of your inquiry—cross-sectional or longitudinal? (e) What ethical considerations must be addressed before you conduct your study?
2. According to Chapter 1, five issues define the nature of development: (a) biological, cognitive, and social processes, (b) periods or stages, (c) the issue of maturation (nature) versus experience (nurture), (d) the issue of continuity versus discontinuity, and (e) the issue of stability versus change. Indicate your ability to think critically by (a) perusing this chapter for two examples of each of the five defining issues and (b) explaining how and why each of your examples illustrates one of the five defining issues.
3. Chapter 2 presents six different theoretical approaches (i.e., Freudian, cognitive, behavioral and social learning, phenomenological and humanistic, ethological, and ecological), but notes that no single approach explains the complexity of development. Indicate your ability to think critically by supplementing Santrock's discussion of psychoanalytic, cognitive, social learning, and ethological explanations for the development of attachment with your own behavioral, phenomenological and humanistic, and ecological accounts for the development of attachment.
4. One aspect of thinking critically is to read, listen, and observe carefully, and then ask questions about what is missing from a text, discussion, or situation. Alternatively, critical thinking also involves asking why the material is included. Indicate your ability to think critically by (a) explaining why Santrock presents material on emotional and personality development in a chapter about social development in infancy, and (b) justifying your recommendation about where these topics ought to be discussed.
5. Santrock places several quotations in the margins of this chapter. One by Alexander Pope says, "The beast and the bird their common charge attend the mothers nurse it, and the sires defend; the young dismissed, to wander earth or air, there stops the instinct, and there the care. A longer care man's helpless kind demands, that longer care contracts more lasting bonds." Another by Edward Zigler says, "We have all the knowledge necessary to provide absolutely first-rate child care in the United States. What is missing is the commitment and the will." Indicate your ability to think critically by (a) learning about the author and indicating why this individual is eminently quotable (i.e., what was the individual's contribution to human knowledge and understanding), (b) interpreting and restating the quote in your own terms, and (c) explaining what concept, issue, perspective, or term in this chapter Santrock intended this quote to illuminate. In other words, about what aspect or issue in development does this quote make you pause and think reflectively?

1. The organism best prepared to interact with its social environment at birth is the
   a. wildebeest.
   b. opossum.
   c. human.
   d. kangaroo.

2. The birth of a baby forces a married couple into a state of
   a. harmony.
   b. fatigue.
   c. disequilibrium.
   d. postpartum blues.

3. Research by Cowan and Cowan has documented that after the birth of the first baby, roles of the husband and wife
   a. become less traditional.
   b. become more traditional.
   c. stay consistent with what they were prior to the birth of the child.
   d. can change in a variety of ways, with no consistent pattern from family to family.

4. Because of the birth of their new baby, Mara and Steve have less time to devote to their other children. In terms of family system theory, this is a(n) _____ effect on their other children.
   a. direct
   b. indirect
   c. reciprocal
   d. postpartum

5. Scaffolding is a procedure that allows infants to master
   a. spatial relations.
   b. attachment.
   c. object permanence.
   d. turn-taking.

6. Tara is sitting in her mother's lap when her mother's friend comes into the room. Tara looks away from the unknown woman and begins to fuss. This represents
   a. separation anxiety.
   b. insecure attachment.
   c. stranger anxiety.
   d. type B behavior.

7. The view that attachment occurs through oral gratification is a component of which theory?
   a. ethological
   b. psychoanalytic
   c. behavioral
   d. cognitive

8. Wasam approaches his mother after a brief separation from her, but pushes her away and hits her as she picks him up. According to Ainsworth, what type of baby is Wasam?
   a. type A
   b. type B
   c. type C
   d. autistic

9. All of the following have been observed as longitudinal outcomes for securely attached infants except
   a. better performance on IQ tests at age 6.
   b. less frustration at age 2.
   c. happier at age 2.
   d. more socially competent in third grade.

10. Criticisms of attachment theory include ignoring all of the following except
    a. changing gender roles.
    b. day care.
    c. experiences with the father.
    d. experiences with the mother.

11. Fathers' roles in child care have changed over the generations. The prime role of fathers as breadwinners was most characteristic during the
    a. colonial period.
    b. Industrial Revolution.
    c. 1940s.
    d. 1970s.

12. Research by Lamb demonstrated a preference for the mother rather than the father under what circumstances?
    a. in the presence of three people including the mother and the father
    b. preparing for bedtime and sleep
    c. entrance of a stranger when the infant is bored and fatigued
    d. in the company of both parents

13. About what number of children are in formal, licensed day care?
    a. 2 million
    b. 4 million
    c. 5 million
    d. 10 million
14. All but one of the following are recommendations of the National Association for the Education of Young Children about quality day care. Which one is the exception?
    a. Caregiver's record children's progress.
    b. The environment stimulates development.
    c. Parents make suggestions about day-care policies and activities.
    d. The day-care program focusses on cognitive development.
15. All of the following emotions have been observed in infants prior to the onset of language except
    a. guilt.
    b. anger.
    c. surprise.
    d. fear.
16. The Smiths' 2-year-old has started biting other children at day care. How will her caregivers deal with it?
    a. They will ignore it, because it is just attention-getting behavior.
    b. They will laugh and tease her to embarrass her, to make her stop.
    c. They will not worry about it, because it's just a phase she is going through.
    d. They will act to stop her biting.

17. Meng is consistently fed when hungry, and kept warm and dry by her mother. She expects the world to be a good place. What outcome is predicted by which theorist?
    a. type B attachment, Ainsworth
    b. separation, Mahler
    c. emotionality, Rheingold
    d. trust, Erikson
18. Which of the following techniques is used to test for the sense of self?
    a. separating the infant from the mother
    b. having a stranger approach the infant
    c. observing the infant move away from the mother
    d. observing the infant react to her reflection in a mirror
19. According to Mahler, what behavior on the part of the mother makes the separation/individuation process difficult for the infant?
    a. overprotection
    b. emotional unavailability
    c. emotional support
    d. need satisfaction
20. All but one of the following is a characteristic of competent caregivers. Which one is the exception?
    a. college degree in child psychology
    b. health
    c. positive self-image
    d. positive model for infant behavior

Self-Test Answers
Test B

1. a	4. b	7. b	10. d	13. a	16. d	19. b
2. c	5. d	8. c	11. b	14. d	17. d	20. a
3. b	6. c	9. a	12. c	15. a	18. d	

Chapter **9** Physical Development in Early Childhood

Objectives

1.0 *Images of Children: Tony's Physical Development*
1.1 List aspects of Tony's behavior that indicate he is a toddler rather than an infant.
1.2 Discuss why toddlers such as Tony pose more problems and offer more rewards to parents than do infants.

2.0 *Body and Growth Change*
2.1 Compare and contrast the physical and motor development of infants and preschool children.
2.2 Describe changes in height and weight during the preschool years, differentiating between boys and girls.
2.3 List factors that are associated with individual differences in height and weight among preschoolers.
2.4 Explain why some children are unusually short and how the deprivation dwarfism syndrome illustrates the concept of interaction between physical and emotional factors.
2.5 Explain whether brain and head growth relative to body growth exemplifies a cephalocaudal or proximodistal principle.
2.6 Explain why children lose their "top-heavy" look during the preschool years.
2.7 Define myelination, and discuss its contribution to development.
2.8 Explain how motor development is related to reading readiness and other aspects of sensorimotor coordination.
2.9 Define functional amblyopia, and list the symptoms of vision problems in preschool children.

3.0 *Motor Development*
3.1 List representative changes in gross motor skills between the ages of 3 and 5.
3.2 List ways to promote gross motor skills during early childhood, and explain whether the Catherine Poest program is age-appropriate.
3.3 Compare and contrast rough-and-tumble play and aggressive behavior, and describe observations that indicate the occurrence of each.
3.4 Discuss the educational and developmental functions of rough-and-tumble play.
3.5 List representative changes in fine motor skills between the ages of 3 and 5.
3.6 Explain what you would learn about a toddler from the Denver Developmental Screening Test.
3.7 Describe changes in children's drawings during the preschool years, and explain what these drawings reveal about toddlers' views of the world.
3.8 Discuss the role of motor development in the changes that appear in children's drawings during early childhood.
3.9 Define and distinguish among Kellogg's four stages of drawing.
3.10 List advantages and disadvantages experienced by left-handed children.
3.11 Explain how researchers learn about the hand preferences of infants and toddlers, and describe the development of handedness from early infancy through early childhood.

4.0 *Sleep and Sleep Problems*
4.1 Describe how to get a preschooler to go to sleep.
4.2 Define transitional objects, and explain whether they promote or hinder emotional adjustment during adolescence.
4.3 Define and distinguish among nightmares, night terrors, sleep walking (somnambulism), and sleep talking, and discuss whether these are symptoms of psychological disturbance.

5.0 *Nutrition*
5.1 Indicate what we know and do not know about changing nutritional needs during the preschool years.
5.2 Define basal metabolism rate (BMR), and discuss its role in establishing nutritional needs.
5.3 Summarize the daily eating routines of 3-, 4-, and 5-year-olds.
5.4 Explain why early exposure to fast foods worries developmentalists, and identify which fast foods are the most nutritionally sound.
5.5 List presumed effects of sugar consumption on the behavior and health of young children.
5.6 List the recommendations to caregivers about ways to discourage eating problems for children.
5.7 Identify the most common nutritional problems of early childhood, and indicate who suffers them.
5.8 Define iron deficiency anemia, and discuss its causes and cures.

6.0 *Illness and Health*
6.1 List the leading causes of death among children in the world and children in the United States.
6.2 Explain how poor nutrition contributes to children's illnesses.
6.3 List factors that contribute to worldwide rates of illness.
6.4 Define oral rehydration therapy (ORT), and describe its use in Bangladesh.
6.5 Describe the psychological health needs of children.
6.6 Identify developmental factors that increase preschool children's risk of illness and injury.
6.7 Explain why so many preschool children are injured on playgrounds.
6.8 Explain why most attempts to increase seat belt use fail with young children, and discuss what procedures might be used to promote better success with safety programs.
6.9 List goals for health-education programs for preschool children.
6.10 Describe caregiver behavior that puts young children's health at risk.
6.11 Explain how everyday illnesses are opportunities for cognitive, social, and emotional development.

Summary

1.0 Images of Children: Tony's Physical Development

Toddlers pose more problems and offer more rewards to parents than infants.

2.0 Body and Growth Change

Height and Weight. Growth slows down during early childhood. The average child grows 2.5 inches in height and gains 5 to 7 pounds a year during this period. Ethnic origin and nutrition contribute to variability in growth. Children with congenital growth problems often can be treated with hormones directed at the pituitary gland. The deprivation of affection may also cause alterations in the release of hormones by the pituitary gland and lead to deprivation dwarfism.

The Brain. The brain and nervous system continue to develop during early childhood, although at a slower rate than during infancy. The brain reaches 75 percent of its adult size by the time a child is 3 years old, and 90 percent of its adult size by age 5. Changes in the brain are due to increased connections between neurons and to myelination, which speeds up the transmission of impulses in the brain.

Visual Perception. Visual capabilities such as acuity, scanning ability, and depth perception continue to develop during early childhood. Functional amblyopia may occur, but it can be treated by patching the stronger eye, doing eye exercises targeted at the weaker eye, or having eye muscle surgery. Various signs indicate that a child may have visual problems.

3.0 Motor Development

Motor development is important during early childhood.

Gross Motor Skills. Gross motor skills include such actions as running, jumping, and climbing. These newly developed skills allow toddlers to become more active and mobile. Rough-and-tumble play differs from aggression and serves some positive educational and developmental outcomes. Young children can improve their gross motor skills through a developmentally appropriate movement curriculum.

Fine Motor Skills. Fine motor skills, such as drawing and building with blocks, continue to develop through early childhood. The Denver Developmental Screening Test is used for children through 6 years of age and evaluates developmental delay. The test assesses behaviors such as language, personal-social ability, and gross and fine motor skills.

Young Children's Artistic Drawings. The development of fine motor skills allows children to draw. Scribbling begins by age 2, and is followed by four stages of drawing: placement, shape, design, and pictorial. These stages of drawing during early childhood gradually become more complex and eventually result in drawings of objects that adults recognize.

Handedness. Handedness, the tendency to use one hand more than another, develops during this time even though some evidence exists that hand preference may be seen in infants reaching for objects. There are both environmental and genetic explanations of handedness.

4.0 Sleep and Sleep Problems

Many young children supplement nighttime sleep with naps and often take transitional objects to bed with them. Problems in sleep include nightmares, night terrors, somnambulism, and sleeptalking.

5.0 Nutrition

Energy Needs. Energy needs increase as children pass through childhood. Adequate nutrition is necessary for growth, and an average preschool child should receive 1,700 calories per day in a diet that includes protein, carbohydrates, fats, vitamins, and minerals. Energy needs vary according to basal metabolism rate (BMR), rate of growth, and activity levels.

Eating Behavior. Three-, 4-, and 5-year-olds have defined daily routines of eating. One important concern in our culture today is the excessive amount of fat and sugar in the diet. Eating problems often carry over from the toddler years. Parents should maintain a separation between the child's eating and discipline. Low-income families may have children who develop iron deficiency anemia. Approximately 11 million children in the United States are malnourished.

6.0 Illness and Health

Young Children's Illness and Health in the United States. Immunizations protect children from serious illnesses such as diphtheria and polio. The disorders most likely to be fatal during early childhood are birth defects, cancer, and heart disease.

The State of Illness and Health in the World's Children. Several causes of children's death throughout the world include diarrhea, infection, acute respiratory infections, undernutrition, and poor hygiene. Oral hydration therapy has been successful in Bangladesh in reducing deaths from diarrhea.

Health, Illness, and Development. Children's health care needs involve their motor, cognitive, and social development. Playgrounds should be designed to keep children safe, and children should be taught to keep themselves safe. A behavior modification plan successfully promoted seatbelt use by preschool children. Parents must be sensitive to the use of language to identify emotional and physical feelings.

Key Terms

1.0 Images of Children: Tony's Physical Development

pictorial stage
handedness

2.0 Body Growth and Change
congenital
deprivation dwarfism
myelination
functional amblyopia

4.0 Sleep and Sleep Problems
transitional objects
nightmares
night terrors
somnambulism

3.0 Motor Development
gross motor skills
rough-and-tumble play
aggression
fine motor skills
Denver Developmental Screening Test
placement stage
shape stage
design stage

5.0 Nutrition
basal metabolism rate (BMR)
iron deficiency anemia
malnutrition

6.0 Illness and Health
oral rehydration therapy (ORT)
hygiene

Guided Review

1.0 Images of Children: Tony's Physical Development

1. By 2 years of age, Tony has departed _____ and become a _   infancy
    _____.   toddler

2. Toddlers such as Tony pose more _____ and offer more _____ than infants to parents.

problems
rewards

2.0 Body and Growth Change

1. The _____ of growth begun in the second year continues in early childhood. The child grows _____ inches and gain _____ to _____ pounds a year. Both boys and girls become _____ during this time. The relative size of the _____ decreases.

slowing
2½
5, 7
leaner
head

2. _____ differences characterize patterns of growth. The most important factors in the individual differences in height are _____ _____ and _____. _____, _____ class, and _____ children are taller than _____, _____ class and _____ _____ children. Children whose mothers _____ during pregnancy were about _____ inch shorter than those whose mothers did not. In the United States _____ children are taller than _____ children.

Individual

ethnic origin, nutrition,
Urban, middle-, firstborn,
rural, lower-, later-born
smoked, ½
black
white

3. Factors that can result in unusually short children are _____ factors, _____ problems, and _____ difficulties.

congenital
physical, emotional

4. One hormone that helps to control growth is secreted by the _____ gland located at the base of the brain. Deprivation dwarfism is a type of growth _____ that may result from alterations in the secretion of growth hormone produced by lack of _____.

pituitary
retardation

affection

5. The brain grows more _____ in early childhood than in infancy. By 3 years of age, children have a brain _____ of adult size, and it is _____ of adult size by age 5. The increase in size is due to an increase in _____ and _____ of nerve endings. Myelination covers nerve cells with _____ and has the effect of _____ the _____ that information travels in the brain.

slowly
3/4
9/10
number, size
fat
increasing, speed

6. Reading depends on the eye _____ moving the eye efficiently across letters. Preschool children are often _____ -sighted, although most children can focus their eyes well by _____ grade.

muscles
far
first

7. The term for having a "lazy eye" is _____ _____. This condition can be corrected by _____ the good eye, eye exercises, wearing glasses, or by _____.

functional amblyopia
patching
surgery

3.0   Motor Development

1. Gross motor skills change dramatically in the early childhood
    years. At age 3, children enjoy _____ movements such as
    hopping and jumping. By age 4, children become more _____,
    and begin to _____ _____ stairs with one foot on each
    step. At age 5, children enjoy _____ with their parents.

    simple
    adventurous
    climb down
    racing

2. _____-year-old children have the highest activity rate of any
    age. One kind of motor activity preschool children enjoy is
    _____ _____ _____ play. It is characterized by a
    _____ face, and contrasts with _____, which involves
    hostile intentions. Children who engage in rough-and-tumble play
    are more _____ with peers than aggressive children are.

    Three

    rough-and-tumble
    smiling, aggression

    popular

3. Preschool and _____ programs should foster toddler's
    _____ motor skills. Catherine Poest recommends activities that
    are _____ and _____ appropriate. In addition to group
    _____, young children should develop their _____ _____
    skills. Although _____ consuming, a developmentally
    appropriate _____ curriculum should promote children's
    _____ _____ _____.

    kindergarten
    gross
    age-, individually-
    calisthenics, perceptual-
    motor, time
    movement
    gross motor skills

4. Children also show development in _____ motor skills. Three-
    year-olds can build block towers, but blocks frequently fail to be
    in a _____ line. Four-year-olds are much more _____.
    They may try to place each block _____ and become upset
    when they fail. By age 5, children are ready to build more
    complex structures.

    fine

    straight, precise
    perfectly

5. The Denver Developmental Screening Test can be used for children
    through the age of _____ years. The Denver Developmental
    Screening Test is a simple way to identify _____ development
    because it includes items concerning _____ and _____
    _____ as well as evaluations of both _____ and _____
    motor skills.

    6
    delayed
    language, social skills
    gross, fine

6. Children develop _____ skills during this period. Artwork
    provides insight into children's perceptual worlds. Scribbling
    appears by age _____. _____ basic scribbles have been
    identified.

    artistic

    2, Twenty

7. Rhoda _____ has identified _____ stages of children's
    drawings. The first begins with the _____ stage, and is
    followed by the _____ stage at age 3. Children mix two basic
    shapes in the _____ stage. Between the ages of 4 and 5,
    recognizable drawings occur that define the _____ stage.

    Kellogg, four
    placement
    shape
    design
    pictorial

8. Historically, teachers forced children to write with their _____ hand. Today, teachers allow children to write with their _____ hand. The rate of left-handed people in the general population is about _____%. The top scoring group of students who took the SAT has _____% left-handed students.

right
preferred

10
20

9. Side preference is evident in _____. About _____% turn their head to the right when lying on their stomach. A preference for grabbing an object with one hand over the other is evident by _____ months. _____ and _____ causes of handedness have been proposed; however, your author presents evidence for only a _____ influence.

newborns, 65

7, Genetic, environmental
genetic

4.0 Sleep and Sleep Problems

1. Although children often try to delay going to sleep, parents can help toddlers _____ _____ by engaging in _____ activities. _____ objects provide bedtime companionship to many children.

calm down, quieting
Transitional

2. Children are often awakened by frightening dreams called ____; however, they are _____ than _____ _____. Although accompanied by dramatic _____ reactions, _____ _____ generally are not regarded as serious _____ problems.

nightmares
milder, night terrors
physiological, night
terrors, psychological

3. About _____% of all children engage in _____ or sleepwalking; however, most simply outgrow the problem. _____ is also common, but not _____.

15, somnambulism
Sleeptalking
abnormal

5.0 Nutrition

1. Nutrition and energy requirements for an individual child are related to the _____ _____ of the individual. An individual's _____ entails the minimum amount of energy required for _____, _____, and _____. There are _____ differences in basal metabolism rates among children of the same age, sex, and size.

basal metabolism
BMR
resting, growth, activity
individual

2. Three issues regarding the eating behavior of children include daily _____, consumption of excess _____ and ____, and _____ and _____ _____.

routines, fat, sugar
snacks, fussy eaters

3. Three- to 5-year-olds have distinctive, but _____ defined daily _____ for eating.

well-
routines

4. American children eat too much _____. In part this results from a taste for _____ _____. It is very likely that this sort of diet is bad for the _____.

fat
fast food
heart

5. Another substance that can have detrimental effects on children's health and behavior is _____. Excessive sugar consumption contributes to _____ _____ and obesity. In addition, sugar has been implicated in both _____ and _____ behavior; however, the issue is still _____.

sugar
dental problems
aggressive, hyperactive
unresolved

6. Although children need _____ food than adults, children may require _____. However, snacks should entail limited sweets.

more
snacks

7. One way to discourage children from becoming _____ eaters is to encourage their _____ in eating.

fussy
independence

8. Children from low-income families may suffer malnutrition. _____ _____ anemia results from too little quality meats and dark green vegetables. Despite its _____ _____, relatively few states supplement federal funding for _____ and _____ services to _____, infants, and _____.

Iron deficiency

cost-effectiveness
food, nutritional
women, children

6.0   Illness and Health

1. In the United States, the most likely causes of death during the preschool years are _____, _____ disease, and _____ _____. Malnutrition places children's _____ at risk because they have less _____ to disease.

cancer, heart, birth
defects, health
resistance

2. _____ is the leading cause of children's death in the world. Its effects can be prevented through the use of _____ _____ _____. Other causes of death include _____ diseases, _____ infections, and _____. Additional contributing factors to children's deaths are problems in _____ of births and poor _____.

Diarrhea, oral
rehydration therapy,
infectious, respiratory,
undernutrition,
timing
hygiene

3. Countries with the highest mortality rates for children under age 5 include _____ and _____. The lowest mortality rates are found in the _____ countries. The United States has the _____ lowest mortality rate.

Afghanistan, Ethiopia
Scandinavian
21st

4. One issue that must be addressed concerning children and health is _____ _____. Adults must take _____ measures to ensure children's personal safety because children are unable to _____ their own personal safety.

developmental level,
preventive
ensure

5. _____ need to be designed with the child's safety in mind. More than _____ children were treated in emergency rooms with playground-related injuries from 1983 to 1987. One solution is to change the _____ on which playground equipment is located from _____ to _____ materials.

Playgrounds
305,000

surface
hard, soft

6. For car travel, _____ _____ for children are necessary. Children can be trained to use seat belts using a _____ _____ technique.

car seats
behavior modification

7. According to one group, health education for preschool children should stress three goals. Children should be able to _____ feelings and be able to _____ them to adults, identify appropriate sources of _____, and independently initiate the _____ of sources of assistance for health problems.

identify
express
help
use

8. One developmental problem that needs to be considered is the child's level of _____ skill. Children may not have the _____ to describe the feelings, and therefore they may not distinguish between _____ distress and _____ illness. Mild illnesses provide an excellent opportunity for children to learn about _____ and _____ and develop a sense of _____.

linguistic
word
emotional, physical

health, illness
empathy

Key Terms Matching Exercise

1.0 Images of Children: Tony's Physical Development (Term 1)
2.0 Body and Growth Change (Terms 2–5)
3.0 Motor Development (Terms 6–15)
4.0 Sleep and Sleep Problems (Terms 16–19)
5.0 Nutrition (Terms 20–22)
6.0 Illness and Health (Terms 23–24)

---

1. autonomy
2. congenital

3. deprivation dwarfism

4. myelination

5. functional amblyopia

6. gross motor skills

a. Growth retardation due to lack of affection
b. Motor behaviors involving large muscle groups such as walking and climbing
c. A sense of self-governing or responsibility for oneself; independence from parents
d. Visual disorder that results from not using one eye enough; avoids double vision
e. Existing at birth, but not hereditary in nature
f. Layer of fat cells that covers and insulates nerve cells

---

7. rough-and-tumble play

8. aggression

9. fine motor skills

10. Denver Developmental Screening Test

a. Stage of children's drawings characterized by the use of circles, squares, triangles, crosses, X's, and forms
b. Instrument designed to measure developmental delay; evaluates language, personal-social ability, gross and fine motor skills
c. Behavior that is designed to harm persons or property and is not socially justifiable
d. Physically vigorous play common to young males that entails running, jumping, chasing, fleeing, hitting at another, and much laughing on the part of participants

11. placement stage

    e. Motor behaviors involving small muscle groups such as scribbling with a pencil

12. shape stage

    f. Stage of children's drawings characterized by the position of patterns on the page

---

13. design stage

    a. Stage of children's drawings when the images are easily recognizable by adults

14. pictorial stage

    b. A dream that arouses feelings of inescapable horror and distress

15. handedness

    c. Disruptions of sleep in which an individual awakes with intense fears and physiological responses such as rapid heart rate, screams, and perspiration

16. transitional objects

    d. Refers to favoring one hand or side over the other hand or side; hand preference

17. nightmares

    e. Stage of children's drawings characterized by the mixture of two or more shapes into a larger pattern

18. night terrors

    f. Bedtime companions of young children that are typically soft and cuddly

---

19. somnambulism

    a. Range of techniques used to prevent dehydration during episodes of diarrhea

20. basal metabolism rate (BMR)

    b. A condition whereby an individual is unable to assimilate enough food to maintain growth and tissue replacement

21. iron deficiency anemia
22. malnutrition

    c. Refers to sleepwalking
    d. Minimal amount of energy an individual uses in resting, growth, and activity

23. oral rehydration therapy (ORT)

    e. Refers to conditions or practices that promote health

24. hygiene

    f. A nutritional deficit resulting from inadequate quantities of dark green vegetables and meat that produces chronic fatigue or tiredness

Key Terms Matching Exercise
Answer Key

1. c	4. f	7. d	10. b	13. e	16. f	19. a	22. b
2. e	5. d	8. c	11. f	14. a	17. b	20. d	23. a
3. a	6. b	9. e	12. a	15. d	18. c	21. f	24. e

1. During the preschool years, the child will gain about _____ inches and _____ pounds a year.
   a. 2.5; 5 to 7
   b. 3; 3 to 5
   c. 3.4; 5 to 7
   d. 4; 6 to 8

2. Deprivation dwarfism refers to stunted growth in children due to
   a. inadequate nutrition.
   b. exposure to cigarette smoke.
   c. unlimited access to caffeine.
   d. inadequate affection.

3. The growth of the brain during early childhood includes all of the following except
   a. number of nerve endings.
   b. number of nerves.
   c. myelination.
   d. size of nerve endings.

4. In order for children to move their eyes efficiently to scan a series of letters, what must develop?
   a. eye muscles
   b. brain cells
   c. occipital lobe
   d. far vision

5. At what age are children most active?
   a. 2
   b. 3
   c. 4
   d. 5

6. Which gross motor skill is most typical of a 6-year-old child?
   a. catching a large ball
   b. carrying a 12 pound object
   c. rolling a ball to hit an object
   d. bouncing and catching a ball

7. Rough-and-tumble play seems to lead to
   a. aggression.
   b. prosocial play.
   c. leadership skills.
   d. secure attachment to peers.

8. The stage of children's drawings characterized by joining two or more shapes together is the
   a. placement stage.
   b. shape stage.
   c. design stage
   d. pictorial stage.

9. What behavior in newborns is associated with handedness in early childhood?
   a. head turning when lying on the stomach
   b. preferred direction for nursing
   c. hand used for reaching
   d. hand used for throwing

10. How is the use of transitional objects at bedtime by young children related to their emotional adjustment during adolescence?
    a. They are better adjusted than peers who did not use transitional objects.
    b. They are less well adjusted than peers who did not use transitional objects.
    c. There is no relationship between use of the objects and emotional adjustment.
    d. These children are emotionally immature at adolescence.

11. Harry has just awakened from a horrible dream in which he was chased by dinosaurs. Harry has had a
    a. night terror.
    b. somnambulism.
    c. night without his teddy bear.
    d. nightmare.

12. A mealtime problem parents of 4-year-olds can expect is
    a. dawdling over food.
    b. talking too much.
    c. imitating food preferences of older siblings.
    d. liking only a few vegetables.

13. What percentage of fat in children's diets is recommended by the American Heart Association?
    a. 15%
    b. 20%
    c. 35%
    d. 40%

14. Sugar intake has been related to all of the following except
    a. dental cavities.
    b. obesity.
    c. activity level.
    d. intelligence.

15. Ways to deal with fussy eaters include all of the following except
    a. letting the child eat food in any order.
    b. keeping mealtimes enjoyable.
    c. letting the child decide when he has had enough.
    d. using food as a reward for good behavior.
16. Oral rehydration therapy is used to treat
    a. respiratory infections.
    b. diarrhea.
    c. pneumonia.
    d. malnutrition.
17. Relatively cheap vaccinations could help prevent the vast incidence among children of
    a. diarrhea.
    b. measles.
    c. pneumonia.
    d. malaria.
18. More than half of illnesses and deaths among children are related to
    a. inadequate hygiene.
    b. infection.
    c. undernutrition.
    d. prenatal factors.
19. What theoretical orientation contributed most heavily to the program that successfully trained children to use seatbelts?
    a. cognitive
    b. behavioral
    c. psychoanalytic
    d. ecological
20. When children are ill, adults have an opportunity to teach them about
    a. health-promoting behavior.
    b. good eating habits.
    c. safe ways to behave.
    d. feelings.

Self-Test Answers
Test A

1. a	4. a	7. b	10. c	13. c	16. b	19. b
2. d	5. c	8. c	11. d	14. d	17. b	20. d
3. b	6. b	9. a	12. b	15. d	18. a	

Critical Thinking Exercises

Exercise 1

This chapter describes physical development during early childhood, and illustrates several features of the nature of development. Reread "The Nature of Development" section in Chapter 1, and then indicate which of the following pairs of events, terms, or outcomes illustrates the same feature or features of development (e.g., stages of development, continuity/discontinuity, etc.). **Circle the letter of the best answer and explain why it is the best answer and why each other answer is not as good.**

A. Growth in height and stages of children's drawings
B. The respective influences of sugar and brain myelination on behavior
C. Deprivation dwarfism and handedness
D. Buckling up for safety and development of gross motor skills
E. Rough-and-tumble play and illness

Exercise 2

Santrock illustrates what we know about physical development with data that invite us to draw our own conclusions. Each of the following statements is a conclusion that one might draw. Which conclusion is best supported by the data in the designated table or figure? **Circle the letter of the best answer and explain why it is the best answer and why each other answer is not as good.**

A. The rate of increase in height between 2 and 6 years of age slows down (see Figures 9.1 and 9.2 on page 245).
B. Between 3 and 6 years of age brain and head growth occur at a constant rate (see Figure 9.3 on page 247).
C. Assuming that Figure 9.7 (see page 253) represents most children's drawing between 2 and 5 years of age, we conclude that drawing skill increases in a smooth and continuous fashion.
D. Energy needs accelerate between the ages of 1 and 10 years (see Figure 9.8 on page 257).
E. The best fast food meal for preschool children is available at McDonald's restaurant (see Table 9.1 on page 258).

Research Project 1 Gross Motor Activity of Children

This project provides an observational exercise for examining the gross motor activity of children. Pair up with another student in the class and go to a local playground. Observe two children, one about 4 years old and the other about 8 years old. For each child, describe five gross motor behaviors that the child performs while you are observing. These can include running, climbing, skipping, jumping, hopping, walking, throwing, catching, etc. Describe the same five behaviors for each child, noting differences in the way they perform the behaviors. Use the data sheet below for recording your observations. Then answer the questions that follow.

DATA SHEET

Child 1   Child 2
Sex ___ Age ___   Sex ___ Age ___

Behavior 1 (   ):   Behavior 1 (   ):
Behavior 2 (   ):   Behavior 2 (   ):
Behavior 3 (   ):   Behavior 3 (   ):
Behavior 4 (   ):   Behavior 4 (   ):
Behavior 5 (   ):   Behavior 5 (   ):

Questions:

1. What were the five behaviors you observed?
2. In general how can these behaviors be characterized or described for the 4-year-old? For the 8-year-old?
3. How did the children differ in the way they performed the behaviors?
4. From your observations of the two children and five behaviors, what do you see as the course of development of gross motor behavior between 4 and 8 years? How do your specific findings compare with the general descriptions reported in the text?

Research Project 2 Reinforcers and Punishers During Play

This project is an observational study. Pair up with another student in the class. One of you will observe the behavior, and the other will record the behavior. Go to a local neighborhood playground and observe two sets of two children playing. Designate one child in each set as the target child. The two sets of children are to be of different ages. One set is to be 4 to 5 years old and the other 8 to 9 years old. Observe each pair of children for 10 minutes. For each 10-minute session, describe any reinforcer or punisher that is used by the nontarget child in response to some behavior by the target child. Also note what the result of the reinforcer or punisher is on the subsequent behavior of the target child. Use the following data sheet to record observations and then answer the questions that follow.

DATA SHEET

| Child 1 | | | Child 2 | | |
| Sex ___ Age ___ | | | Sex ___ Age ___ | | |
Event	Reinforcers/Punishers	Effect	Event	Reinforcers/Punishers	Effect
1.			1.		
2.			2.		
3.			3.		
4.			4.		
5.			5.		
6.			6.		

Questions:

1. What did the 4- to 5-year-old child use as reinforcers? Are there any general categories that can be seen from the specific behaviors observed? What did the 4- to 5-year-old use as punishers? Did any general categories appear here? What kinds of behaviors were reinforced? What kinds of behaviors were punished? What effect did the reinforcers have on the child's subsequent behavior? What effect did the punishment have on the child's subsequent behavior?

2. What did the 8- to 9-year-old child use as reinforcers? Are there any general categories that can be seen from the specific behaviors observed? What did the 8- to 9-year-old use as punishers? Did any general categories appear here? What kinds of behaviors were reinforced? What kinds of behaviors were punished? What effect did the reinforcers have on the child's subsequent behavior? What effect did the punishment have on the child's subsequent behavior?

3. Were different reinforcers and punishers used by the younger child than were used by the older child? If so, how would you characterize the nature of the difference?

4. Were there differences in the types of behaviors reinforced or punished by the younger and the older child? If so, how would you characterize the nature of the difference?

5. Could any differences you observed in the ages possibly be attributed to sex differences? Why or why not?
6. What did you find out about peer reinforcement in 4- to 5-year-old and 8- to 9-year-old children? Does it occur? Is it effective?

Essay and Critical Thinking Questions

Comprehension and Application Essay Questions

We recommend that you follow either our guidelines for answering essay and critical thinking questions, or those guidelines provided by your instructor in preparing your response. Your answers to these kinds of questions demonstrate an ability to comprehend and think critically about concepts and topics discussed in this chapter.

1. Explain why toddlers pose more problems and offer more rewards to parents than infants.
2. Explain why some children are unusually short.
3. What is myelination? What is its role in development?
4. What are the similarities and differences between rough-and-tumble play and aggression?
5. Describe changes in children's drawings during early childhood. Should parents and preschool teachers allow children's artistic and drawing skills to develop naturally or should they try to train these skills?
6. Explain whether nightmares, night terrors, sleepwalking, and sleeptalking indicate psychological disturbance.
7. Identify and explain at least three concerns of developmentalists about toddlers' nutrition.
8. Explain how parents and caregivers can discourage eating problems on the part of young children.
9. Explain what developmental factors contribute to toddlers' risk of illness and injury.
10. In what ways do everyday illnesses provide opportunities for cognitive, social, and emotional development during early childhood?

Critical Thinking Questions

Your answers to the following kinds of questions reflect an ability to apply your critical thinking skills to a novel problem or situation that is *not* specifically discussed in this chapter.

1. In this chapter Santrock discusses aspects of nutrition in early childhood, some of which are not well understood. Apply your knowledge about the scientific base of child development by designing a study to determine the relationship between sugar ingestion in early childhood and children's present and/or future behavior: (a) What specific problem or questions do you want to study? (b) What predictions would you make and test in your study? (c) What measures would you use (i.e., observation, interviews, and questionnaires, case studies, standardized tests, physiological research, or a multimeasure, multisource, and multicontext approach) and how would you define each measure clearly and unambiguously? (d) What strategy would you follow— experimental or correlational, and what would be the time span of your inquiry—cross-sectional or longitudinal? (e) What ethical considerations must be addressed before you conduct your study?
2. According to Chapter 1, five issues define the nature of development: (a) biological, cognitive, and social processes, (b) periods or stages, (c) the issue of maturation (nature) versus experience (nurture), (d) the issue of continuity versus discontinuity, and (e) the issue of stability versus

change. Indicate your ability to think critically by (a) perusing this chapter for two examples of each of the five defining issues and (b) explaining how and why each of your examples illustrates one of the five defining issues.

3. Chapter 2 presents six different theoretical approaches (i.e., Freudian, cognitive, behavioral and social learning, phenomenological and humanistic, ethological, and ecological), but notes that no single approach explains the complexity of development. Indicate your ability to think critically by (a) perusing this chapter for topics influenced by at least one of the six theoretical approaches and (b) explaining which theoretical approach dominated the topic in question. If the presentation is entirely atheoretical, identify and explain how one of the theoretical approaches could be used to guide the analysis of the topic in question.

4. One aspect of thinking critically is to read, listen, and observe carefully, and then ask questions about what is missing from a text, discussion, or situation. For example, your author describes a successful "buckle up for safety" program, but does not connect it with any defining developmental issues discussed in Chapter 1 or any of the six theoretical approaches discussed in Chapter 2. Indicate your ability to think critically by explaining this topic's relationship to (a) one of the five defining developmental issues and (b) one of the six theoretical approaches

5. Santrock places several quotations in the margins of this chapter. One by Sir Charles Sherrington says, "Swiftly the brain becomes an enchanted loom, where millions of flashing shuttles weave a dissolving pattern—always a meaningful pattern—though never an abiding one." One by Samuel Butler says, "The youth of an art is, like the youth of anything else, its most interesting period." Indicate your ability to think critically by (a) learning about the author and indicating why this individual is eminently quotable (i.e., what was the individual's contribution to human knowledge and understanding), (b) interpreting and restating the quote in your own terms, and (c) explaining what concept, issue, perspective, or term in this chapter Santrock intended this quote to illuminate. In other words, about what aspect or issue in development does this quote make you pause and think reflectively?

Self-Test B

1. How does the rate of growth change from infancy to early childhood?
   a. It stays the same.
   b. It slows down.
   c. It speeds up.
   d. Growth rates are variable from child to child.

2. The two factors that contribute most heavily to individual differences in height are
   a. ethnic origin and nutrition.
   b. sex and ethnic origin.
   c. affection and sex.
   d. nutrition and sex.

3. Myelination is important because it
   a. provides needed nutrition to brain cells.
   b. protects brain cells.
   c. speeds up information traveling in the nervous system.
   d. assists in the production of neurotransmitters.

4. Functional amblyopia is a visual disorder characterized by
   a. problems with far vision.
   b. problems with near vision.
   c. inability to perceive depth.
   d. using one eye more than the other.

5. All of the following are examples of gross motor skills except
   a. running.
   b. drawing.
   c. hopping.
   d. skipping.

6. All but one of the following is an appropriate way to stimulate gross motor skill development in young children. Which one is the exception?
   a. Organize group exercises.
   b. Play balance games.
   c. Have a daily run.
   d. Imitate animal movements.

7. Aggression differs from rough-and-tumble play in which characteristic?
   a. clenched fists
   b. hitting
   c. chasing
   d. fleeing

8. What instrument is used to assess motor development in 3- to 6-year-old children?
   a. Apgar Scale
   b. Bayley Motor Scale
   c. Denver Developmental Screening Test
   d. Brazelton Scale

9. Carol's drawings generally have circles, squares, and crosses, each isolated from one another. Her drawings are examples of which drawing stage?
   a. placement stage
   b. shape stage
   c. design stage
   d. pictorial stage

10. What evidence is used to argue for a genetic basis for handedness?
    a. The handedness of adopted children is similar to that of adoptive parents.
    b. The handedness of adopted children is similar to that of biological parents.
    c. Handedness is easily trained in schools.
    d. Infants prefer to use the hand that they see day-care teachers use.

11. Which of the following is most likely to be a sign of emotional disturbance or upset?
    a. use of transitional objects
    b. nightmares
    c. night terrors
    d. somnambulism

12. Fast food meals are poor for children's diets because they contain too much
    a. sugar.
    b. fat.
    c. protein.
    d. carbohydrate.

13. Sugar is associated with several undesirable health outcomes. Which of the following, however, is not definitely known to be associated with eating too much sugar?
    a. aggression
    b. eating problems
    c. obesity
    d. cavities

14. A nutritional deficiency associated with poverty in the United States is lack of sufficient
    a. fat.
    b. protein.
    c. carbohydrate.
    d. iron.

15. Oral rehydration therapy involves what substances?
    a. molasses, salt, and water
    b. milk and water
    c. water and salt
    d. water and sugar

16. Which of the following is not a major contributing factor to childhood mortality?
    a. access to prenatal care
    b. undernutrition
    c. timing of births
    d. hygiene

17. The death rate of children under 5 in the United States is worse than how many other countries?
    a. 2
    b. 5
    c. 8
    d. 20

18. Perhaps one of the most long-lasting and effective ways to deal with the health problems of the world's children would be to
    a. provide clean water.
    b. make vaccines universally available.
    c. combat diarrhea.
    d. educate parents.

19. Respiratory illnesses in children were related to what parental behavior?
    a. smoking
    b. drinking
    c. working outside the home
    d. neglect

20. All but one of the following should be a goal of health education programs for children. Which one is the exception?
    a. Teach children how it feels to be healthy or sick.
    b. Identify for children who can help them when they have health problems.
    c. Get children to act on their own to get help.
    d. Encourage children to help each other with their problems.

1. b	4. d	7. a	10. b	13. a	16. a	19. a
2. a	5. b	8. c	11. b	14. d	17. d	20. d
3. c	6. a	9. b	12. b	15. a	18. d	

Objectives

1.0   *Images of Children: Amy and Her Experiences at Montessori School*
1.1   Sketch the philosophy of a Montessori school, and describe the roles of the teacher and student.
1.2   Discuss what a child might do and learn at a Montessori school, and explain why some developmentalists have reservations about Montessori schools.

2.0   *Preoperational Thought*
2.1   Define operations, and distinguish preoperational thought from sensorimotor and concrete operational thought.
2.2   Define and distinguish between the symbolic function substage and the intuitive thought substages of preoperational thought.
2.3   Describe young children's drawings, explain why developmentalists call them symbolic, and evaluate Piaget's hypothesis that children's drawings represent what they know rather than what they see.
2.4   Define and distinguish between egocentrism and animism, describe observations that indicate each one's presence in children's thought, and discuss the idea that egocentrism and animism represent limitations on thought.
2.5   Describe the three mountains task and explain what it purportedly demonstrates about a child's cognition.
2.6   Define and distinguish between centration and conservation, and describe observations that indicate their presence in young children's thought.
2.7   Explain how centration causes both failure to classify objects and contributes to an inability to conserve.
2.8   Describe the types of conservation tests according to Piaget, and indicate what failing or passing this kind of test means according to Piaget's theory.
2.9   Use the concepts of intuitive thought and operations to explain why young children fail conservation tasks, whereas concrete operational children pass them.
2.10   Compare and contrast Piaget's and Gelman's views about why young children fail conservation tasks.
2.11   Discuss what children's questions reveal about their cognition.

3.0   *Information Processing*
3.1   Explain how an information processing approach distinguishes between limitations on cognitive development and limitations on the method of study.
3.2   Indicate how habituation and dishabituation influence attention during the preschool years, and how visual attention to television changes during the same period.
3.3   Define and distinguish between salient and task relevant dimensions, and discuss how these influence young children's attention.
3.4   Define short-term memory, list its properties, and indicate how it changes in young children.
3.5   Explain (a) what a digital memory-span task demonstrates about the information processing ability of young children and (b) how 6-year-olds and young adults can display equivalent memory spans.
3.6   Discuss how task analysis has led to an understanding of children's ability to reason syllogistically.

4.0 *Language Development*
4.1 Define mean length of utterance (MLU), and describe language development from 1 to 4 years of age according to Brown's five stages.
4.2 Review the components of a rule system for language discussed in Chapter 7, and describe observations that indicate children understand rules of morphology, syntax, semantics, and pragmatics.
4.3 Describe the growth of vocabulary from 1 to 6 years of age.
4.4 Explain why educators believe that literacy begins in infancy.
4.5 Define literacy, list deterrents to a literate populace, and summarize elements of a literacy program for preschoolers.

5.0 *Vygotsky's Theory of Development*
5.1 Define the zone of proximal development (ZPD), and indicate how learning in toddlers exemplifies the workings of ZPDs.
5.2 Compare and contrast uses of the zone of proximal development (ZPD) and the intelligence quotient (IQ).
5.3 Characterize the respective activities of child and teacher as a child moves through a ZPD.
5.4 Discuss Vygotsky's conception of the developmental relationship between language and thought.
5.5 Compare and contrast Piaget's and Vygotsky's ideas about what causes development of thought and language.

6.0 *Early Childhood Education*
6.1 List criticisms of contemporary kindergartens.
6.2 Discuss the philosophy and activities of a child-centered kindergarten.
6.3 Explain the concept of developmentally appropriate practice, and explain what makes the kindergarten in Greensbrook School in New Jersey a developmentally appropriate class.
6.4 Define and distinguish between developmentally appropriate and inappropriate teaching practices for the eight different components of education for young children.
6.5 Explain why contemporary parents may not be able to care for their young children as well as preschools.
6.6 Describe evidence that formal instruction in reading should be delayed until age 7.
6.7 Describe the controversy over preschool experience, and discuss the ideal intent from programs of early childhood education.
6.8 Describe evidence that developmentally inappropriate schools harm their young pupils in comparison to developmentally appropriate schools.
6.9 Compare and contrast both preschools in Japan and the United States and mothers' involvement in early childhood education in the two countries.
6.10 Summarize the effects of early childhood education on development.
6.11 Define Project Head Start, describe findings from Project Follow Through, and relate them to findings (a) from comparisons of developmentally appropriate and inappropriate teaching and (b) about the value of preschool and kindergarten.
6.12 List the documented benefits of compensatory education for disadvantaged children, and compare them to benefits associated with preschool attendance in general.
6.13 List and define three factors that indicate school readiness, and discuss how these should influence government school policy.
6.14 List reasons why students might fail in school.
6.15 Indicate what best predicts sixth-grade academic competence.
6.16 Compare and contrast advice on how to involve mothers and fathers in young children's learning and education.
6.17 Summarize early childhood education teachers' perceptions of parents.
6.18 List considerations relevant to selecting a preschool program.

Summary

1.0 Images of Children: Amy and Her Experiences at Montessori School

Maria Montessori's approach to the education of retarded children has been adopted and extensively used in private nursery schools in the United States. The teacher facilitates rather than directs learning and encourages students to freely and spontaneously choose their activities. This approach seems to foster independence and the development of cognitive skills, but critics complain that it neglects children's social development.

2.0 Preoperational Thought

The Nature of Preoperational Thought. The preoperational period is the second stage in Piaget's theory of cognitive development and encompasses ages 2 to 7 years. During this time, stable concepts are formed, mental reasoning emerges, magical belief systems are constructed, and egocentrism is perceptually based.

Symbolic Function Substage. The first substage of this period is the symbolic function substage. During the ages of 2 to 4 years, the child gains the ability to develop mental representations of objects and events. Drawing, language, and symbolic play appear. Thinking is egocentric during the preoperational period in that the child is unable to distinguish between his or her own perspective and the perspective of another. Animism also characterizes thought during this period. Children incorrectly attribute human qualities to inanimate objects.

Intuitive Thought Substage. The second substage is called the intuitive thought substage. During the ages of 4 to 7 years, children begin to reason and have opinions about matters but they cannot explain how they know what they know. The child at this age can neither correctly classify objects into groups that belong together nor correctly reason about an object belonging simultaneously to two different classes. Thought is characterized by centration, in which attention focuses on one dimension only. In addition, children fail to understand conservation problems.

Several individuals have challenged Piaget's view of the child between 2 and 7 years of age. For example, Gelman's research has shown that improving a child's attention to relevant aspects of a task can improve the likelihood of a child offering correct responses on conservation tasks even though they are less than 7 years old.

3.0 Information Processing

Information processing capacities related to attention and memory develop dramatically during early childhood.

Attention. Attention span increases with age, and children become increasingly able to attend to relevant dimensions of a task rather than to only the most salient dimension. The latter ability may result from the cognitive control of attention.

Memory. Short-term memory retains information for about 20 to 30 seconds. With rehearsal, material can be maintained longer in short-term memory. Memory span increases from two digits in 2- to 3-year-old children to about five digits in 7-year-old children. Speed and efficiency of processing may contribute to the increase in digit span.

Task Analysis. The information processing approach led to the analysis of the kinds of activities involved in the development of children's cognition. By making tasks simpler and more interesting, developmentalists have discovered that children may possess greater cognitive maturity than previously thought possible.

4.0 Language Development

Issues in language development during early childhood encompass Brown's stages, rule systems, and literacy.

Elaboration of Brown's Stages. Roger Brown's model of young children's language development encompasses mean length of utterance (MLU), age ranges, characteristics of language, and sentence variations. Brown has described five stages of language development in which different syntactic structures appear at each stage.

Rule Systems. Evidence for morphological rules comes from the errors children make by generalizing the rule to irregular forms, such as using "foots" for "feet." There is evidence that children learn and apply syntactic rules. An example is that children apply rules for forming "wh-" questions by correctly placing the "wh-" word without inverting the auxiliary verb. Semantic knowledge also expands after the two-word stage. Vocabulary grows rapidly. Understanding of pragmatics also grows. Preschool children develop a command of displacement and begin to be sensitive to the conversational needs of others. The ability to change speech style according to the listener first appears around age four.

Literacy and Early Childhood Education. Literacy in the United States is a problem of contemporary concern. Formal reading instruction for preschool children is inappropriate. However, education that focuses on communication across a wide range of modalities, with an emphasis on risk taking and having fun, may be more appropriate for children of this age.

5.0 Vygotsky's Theory of Development

Vygotsky's theory has received more attention in recent years.

Zone of Proximal Development. The zone of proximal development is a measure of learning potential. The lower limit of the zone of proximal development is the problem-solving ability that a child displays when working alone. The upper level encompasses the problem-solving ability of a child when aided by an instructor.

Language and Thought. Vygotsky believes that language and thought first develop independently, but that later on they merge. One principle is that all mental functions have social origins. A second principle is that children use language prior to developing internal speech, or talking to themselves. Vygotsky's views contrast with those of Piaget.

Culture and Society. Vygotsky's view emphasizes the sociocultural context of development in contrast to Piaget, who views young children as solitary scientists.

6.0 Early Childhood Education

Child-Centered Kindergarten. Child-centered kindergarten programs, such as Montessori programs, should involve the whole child. They should not place a major emphasis on success. Children who attend early educational programs may be more mature than children who have no experience of that kind.

Developmentally Appropriate and Inappropriate Practices in the Education of Young Children. Developmentally appropriate practice entails both age-appropriate and individually appropriate considerations and activities. Inappropriate practices ignore concrete, hands-on approaches to learning. The National Association for the Education of Young Children (NAEYC) advocates developmentally appropriate practice and has provided extensive recommendations for its implementation.

Does It Really Matter If Children Attend Preschool Before Kindergarten? Education for Disadvantaged Children. Although parents can be effective educators of their children, many lack the commitment, time, and resources to provide children with all the ingredients in a competent early childhood education program. Viewing education as a race may be stressful to children and contribute to rather than eliminate illiteracy. Early childhood education confronts some issues that overlap with those of upper levels of schooling; however, the agenda is and should be different than ones for traditional elementary schools. Early childhood education differs in the Orient and the United States; however, the superior academic performance of Asian children in elementary and secondary schools does not result because they were pushed to achieve during their preschool years.

The Effects of Early Childhood Education. In general, children who attend preschool or kindergarten interact more with peers and appear both more and less socially competent. For example, they are more confident and extroverted; however, they are also less polite, louder, and more aggressive.

Education for Disadvantaged Children. Project Head Start is a program in compensatory education targeted at children from low-income families. It offers preschool experiences with the hope that these early experiences might counteract the disadvantages these children normally experience and allow them to profit from regular schooling later. Project Follow Through assessed the effectiveness of different kinds of educational programs in helping children from low-income families to progress. Children in academically oriented approaches performed better on achievement tests and were more persistent on tasks. Children in affective education approaches were absent from school less often and were more independent. Thus, different approaches have different outcomes in the kinds of behavior that they foster. Long-term follow-up studies show positive effects of Head Start in the number of people who go to college and who are employed full time, when comparing individuals who participated in Head Start with others of similar backgrounds who did not receive that experience.

School Readiness. The concept of school readiness entails the assumption that all children have specifiable abilities and skills before they enter school. Discussion of school readiness must encompass the diversity of children's early life experiences, individual differences in development and learning, and reasonable and appropriate expectations about children's capabilities upon school entry.

The Role of Parenting in Young Children's Learning and Education. Both mothers and fathers play important roles in their young children's learning and education. An important aspect of preschool and early childhood education is the relationship between young children's parents and schools. Guidelines for selecting a good preschool program exist.

2. Both _____ and _____ of attention during infancy
   _____ with intelligence during preschool years.

   decrements, recovery
   correlate

3. A 2-year-old _____ attention frequently, but the preschool
   child can attend to _____ for up to 30 minutes.

   shifts
   television

4. Preschool children are captured by the _____ features of a
   display not necessarily the ones _____ to a current task.
   After the age of 6 or 7, attention seems to come under
   _____ control so that older children attend to stimuli that
   are _____ to a particular task.

   salient
   relevant

   cognitive
   relevant

5. In addition to the development of _____, the other
   information processing of preschool children that improves entails
   _____.

   attention

   memory

6. Short-term memory appears to retain information for up to ___
   seconds. The retention duration of short-term memory can be
   increased by various _____ strategies.

   30

   rehearsal

7. A test in which you hear a short list of stimuli read and are then
   asked to repeat the digits is called a _____ _____ task.
   The memory-span task can be used to assess _____ _____
   memory. The memory span increases sharply between _____
   and _____ years of age. This seems best explained by
   increases in _____ and _____ of processing.

   memory-span
   short-term
   2
   7
   speed, efficiency

8. One way to better understand the abilities and _____ of
   children's cognitive development requires experiments to perform a
   _____ _____. Such _____ _____ suggest
   methods of research that are both interesting and _____ for
   children. This strategy revealed the preschool children understand
   _____.

   limitations

   task analysis
   task analyses
   simple
   syllogisms

4.0 Language Development

1. Major issues in preschooler's use of language focus on _____
   of language development _____ _____, and _____.

   stages
   rule systems, literacy

2. Brown has identified five stages of language development, based on
   _____ _____ _____ _____. Stage one consists
   mainly of _____ and _____, with _____ _____
   used. Stage two is characterized by the correct use of _____,
   use of the _____ tense, and the appearance of _____
   _____. Stage three marks the appearance of _____
   _____ and _____ questions, along with the use of
   _____ and _____. Stage four includes the uses of
   _____ sentences. In Stage five simple sentences and
   propositional relations are _____.

   mean length of utterance
   nouns, verbs, word order
   plurals
   past, indefinite articles
   yes-no
   wh-
   negatives, imperatives
   embedded
   coordinated

3. The first phase of the preoperational period is called the ____
    _____ substage. The child of _____ to _____ years
    of age has the ability of mental _____. Symbolic thought is
    expressed by children's _____, _____ play, and their use
    of _____.

    symbolic function
    2, 4
    representation
    drawings, pretend
    language

4. Scribbles become pictures about the age of _____. By ____
    the child has represented a _____.

    3, 4
    person

5. The inability to distinguish between one's own perspective and the
    perspective of another is called _____. The _____
    _____ task was devised by Piaget and Inhelder to study
    egocentrism in children. When asked what a doll seated across the
    table sees, preoperational children often describe _____
    _____ _____ rather than the view of the doll.

    egocentrism
    three mountain

    their own view

6. The view that inanimate objects are alive or that plants and
    similar forms have human qualities is called _____. Recent
    evidence suggests that what appears to be animism might be due
    to lack of _____ and understanding.

    animism

    knowledge

7. During the substage called _____ _____, children in the
    age range of _____ to _____ years of age are sure of
    their knowledge, but unaware of how they know. When asked to
    put an assortment of objects into groups of similar items the
    intuitive child cannot because she has not yet developed the skill
    of _____. The _____year-old child can't _____
    _____; the _____year-old child probably can.

    intuitive thought
    4, 7

    classification, 6-
    cross-classify, 9-

8. Egocentrism, animism, and difficulty with classification may
    represent _____, the inability to focus attention on more than
    one characteristic at a time. Centration is evident in the child's
    response to _____ tasks, when the child will reason that
    there is more liquid in a tall, thin glass because it is higher, even
    when the child saw an equal amount of liquid poured into the
    taller container. Failure to pass a _____ task test indicates
    that a child is in the _____ stage of _____ development
    according to _____.

    centration

    conservation

    conservation
    preoperational, cognitive
    Piaget

9. According to Gelman, _____ problems are responsible for
    failure on conservation tasks. _____ training allows children
    to demonstrate conservation earlier than Piaget expected.

    attention
    Attentional

10. About the age of _____ children begin to _____ ____.
    Many of the questions ask _____? This phenomenon
    demonstrates the child's _____ _____.

    3, ask questions
    why
    cognitive abilities

3.0 Information Processing

1. Developmentalists believe that what appears to be a limitation in
    children's _____ abilities really may reflect limitations in the
    _____ used to assess their _____ _____.

    cognitive
    procedures
    cognitive development

Key Terms

1.0 Images of Children: Amy and Her Experiences at Montessori School
Montessori approach

2.0 Preoperational Thought
operations
symbolic function substage
egocentrism
animism
intuitive thought substage
centration
conservation
attentional training

3.0 Information Processing
attention
salient dimension
relevant dimension
short-term memory
task analysis
syllogism

4.0 Language Development
MLU
language rule systems
overgeneralization
literacy

5.0 Vygotsky's Theory of Development
zone of proximal development (ZPD)

6.0 Early Childhood Education
child-centered kindergarten
developmentally appropriate practice
Project Head Start
Project Follow Through
direct instruction
affective education
educational outcomes
school readiness
teacher-caregiver

Guided Review

1.0 Images of Children: Amy and Her Experiences at Montessori School

1. In Montessori schools, children are encouraged to work _____, _____ tasks in a prescribed manner once they have begun, and to put materials away in _____ places. The teacher serves as a _____ of a process of _____ rather than a _____ of learning.

   independently, complete assigned, facilitator, discovery, director

2. The Montessori approach includes tasks designed to help develop _____ _____. However, critics believe that _____ development is neglected and critics argue that _____ _____ is restricted.

   cognitive skills, social imaginative play

2.0 Preoperational Thought

1. The preoperational period lasts from _____ to _____ years of age. The child develops _____ concepts, mental _____, and _____ _____ systems. _____ declines.

   2, 7, stable, reasoning, magical belief, Egocentrism

2. Internalized actions that allow children to do mentally what before they could only do physically are called _____. Such _____ are highly _____ and conform to certain _____ and principles of _____.

   operations, operations organized, rules logic

211

3. The correct use of plurals, possessives and "ed" for the past tense is evidence that children beyond the two-word stage know some _____ rules.

morphological

4. Jean Berko's study of preschool and first-grade children demonstrated knowledge of morphological rules using _____ words. Her work provided an explanation for _____ of rules to irregular forms.

fictional
overgeneralization

5. The understanding and use of a wh- question requires not only the placing of a _____ word at the beginning of the sentence but also the _____ of the auxiliary verb. This finding indicates children understand rules of _____. Children learn to apply the _____ rule _____ than they learn to use the wh- words.

wh-
inversion
syntax
inversion, later

6. The speaking vocabulary of a 6-year-old child has been estimated to be between _____ to _____ words. This means a new word rate of _____ to _____ per day between the ages of 1 to 6. A growing vocabulary is also evidence for rules of

_____.

8,000, 14,000
5, 8

semantics

7. The ability to talk about things not physically present is _____. It appears about the age of _____. About the age of _____, evidence of sensitivity to the _____ of others is displayed by their correct use of _____ and by using different _____ of speech with a _____ _____ _____ child and an _____. This is evidence for understanding rules of _____.

displacement, 3
4, needs
articles
styles, 2-year-old
adult
pragmatics

8. A major concern currently is _____, which has led to examination of the experience young children have with reading and writing. Children need to feel _____ and _____ in their early reading and writing. Reading and writing should be incorporated into understanding _____ systems in general. Children should be encouraged to take _____ and be allowed to make _____.

illiteracy

success, pride

communication
risks
errors

5.0 Vygotsky's Theory of Development

1. According to Vygotsky, tasks that are too difficult for children to handle alone, but that can be done with assistance of someone more skilled fall into the _____ _____ _____ _____ or _____.

zone of proximal
development, ZPD

2. For Vygotsky, language and thought initially are _____; however, the two eventually _____.

unrelated
merge

3. The merging of thought and language is governed both by its _____ origins, and by a transition from _____ to _____ speech.

social, external, internal

214

4. The zone of proximal development is just one indication of Vygotsky's emphasis on the _____ and _____ factors that influence cognitive development.

social, cultural

5. Vygotsky argues that children's mental development is dependent on _____ interactions embedded in a _____ background.

social, cultural

6.0 Early Childhood Education

1. Some experts on early childhood education believe that kindergartens and preschools place too much emphasis on _____, and thereby place unnecessary pressure on children too soon.

achievement

2. In a _____ _____ _____, education includes concerns for the child's physical, cognitive, and social development.

child-centered kindergarten

3. In a child-centered kindergarten, the _____ of learning rather than the end product is emphasized.

process

4. Schooling that is based on age-appropriate activities with an emphasis on individual appropriateness are following _____ _____ educational practices.

developmentally appropriate

5. _____ _____ practices ignore the hands-on approach to learning, teach using paper-and-pencil activities, and teach to large groups instead of individuals.

Developmentally inappropriate

6. Sending a child to preschool is not necessary if _____ _____ approximates the experiences that can be obtained at a preschool.

home schooling

7. One of the dangers of instituting public preschools is that they will become extensions of _____ elementary education.

traditional

8. Children in high academically oriented early education programs had _____ test anxiety, _____ creativity, and a _____ positive attitude toward school than children in low academically oriented programs.

more, less, less

9. American mothers devoted _____ time to the educational activities of their preschoolers than oriental mothers, but _____ time to their elementary school children than oriental mothers.

more
less

10. The most popular form of education before the first grade has been described as _____ _____ because the emphasis is on providing the child with an _____ experience in learning. Children who have attended preschool demonstrate greater developmental _____ than children who have not attended such programs.

child-centered individualized

maturity

215

11. The first attempt at compensatory education in the United States was _____ _____ _____. The purpose of this program was to _____ the early environment of children from low-income families.

Project Head Start
enrich

12. The attempt to determine whether some types of enrichment programs worked better than others was called _____ _____ _____. The academic models of Project Follow Through produced better academic _____ and task _____, but the students in the affective models were _____ less and were more _____.

Project Follow Through

performance, persistence
absent
independent

13. One long-term follow-up study of Head Start students has found that _____ have shown a greater effect than _____ who seem no better off.

males, females

14. Lazar, Darlington, and their collaborators have found _____ long-term effects of _____ preschool education with _____ _____ children.

positive
competent, low-income

Key Terms Matching Exercise

1.0 Images of Children: Amy and Her Experiences at Montessori School (Term 1)
2.0 Preoperational Thought (Terms 2–9)
3.0 Information Processing (Terms 10–15)
4.0 Language Development (Terms 16–19)
5.0 Vygotsky's Theory of Development (Term 20)
6.0 Early Childhood Education (Terms 21–29)

---

1. Montessori approach

a. Belief that non-living objects have life-like qualities and are capable of action

2. operations

b. Inability to distinguish between one's own perspective and the perspective of someone else

3. symbolic function substage

c. Approach to education in which children are encouraged to work independently, to complete tasks in a prescribed manner once started, and to put materials away in assigned places; teacher serves as facilitator

4. egocentrism

d. Internalized set of actions that allows the child to do mentally what before was done physically

5. animism

e. First part of preoperational period, during which the child begins to use mental representations to represent object not actually present

6. intuitive thought substage

f. Second part of the preoperational stage, characterized by beginning of reasoning about various matters, and frequent questions

7. centration

    a. Giving children practice at learning to attend to the pertinent or relevant part of a procedure used to determine children's cognitive abilities

8. conservation

    b. An obvious and attractive feature of a problem that may be irrelevant to the solution of a problem such as that entailed in Piagetian conservation

9. attentional training

    c. The key feature of a problem that must be recognized and addressed in order to solve a problem such as that entailed in Piagetian conservation

10. attention

    d. Focusing attention on one characteristic to the exclusion of all others

11. salient dimension

    e. Understanding that amount remains the same regardless of how shape changes

12. relevant dimension

    f. A cognitive or information processing skill that refers to focused awareness

13. short-term memory

    a. Memory storage where stimuli are stored and retrieved for up to thirty seconds, if not rehearsed

14. task analysis

    b. A form of deductive reasoning in which there are major and minor premises and a conclusion

15. syllogism

    c. One of the defining characteristics of language along with infinite generativity

16. MLU

    d. Technique used by an information processing approach to determine exactly what each part of an experimental task requires of a child; procedure helps identify whether children have abilities that are not revealed by procedures inappropriate for them

17. language rule systems

    e. In language, the application of normative rules to exceptions

18. overgeneralization

    f. Brown's index of language development based on the number of words per sentence that a child produces in a sample of 50–100 sentences

19. literacy

    a. Program designed to give children from low-income families an enriched early environment to help them acquire skills and experiences necessary for success in school

20. zone of proximal development (ZPD)

21. child-centered kindergarten

22. developmentally appropriate practice
23. Project Head Start

24. Project Follow Through

b. This type of schooling is based upon knowledge of the typical development of children within an age span as well as the uniqueness of the child; it contrasts with an approach that ignores the concrete, hands-on approach to learning, and teaches largely through abstract activities presented to large groups of young children

c. Program to see which of several different educational programs were effective

d. The general ability to read and write

e. Vygotsky's term for tasks too difficult to master alone, but that can be mastered with the guidance of adults or more skilled children

f. In this type of kindergarten, education involves the whole child and includes a concern for the child's physical, cognitive, and social development; instruction is organized around the child's needs, interests, and learning styles

---

25. direct instruction

26. affective education

27. educational outcomes

28. school readiness

29. teacher-caregiver

a. A concept based on the assumption that children must possess a specifiable set of characteristics prior to entering schools

b. Educational programs that focus on emotional and social components

c. An approach to learning that teaches largely through abstract activities presented to groups of young children

d. Person who serves in the role of both a caregiver and a teacher in a preschool program

e. Measurements of the effect of different kinds of educational programs

Key Terms Matching Exercise
Answer Key

1. c	5. a	9. a	13. a	17. c	21. f	25. c	29. d
2. d	6. f	10. f	14. d	18. e	22. b	26. b	
3. e	7. d	11. b	15. b	19. d	23. a	27. e	
4. b	8. e	12. c	16. f	20. e	24. c	28. a	

1. Montessori initially began her program of early childhood education to help
   a. mentally retarded children.
   b. poor children.
   c. gifted children.
   d. sick children.
2. According to Piaget, an internalized set of actions that are organized and conform to certain rules of logic are
   a. structures.
   b. schemes.
   c. operations.
   d. symbols
3. All of the following are primary characteristics of the symbolic function substage except
   a. pretend play.
   b. scribbling.
   c. language.
   d. operations.
4. Betsy, standing in the bedroom, holds up a sock and says to her mother, who is in the kitchen, "Is this mine?" Betsy is demonstrating
   a. conservation.
   b. egocentrism.
   c. animism.
   d. centration.
5. A child is asked to classify a set of shapes into groups which go together. She first puts a square down, then a circle on top of it for head. Next she chooses two triangles for the legs and two rectangles for the arms. This child is most likely in which of Piaget's stages?
   a. sensorimotor
   b. preoperational
   c. concrete operational
   d. formal operational
6. Research by Gelman using Piaget-type tasks found that
   a. her results supported Piaget's descriptions.
   b. children did better at earlier ages than Piaget's descriptions.
   c. children did worse at earlier ages than Piaget's descriptions.
   d. children did worse than Piaget's descriptions, but her research was seriously flawed.
7. A child drawing a picture makes a circle which he says is an airplane. This child is most likely in which stage according to Piaget?
   a. concrete operational stage
   b. sensorimotor
   c. symbolic function substage
   d. intuitive substage
8. Antonio is asked if he can be a boy and an Egyptian at the same time. He replies, "No!" Antonio is in which stage according to Piaget?
   a. concrete operational stage
   b. sensorimotor
   c. symbolic function substage
   d. intuitive substage
9. Decrement of attention is another way to describe
   a. habituation.
   b. dishabituation.
   c. short-term memory.
   d. conscious memory.
10. Younger children attend to _____ dimensions, whereas older children attend to _____ dimensions.
    a. salient, relevant
    b. novel, unusual
    c. unusual, novel
    d. relevant, salient
11. Short-term memory is often measured by
    a. having a child recall what she ate yesterday.
    b. a recognition task.
    c. a memory-span task.
    d. a bimodal presentation of information.
12. The unit of analysis in calculating a child's mean length of utterance (MLU) is
    a. morphemes.
    b. phonemes.
    c. whole words.
    d. syllables.
13. According to Brown, *yes/no* and *wh-* questions appear during which stage of language development?
    a. one
    b. two
    c. three
    d. four

14. Which of the following characteristics of speech is mastered latest in development?
    a. use of plurals
    b. use of past tense
    c. use of definite articles
    d. use of negatives
15. As he sees his father walk out, a child says, "Where daddy is going?" This error is an example of which kind of development?
    a. phonological
    b. syntactic
    c. semantic
    d. pragmatic
16. At what age to children begin to use definite and indefinite articles?
    a. 3
    b. 5
    c. 7
    d. 8
17. Lev Vygotsky developed the concept of
    a. the child-centered kindergarten.
    b. the mean length of utterance.
    c. the zone of proximal development.
    d. school readiness.

18. According to Vygotsky,
    a. egocentric speech demonstrates cognitive immaturity.
    b. the process of learning, rather than what is learned, is most important.
    c. children fail conservation tasks because they fail to attend to relevant dimensions.
    d. language and thought initially are independent but eventually merge.
19. Schooling based on research about the typical characteristics of individuals in a certain age range defines the concept of
    a. the zone of proximal development.
    b. developmentally appropriate practice.
    c. school readiness.
    d. the Montessori school.
20. Project Head Start was designed for _____ children.
    a. gifted
    b. retarded
    c. physically impaired
    d. impoverished

Self-Test Answers
Test A

1. a	4. b	7. c	10. a	13. c	16. a	19. b
2. c	5. b	8. d	11. c	14. d	17. c	20. d
3. d	6. b	9. a	12. a	15. b	18. d	

Critical Thinking Exercises

Exercise 1

This chapter makes many claims about diverse aspects of the cognitive functioning of preschool children. Although the picture of their cognitive skills is fairly consistently presented, some of the studies contradict one another. Which of the following statements is contradicted by information elsewhere in the chapter? **Circle the letter of the best answer and explain why it is the best answer and why each other answer is not as good.** *Hint:* Cite the specific finding (or findings) that confirms or contradicts the claim in question.

A. As indicated by their performance on the three mountains task, young children cannot take the perspective of others.

B. Young children find it difficult to pay attention to more than one feature, characteristic, or dimension of a task at the same time.

C. An aspect of preoperational thought is that nonliving things have the characteristics of living things.

D. Memory span increases rapidly between the ages of 2 and 7 years old.

E. Around 3 years of age children are able to talk about things that are not physically present.

Exercise 2

Santrock devotes much effort in this chapter to describing the nature of cognition in early childhood and to identifying the experiences presumed to promote cognition; however, he seldom directly shows the relationship between ideas and observations. To the contrary, the job of synthesizing this information is left to the reader. According to your synthesis of information in the chapter, which of the following statements makes the most sense? **Circle the letter of the best answer and explain why it is the best answer and why each other answer is not as good.**

A. Piaget's and Vygotsky's theories contradict one another.
B. The best early childhood education programs are patterned after Montessori's methods.
C. The development of language is very different from and unrelated to the development of thought.
D. The concept of a child-centered kindergarten is clearly based on Piaget's theory of cognitive development.
E. Both Piagetian tests and information processing tasks reveal that the preschooler's mind is qualitatively different from the mind of a school-age child.

Exercise 3

In this chapter Santrock presents a sample and some interpretations of preschool children's art. Which of the following statements underlying this presentation constitutes an assumption rather than an inference or an observation? **Circle the letter of the best answer and explain why it is the best answer and why each other answer is not as good.**

A. When they are 3 years old children draw scribbles that resemble pictures.
B. Children know more about the human body than they are capable of drawing.
C. Preschool children's drawings are fanciful and inventive.
D. Children both distort and omit the details of what they are trying to draw.
E. Children's drawings reflect levels of cognitive development despite the fact that children's motor skills are limited.

Research Project 1 Memory Span

The function of this project is to provide a demonstration of memory span. Pair up with a classmate and test four individuals: a 3-year-old, a 6-year-old, a 9-year-old, and a classmate. The task is a digit span task. Present a list of digits to each subject at the rate of one per second, and have each subject repeat as many digits as he or she remembers. One of you will present the digits and the other will record the subject's response. Use the following work sheets for data collection and then answer the questions that follow.

Task	Child 1	Child 2	Child 3	Adult
	Age ___	Age ___	Age ___	Age ___
	Sex ___	Sex ___	Sex ___	Sex ___
Digits	Response:	Response:	Response:	Response:

2
74
196
2389
64157
326890
7509621
92503184
849276304

Number of correct
digits out of:
one
two
three
four
five
six
seven
eight
nine

Questions:

1. How many digits would a 3-year-old remember? Was it the same number regardless of the number of digits presented? How many could the 6-year-old, the 9-year-old, and the classmate remember? Was the number different depending on the number presented? In what way was the number different?

2. Did you find age differences for memory span? What is the nature of the differences observed? Could anything besides memory span account for the differences? (Consider possible sex differences, if applicable, or differences in the child's understanding of his or her role in the task.)

3. From your data, what statement could you make about the development of memory span from 3 years to adulthood? What qualifications, if any, would you need to make about your statement, based on the limitations of your data?

Research Project 2 Language Errors

This class project exposes you to the kinds of errors that children make when they are acquiring language. Pair up with another student in the class. One of you will act as the experimenter, while the other will act as the observer. Test two different children, one 3 to 4 years of age, the other 7 to 8 years of age. In order to test the two children, you will need to clear this through the human subjects review board at your school and get a signed informed consent form from the children's parents.

The children will receive three different tasks evaluating their understanding and use of the passive construction. Present an act-out task, an imitation task, and a production task. The task and sentence descriptions follow. Use the accompanying data sheets to record observations. Then answer the questions that follow.

1. Act-out task: Have several objects available, a toy car and truck, a toy doll, a toy horse, cow, dog, and cat. Read the sentences below one at a time, and have the child act out the sentences with the toys.
2. Imitation task: Present each of the sentences below to each child, and have the child repeat the sentences back to you.
3. Production Task: Perform the actions in each of the sentences below with the toys for the child. Ask the child to tell you what happened, starting with the first noun in the sentence. For instance, for item e roll the car along so that it hits the truck, and then ask the child to tell you what happened beginning with the truck.

a. The car hit the truck.
b. The dog was kicked by the cat.
c. The boy was bitten by the dog.
d. The boy hit the cat.
e. The truck was hit by the car.
f. The cow stepped on the horse.
g. The cat kicked the dog.
h. The cat was hit by the boy.
i. The dog bit the boy.
j. The horse was stepped on by the cow.

Task	Child 1	Child 2
	Sex ___ Age ___	Sex ___ Age ___

Act-out task

Sentence a
Sentence b
Sentence c
Sentence d
Sentence e
Sentence f
Sentence g
Sentence h
Sentence i
Sentence j

Task	Child 1 Sex ___ Age ___	Child 2 Sex ___ Age ___

Imitation task

Sentence a
Sentence b
Sentence c
Sentence d
Sentence e
Sentence f
Sentence g
Sentence h
Sentence i
Sentence j

Production task

Sentence a
Sentence b
Sentence c
Sentence d
Sentence e
Sentence f
Sentence g
Sentence h
Sentence i
Sentence j

Questions:

1. What did the 3- to 4-year-old child do on the act-out task? The imitation task? The production task? Was performance on one task better than on the others? If so, which? What sorts of errors appeared in the act-out task? What about the imitation task? The production task? Were the errors similar in the various tasks?
2. What did the 7- to 8-year-old child do on the act-out task? The imitation task? The production task? Was performance on one task better than on the others? If so, which? What sorts of errors appeared in the act-out task? What about the imitation task? The production task? Were the errors similar in the various tasks?
3. Compare the two children. What differences if any did you see on their performances on these three tasks? How would you account for the differences? What is the nature of language learning that seems to be occurring during this time?
4. What criticisms could be leveled at the procedures you used in this demonstration? For example, do you think each task should have had different questions?

Essay and Critical Thinking Questions

Comprehension and Application Essay Questions

We recommend that you follow either our guidelines for answering essay and critical thinking questions, or those guidelines provided by your instructor in preparing your response. Your answers to these kinds of questions demonstrate an ability to comprehend and think critically about concepts and topics discussed in this chapter.

1. Explain what children might do and learn at Montessori schools, and evaluate these schools from a developmentalist's perspective.
2. What does Piaget mean by "operations"? Explain how preoperational thought differs from sensorimotor thought.
3. Explain at least two examples of a Piagetian conservation task. Compare and contrast Piaget's and Gelman's analyses of children's success or failure on a conservation task.
4. Describe short-term memory, and indicate how it changes in young children.
5. Characterize Brown's method for studying language development in children, and summarize his findings.
6. What is a zone of proximal development (ZPD)? Explain the respective activities of child and teacher as a child moves through a ZPD.
7. Compare and contrast Piaget's and Vygotsky's views about what causes the development of thought and language.
8. Characterize the philosophy and activities of a child-centered kindergarten.
9. Characterize and explain at least three of the controversies regarding preschools and preschool experiences.
10. Imagine that you are a parent with a prospective preschooler. Explain what you would do before attending a session with a preschool director and what kinds of questions you would ask during the meeting.

Critical Thinking Questions

Your answers to the following kinds of questions reflect an ability to apply your critical thinking skills to a novel problem or situation that is *not* specifically discussed in this chapter.

1. This chapter discusses various aspects of cognitive development in early childhood. Apply your knowledge about the scientific base of child development by designing a study to determine whether formal instruction in reading should be delayed until age 7: (a) What specific problem or question do you want to study? (b) What predictions would you make and test in your study? (c) What measures would you use (i.e., observation, interviews, and questionnaires, case studies, standardized tests, physiological research, or a multimeasure, multisource, and multicontext approach) and how would you define each measure clearly and unambiguously? (d) What strategy would you follow—experimental or correlational, and what would be the time span of your inquiry—cross-sectional or longitudinal? (e) What ethical considerations must be addressed before you conduct your study?
2. According to Chapter 1, five issues define the nature of development: (a) biological, cognitive, and social processes, (b) periods or stages, (c) the issue of maturation (nature) versus experience (nurture), (d) the issue of continuity versus discontinuity, and (e) the issue of stability versus change. Indicate your ability to think critically by (a) perusing this chapter for two examples of each of the five defining issues and (b) explaining how and why each of your examples illustrates one of the five defining issues.

3. Chapter 2 presents six different theoretical approaches (i.e., Freudian, cognitive, behavioral and social learning, phenomenological and humanistic, ethological, and ecological), but notes that no single approach explains the complexity of development. Indicate your ability to think critically by (a) explaining why Santrock discusses Vygotsky's theory of development in this chapter rather than in Chapter 2 and (b) explaining how you would integrate Vygotsky's theory into Chapter 2.

4. One aspect of thinking critically is to read, listen, and observe carefully, and then ask questions about what is missing from a text, discussion, or situation. For example, a major theme of this chapter concerns individual differences among children; however, an individual differences approach to children does not appear in this chapter. Indicate your ability to think critically by (a) perusing your textbook for discussions about an individual differences approach and (b) evaluating the pros and cons of what you would learn by applying this approach to cognitive development in early childhood.

5. Santrock places several quotations in the margins of this chapter. One by Helen Keller says, "But whatever the process, the result is wonderful, gradually from naming an object we advance step-by-step until we have traversed the vast difference between our first stammered syllable and the sweep of thought in a line of Shakespeare." Another by Aristotle says, "Learning is an ornament in prosperity, a refuge in diversity." Indicate your ability to think critically by (a) learning about the author and indicating why this individual is eminently quotable (i.e., what was the individual's contribution to human knowledge and understanding), (b) interpreting and restating the quote in your own terms, and (c) explaining what concept, issue, perspective, or term in this chapter Santrock intended this quote to illuminate. In other words, about what aspect or issue in development does this quote make you pause and think reflectively?

Self-Test B

1. Which approach focuses on teaching children to work independently, complete tasks, put materials away, and conceptualizes the teacher as a facilitator?
   a. Montessori
   b. Project Head Start
   c. child-centered kindergarten
   d. Project Follow Through

2. Which of the following characterizes preoperational thought?
   a. reversible thought
   b. coordination between action and perception
   c. decentration
   d. symbolic functioning

3. Juanita believes that men made the lakes and the rivers, but she cannot tell why she believes that. Juanita is most likely in which substage?
   a. tertiary circular reactions
   b. symbolic function
   c. intuitive
   d. internalization of schemes

4. Carlos is describing a shape to a friend so that his friend can pick out an object of the same shape. Carlos says, "It looks like my mommy's hat." This is an example of
   a. egocentric thinking.
   b. animistic reasoning.
   c. logical reasoning.
   d. decentration.

5. Karen thinks that thunder roars because the clouds are angry. She is displaying
   a. egocentric thinking.
   b. animistic reasoning.
   c. logical reasoning.
   d. decentration.

6. The understanding that a glass of milk remains the same if it is poured from a tall thin glass into a short fat glass is
   a. egocentrism.
   b. animism.
   c. conservation.
   d. classification.

7. Preschool children are apt to attend most to _____ stimulus features when performing a task.
   a. salient.
   b. relevant.
   c. critical
   d. intuitive
8. Decentration is a characteristic of
   a. memory.
   b. language.
   c. operations.
   d. attention.
9. Short-term memory, without the use of rehearsal, lasts for a span of
   a. 2 to 3 seconds
   b. 15 to 30 seconds.
   c. 5 minutes.
   d. 24 hours.
10. The memory span of a seven-year-old is about
    a. two digits.
    b. three digits.
    c. four digits.
    d. five digits.
11. One of the most useful measures of language development is
    a. semantic development.
    b. use of pragmatics.
    c. mean length of utterance.
    d. onset of babbling.
12. According to Brown's stages of language development, correctly formed plurals are a characteristic of stage
    a. two.
    b. three.
    c. four.
    d. five.
13. Learning to use the *s* to form a plural structure is an example of what kind of development?
    a. phonological
    b. morphological
    c. syntactic
    d. semantic
14. After racing down the street with his uncle, Peter says, "I runned very, very, fast!" The use of the term *runned* is an example of what kind of development?
    a. phonological
    b. morphological
    c. syntactic
    d. semantic

15. Nadia answers the phone when her father calls. When she realizes it is her father, she says, "You don't come home. Why you don't come home?" This speech sample is a good example of what kind of development?
    a. syntactic
    b. phonological
    c. pragmatic
    d. semantic
16. What is the estimate of the speaking vocabulary of a 6-year-old?
    a. 1 to 2,000 words
    b. 7 to 12,000 words
    c. 8 to 14,000 words
    d. 10 to 20,000 words
17. The zone of proximal development is most appropriately regarded as
    a. a measure of literacy.
    b. a measure of language development.
    c. a measure of school readiness.
    d. a measure of learning potential.
18. Should formal instruction in reading be delayed until age 7?
    a. Yes, because illiteracy is rare in countries in which reading instruction is delayed until age 7.
    b. No, because children need a head start on reading.
    c. No, because children younger than age 7 have limited short-term memory.
    d. Yes, because such instruction takes advantage of the natural growth of vocabulary from 1 to 6 years of age.
19. Which approach to compensatory education produced children who performed best on achievement tests?
    a. parent education programs
    b. affective centered programs
    c. Piagetian based programs
    d. direct instruction programs
20. Which approach to compensatory education produced children who were absent from school less and were more independent?
    a. parent education programs
    b. affective centered programs
    c. Piagetian based programs
    d. direct instruction programs

1. a	4. a	7. a	10. d	13. b	16. c	19. d
2. d	5. b	8. d	11. c	14. b	17. d	20. b
3. c	6. c	9. b	12. a	15. a	18. a	

Objectives

1.0 *Images of Children: The World of Pretend Play*

1.1 Discuss how children's play mimics adult roles and reveals what they understand about gender-appropriate behavior.

1.2 Discuss why adults express greater concern than children about gender-specific behavior.

2.0 *Families*

2.1 Sketch changes of emphasis in parenting recommendations over the past 60 years.

2.2 Define and distinguish among authoritarian, authoritative, permissive-indifferent, and permissive-indulgent parenting, and describe the personalities of children who experience each type of parenting.

2.3 Summarize Meyerhoff and White's recommendations for competent parenting.

2.4 Define developmentally appropriate parenting, describe ways in which parenting may change as children develop, and explain why parenting behaviors should change as children grow older.

2.5 List factors that influence sibling relationships.

2.6 Compare and contrast parent-child and child-child (sibling) interactions, and explain why siblings may be more important than parents to some aspects of socialization.

2.7 Explain why the firstborn child's relationship with parents is unique compared to that of any subsequent child; discuss firstborn children's relationships with later-born siblings; list the personality and behavioral characteristics of first- versus later-born children, and compare firstborn to only children.

3.0 *The Changing Family in a Changing Society*

3.1 List changes in the American family that have occurred over the last 50 years.

3.2 Indicate the most common parenting style in the world.

3.3 Compare and contrast the child-rearing practices and values of both different ethnic groups and different social classes, and explain how ethnic minority families can protect their children from social problems and injustice.

3.4 Discuss the positive and negative effects of a mother's working outside the home on a child's social development, and explain why children of two working parents may *not* suffer compared to children cared for by a nonworking parent.

3.5 Discuss causes and cures for parents' feelings of guilt, and summarize Galinsky and David's recommendations for working parents about how to overcome work/family interference.

3.6 Describe recent and projected proportions of children living in single-parent homes in America, and explain why developmentalists are concerned about single mothers.

3.7 List factors related to how well children adjust to their parent's divorce.

3.8 Discuss how conflict, gender, and age relate to individual differences in children's adjustment to divorce, and evaluate the idea that divorce is never a good solution to marital problems when there are children in the family.

3.9 Discuss guidelines for talking with children about divorce.

3.10 Define and distinguish between child abuse and child maltreatment, and list the incidence of different types of maltreatment.

3.11 Evaluate the severity of child abuse, and explain why it is too simple to view child abuse as a result of the hostility of bad, sadistic parents.

3.12 Identify cultural and social factors that relate to lower rates of child maltreatment.

4.0   *Peer Relations*
4.1   Define and distinguish between peers and siblings, and compare and contrast the function of peers and siblings in the socialization of children.
4.2   Describe changes in peer relations during early childhood, and evaluate the evidence that peers are necessary for adequate social development.
4.3   Compare and contrast peer and child-parent relationships, and explain how children's relationships with their parents can influence relationships with their peers.

5.0   *Play*
5.1   Define play, and compare and contrast the cognitive functions of play according to Freud, Erikson, Piaget, Vygotsky, and Berlyne.
5.2   Define and distinguish among unoccupied, solitary, onlooker, parallel, associative, and cooperative play.
5.3   Describe differences in play exhibited by children in the 1930s and 1970s in terms of Parten's categories of play.
5.4   Compare and contrast Parten's types of play and the play types identified by contemporary researchers (e.g., sensorimotor, practice, pretense/symbolic, social, and constructive play, and also games).
5.5   Explain how play fulfills both developmental and educational goals and functions.

6.0   *Television*
6.1   Indicate how much time children spend watching television, and list the possible positive and negative influences of television watching on cognitive and social development.
6.2   Describe the evidence that ethnic minorities are under- and misrepresented on television.
6.3   Define and distinguish between direct and indirect teaching, discuss which best describes the influence of "Sesame Street," and evaluate whether "Sesame Street" is "good television" for children.
6.4   Discuss what you would find out about cultural and national concerns by viewing various foreign language versions of "Sesame Street."
6.5   Evaluate the claims that television violence causes aggression in children and that viewing prosocial behavior on television causes children to engage in prosocial behavior.
6.6   List factors associated with more or less television watching, and discuss ways that parents can enhance the impact of television on the lives of their children.

7.0   *The Self*
7.1   Define and distinguish among guilt, conscience, and initiative in Erikson's theory, and describe how these interact in the development of self.
7.2   Indicate how early childhood is dominated by initiative versus guilt feelings, and identify what type of parenting promotes initiative rather than guilt during childhood.
7.3   Define self-understanding, and describe young children's self-understanding.

8.0   *Gender*
8.1   Define and distinguish among sex, gender, gender identity, and gender role.
8.2   Explain and evaluate the idea that "anatomy is destiny."
8.3   Define hermaphrodite, and explain the biological and social influences on gender role development.
8.4   List possible ways to interpret the phrase "biological and environmental factors interact to produce gender-related behavior" and evaluate which interpretation best applies to gender-role development.
8.5   Compare and contrast the identification and social learning theories of gender development.
8.6   Identify differences in parents' treatment of daughters and sons, and explain how differences in treatment may result in gender role differences.

8.7   Summarize peer, teacher, and media influences on gender role development.
8.8   List trends in sex equity education research.
8.9   Compare and contrast the cognitive developmental and gender schema theories of gender role development.
8.10   Define sexist language, and explain how language may influence gender role development.

9.0   *Moral Development*
9.1   Define moral development, and distinguish the study of moral behavior from the study of moral reasoning, behavior, and emotion.
9.2   Define and distinguish among heteronomous morality, autonomous morality, and immanent justice, and describe observations that indicate their presence in children's moral reasoning.
9.3   Sketch Piaget's ideas about the importance of peer versus parent relations to moral development.
9.4   List factors that social learning theory suggests control the expression of moral behavior.
9.5   Describe the sources and effects of guilt, and discuss the role of positive and negative emotions in moral development.
9.6   Define altruism, explain its relationship to empathy, and describe the part that role-taking and perspective-taking skills play in each.

Summary

1.0 Images of Children: The World of Pretend Play

Children's pretend play reflects their understanding of the world. Although gender-specific behavior from young children is common, parents and preschool teachers increasingly regard it as a problem in light of their endeavor to raise children without sexist bias.

2.0 Families

Parenting Styles. Four types of parenting styles are associated with different aspects of the child's social behavior. Authoritarian parents are restrictive, punitive, and controlling. Their children tend to be anxious about social comparison, fail to initiate activity, and are ineffective in social interactions. Authoritative parents encourage the child to be independent, place limits and demands on the child, and give the child warmth, along with verbal give-and-take. Their children are socially competent, self-reliant, and socially responsible. Permissive-indulgent parents are highly involved in their children's lives but do not control or set limits on their behavior. Their children show a disregard for rules and regulations. Permissive-indifferent parents are uninvolved in their children's lives and do not control them. Their children show a lack of self-control. Meyerhoff and White provided guidelines for competent parenting that dovetail with the concept of authoritative parenting.

Adapting Parenting to Developmental Changes in the Child. Parents need to adapt their style of parenting as a child grows older. An emphasis on reasoning should increase, and the use of physical manipulation should decrease.

Sibling Relationships and Birth Order. Sibling relationships are generally more negative than parent-child relationships. Siblings may have a stronger socializing influence than parents on a child in areas such as dealing with peers, coping with difficult teachers, and discussing taboo subjects. In general, firstborn children receive more attention from the mother than late-born children do. A younger sibling will tend to observe and imitate an older sibling, whereas an older sibling will not do this with a younger one.

3.0 The Changing Family in a Changing Society

Changes in American families include an increasing number of ethnic minority families, working mother families, families in which there is divorce, stepparent families, and families in which child abuse occurs.

Cultural, Social Class, and Ethnic Variations in Families. The most common parenting style in the world is authoritative parenting. Social class differences characterize the parenting values in most Western cultures. Working-class and low-income parents more highly value external characteristics such as obedience and neatness, whereas middle-class parents value internal characteristics such as self-control. Ethnic minority families differ from White American families in their size, structure, composition, reliance on kinship networks, income, and education. Extended families are common to Black American and Hispanic American families.

Working Mothers. More mothers work outside the home now than in previous generations. Working mothers may provide a pattern of socialization for children more appropriate to their adult roles than traditional stay-at-home mothers. Working parents often feel guilty about being away from their children. Ellen Galinsky offers guidelines for parents who experience work/family interference and guilt.

Effects of Divorce on Children. Divorce is common in America; a large percentage of the children born in the 1970s have spent some time in a single-parent home. Research suggests that separations and divorces have fewer negative effects for the child than does living in a family with conflict. Nonetheless, the time immediately after a divorce is still conflict-ridden for many families, and children receive less adequate parenting than before the divorce. The support systems available, the age of the child at the time of the divorce, and the sex of the child with respect to the sex of the custodial parent are all variables that can affect the outcome of the divorce for the child. Boys generally fare better in father-custody families, and girls generally fare better in mother-custody families. Ellen Galinsky and Judy David outline recommendations for how parents can communicate with their children about divorce.

Child Abuse. Some problems and disturbances appear during infancy. Child abuse is an example of a growing contemporary problem in our culture. It is a multifaceted problem and one perhaps better termed child maltreatment. Understanding child abuse requires information about the cultural context and family influences.

4.0 Peer Relations

Peers are children of about the same age or behavioral level and who serve as powerful social agents. Social contacts and aggression are characteristics of same-age peers. Peer groups allow the child to receive feedback about his or her abilities relative to others of the same age. Peer relationships are different from interactions with adults. As research on bully behavior has demonstrated, the nature of parent-child interactions can affect the quality of peer interactions.

5.0 Play

Play's Functions. Play is an important activity that is engaged in for its own sake. Different theorists indicate that play promotes affiliation with peers, tension release, cognitive development, and exploration. Play therapy has been used in therapeutic settings with young children to provide a medium through which the therapist can learn about the conflicts that a child experiences and how a child copes with those conflicts.

Parten's Classic Study of Play. Parten described six categories of play: unoccupied, solitary, onlooker, parallel, associative, and cooperative. Young children engage more in solitary and parallel play, and older children engage more in cooperative and associative play.

Types of Play. In contrast to Parten's emphasis on the role of play in a child's social world, contemporary views emphasize both the cognitive and social aspects of play. The more studied kinds of play now include sensorimotor, practice, pretense/symbolic, social, and constructive play. Play is different from games that include rules and competition.

6.0 Television

Television's Many Roles. Children watch a great deal of television. Television has two primary functions: entertainment and communication. Television provides the child with information about a wider variety of views and knowledge than may be available from the child's immediate environment. It also exposes children to violence and aggression, which they may then imitate, and the content of television typically stereotypes minorities. Television also can teach prosocial behavior.

Parents' Role in Children's Television Viewing. Although parents rarely discuss television's content with their children, the Singers have developed guidelines for parents who want to make television a more positive influence in their children's lives.

7.0 The Self

Initiative versus Guilt. The conflict that characterizes early childhood in Erikson's view, is initiative versus guilt. Children resolve this conflict by engaging in self-generated actions or by feeling guilty over these activities. Children develop a conscience during this time.

Self-Understanding. The self is particularly important in understanding development. Self-understanding begins with self-recognition, but most children's view of the self focuses on external characteristics, a physical self or an active self.

8.0 Gender

What is Gender? Sex refers to a biological dimension, whereas gender refers to a social dimension. Gender identity is the sense of being male or female, typically acquired by age 3. Gender role is the set of expectations that prescribe how females or males should think, act, or feel.

Biological Influences. Several biological arguments have been made to explain differences between males and females. Erikson has argued that psychological differences between males and females result from anatomical differences—that anatomy is destiny. Based on the structures of the penis and uterus, Erikson believes males are more intrusive and aggressive, whereas females are more inclusive and passive. A second biological influence is hormonal level. Estrogen in females and androgen in males are responsible for genital development. Biological influences on social behavior may be direct or indirect.

Social Influences. Parents, culture, school, peers, the media, and other family members affect gender role development. Identification theory is derived from Freud's views. Social learning theory of gender emphasizes the observation and imitation that govern gender role development. Parents affect gender development. For example, fathers play an important role in sex typing both boys and girls by behaving differently toward sons and daughters. Parents often encourage boys and girls to engage in different kinds of play behaviors even in infancy. Boys are typically more constrained in their play behavior than are girls. Parents treat boys and girls differently by allowing boys more freedom and by protecting girls more. Peers also play a role in socializing sex-typed behavior by criticizing those who play in sex-crossed activities and reinforcing those who play in sex-appropriate activities. In elementary school, female teachers reinforce feminine behaviors in both boys and girls. Despite improvements, television still portrays males as more competent than females.

Cognitive Influences. Cognitive factors are also important in sex role development. According to Kohlberg's cognitive developmental theory of gender, children are trying to make sense of their world and to create categories that simplify information processing. Sex categories, according to gender schema theory, allow the child to generate expectations about a person on the basis of their sex and to develop expectations about his or her own appropriate behavior on the basis of their own. Sexist language, such as the use of the pronoun "he" when referring to everyone, may limit or constrain thinking.

9.0 Moral Development

What Is Moral Development? Moral development concerns the rules and conventions about what people should do in their interactions with others. Several different theories have emerged to explain the development of moral reasoning, behavior, and feelings in children.

Piaget's View of How Children's Moral Reasoning Develops. Piaget viewed moral development in two stages. The stage of heteronomous morality is associated with younger children. In this stage, children evaluate good or bad based on the consequences of behavior, without regard to intention. The child sees rules as unchangeable and given from a higher authority and believes that punishment is mechanically connected to transgression—the concept of immanent justice. In Piaget's second stage of moral development, autonomous morality, the child believes that the intention of the action is the primary consideration in evaluating an action as good or bad. The child understands that rules are conventional and open to negotiation. In Piaget's view, social understanding comes out of the peer group.

Moral Behavior. Moral behavior has primarily been studied by social learning theorists, who invoke the processes of reinforcement, punishment, and imitation to explain how children learn moral behavior. A key ingredient of moral development from the social learning perspective is the child's ability to resist temptation and to develop self-control. Cognitive rationales are more effective in getting a child to resist temptation than threats or punishments alone. A second behavior that has been examined is delay of gratification, which is closely related to resistance to temptation. Mischel believes that self-control, including the ability to delay gratification is influenced by cognitive factors. The child can instruct himself or herself to be more patient.

Moral Feelings. Moral feelings are also an important aspect of moral development. Guilt can be instrumental in preventing the performance of a behavior or in making reparations after a transgression. Feelings of empathy for the distress of another appear early and may lead a young child to attempt to alleviate the other's distress. Altruistic behavior, behavior that involves attempts to be helpful to another, can appear as early as 2 years of age, although the occurrence increases with development. It may be motivated by the child's developing feelings of empathy.

Key Terms

1.0 Images of Children: The World of Pretend Play
pretend play
gender-specific behavior

2.0 Families
authoritarian parenting
authoritative parenting
permissive-indulgent parenting
permissive-indifferent parenting
competent parenting
sibling relationships

3.0 The Changing Family in a Changing Society
working mothers
divorce
child abuse
child maltreatment

4.0 Peer Relations
peers

5.0 Play
play
play therapy
unoccupied play
solitary play
onlooker play
parallel play
associative play
cooperative play
sensorimotor play
practice play
pretense/symbolic play
social play
constructive play
games

6.0 Television
prosocial behavior

7.0 The Self
initiative versus guilt
self-understanding
conscience

8.0 Gender
gender
gender identity
gender role
anatomy is destiny
estrogen
androgen
hermaphrodite
identification theory
social learning theory of gender
sex equity education research
cognitive developmental theory of gender
schema
gender schema
gender schema theory

9.0 Moral Development
moral development
moral reasoning
heteronomous morality
autonomous morality
immanent justice
moral behavior
moral feelings
empathy

Guided Review

1.0 *Images of Children: The World of Pretend Play*

1. _____ play by children reveals what they understand about _____ _____ behavior. Although gender specific behavior by children _____ has occurred; it is _____ regarded as a problem by adults such as _____ teachers and some _____.

Pretend
gender specific
always, now
preschool
parents

2.0 *Families*

1. Some experts regard _____ as a primary ingredient in children's _____ development; however, other experts deemphasize the importance of attachment and focus on features such as the child's _____, other _____ variables, and the _____ of a child's social world.

attachment
social

temperament, social
complexity

2. There are _____ basic parenting styles. In addition to ____ and _____ parenting, there are two forms of _____ parenting.

four, authoritarian
authoritative, permissive

3. The _____ parenting style places many _____ on the child. There is very little verbal give-and-take. The parents use _____ and take the position that the _____ are the bosses. Authoritarian parenting is associated with anxiety about social _____, _____ to initiate activity, and _____ social interactions.

authoritarian, controls

punishment, parents

comparison, failure,
ineffective

4. The _____ parenting style encourages _____ within limits. It uses extensive _____ and is associated with _____ and _____. Authoritative parenting produces children with _____ social skills, particularly _____ _____ and social _____.

authoritative,
independence,
explanations
warmth, nurturance, good
self-reliance,
responsibility

5. A permissive-indulgent parent is _____, but _____ and _____. Neglecting parents are undemanding but _____. This is called _____ _____ parenting. Permissive-indulgent children grow up showing a disregard for _____, whereas permissive-indifferent children grow up with a lack of _____ _____.

undemanding, accepting
responsive, rejecting
permissive-indifferent
rules

self-control

6. Meyerhoff and White developed a _____ for _____ parenting that includes both things _____ _____ and things _____ _____ _____.

primer, competent
to do
not to do

238

7. During the first year of a child's life the interaction moves from an emphasis on _____ to include more play and visual-vocal exchanges. During the second and third years, discipline centers on physical _____, and focuses more on _____ as the child grows older.

caretaking

manipulation, reasoning

8. The relations of siblings with their parents are generally more _____ than their relations with each other. Children behave more _____ and _____ with siblings than with parents.

positive

negatively, punitively

9. Siblings can be a stronger socializing influence than parents. This is especially true in areas such as _____ interaction, coping with difficult _____, and discussion of _____ subjects.

peer

teachers, taboo

10. The appearance of a younger sibling _____ the amount of _____ the mother gives the older sibling and mother may become more _____ or _____ toward the older child.

decreases

attention

coercive, negative

11. Older siblings are expected to have more _____ _____ than younger siblings. The oldest sibling is more _____, _____, and _____ than younger siblings.

self-control

dominant

competent, powerful

12. Older siblings are more _____ and _____ than their younger siblings. Same-sex siblings are characterized by more _____, _____, and cheating than opposite-sex siblings. Firstborns have high standards placed on them and are more likely to excel in _____ endeavors.

antagonistic, nurturant

aggression, dominance

professional

3.0   The Changing Family in a Changing Society

1. The most prominent changes in the American family include an _____ number of ethnic _____ families, _____ mother families, _____ families, and families in which _____ _____ occurs.

increasing, minority, working, stepparent, child abuse

2. The most common style of parenting in the world entails _____ rather than _____ and _____ rather than _____. In most Western cultures, middle-class families value _____ characteristics whereas lower-class families value _____ characteristics.

warmth
coldness, control, permissiveness, internal
external

3. Large, extended families typify _____ _____ groups more so than White American groups, and may benefit children by protecting them from social _____ and reducing their _____.

ethnic minority

injustice
stress

4. _____ _____ families are more likely than White American families to have _____ parents.

Ethnic minority
single

5. An educated, nonworking mother may discourage _____ in her children by doing too much _____.

independence
mothering

239

6. Hoffman argues that working mothers are more _____ models for socialization of today's child than are full-time mothers. This is especially true for _____.

realistic

daughters

7. Working parents often feel _____ about spending little time with their children. Brazelton suggests that working parents either _____ their guilt or _____ it away. Ellen _____ provided guidelines for _____ who experience _____ _____ interference.

guilty

admit, rationalize, Galinsky, parents work/family

8. Current evidence indicates that _____ in every _____ children will spend some time in a _____ parent home by the year 2000.

one, four

single

9. Traditionally, studies of divorce have followed a _____ _____ model; however, more recent approaches focus on the _____ and _____ of a child before a divorce, the _____ surrounding a divorce, and family functioning _____ a divorce. Positive adjustment of the child following divorce is related to _____ systems, a positive relationship between the _____, _____ parenting, and the child's _____ at the time of the divorce.

father absence

strengths, weaknesses
events, after
support
parents, authoritative
competencies

10. _____ is more important than family structure on the child's development. Divorce may not solve the conflict problem because in the first year after a divorce conflict usually _____. Adjustment problems for children are particularly evident in the _____ year after a divorce.

Conflict

increases

first

11. According to work by Santrock and Warshak, children living with the _____ _____ _____ were characterized as being more socially competent than those with the other custody arrangement. Divorce when children are _____ has a more negative effect than when they are _____. _____ children may blame themselves more for the divorce and have fears of _____.

same-sex parent

younger
older, Younger

abandonment

12. Parental guidelines for talking to children about a divorce were developed by _____ and _____ who recommend such things as explaining the _____, maintaining _____ of communication, and providing support for both _____ and _____.

Galinsky, David
separation, channels
children
parents

13. When a caregiver harms his or her charge, it is called _____ _____. American society is _____. This is a _____ influence. The child may be _____ or _____, the parents may be experiencing severe _____ or there may be a parental history of _____. These are _____ influences. There may be no family or friends or crisis centers nearby. This is a _____ influence.

child abuse
violent, cultural
unattractive, unwanted
stress
abuse, family

community

4.0 Peer Relations

1. People of about the same age of _____ _____ are called
   _____.

   behavioral level
   peers

2. Peer groups serve to provide a source of _____ and _____
   about the world outside the family.

   information, comparison

3. Work with animals suggests that monkeys reared with peers
   become _____ when separated from one another. A case
   history compiled by _____ _____ on a group of six World
   War II orphans indicated that peer associations alone prevented
   _____ and _____. Good peer relations may be _____
   for normal social development.

   depressed
   Anna Freud

   delinquency, psychosis
   necessary

4. _____, _____, _____, and _____ are observed
   in relations with both peers and parents. _____ _____
   _____ _____ is seen mostly in peer relations, but children
   prefer their _____ when under stress.

   Smiling, touching,
   frowning, vocalizing,
   Rough-and-tumble play
   parents

5. Strong peer relations are related to _____ _____.
   Children who become _____ have parents who reject them,
   use power assertion, and allow aggression. Children who become
   _____ _____ have anxious and overinvolved mothers who
   prohibit aggression.

   secure attachment
   bullies

   whipping boys

5.0 Play

1. A pleasurable activity in which individuals engage for its own sake
   is called _____. The _____ of play varies according to
   different _____ theorists even though all of them agree that
   play increases the probability that children will _____ with
   one another. According to Freud, the function of play is _____
   reduction. For Piaget, play allows a child to _____ her
   cognitive skills. According to Berlyne, play satisfies an _____
   drive present in all people.

   play, function
   developmental
   affiliate
   tension
   practice
   exploratory

2. Mildred _____ performed the _____ study in which she
   identified _____ categories of play. When in _____ play,
   a child may stand in one spot, look, or perform random movements
   with no goal. A kind of play described by Parten in which a child
   plays alone and independently of those around him is called
   _____ play. _____ play describes a child who is
   essentially watching others play. In _____ play, a child plays
   by himself with toys similar to those being used by others.

   _____ play, described by Parten, is characterized by social
   interaction and little or no organization. If group identity and
   organization are added, associative play becomes _____ play.

   Parten, classic
   six, unoccupied

   solitary, Onlooker
   parallel

   Associative

   cooperative

3. Keith _____ observations are more recent than those of
   Parten. He has found that children in the 1980s engage in
   _____ associative and cooperative play than children did in the
   1930s; however, the bulk of Parten's observations were _____.

   Barnes'

   less
   replicated

4. Pretend play appears at about _____ months of age. During
   pretend play the child may try out several different _____. It
   is at about this time that children develop imaginary _____.
   The incidence of pretend play peaks between ____ and ____
   years. Pretend play involves the use of _____, usually has a
   _____, and allows children to try out different _____.

   18
   roles
   playmates
   5, 6
   props
   plot, roles

5. Parten's play categories fall under the category of _____
   play.

   social

6. When sensorimotor play is combined with symbolic representation,
   it is called _____ play.

   constructive

7. _____ are activities engaged in for pleasure that include rules
   and competition. Games are _____ salient in the preschool
   years than they are in the elementary school years.

   Games
   less

6.0   Television

1. Television can have a _____ influence on children's
   development by presenting motivating educational programs,
   increasing children's information about the world, and providing
   models of prosocial behavior.

   positive

2. Of special concern is how _____ _____ are portrayed on
   television.

   ethnic minorities

3. A review of television watched by children indicated that ____
   tended to hold lower status jobs and were more likely to be cast
   as criminals or victims.

   minorities

4. "Sesame Street" demonstrates that _____ and _____ can
   work well together. It seeks to teach in both direct and ____
   ways.

   education, entertainment
   indirect

5. In correlational studies of violence on television, investigators
   _____ conclude that watching violence on television causes
   aggressive behavior. In _____ studies it has been shown that
   watching violence on television causes an increase in aggressive
   behavior.

   cannot
   experimental

6. When children are taught critical viewing skills they can ____
   the effects of television violence.

   reduce

7. The amount of television viewed by children is _____ correlated with socioeconomic status of the family and _____ correlated with conflict in the home.

inversely
positively

8. To escape from the stress of living in a dysfunctional family, children watch more _____ oriented television than those from functional families.

fantasy-

7.0 The Self

1. Erikson sees the psychosocial conflict of early childhood as _____ versus _____. Initiation is governed by _____. _____ influence the resolution of this stage.

initiative, guilt, conscience, Parents

2. Children who are given freedom and are encouraged to initiate motor play are likely to develop a sense of _____.

initiative

3. If parents let their children know that their questions are a nuisance, discourage initiative, and tell them their games are stupid, they are likely to develop a sense of _____.

guilt

4. _____ _____ is the child's cognitive representation of self.

Self-understanding

5. In early childhood, children usually conceive of themselves in _____ terms.

physical

6. A central component of the self in early childhood is the _____ dimension.

active

8.0 Gender

1. _____ refers to the biological dimensions of being male or female, whereas gender is the _____ dimension of being male or female.

Sex
social

2. _____ _____ is the sense of being male or female, whereas _____ _____ is the set of expectations that prescribe how females and males should think, act, and feel.

Gender identity
gender role

3. According to Freud, human sexual behavior is related to _____ process. For Erikson, psychological differences stem from _____ differences, and his view is called the "_____ _____ _____" view.

reproductive

anatomical
anatomy is destiny

4. Biological influences on gender roles are also apparent in the influence of hormones, _____ in females and _____ in males. When the hormones are unbalanced during fetal development, the genitals are not clearly male or female, and the individual is called a _____. One issue is how _____ the influence of biological factors is on behavior.

estrogen, androgen

hermaphrodite, direct

5. Most investigators believe that children's behavior as males and females is due to an _____ between biological and environmental factors.

interaction

6. According to the social view of gender development, boys and girls learn gender roles through _____ learning, by watching what other people say and do.

observational

7. Freud's view that preschoolers identify with the same-sex parents and unconsciously adopt their characteristics is called _____ theory. Critics of Freud's theory claim that children become gender-typed much _____ than 5 to 6 years of age.

identification

earlier

8. The _____ _____ view of gender emphasizes that gender development occurs through the rewards and punishments children receive for appropriate and inappropriate gender behavior. Critics of the social learning view argue that gender development is not as _____ acquired as the view suggests.

social learning

passively

9. _____ are more involved in the socialization of their sons than their daughters.

Fathers

10. Children show a clear preference for being with and liking _____-sexed peers. Playgrounds may appropriately be called _____ _____.

same
gender school

11. Girls experience _____ sex-typing behavior than boys.

less

12. Both _____ and _____ favor _____ over _____. _____ students were given more attention and had more interactions with teachers than _____ students.

schools, teachers, males
females, Male
female

13. Three issues in _____ _____ research concern subtle _____ and _____, shifting educational outcomes, and emphasized _____ _____ outcomes.

sex equity,
discrimination,
stereotyping, sexual,
equity

14. On television, _____ are more likely to appear in higher status jobs and are portrayed as more aggressive and more competent than _____.

males

females

15. The _____ view stresses that children _____ construct their gender world. According to the _____ _____ _____ _____ _____, once children consistently see themselves as male or female, they organize their world on the basis of _____.

cognitive, actively
cognitive developmental
theory of gender

gender

16. Preschool children rely on _____ characteristics to put males and females into categories.

physical

17. A _____ is a cognitive structure that guides individual perceptions. A _____ _____ is a construct that organizes the world according to sex, and reflects children's understanding of _____ standards.

schema
gender schema

cultural

18. Gender is also characteristic of _____. Children typically hear language that is _____ is nature.

langauge
sexist

9.0 Moral Development

1. The development of the rules and conventions about how people should behave in their interaction with other people is called _____ development. The three domains of moral development involve how children _____ or _____ about rules for ethical conduct, how they _____ in the face of temptation, and how they _____ after a moral decision.

moral
think, reason
behave
feel

2. The more primitive stage in the development of moral reasoning according to Piaget is the stage of _____ _____. Heteronomous morality is characterized by reasoning that the _____ of a behavior determine its morality. The child at this level believes that rules are set by an _____ and are unchangeable. The child who shows heteronomous morality believes in _____ _____ if a rule is broken.

heteronomous morality

consequences
authority

immanent justice

3. The child functioning in the stage of _____ _____ is more sophisticated in reasoning about moral problems. The moral autonomist considers the _____ of the actor. He understands rules are socially agreed upon _____ that are subject to change. He also realizes that a transgression must be _____ to result in punishment.

autonomous morality

intentions
conventions
witnessed

4. Piaget believed that the increased social understanding the child develops comes about through _____ _____.

peer relationships

5. The study of moral reasoning identifies what children _____ is right and wrong. The study of moral _____ investigates what children actually do in a situation.

believe
behavior

6. The reinforcement of behavior consistent with laws and social customs is likely to result in that behavior being _____. Moral behavior also depends on the _____.

repeated
situation

7. From the social learning perspective, an important component of the development of moral development is the child's ability to _____ _____. The ability to resist temptation has been tied to _____ _____ _____.

resist temptation
delay of gratification

8. _____ _____ is involved both in the ability to resist temptation and the ability to delay gratification. Delay of gratification is facilitated by the _____ _____ of desired objects.

Self-control

cognitive transformation

9. Moral _____ comprise a third developmental concern. According to psychoanalytic thought, guilt is _____ turned inward. According to psychoanalytic thought, guilt comes from the part of the personality structure called the _____.

feelings
hostility

superego

10. The understanding of another's feelings is called _____. This is the _____ side of moral development.

empathy
positive

Key Terms Matching Exercise

1.0 Images of Children: The World of Pretend Play (Terms 1-2)
2.0 Families (Terms 3-8)
3.0 The Changing Family in a Changing Society (Terms 9-12)
4.0 Peer Relations (Term 13)
5.0 Play (Terms 14-27)
6.0 Television (Term 28)
7.0 The Self (Terms 29-31)
8.0 Gender (Terms 32-45)
9.0 Moral Development (Terms 46-53)

---

1. pretend play

a. Parenting style in which parents encourage independence but still place limits, demands, and controls on the child; there is extensive verbal give-and-take, and the parents demonstrate much warmth toward the child

2. gender specific behavior

b. Parenting style in which parents are highly involved in their children's lives but do not control or place limits on their behavior

3. authoritarian parenting

c. A form of play in which children transform the physical environment into a symbol

4. authoritative parenting

d. Behavior that is seemingly limited to and appropriate for only individuals of one specific gender

5. permissive-indulgent parenting

e. Parenting style in which parents are restrictive, punitive, controlling, and engage in little verbal give-and-take with the child

6. permissive-indifferent parenting

f. Parenting style in which parents are uninvolved in their children's lives and place no limits on their behavior

7.	competent parenting	a.	A diverse condition that ranges from mild to severe mistreatment of children; only partially caused by the personality characteristics of the parents
8.	sibling relationships	b.	The legal dissolution of a marriage
9.	working mothers	c.	Refers to parenting practices that are likely to help children's progress and competence
10.	divorce	d.	Feelings for and interactions with brothers of sisters
11.	child abuse	e.	Refers to women who are parents and also are employed outside the home
12.	child maltreatment	f.	A term sometimes favored over child abuse that acknowledges forms such as physical and sexual abuse, fostering delinquency, lack of supervision, medical, educational, and nutritional neglect, and drug or alcohol abuse

13.	peers	a.	Type of play in which the child plays alone and independently of those around her or him
14.	play	b.	Pleasurable activity engaged in for its own sake
15.	play therapy	c.	Children about the same age; can also be children who interact at about the same behavioral level
16.	unoccupied play	d.	Type of play in which the child watches other children playing
17.	solitary play	e.	Use of play to allow a child to work off frustrations and to allow the therapist to analyze the child's conflicts and methods of coping with them
18.	onlooker play	f.	Type of play in which the child does not engage in ordinary play and may be looking around the room or performing random movements with no goal

19.	parallel play	a.	Type of play in which children transform the physical environment into a symbol and try out many different roles
20.	associative play	b.	Infants engage in this play behavior to derive pleasure from exercising their sensorimotor schemas
21.	cooperative play	c.	Type of play in which children play together with a sense of group identity and organized activity

22.	sensorimotor play	d.	Type of play in which the child plays alone, with toys like those other children are using or in a manner that mimics the behavior of other playing children, but does not actually play with other children
23.	practice play	e.	Type of play in which children play together but with little or no organization
24.	pretense/symbolic play	f.	The child repeats behavior when new skills are being learned, or when physical or mental mastery and coordination of skills is required for games or sports; an activity engaged in throughout one's life

---

25.	social play	a.	Third of Erikson's stages, during which the child may discover ways to overcome feelings of powerlessness by engaging in various activities or may feel guilt at being dominated by the environment
26.	constructive play	b.	These are activities engaged in for pleasure; they often include rules and competition with other individuals
27.	games	c.	Socially desirable behaviors such as sharing, helping, and cooperating
28.	prosocial behavior	d.	The child plays in a way that involves social interaction with peers
29.	initiative versus guilt	e.	The child combines sensorimotor/practice repetitive activity with symbolic ideas; children engage in self-regulated creation or construction of a product or problem solution
30.	self-understanding	f.	This refers to the substance and content of a child's self-conception, the cognitive representation of self

---

31.	conscience	a.	The sense of being male or female; most children acquire their gender identity by the time they are 3 years old
32.	gender	b.	Social expectations of how an individual should act and think based on whether one is male or female
33.	gender identity	c.	Sex hormone produced by the ovaries
34.	gender role	d.	The ability to recognize right from wrong joined with a sense that one should act accordingly
35.	anatomy is destiny	e.	Erikson's view that psychological differences between males and females derive from physical, and anatomical differences
36.	estrogen	f.	Refers to the social dimensions of being male or female

37.	androgen	a.	Trend in research toward investigating subtle gender discrimination and stereotyping, shifting toward both male- and female-valued educational outcomes, and fostering equitable outcomes for both sexes
38.	hermaphrodite	b.	This theory holds that children's gender development occurs through observation and imitation of gender behavior, and through the rewards and punishments they receive for gender appropriate and inappropriate behavior
39.	identification theory	c.	Children's gender typing occurs after they have developed a concept of gender; once they consistently conceive of themselves as male or female, children organize their world on the basis of gender
40.	social learning theory of gender	d.	Individuals with genitals that are intermediate between male and female
41.	sex equity education research	e.	Freud held that children acquire masculine and feminine attitudes from their parents because the preschool child develops a sexual attraction to the same-sex parent, then renounces this attraction by 6 or 7 years of age because of anxious feelings, and subsequently identifies with the same-sex parent, adopting that parent's characteristics
42.	cognitive developmental theory of gender	f.	Sex hormone produced by the testes

43.	schema	a.	Piaget's term for the first stage of moral development; rightness or goodness of behavior judged by considering the consequences of behavior, not intentions; rules are believed to be unchangeable and handed down by all-powerful authorities; there is a belief that, if a rule is broken, punishment will be meted out immediately
44.	gender schema	b.	Use of sex as an organizing category to build a network of associations
45.	gender schema theory	c.	This cognitive structure is a network of associations that organizes and guides an individual's perceptions
46.	moral development	d.	An issue in moral development concerned with children's knowledge and understanding of moral issues and principles
47.	moral reasoning	e.	The theory argues that children's attention and behavior are guided by an internal motivation to conform to gender-based, sociocultural standards and stereotypes

48.	heteronomous morality

f.	Development that concerns rules and conventions about what people should do in their interaction with other people

---

49.	autonomous morality

50.	immanent justice

51.	moral behavior

52.	moral feelings

53.	empathy

a.	Ability to feel the distress of another

b.	Refers to emotions of guilt and to positive emotions such as empathy

c.	Concerns what conventions and rules individuals should follow in their interactions with other people

d.	Belief that, if a rule is broken, punishment will be meted out immediately, that somehow punishment is mechanically linked to the violation

e.	Piaget's term for the second stage of moral development; right or good behavior is judged by the consequences of the act; this view recognizes that rules are socially agreed upon conventions that can be changed by consensus

Key Terms Matching Exercise
Answer Key

1. c	9. e	17. a	25. d	33. a	41. a	49. e
2. d	10. b	18. d	26. e	34. b	42. c	50. d
3. e	11. a	19. d	27. b	35. e	43. c	51. c
4. a	12. f	20. e	28. c	36. c	44. b	52. b
5. b	13. c	21. c	29. a	37. f	45. e	53. a
6. f	14. b	22. b	30. f	38. d	46. f	
7. c	15. e	23. f	31. d	39. e	47. d	
8. d	16. f	24. a	32. f	40. b	48. a	

Self-Test A

1.	Why do adults express greater concern than children about gender-specific behavior?
   a.	Parents feel that their child's behavior constitutes a public demonstration of their parenting style.
   b.	Parents want to have more influence than peers and siblings on their child's behavior.
   c.	Parents endeavor to raise their children free of sexist bias.
   d.	All of these answers are correct.

2.	Timmy finds it difficult to initiate activity, he has much anxiety about social comparison, and he is ineffective in social interactions. His parents most likely are
   a.	authoritarian.
   b.	authoritative.
   c.	permissive-indulgent.
   d.	permissive-indifferent.

3. Which of the following is true of the difference between parent-child and sibling relationships?
   a. Children are more negative with parents than siblings.
   b. Children interact in more varied ways with siblings.
   c. Children interact more positively with siblings.
   d. Children follow parents' requests more than siblings' requests.

4. Which of the following characterizes interactions with peers, but not interactions with both peers and parents?
   a. rough-and-tumble play
   b. smiling
   c. touching
   d. vocalizing

5. Which of the following is not mentioned as an important aspect of divorce that influences the child's behavior?
   a. family conflict
   b. the child's relationship with both parents
   c. age of the child
   d. birth order of the child

6. Developmentalists favor the term child _____ over the term child _____.
   a. maltreatment; abuse
   b. neglect; abuse
   c. abuse; maltreatment
   d. abuse; neglect

7. What best defines a peer?
   a. an individual who is a brother or sister
   b. an individual who lives in the same neighborhood
   c. an individual about the same age or maturity level
   d. an individual with whom one plays regularly

8. One of the most important factors that influence the socialization of children is
   a. media personalities.
   b. parents.
   c. peers.
   d. personal heroes.

9. Chaim is playing with a cup and is pouring water out of the cup and watching the water spill into the sink. He then refills the cup and repeats this again and again. Which function of play is represented by Chaim's activity?
   a. affiliation with peers
   b. tension release
   c. coping with conflict
   d. exploration

10. Karen is drawing a picture. Next to her, Rashad is also drawing a picture, while across the room Nancy and Rosa are playing with dolls together. Karen and Rashad are engaging in what kind of play?
    a. solitary play
    b. onlooker play
    c. parallel play
    d. associative play

11. Which of the following is not one of the three elements that defines pretend play according to Garvey?
    a. props
    b. language
    c. roles
    d. plots

12. On average, an individual will have watched how many hours of television by the time of high school graduation?
    a. 5,000
    b. 10,000
    c. 20,000
    d. 40,000

13. Does violence on television cause children to be aggressive?
    a. Yes, because children watch much television and many of the programs depict violent acts.
    b. Yes, because studies of the relationship between television viewing and aggression are scientifically sound.
    c. No, because the studies involve correlational rather than experimental evidence.
    d. We do not know the answer because the findings have been contradictory and inconclusive.

14. At what age do children primarily define themselves by external characteristics, such as how they look?
    a. 3 to 6 years
    b. 6 to 9 years
    c. 8 to 12 years
    d. 10 to 17 years
15. The "anatomy is destiny" explanation of sex-role differences is attributed to
    a. Freud.
    b. Piaget.
    c. Erikson.
    d. Kohlberg.
16. The hormone responsible for genital development in females is
    a. androgen.
    b. estrogen.
    c. testosterone.
    d. progesterone.
17. Peers influence each other's sex-role development in all of the following ways except
    a. playing in cross-sexed groups.
    b. playing in same-sexed groups.
    c. rewarding sex-appropriate activities.
    d. criticizing cross-sex activities.

18. Which of the following statements of elementary teachers' effects on sex-typing in children is false?
    a. Most teachers are female and present female models of behavior.
    b. Female teachers tend to reinforce feminine behavior.
    c. Girls are given more disapproval and other forms of negative attention than boys.
    d. Boys get more positive attention than girls.
19. Moral development involves all of the following domains except
    a. reasoning.
    b. behavior.
    c. feeling.
    d. situations.
20. Which of the following best characterizes Piaget's view of heteronomous morality?
    a. The child sees rules as changeable by consensus.
    b. The child judges behavior based on consequences of actions.
    c. The child believes that punishment is a socially mediated event.
    d. The child believes that punishment for a transgression is not inevitable.

Self-Test Answers
Test A

1. c	4. a	7. c	10. c	13. c	16. b	19. d
2. a	5. d	8. c	11. d	14. a	17. a	20. b
3. d	6. a	9. d	12. c	15. c	18. c	

Critical Thinking Exercises

Exercise 1

Study Table 11.A on page 311 of the text, "A Primer for Competent Parenting and Parent Education," which presents various "dos" and "don'ts" for competent parenting. Three dos and two don'ts appear below. Develop two arguments for each item using material either from this chapter or from other chapters in the book. Each of the two arguments should demonstrate that the specific parenting practice named by the item is associated with or causes some specific positive developmental outcomes (e.g., enhanced cognitive development). **Note that this exercise differs from previous ones in that you do not have to identify a best answer; to the contrary, you should develop two arguments for each item!**

A. Encourage your child's pretend activities, especially those in which they act out adult roles.
B. Don't worry that your children won't love you if you say "no" on occasion.
C. Talk to your children often. Make an effort to understand what they are trying to do and concentrate on what they see as important.
D. Don't spoil your children, giving them the notion that the world was made for them.
E. Use words children understand, but regularly add new words and related ideas.

Exercise 2

Child psychologists advocate authoritative parenting because this parenting style is associated with so many valued developmental outcomes. But because this parenting style is so popular and well supported, it is easy to overgeneralize its benefits and to conclude that all desirable developmental outcomes are related to it. Which of the following outcomes associated with early childhood is *least* likely to result from authoritative parenting? **Circle the letter of the best answer and explain why it is the best answer and why each other answer is not as good.**

A. Competence at cooperative play
B. Relatively positive adjustment to a divorce
C. Development of a pervasive sense of guilt, especially after misbehavior
D. Development of higher levels of moral reasoning
E. Development of perspective taking

Exercise 3

The study of gender role development is fraught with assumptions. For example, one popular belief has been that males are biologically superior to females. Which of the following statements constitutes an assumption in Santrock's treatment of gender, rather than an inference or an observation? **Circle the letter of the best answer and explain why it is the best answer and why each other answer is not as good.**

A. Among human males, castration is associated with highly variable sexual behavior.
B. The development of gender roles results from an interaction of biological and environmental factors.
C. The language children hear most of the time is sexist.
D. Parents' differential treatment of boys and girls causes boys and girls to acquire different gender roles.
E. When not required to do otherwise, preschool boys and girls play with children of their own sex.

Research Project 1 Parten's Play Styles

This project is an observational study of children's play. Pick a partner from the class and go to a neighborhood playground. Observe two children, one about 3 years old, the other about 5 years old for 10 minutes each. Determine for each child the amount of time spent in each of Parten's categories of play. Compare the differences as a function of age. Use the following data sheet for recording your observations. After making your observations, answer the questions that follow.

One student should act as observer, the other as recorder. Enter the amount of time each child spent in each type of play for the 10-minute observation period. Then calculate the percentage of time spent in each category for the time period.

Category	Child 1 Sex ___ Age ___	Child 2 Sex ___ Age ___
Unoccupied play		
Solitary play		
Onlooker play		
Parallel play		
Associative play		
Cooperative play		

Questions:

1. For the 3-year-old child, in what category was the largest amount of time spent? What category of play was the least frequent?
2. For the 5-year-old child, in what category was the largest amount of time spent? What category of play was the least frequent?
3. What were the differences between the children in the kinds of play in which they engaged? To what do you attribute this difference? (Use information about cognitive, physical, and social development to answer this question.) Are there variables besides age that could account for the differences you observed?
4. How do your findings compare with those of Parten and Barnes?

Research Project 2 Moral Messages in Children's Literature

This project is a preliminary examination of the values that are being emphasized in children's literature. Have students go to a public library and ask the librarian for assistance in locating children's literature that has been excellently reviewed (e.g., has received awards or good critical reviews) and also deals with situations requiring a moral decision. Choose five books to evaluate for morality messages and values. Students should write up a summary of their impressions including whether books emphasize, minimize, or even ignore the following issues: achievement, nurturance, cooperation, competition, endurance, taking chances, doing one's best, kindness, honesty, caring.

Does the book emphasize doing right in order to: have a good life, be liked or appreciated, avoid punishment, do the right thing, follow the law?

	Book 1	Book 2	Book 3	Book 4	Book 5
Values that are emphasized					
Reasoning for acting moral					
Consequences for acting bad					
Other					

Questions:

1. What values were most evident in the five books you read? What values were largely missing?
2. What reasons are given in the books for acting moral? Which of Kohlberg's stages are emphasized (is it influenced by children's typical reasoning stages)? Is a caring orientation or a justice orientation provided more often?
3. What consequences are given to those who choose to act improperly?

Research Project 3 Altruism—Empathy Observations

In this exercise you will observe two children playing on a playground for 20 minutes each and note any evidence of altruism or empathy. One child should be about 2 years of age, the other about 5. Make observations and record any behavior relevant to altruism or empathy you see (you may see both operations in the same situation). Record observations in the spaces provided and answer the questions that follow.

Child 1   Sex ___ Age ___

_____

_____

Child 2   Sex ___ Age ___

_____

_____

Questions:

1. How many instances of empathy did you observe in the 2-year-old? In the 5-year-old?
2. How many instances of altruism did you observe in the 2-year-old? In the 5-year-old?
3. What seems to be the developmental progression in empathy and altruism from 2 to 5 years of age? How would you account for this? Could your data be explained on the basis of individual differences rather than on the basis of developmental changes? Why or why not?

Essay and Critical Thinking Questions

Comprehension and Application Essay Questions

We recommend that you follow either our guidelines for answering essay and critical thinking questions, or those guidelines provided by your instructor in preparing your response. Your answers to these kinds of questions demonstrate an ability to comprehend and think critically about concepts and topics discussed in this chapter.

1. Explain the four types of parenting, and describe the personalities of children who experience each type of parenting.
2. Compare and contrast child-child and parent-child interactions.
3. Discuss the pros and cons of a mother working outside of the home on her child's social development.
4. What are peer relations? Explain whether they are necessary for adequate social development.
5. Explain how play fulfills both developmental and educational goals and functions.
6. Evaluate these claims: (a) Violence on television causes aggression in children; and (b) Prosocial behavior on television causes children to engage in prosocial behavior.
7. Explain what Erikson meant in saying that early childhood is dominated by feelings of initiative versus guilt.
8. Compare and contrast any two theories of gender development.
9. Explain the relationship between oral reasoning and moral behavior.
10. Compare and contrast any two theories of moral development.

Critical Thinking Questions

Your answers to the following kinds of questions reflect an ability to apply your critical thinking skills to a novel problem or situation that is *not* specifically discussed in this chapter.

1. This chapter discusses the relationship between parenting style and personality development. Apply your knowledge about the scientific base of child development by designing a study to determine the relationship between parenting styles and children's present or future personalities: (a) What specific problem or questions do you want to study? (b) What predictions would you make and test in your study? (c) What measures would you use (i.e., observation, interviews, and questionnaires, case studies, standardized tests, physiological research, or a multimeasure, multisource, and multicontext approach) and how would you define each measure clearly and unambiguously? (d) What strategy would you follow—experimental or correlational, and what would be the time span of your inquiry—cross-sectional or longitudinal? (e) What ethical considerations must be addressed before you conduct your study?
2. According to Chapter 1, five issues define the nature of development: (a) biological, cognitive, and social processes, (b) periods or stages, (c) the issue of maturation (nature) versus experience

(nurture), (d) the issue of continuity versus discontinuity, and (e) the issue of stability versus change. Indicate your ability to think critically by (a) perusing this chapter for two examples of each of the five defining issues and (b) explaining how and why each of your examples illustrates one of the five defining issues.

3. Chapter 2 presents six different theoretical approaches (i.e., Freudian, cognitive, behavioral and social learning, phenomenological and humanistic, ethological, and ecological), but notes that no single approach explains the complexity of development. Indicate your ability to think critically by analyzing divorce (i.e., its causes and effects) in terms of each of the six theoretical approaches.

4. One aspect of thinking critically is to read, listen, and observe carefully, and then ask questions about what is missing from a text, discussion, or situation. For example, Santrock discusses the difficulties and consequences for women who combine motherhood and careers; however, he does not discuss the issues faced by men who combine career and family or become stay-at-home fathers. Indicate your ability to think critically by (a) speculating about why Santrock neglected to discuss these kinds of problems and (b) evaluating whether this seeming oversight represents a case of sexism in developmental research that should be avoided, according to the author's claim in Chapter 1.

5. Santrock places several quotations in the margins of this chapter. One by George Bernard Shaw says, "Parenting is a very important profession, but no test of fitness for it is ever imposed in the interest of children." Another by Ernest Hemingway says, "What is moral is what you feel good after and what is immoral is what you feel bad after." Indicate your ability to think critically by (a) learning about the author and indicating why this individual is eminently quotable (i.e., what was the individual's contribution to human knowledge and understanding), (b) interpreting and restating the quote in your own terms, and (c) explaining what concept, issue, perspective, or term in this chapter Santrock intended this quote to illuminate. In other words, about what aspect or issue in development does this quote make you pause and think reflectively?

Self-Test B

1. Dora is very easygoing, self-reliant, and takes on social responsibility easily. Most likely her parents were
   a. authoritarian.
   b. authoritative.
   c. permissive-indulgent.
   d. permissive-indifferent.
2. How would permissive-indulgent parents be classified along the dimensions of controlling and accepting?
   a. accepting, controlling
   b. rejecting, controlling
   c. rejecting, uncontrolling
   d. accepting, uncontrolling
3. Siblings are stronger socializing influences on a child than parents are in all of the following areas except
   a. dealing with peers.
   b. coping with difficult teachers.
   c. discussing taboo subjects.
   d. mediating arguments with siblings.

4. What is one advantage for children who have a mother who works outside of the home?
   a. The quality of time together is better, even if the actual amount of time is less.
   b. Children are exposed to less rigid sex-role stereotypes.
   c. Children have more free time away from adult supervision.
   d. Children have more time with their fathers than in other families.
5. About what percentage of children are expected to spend some part of their childhood in a single-parent family?
   a. 10 to 15%
   b. 25 to 30%
   c. 40 to 45%
   d. 50 to 55%

6. Are peers necessary for adequate social development?
   a. Yes, because children deprived of parents can produce appropriate social and psychological behavior.
   b. No, because studies of monkeys have nothing to do with humans.
   c. No, because a child must interact with an opposite sex parent in order to develop a positive self-concept.
   d. The evidence is inconclusive, and developmentalists do not know the answer to this question.
7. Play contributes to cognitive development, but cognitive maturity also limits children's play according to the view expressed by
   a. Freud.
   b. Vygotsky.
   c. Piaget.
   d. Berlyne.
8. Betty and Jane are playing together, digging a hole in the backyard in order to reach China. Which function is play serving for them?
   a. affiliation with peers
   b. tension release
   c. advances in cognitive development
   d. exploration
9. Hans is building a tower of blocks. He is oblivious to anything going on around him. Hans is engaged in what kind of play?
   a. unoccupied play
   b. solitary play
   c. onlooker play
   d. parallel play
10. What kind of play involves transforming the physical environment into a symbol?
   a. play therapy
   b. cooperative play
   c. pretend play
   d. parallel play

11. Parental guidelines for influencing children's television viewing include all of the following except
   a. encouraging planned rather than random viewing.
   b. delaying formal instruction in television viewing until the age of 7.
   c. balancing reading and television viewing.
   d. encouraging and answering children's questions about the content of television programs.
12. A psychologist who emphasizes the role of the self and self-concept as central in understanding the child's development is most likely a
   a. humanist theorist.
   b. psychoanalytic theorist.
   c. ecological theorist.
   d. behavior theorist.
13. An individual who has genitals that are intermediate between male and female is most likely a
   a. female who was exposed to too little androgen.
   b. male who was exposed to too much androgen.
   c. female who was exposed to too much androgen.
   d. female who was exposed to too much estrogen.
14. At what age do children first show sex-typed play?
   a. 1 to 3 years
   b. 3 to 7 years
   c. 7 to 12 years
   d. after 12 years
15. Female teachers tend to reinforce what kinds of behaviors?
   a. feminine behavior in both boys and girls
   b. feminine behavior in girls only
   c. masculine behavior in boys
   d. androgynous behavior in both sexes

16. Which of the following statements accurately represents the role parents play in the development of their child?
    a. Mothers are responsible for nurturance and are more demanding than fathers.
    b. Fathers are more playful with children and are less demanding than mothers.
    c. Mothers are responsible for playing with the child and for physical child care.
    d. Fathers play with the child and see that the child conforms to cultural norms.

17. What accounts for sex-role development according to Kohlberg's cognitive development theory of gender?
    a. identification with the same-sex parent
    b. imitation of same-sex models
    c. reinforcement of sex-appropriate behavior
    d. categorizing oneself as male or female

18. Which of the following best characterizes Piaget's view of autonomous morality?
    a. The child judges behavior based on consequences of actions.
    b. The child believes in immanent justice.
    c. The child sees rules as changeable by consensus.
    d. The child believes that rules are handed down by authorities.

19. According to work by Mischel, what most effectively enables children to cope with resistance to temptation?
    a. a lecture by an adult
    b. the use of reinforcers
    c. modeling appropriate behavior
    d. cognitive transformations of the desired object

20. Altruistic behavior is most closely tied to which of the following emotions?
    a. guilt
    b. empathy
    c. love
    d. shame

Self-Test Answers
Test B

1. b	4. b	7. c	10. c	13. c	16. d	19. d
2. d	5. c	8. a	11. b	14. a	17. d	20. b
3. d	6. a	9. b	12. a	15. a	18. c	

Objectives

1.0 *Images of Children: Training Children for the Olympics in China*
1.1 Discuss the pros and cons of training young children for sports.

2.0 *Body Changes in Middle and Late Childhood*
2.1 Compare and contrast physical development during middle and late childhood, the preschool years, and pubescence.
2.2 Identify average heights and weights for females and males between the ages of 6 and 10 years old, and describe physical growth during middle and late childhood.
2.3 Describe advances in gross and fine motor skills during middle and late childhood.
2.4 Explain why elementary school children should be involved in active rather than passive activities.

3.0 *Health*
3.1 Describe the nature and severity of health problems typical of middle and late childhood.
3.2 Explain why hearing and vision problems are overlooked in middle and late childhood.
3.3 Identify what children and adolescents understand about health and evaluate how well they apply what they know.
3.4 Describe children's energy needs, and define obesity and set point.
3.5 Explain how heredity, exercise, and diet influence the incidence of obesity in children.
3.6 Explain the relationship between obesity and self-esteem, and indicate how parents can help an obese child.
3.7 Identify factors that may explain why the fitness of children from 6 to 12 years of age did not improve between 1975 and 1985.
3.8 Describe current school fitness programs, and contrast them with potential fitness programs suggested by research.
3.9 Discuss how adults can promote good fitness habits in children.
3.10 List pros and cons of children's participation in high-pressure sports.
3.11 Explain how sports programs could apply information about the development of fine and gross motor skills during middle and late childhood to create developmentally appropriate activities.
3.12 Define and distinguish between appropriate and inappropriate ways for parents to involve themselves in their children's participation in sports.

4.0 *Stress and Coping*
4.1 Define and distinguish among stress, eustress, and stressor, and explain how psychologists use these concepts differently than physicists.
4.2 Define and distinguish the three stages of the general adaptation syndrome (GAS), and describe observations that indicate their development in response to a stressor.
4.3 Explain why some researchers have criticized Selye's concept of stress.
4.4 Define and distinguish conflict and frustration, and explain how each may be a stressor in children's lives.

4.5   Define and distinguish among approach/approach conflicts, approach/avoidance conflicts, and avoidance/avoidance conflicts.

4.6   Define and distinguish between life events and daily hassles, and indicate examples of such stressors in children's lives.

4.7   Define and distinguish acculturative and socioeconomic stress, and list examples of acculturative stress in American families.

4.8   Discuss daily hassles and life events that constitute stressors for minorities, and discuss cultural coping mechanisms for acculturative stress.

4.9   List the stressors that Madeline Cartwright removed from the lives of children at James G. Blaine school in Philadelphia.

4.10   Define and distinguish between primary and secondary cognitive appraisal, and explain how the two interact to intensify or alleviate a child's experience of stress.

4.11   Describe the Type A behavioral pattern, indicate its associated ailments, and list possible causes of Type A behavior in children and adolescents.

4.12   Explain whether the data indicate Type A-behavior children grow up to be Type A-behavior adults.

4.13   Outline the Heart Smart program, and evaluate whether and how the Bogalusa Heart Study addresses the risk factors Type A behavior generates in children and adolescents.

4.14   Explain what it means to cope with stress, and define and distinguish between avoidance strategies and facing strategies.

4.15   List three ways adults can help children cope with stressors.

4.16   List six factors that influence stress.

4.17   List factors associated with a child's ability to cope with death.

4.18   Describe the development of the understanding of death, and explain how elementary school-age children cope with the death of another person.

4.19   Explain why the death of a sibling might be harder for a child to cope with than the death of a parent.

5.0   *Handicapped Children*

5.1   Explain why middle and late childhood is an especially difficult time for a handicapped child.

5.2   List examples and incidences of handicapped children in America, and explain why it is difficult to determine the rates of various handicapping conditions among children in the United States.

5.3   Summarize Public Law 94–142, and explain the nature of an individualized education program.

5.4   Define mainstreaming and indicate its positive and negative aspects.

5.5   Explain the pros and cons of labeling children as disabled or handicapped.

5.6   Define and distinguish between learning disabilities and attention-deficit hyperactivity disorder, and describe the observations that indicate their presence in children.

5.7   Indicate evidence favoring an environmental or a hereditary explanation of the attention-deficit hyperactivity disorder (ADHD).

5.8   List and explain treatments for hyperactivity, and identify problems with each method of treatment.

5.9   Describe the incidence of attention-deficit hyperactivity disorder from infancy to adulthood.

Summary

1.0 Images of Children: Training Children for the Olympics in China

The national policy of China is to select youngsters who show athletic promise and enroll them in sports schools. The sports schools are the only route to Olympic stardom in China, and when students

263

no longer show potential they are asked to leave. The question of when children are developmentally ready for competitive sports is raised.

2.0 Body Changes in Middle and Late Childhood

The Skeletal and Muscular System. During middle and late childhood, ages 6 through 11 years, growth is 2 to 3 inches per year and weight gain is 3 to 5 pounds per year. Slow and consistent growth increases both muscle mass and strength, lengthens legs, and slims the trunk.

Motor Skills. Motor behavior becomes smoother and more coordinated during the elementary school years. Although children gain greater control over their bodies and can sit for longer periods of time, their lives should be focused on active rather than passive activities. Improved motor skills result from increased myelinization of the central nervous system. Boys are usually superior at gross motor skills, whereas girls are usually superior at fine motor skills.

3.0 Health

Despite a national trend toward health consciousness, few children practice good health habits.

Children's Health Status. Elementary school children often suffer from respiratory infections, the most common reason for absences from school. Dental problems, visual problems, and hearing problems are also common during this age period.

Children's Understanding of Health. Children in elementary school recognize that health requires almost continual work and that nutrition and fitness are important in its maintenance. They do not define health as an absence of illness. There is, however, a gap between their apparent knowledge and their behavior.

Nutrition and Children's Obesity. During middle and late childhood, children need to consume more food than earlier in their lives. A special concern is with obesity, a body weight 20 percent above the ideal weight given one's age and sex. Genetic inheritance, physiological mechanisms, cognitive factors, and environmental influences play roles in obesity.

Exercise. Many children are in poor physical shape by the time they enter the first grade. They frequently do not get enough exercise, and often schools do not provide enough opportunities for exercise. Parents play an important role in helping youngsters to exercise more.

Sports. In middle and late childhood, many children engage in activities such as baseball, soccer, football, swimming, and gymnastics. Participation in organized sports can have both positive and negative consequences for children. Guidelines for parental involvement in sports exist.

4.0 Stress and Coping

What Is Stress? Stress is ever present in our daily lives and refers to an individual's response to circumstances and events that are, in turn, deemed stressors.

The Body's Response to Stress. The general adaptation syndrome describes three stages in response to stress: the alarm stage, the stage of resistance, and the exhaustion stage. Eustress is the term for the positive features of stress.

Environmental Factors. Environmental stressors include three kinds of conflict (approach/approach, avoidance/avoidance, and approach/avoidance), frustration, life events, and daily hassles.

Sociocultural Factors. Sociocultural stressors include acculturative stress and poverty. The former entails the negative consequences of conflict between two different cultures. For example, ethnic minority group members have long encountered hostility, prejudice, and lack of support during personal crises, all of which contribute to alienation, isolation, and stress. Chronic poverty is also stressful. Madeline Cartwright, an inner-city school principal, built a model school by buffering the effects of stress on students.

Cognitive Factors. Richard Lazarus argues that the interpretation or cognitive appraisal of a situation by an individual determines how stressful the events or circumstances are for that individual. Primary appraisal determines to what extent events are perceived as harmful, threatening, or challenging. Secondary appraisal determines what resources one has to cope effectively with stressors.

Personality Factors—Type A Behavior Pattern. Type A behavior pattern is a cluster of characteristics that may lead to cardiovascular problems, even in children. This concept is controversial because only specific components, such as hostility, may really be associated with coronary risk. Heart Smart is a cardiovascular health intervention program for children and adolescents.

Coping with Stress. Different children cope with stress differently, and different techniques may be used at different stages of development. Some children avoid stress through denial, regression, withdrawal, and impulsive acting out. Some face stress through altruism, suppression, anticipation, and sublimation. Children can be aided in coping with stress by removing at least one stressor, teaching them new coping strategies, and learning how to apply existing coping strategies to new stressors.

Coping with Death. Another person's death is a stressor for many individuals. Young children generally do not understand death; however, children in the middle of their elementary school years seem to understand its finality.

5.0 Handicapped Children

Scope and Education of Handicapped Children. Some 10 to 15 percent of the children in the United States are handicapped in some way. Public Law 94–142 requires that all handicapped children receive free and appropriate education. This is often accomplished through mainstreaming—placing handicapped students in regular classrooms, and providing them with supportive services. Labeling children as handicapped or disabled may have negative consequences for the child.

Learning Disabilities. Children with learning disabilities have normal intelligence but difficulty with one or more academic subjects. Learning disabilities are complex and multifaceted and require precise analysis.

Attention-Deficit Hyperactivity Disorder. Attention-deficit hyperactivity disorder is characterized by distractibility, impulsivity, and extreme activity. Possible causes include heredity, prenatal damage, diet, family dynamics, and physical environment. Amphetamines have been used in treatment with some success, but amphetamines do not work with all hyperactive children.

Key Terms

1.0 Images of Children: Training Children for the Olympics in China

2.0 Body Changes in Middle and Late Childhood
middle and late childhood
active versus passive activities

3.0 Health
obesity
set point
insulin level
self-esteem
sports

4.0 Stress and Coping
stress
stressors
general adaptation syndrome (GAS)
alarm
resistance
exhaustion
eustress
approach/approach conflict
avoidance/avoidance conflict
approach/avoidance conflict
frustration
life events
daily hassles

acculturation
acculturative stress
cognitive appraisal
harm
threat
challenge
secondary appraisal
Type A behavioral pattern
Heart Smart
coping with stress
stress-avoiding strategies
denial
regression withdrawal
impulsive acting out
stress-facing strategies
altruism
suppression
anticipation
sublimation
coping with death

5.0 Handicapped Children
handicapped children
Public Law 94–142
mainstreaming
learning disabilities
attention-deficit hyperactivity disorder

Guided Review

1.0 Images of Children: Training Children for the Olympics in China

1. The national policy of _____ entails selecting youngsters who show evidence of _____ skill and placing them in special _____ _____. Developmentalists question whether young children are _____ _____ for competitive sports.

China
athletic
sports schools
developmentally ready

2.0 Body Changes in Middle and Late Childhood

1. The average rate of growth during the elementary school years is _____ inches and _____ to _____ pounds per year. At 11 years of age the average girl is _____ inches tall and the average boy is slightly _____. By age 11 boys are _____ than girls, although girls are _____ than boys.

2½, 5, 7
58
shorter
stronger, taller

2. Motor coordination _____ with age. There appear to be sex differences in _____ motor skills with boys outperforming girls. In _____ motor skills girls generally outperform boys. Improvements in fine motor skills have been linked to increased _____ of the central nervous system.

improves
gross
fine

myelinization

3.0 Health

1. Although the United States is health conscious, _____ children display _____ health practices.

few
good

2. The most common ailment leading to school absenteeism is _____ infections and _____ infections.

respiratory, gastrointestinal

3. _____ problems are also common. Most children have had _____ cavities filled by age 12.

Dental
four

4. _____ maturity occurs by age 6 or 7. By age 11, _____% of children have visual problems.

Visual
17

5. About _____% of children fail hearing tests.

5

6. Elementary school children seem to understand that they must _____ at health. Adolescents are very poor at _____ health information to _____. Many adolescents have _____ and overly _____ beliefs about their future health risks.

work, applying
themselves, unrealistic
optimistic

7. Children's average body weight _____ during middle and late childhood. Children need _____ food than _____.

doubles
more, adults

8. For a given age and sex, children who weigh _____% more than their ideal weight are considered to be _____. Obesity is influenced by _____, _____, cognitive, and _____ variables.

20, obese, genetic
environmental,
physiological

9. One's _____ _____, or easily maintained body weight, can be lowered only by _____.

set point
exercise

10. Obese children typically have _____ negative _____ _____ than average-weight children.

more
self-concepts

11. Elementary school children are often in _____ physical condition. _____ is one reason children do not exercise enough.

poor
Television

12. Schools do not provide daily _____ _____ classes. Parents are often _____ role models when it comes to exercise.

physical education
poor

13. Most physical education classes do not include _____ activity. In one study, boys who exercised regularly had less _____ _____ and girls had more _____ _____ in their classes.

vigorous
body fat
creative involvement

14. Sports are an important part of American _____, and have both _____ and _____ consequences for children.

culture
positive, negative

15. One special concern is _____ _____ sports in which children are urged to win _____ _____ _____.

high-pressure
at all costs

16. Although sports psychologists urge parents to support children's _____ in sports, parents must guard against _____. The Women's Sports Foundation suggests both _____ and _____ for parents and _____ of children.

participation
overinvolvement
do's, don'ts
coaches

4.0   Stress and Coping

1. An individual's response to threatening environmental events is termed _____, whereas the events themselves are called _____.

stress
stressors

2. Hans _____ general adaptation syndrome is composed of three stages. First is the _____ stage, when the body detects stress and tries to get rid of it. Second is _____ followed by the _____ stage.

Selye's
alarm
resistance
exhaustion

3. Most stress research has focused on _____ experience. Selye coined the term _____ to talk about the _____ features of stress, such as being elected class president.

negative
eustress, positive

4. Examples of environmental factors that produce stress are _____ and _____.

conflict, frustration

5. A choice between two attractive outcomes defines an _____ _____ conflict, whereas a choice between two undesirable outcomes defines an _____ _____ conflict.

approach/approach

avoidance/avoidance

6. The inability to achieve a goal constitutes _____ for many children.

frustration

7. _____ _____ and _____ _____ both contribute to stressful experience.

Daily hassles, life events

8. The _____ consequence of acculturation is called _____ stress, a problem for many ethnic minority group members.

negative, acculturative

9. Madeline Cartwright improved the lives of children in her school by removing various _____.

stressors.

10. A cognitive approach distinguished between _____ appraisal, in which children determine whether events involve _____, _____, or _____, and _____ appraisal, in which children determine how to cope with the event in question.

primary
harm
threat, challenge,
secondary

11. The _____ _____ behavioral pattern is correlated with cardiovascular disease in adults. A person with this pattern is always _____ with the slow pace of events, is _____, has an _____ pace, and shows _____.

Type A

impatient, competitive
accelerated, hostility

12. In a recent study, Type A children were found to have more cardiovascular _____ than non-Type A children. They were more likely to have _____ _____ _____ fathers and low _____ _____. Their parents were more likely to be _____ of failure.

symptoms
high Type A
self-esteem
critical

13. Children can use a number of defense mechanisms to avoid stress. These include _____, acting as if the stress did not exist; _____, behaving in ways appropriate for a younger child; _____, removing themselves from the stress; or _____ _____ _____, engaging in destructive behavior.

denial
regression
withdrawal, impulsive
acting out

14. More positive coping mechanisms also can be employed to face stress. These include _____, forgetting one's stress by helping others; _____, setting one's stress aside temporarily; _____, thinking about and planning for the next stressful episode; and _____, releasing one's tension by becoming involved in activities.

altruism
suppression
anticipation
sublimation

15. Children can be assisted in dealing with multiple stressors by _____ one stressor and by teaching alternative _____ strategies.

removing
coping

16. One of the most stressful events in anyone's life is another's _____.

death

17. Children understand death _____ at different ages.

differently

18. Children aged _____ to _____ think dead people will come back at some point. _____ _____ prevents young children from understanding the meaning of death. Young children may _____ themselves for someone's death.

3, 5
Preoperational reasoning

blame

19. Children recognize the _____ nature of death around the middle of _____ school. They also recognize the inevitability of _____ _____ death.

irreversible
elementary
their own

5.0 Handicapped Children

1. Children with handicaps become _____ sensitive to their differences during the elementary school years. Public Law _____ assures a free and appropriate education to all _____ children. It is often accomplished by _____.

   more
   94-142
   handicapped
   mainstreaming

2. Mainstreaming places handicapped students in _____ classrooms. _____ retarded children are usually institutionalized; retarded students who are mainstreamed are generally _____ _____.

   regular
   Severely
   mildly retarded

3. Children of normal intelligence, who have severe difficulty with some but not all academic areas, and who have no handicapping condition that explains this discrepancy are labeled _____ _____. These children often have problems in _____ and _____ and in the academic areas of _____, _____, and _____. The number of children identified as learning disabled in the United States is about _____ million.

   learning disabled
   listening
   thinking, reading,
   spelling, math
   two

4. One kind of learning disability that specifically affects concentration and activity is _____ _____ _____ _____, or ADHD. This disorder is much more common in _____ than in _____.

   attention deficit
   hyperactivity disorder
   males, females

5. ADHD may be related to genes on the _____ chromosome, or to prenatal substances such as _____. In addition, diet can have an impact, especially the excessive consumption of _____ and _____. _____ deficiency may also contribute to attentional problems.

   Y
   alcohol
   sugar
   caffeine, Vitamin

6. ADHD is also affected by the social environment. Families who _____ frequently and who _____ behavior rather than focus on academic work may have children with ADHD. _____ settings and situations with many _____ may also contribute to problems with in these children.

   move, control
   Unstructured
   demands

7. ADHD is most frequently treated with _____ therapy and with _____ such as _____, which is widely prescribed.

   drug
   amphetamines, Ritalin

Key Terms Matching Exercise

1.0 Images of Children: Training Children for the Olympics in China (no terms)
2.0 Body Changes in Middle and Late Childhood (Terms 1-2)
3.0 Health (Terms 3-7)
4.0 Stress and Coping (Terms 8-40)
5.0 Handicapped Children (Terms 41-45)

1. middle and late childhood

    a. The evaluative and affective dimension of self-concept; also termed self-image or self-worth

2. active versus passive activities

    b. Extremely fat or corpulent; typically defined as 20% or more above one's ideal body weight

3. obesity

4. set point

    c. Corresponds to the elementary school years

    d. Actions such as running and jumping as opposed to sitting and listening

5. insulin level

    e. The amount of a hormone that regulates carbohydrate metabolism by controlling blood glucose levels

6. self-esteem

    f. The weight that is maintained when no effort is made either to gain or lose weight

---

7. sports

    a. The first phase of GAS in which an individual's body mobilizes to meet a perceived threat

8. stress

    b. A situation in which an individual feels overwhelmed and unable to cope effectively; a subjective response

9. stressors

    c. Selye's model about how the body reacts to stressors in which there are three stages of response

10. general adaptation syndrome (GAS)

    d. Physical factors in the environment that threaten an individual and activate the GAS

11. alarm

    e. The second phase of GAS in which an individual's body resists or copes with an unavoidable threat

12. resistance

    f. These are activities engaged in for pleasure; they often include rules and competition with other individuals

---

13. exhaustion

    a. Refers to situations in which one cannot achieve a desired goal

14. eustress

15. approach/approach conflict

    b. Positive or beneficial features of stress

    c. The third phase of GAS in which an individual's body becomes depleted and vulnerable to fatigue and eventually illness

16. avoidance/avoidance conflict

    d. A situation in which selecting an object or encountering a circumstance entails both attractive and unfavorable components

17. approach/avoidance conflict

    e. A situation in which one must choose either one or the other of two desirable objects or circumstances

18. frustration

    f. A situation in which one must choose either one or the other of two undesirable objects or circumstances

19.	life events	a.	Lazarus's term for an individual's interpretation of environmental events or situations as possible stressors
20.	daily hassles	b.	The changes in an individual's life produced by ongoing contact between different cultures
21.	acculturation	c.	Features of life that are stressful to everyone such as the death of a family member, getting married, and Christmas; typically measured in terms of "life-change units"
22.	acculturative stress	d.	An appraisal about a loss that has occurred already
23.	cognitive appraisal	e.	Threatening and uncomfortable outcomes produced by the negative consequences of acculturation
24.	harm	f.	Aspects of the daily grind that disrupt lives such as the irritations and frustrations of everyday routines, thoughtlessness of others; a good predictor of psychological and physical symptoms

25.	threat	a.	An appraisal about one's potential for overcoming an adverse situation
26.	challenge	b.	The use of behavioral and cognitive skills to deal with environmental features and conditions that one deems stressful
27.	secondary appraisal	c.	A method for handling stress that involves such things as denial, regression, withdrawal, and impulsive acting out
28.	Type A behavioral pattern	d.	A program designed to educate individuals about their health; specifically focuses on cardiovascular disease
29.	Heart Smart	e.	An appraisal about a loss that may occur in the future
30.	coping with stress	f.	An examination of one's personal resources available to cope with a stressful event or situation
31.	stress avoiding strategies	g.	Cluster of characteristics such as excessive competitiveness, impatience, and doing several things at once

32.	denial	a.	Mode of coping with stress by helping others
33.	regression	b.	A method for handling stress that involves such things as altruism, humor, suppression, anticipation, and sublimation

34. impulsive acting out

    c. Mode of coping with stress by foreseeing and planning for the next stressful experience

35. stress facing strategies

    d. Mode of coping with stress by acting as if the stress does not exist

36. altruism

    e. Mode of coping with stress by acting without thinking about the consequences, sometimes flamboyantly

37. suppression

    f. Mode of coping with stress by setting aside feelings of stress temporarily

38. anticipation

    g. Mode of coping with stress by engaging in behaviors appropriate for a much younger individual

---

39. sublimation

    a. Children who are physically and mentally limited and restricted from normal achievement

40. coping with death

    b. Category that includes children diagnosed as dyslexic, children with minimal brain dysfunction, and children who are hyperactive

41. handicapped children

    c. Federal legislation that requires communities to provide free, appropriate education for all handicapped children

42. Public law 94–142

    d. Mode of coping with stress by becoming absorbed in another activity

43. mainstreaming

    e. A dynamic and changing behavioral and cognitive attempt to deal with the stress produced by death of another

44. learning disabilities

    f. Type of learning disability characterized by high levels of activity, impulsivity, distractibility, and excitability

45. attention-deficit hyperactivity disorder

    g. Process by which children who need special education are placed in regular classrooms rather than in special classrooms

Key Terms Matching Exercise
Answer Key

1. c	8. b	15. e	22. e	29. d	36. a	43. g
2. d	9. d	16. f	23. a	30. b	37. f	44. b
3. b	10. c	17. d	24. d	31. c	38. c	45. f
4. f	11. a	18. a	25. e	32. d	39. d	
5. e	12. e	19. c	26. a	33. g	40. e	
6. a	13. c	20. f	27. f	34. e	41. a	
7. f	14. b	21. b	28. g	35. b	42. c	

1. Do developmentalists recommend training young children for competitive sports such as the Olympics?
   a. Yes, because children need vigorous exercise at all ages.
   b. No, because handicapped children cannot participate in such competition.
   c. Yes, because early experience with the pressure of competition will protect them from stress later in life.
   d. No, because competition is too stressful.

2. During the elementary school years, children grow about ___ to ___ inches and gain about ___ to ___ pounds per year.
   a. 5 to 7; 2 to 3
   b. 2 to 3; 5 to 7
   c. 1 to 2; 3 to 5
   d. 3 to 5; 3 to 4

3. In the performance of gross motor skills during the elementary school years
   a. boys outperform girls.
   b. girls outperform boys.
   c. sex differences do not emerge until puberty.
   d. girls outperform boys initially but boys surpass the girls by puberty.

4. The biological underpinning of development of fine motor skills appears to be
   a. practice.
   b. instruction.
   c. myelinization.
   d. size and weight gains.

5. The most common illness of elementary school children is
   a. dental problems.
   b. respiratory infections.
   c. visual problems.
   d. infectious diseases such as measles and mumps.

6. At what age do children typically reach visual maturity?
   a. 3 to 5 years
   b. 6 to 7 years
   c. 9 to 10 years
   d. at puberty

7. At what age do people have the most difficulty applying health knowledge to their own lives?
   a. early childhood
   b. middle and late childhood
   c. adolescence
   d. early adulthood

8. In a School Fitness Survey in 1985, what percent of boys between age 6 and 12 could not run a 10-minute mile?
   a. 5%
   b. 10%
   c. 20%
   d. 30%

9. The researcher who coined the term eustress was
   a. Chandler.
   b. Selye.
   c. Brenner.
   d. Rutter.

10. The best example of eustress is
    a. hearing one's parents fight.
    b. taking a test.
    c. visiting an amusement park.
    d. going to a dentist.

11. The item of concern about children's health to which the Type A behavior pattern is relevant is
    a. stress.
    b. infection.
    c. physical fitness.
    d. fat intake and heart disease.

12. Which of the following is an example of denial?
    a. Jane continues to play the piano while being told she failed this year in school.
    b. Ten-year-old Miguel crawls in his mother's lap when he is told his father has been in a car accident.
    c. Laila sits in her room and does nothing when she hears her parents are divorcing.
    d. Mark starts throwing things at the wall when he hears his grandmother has died.

13. Which of the following is an example of withdrawal?
    a. Jane continues to play the piano while being told she failed this year in school.
    b. Ten-year-old Miguel crawls in his mother's lap when he is told his father has been in a car accident.
    c. Laila sits in her room and does nothing when she hears her parents are divorcing.
    d. Mark starts throwing things at the wall when he hears his grandmother has died.
14. A child who overcomes fears by becoming absorbed in reading is using which coping mechanism?
    a. denial
    b. regression
    c. anticipation
    d. sublimation
15. The view of death that is characterized by thoughts that the dead person is still living, but under changed circumstances, is characteristic of children of what age?
    a. 1 to 3 years
    b. 3 to 7 years
    c. 7 to 9 years
    d. 12 to 15 years
16. The proportion of handicapped school-aged children in the United States is
    a. 1 to 3%
    b. 3 to 5%
    c. 5 to 7%
    d. 10 to 15%
17. Children most likely to be mainstreamed into regular classes are
    a. profoundly retarded.
    b. severely retarded.
    c. moderately retarded.
    d. mildly retarded.
18. Public Law 94–143 was developed to
    a. protect normal children from their handicapped parents.
    b. subsidize the medical expenses of families with handicapped children.
    c. provide teacher training for those who work with handicapped children.
    d. ensure a free, appropriate education for handicapped children.
19. Low performance in a specific educational area combined with normal intelligence and no behavioral problems is a definition of
    a. learning disability.
    b. mental retardation.
    c. slow learning.
    d. developmental lag.
20. Hyperactive children are frequently treated with
    a. sedatives.
    b. tranquilizers.
    c. amphetamines.
    d. analgesics.

Self-Test Answers
Test A

1. d	4. c	7. c	10. c	13. c	16. a	19. a
2. b	5. b	8. d	11. a	14. d	17. d	20. c
3. a	6. b	9. b	12. a	15. b	18. d	

Critical Thinking Exercises

Exercise 1

This chapter initially sketches life for children who attend sports schools in China to prepare for the Olympics. Although Santrock does not explicitly criticize these sports schools, the tone of his treatment conveys his disapproval of them. Which of the following topics presented in Chapter 12 provides a basis for the most severe criticism of sports schools in China? **Circle the letter of the best answer and explain why it is the best answer and why each other answer is not as good.**

A. The training program in the sports schools does not conform to the developmental timetable for gross and fine motor skills.
B. Children in the sports schools are required to be too active.
C. The daily schedule of the sports schools causes children to develop Type A personalities.
D. The training programs are too stressful for children.
E. There is no place for handicapped children in the training program.

Exercise 2

In many ways, Chapter 12 is less a treatment about development during middle and late childhood and more a treatment about characteristics of that period of life. That is, the presentation of various topics typically does *not* emphasize what develops during this time or how the developmental status of a child influences a child's experience. Some topics, however, do receive a developmental treatment. Review "The Nature of Development" section in Chapter 1, and then indicate which of the following topics receives the strongest developmental treatment in Chapter 12. **Circle the letter of the best answer and explain why it is the best answer and why each other answer is not as good.**

A. Mainstreaming
B. Learning disabilities
C. Children's understanding of health
D. Life's events and daily hassles
E. Coping with death

Exercise 3

In this chapter Santrock discusses the importance of exercise to children's health. Which of the following statements underlying this presentation constitutes an assumption rather than an inference or an observation? **Circle the letter of the best answer and explain why it is the best answer and why each other answer is not as good.**

A. Many children do not get enough exercise because they watch television.
B. Typical school fitness programs do not engage children in enough exercise.
C. Children imitate the exercise patterns exhibited by adults.
D. Adolescent girls are less fit today than they were in 1975.
E. Long distance running is too strenuous for young children.

Research Project 1 Current Exercise Levels

In this exercise, interview three people about their current exercise levels. (If you are between 18 and 20 years old, you may use yourself as one of the subjects.) One subject should be 5 years old, one 10 years old, and one 18 to 20. Use the interview questions on the data sheet, record each person's responses, and then answer the questions that follow.

	Person 1 Sex ___ Age ___	Person 2 Sex ___ Age ___	Person 3 Sex ___ Age ___
1. How often do you exercise a week?			
2. What kinds of activities do you do?			
3. How much time do you spend exercising each week?			

Questions:

1. In what kinds of activities does the 5-year-old engage? How much time a week does the 5-year-old spend exercising? How often does the 5-year-old exercise?
2. In what kinds of activities does the 10-year-old engage? How much time a week does the 10-year-old spend exercising? How often does the 10-year-old exercise?
3. In what kinds of activities does the 18-year-old engage? How much time a week does the 18-year-old spend exercising? How often does the 18-year-old exercise?
4. What differences do you find in activity level between the three different ages? Are there differences in the kinds of exercise engaged in at the different ages? If so, what are these?
5. Could variables other than age determine differences between your subjects reported activity levels? What are these?

Research Project 2 Toy Store Messages

You are to visit three different toy stores or stores that have large toy sections and make observations about the toy selections at each of the stores. The idea of this research project is to do some preliminary naturalistic observations, and, at the end of your observations, develop a hypothesis on which you think further research should be conducted.

Are toys displayed separately by
a. age appropriateness?
b. gender appropriateness?
c. type of toy? (e.g., sports are separated from crafts which are separated from educational toys)

What kinds of values seem to be emphasized by toys (indicate 0 = not at all; 1 = a little; 2 = some; 3 = a lot)
a. aggression; war
b. prosocial; cooperative
c. nurturant; homemaking
d. spatial abilities; mechanical
e. educational; learning
f. competitive; winning-losing
g. creativity; artistic
h. physical activity; sports
i. physical attractiveness
j. morality; values
k. adventure; fantasy
l. problem-solving
m. other:

General observations (e.g., marketing, layout, fads):

Questions:

1. What kinds of toys are available for infants? Preschoolers? School-aged children? Adolescents? How do the changes in toys for different ages reflect cognitive abilities? Psychosocial tasks?
2. Are boys and girls targeted for different toys? What are the differences? Are these gender differences present for all age levels?
3. What values do toys tend to be based on? Do you think that the types of toys children have influence their future values, behaviors, and thoughts? Why or why not?
4. What other observations did you make?
5. From your initial observations, compose a hypothesis about the effects of toys on children. Choose one that you think future research should address.

Essay and Critical Thinking Questions

Comprehension and Application Essay Questions

We recommend that you follow either our guidelines for answering essay and critical thinking questions, or those guidelines provided by your instructor in preparing your response. Your answers to these kinds of questions demonstrate an ability to comprehend and think critically about concepts and topics discussed in this chapter.

1. Describe physical growth and changes in gross and fine motor skills during middle and late childhood.
2. Explain what children understand about health. Also evaluate how well they apply what they know to themselves.
3. Describe obesity, and explain how heredity, exercise, and diet influence the incidence of obesity in children.
4. Imagine that you are a parent and that your children want to compete in sports. Explain how you would evaluate the pros and cons of children's participation in high-pressure sports.
5. Distinguish among stress, eustress, and stressors, and provide at least two examples of each concept from your daily life.
6. Discuss daily hassles and life events that constitute stressors for minorities, and discuss cultural coping mechanisms for acculturative stress.
7. What does it mean to cope with stress? What alternative strategies are available to an individual trying to cope with stress?
8. Provide at least three examples of handicapping conditions among children, and explain why middle and late childhood is an especially difficult time for a handicapped child.
9. What is mainstreaming? Discuss its pros and cons.
10. What is an attention-deficit hyperactivity disorder? Discuss its causes and treatments.

Critical Thinking Questions

Your answers to the following kinds of questions reflect an ability to apply your critical thinking skills to a novel problem or situation that is *not* specifically discussed in this chapter.

1. This chapter begins with a discussion about China's policy of discovering and training potential Olympic athletes at very young ages. Apply your knowledge about the scientific base of child development by designing a study to determine the relationship between involvement in competitive sports at a young age and developmental outcomes: (a) What specific problem or questions do you want to study? (b) What predictions would you make and test in your study? (c) What measures would you use (i.e., observation, interviews, and questionnaires, case studies, standardized tests, physiological research, or a multimeasure, multisource, and multicontext approach) and how would you define each measure clearly and unambiguously? (d) What strategy would you follow—experimental or correlational, and what would be the time span of your inquiry—cross-sectional or longitudinal? (e) What ethical considerations must be addressed before you conduct your study?
2. According to Chapter 1, five issues define the nature of development: (a) biological, cognitive, and social processes, (b) periods or stages, (c) the issue of maturation (nature) versus experience (nurture), (d) the issue of continuity versus discontinuity, and (e) the issue of stability versus change. Indicate your ability to think critically by (a) perusing this chapter for two examples of each of the five defining issues and (b) explaining how and why each of your examples illustrates one of the five defining issues.

3. Chapter 2 presents six different theoretical approaches (i.e., Freudian, cognitive, behavioral and social learning, phenomenological and humanistic, ethological, and ecological), but notes that no single approach explains the complexity of development. Indicate your ability to think critically by analyzing the following case in terms of each of the six theoretical approaches. According to a December 27, 1991 article in *USA Today*, Mike and Bob Bryan are twin brothers and two of the top junior tennis players in the country who compete against others, but not each other. Thus far in their tennis careers the twin brothers have conformed to a parental decree that they take turns defaulting to one another whenever they meet in a tournament—even in the final round.

4. One aspect of thinking critically is to read, listen, and observe carefully, and then ask questions about what is missing from a text, discussion, or situation. Alternatively, critical thinking also involves asking why this material is included here. Indicate your ability to think critically by (a) explaining why Santrock presents material on stress in a chapter about physical development in middle and late childhood and (b) justifying your recommendation about where these topics ought to be discussed.

5. Santrock places several quotations in the margins of this chapter. One by John F. Kennedy says, "We are underexercised as a nation. We look instead of play. We ride instead of walk. Our existence deprives us of the minimum of physical activity essential for healthy living." Another by Aristotle says, "The quality of life is determined by its activities." Indicate your ability to think critically by (a) learning about the author and indicating why this individual is eminently quotable (i.e., what was the individual's contribution to human knowledge and understanding), (b) interpreting and restating the quote in your own terms, and (c) explaining what concept, issue, perspective, or term in this chapter Santrock intended this quote to illuminate. In other words, about what aspect or issue in development does this quote make you pause and think reflectively?

Self-Test B

1. The period of middle and late childhood produces physical changes that
   a. differ qualitatively from those in early childhood.
   b. differ quantitatively from those in early childhood.
   c. occur in fits and spurts.
   d. are discontinuous with those in early childhood.

2. What is the average height of a girl at age 11?
   a. 5 feet
   b. 4 feet 10 inches
   c. 4 feet 8 inches
   d. 4 feet 6 inches

3. The age at which motor coordination is sufficient that most children can learn to play tennis is
   a. 4.
   b. 7.
   c. 11.
   d. 13.

4. About what percentage of children fail auditory screening tests?
   a. 5%
   b. 8%
   c. 10%
   d. 15%

5. At what age do children typically begin to lose their baby teeth?
   a. 3 years
   b. 4 years
   c. 5 years
   d. 6 years

6. Which group of children is more physically fit than their counterparts?
   a. poor students
   b. good students
   c. heavy television viewing children
   d. light television viewing children

7. The negative consequence of acculturation exemplifies
   a. the concept of cognitive appraisal.
   b. a sociocultural factor that influences stress.
   c. the consequences of Type A behavior.
   d. life events and daily hassles.
8. Type A children
   a. go to the doctor more than low Type A children.
   b. have more illnesses, cardiovascular symptoms, and sleep disturbances.
   c. are relatively undamaged by the stress.
   d. are able to report the high level of stress.
9. Which of the following is an example of regression?
   a. Jane continues to play the piano while being told that she failed this year in school.
   b. Ten-year-old Miguel crawls in his mother's lap when he is told that his father has been in a car accident.
   c. Laila sits in her room and does nothing when she hears her parents are getting divorced.
   d. Mark starts throwing things at the wall when he hears that his grandmother has died.
10. Which of the following is an example of impulsive acting out?
    a. Jane continues to play the piano while being told that she failed this year in school.
    b. Ten-year-old Miguel crawls in his mother's lap when he is told that his father has been in a car accident.
    c. Laila sits in her room and does nothing when she hears her parents are getting divorced.
    d. Mark starts throwing things at the wall when he hears that his grandmother has died.
11. Soo Lin's mother is hospitalized for cancer. Soo Lin is taking care of her younger sister after school and cooking dinner for her father. Soo Lin is demonstrating which coping strategy?
    a. regression
    b. withdrawal
    c. altruism
    d. anticipation

12. Children who have the best chance of adapting and functioning competently under stress are those who
    a. have one coping technique.
    b. have a number of coping techniques.
    c. use withdrawal to cope.
    d. use denial to cope.
13. The age at which children recognize that death is the end of life and not reversible is
    a. 1 to 3 years.
    b. 3 to 5 years.
    c. 8 to 10 years.
    d. 12 to 15 years.
14. What percentage of children between the ages of 5 and 18 have speech handicaps?
    a. 1%
    b. 3 to 4%
    c. 6%
    d. .1%
15. Mainstreaming is the result of the provision in Public Law 94–142 for placing handicapped children in
    a. classes for special children.
    b. special schools.
    c. institutions that can cater to their specific needs.
    d. the least restrictive environment.
16. The notion that handicapped and nonhandicapped children must be educated in the same classrooms
    a. is federally mandated mainstreaming.
    b. is mainstreaming but is not yet required.
    c. has been shown to be disadvantageous to both handicapped and nonhandicapped children.
    d. does not permit special services for handicapped children.
17. The technical term used to describe the categorizing of children by handicap is
    a. mainstreaming.
    b. stereotyping.
    c. handicapping.
    d. labeling.

18. In addition to an obvious increase in general activity, what other characteristic distinguishes the hyperactive child?
    a. subclinical brain damage
    b. a poor attachment bond with the mother
    c. a reading problem
    d. decreased attention span

19. If a child is doing poorly in reading in a class, which of the following conditions must be met before a learning disability is diagnosed?
    a. The child must demonstrate behavior problems.
    b. The child must demonstrate a sensory or perceptual deficit.
    c. The child must show a normal intelligence level.
    d. The child must have a history of emotional deprivation.

20. Tommy is in the second grade. He has trouble sitting still in his seat in class and is always fidgeting. Every time he hears a noise in the room, he looks around to see what it is. He frequently becomes so excited that he cannot calm down. He would be classified as
    a. having an attention-deficit disorder.
    b. mentally retarded.
    c. normal for a seven-year-old.
    d. having a hearing disorder.

Self-Test Answers
Test B

1. b	4. a	7. b	10. d	13. c	16. a	19. c
2. b	5. a	8. b	11. c	14. b	17. d	20. a
3. c	6. d	9. b	12. b	15. d	18. d	

Chapter 13 Cognitive Development in Middle and Late Childhood

Objectives

1.0 *Images of Children: Children's Intelligence and IQ Tests*
1.1 Discuss the political, social, and personal uses of intelligence tests.

2.0 *Piaget's Theory and Concrete Operational Thought*
2.1 Indicate the four characteristics of concrete operational thought, and describe observations that indicate their presence in children.
2.2 Explain why a concrete operational child understands a family tree but a preoperational child does not.
2.3 List the three Piagetian principles of cognitive development applicable to children's education.
2.4 Describe four findings that challenge Piaget's views, and discuss whether these criticisms invalidate Piaget's theory.
2.5 Discuss how special efforts to train concrete operations and how variations in sociocultural experiences relate to cognitive development.

3.0 *Information Processing*
3.1 Define and distinguish short- and long-term memory, and compare and contrast their development during middle and late childhood.
3.2 Define and distinguish among control processes, metacognitive knowledge, and learner characteristics.
3.3 Define and distinguish among rehearsal, organization, and imagery, and explain how each may be used.
3.4 Define the keyword method, indicate how it is an example of imagery, and explain why it is a control process rather than a learner characteristic.
3.5 List learner characteristics that influence the memory of children, and explain how previous knowledge plays a role in memory and memory improvement.
3.6 Compare and contrast metacognitive knowledge and cognitive monitoring.
3.7 List the steps in reciprocal teaching, and explain how it promotes cognitive monitoring.
3.8 Define and distinguish between schema and script, and compare and contrast the scripts of four-year-olds and adolescents.
3.9 Define story schema, and explain its role in children's comprehending, remembering, and creating stories such as "Albert, the fish."
3.10 Define critical thinking, list important critical thinking processes, distinguish critical thinking from passive forms of learning, and explain its importance to education and everyday life.
3.11 List ways to cultivate critical thinking by children in everyday life.

4.0 *Children and Computers*
4.1 Explain why computers are important in children's lives.
4.2 Define computer-assisted instruction, and discuss its role in promoting concrete operations, metacognitive knowledge, cognitive monitoring, and critical thinking.
4.3 Define experiential learning, and discuss the potential social and motivational benefits of using computers as multipurpose tools for educating children.
4.4 Explain how computers could dehumanize education, increase social inequality and impair the transfer of skills and motivation to situations outside of the classroom.

5.0 *Intelligence*

5.1 Define and distinguish between intelligence and information processing skills, and explain why it is hard to define intelligence.

5.2 Define individual differences.

5.3 Explain why one might think of intelligence as both a general ability and a number of specific skills.

5.4 Indicate why Binet developed an intelligence test, and explain how such tests are used today.

5.5 Define and distinguish among chronological age (CA), mental age (MA), and intelligence quotient (IQ). Also explain how to use these concepts to compute an IQ score, and explain what is meant by IQs of 80, 100, and 120.

5.6 Define normal distribution and explain how it could be used to measure intelligence.

5.7 Compare and contrast the Stanford-Binet and Wechsler scales of intelligence.

5.8 List verbal and performance subtests of the Wechsler intelligence test.

5.9 Define and distinguish the three components of Sternberg's triarchic theory of intelligence.

5.10 List Gardner's seven types of intelligence, and describe each one.

5.11 Summarize cultural and ethnic differences in intelligence test scores.

5.12 Define and distinguish between a culture-biased and culture-fair test, and indicate what makes the Raven Progressive Matrices test culture-fair.

5.13 List criticisms of the standard approach to cultural and ethnic comparisons of intelligence.

5.14 Describe examples of culture-fair intelligence tests such as the System of Multicultural Pluralistic Assessment and the Kaufman Assessment Battery for Children.

5.15 Present pro an con arguments for the claim that culture-fair intelligence tests are impossibilities.

5.16 Discuss the pros and cons of using IQ tests to evaluate a child's intelligence.

6.0 *The Extremes of Intelligence*

6.1 Define mental retardation, indicate the incidence of the degrees of mental retardation, and evaluate whether this is an appropriate use of the concept of IQ.

6.2 Compare and contrast the intelligence of individuals who suffer organic retardation and those who suffer cultural-familial retardation.

6.3 Explain why it is important to think in terms of a genetic-environment interaction to understand organic retardation.

6.4 Summarize Terman's longitudinal study of gifted people, explain how Terman's findings challenged common beliefs about gifted people, and evaluate the claim that gifted individuals are emotionally and socially maladjusted.

6.5 Discuss the joys and sorrows faced by parents and siblings of gifted children.

6.6 Define and distinguish among creativity, convergent and divergent thinking, and intelligence, and describe evidence that indicates their presence in children.

6.7 Explain why the concept of creativity as spontaneously bubbling up from a magical well is a myth.

6.8 Discuss Perkins' snowflake model of creativity.

7.0 *Language and Development*

7.1 Describe changes in vocabulary and grammar in middle and late childhood, and compare and contrast the way preschool and middle childhood children think about words.

7.2 Define and distinguish among the ABC, whole-word, and phonics methods for learning to read, and explain why reading instruction today typically uses aspects of the whole-word and phonics methods, but not the ABC method.

7.3 Discuss how advances in information processing contribute to improvement in reading during the middle childhood years.

7.4 Define bilingual education.

7.5 Summarize what is known about bilingualism, and evaluate the success of bilingual education programs.

8.0 *Achievement*

8.1 Define achievement motivation (need for achievement), and describe observations that indicate its presence in a child.

8.2 Summarize both the characteristics of individuals who have high achievement motivation and the parental practices that promote it.

8.3 Define and distinguish between extrinsic and intrinsic motivation, and explain why achievement is usually both intrinsically and extrinsically motivated.

8.4 List factors that promote intrinsic motivation, and discuss when it is appropriate rather than inappropriate to offer external rewards for achievement.

8.5 Define and distinguish between helpless and mastery orientations toward achievement.

8.6 Discuss the role of metacognition in the mastery orientation to achievement, and identify other psychological factors that make up a mastery orientation versus a helpless orientation to achievement.

8.7 Describe evidence that differences in ethnic minority children's achievement motivation compared to White American children's motivation are probably due to socioeconomic differences, not cultural deficits.

8.8 Compare and contrast the achievement experiences and motivations of Black, White, and diverse Asian populations in America today.

8.9 Describe the performance of American, Chinese, and Japanese children on mathematics achievement tests, indicate what factors produce these differences, and evaluate the claim that these factors cause the differences.

Summary

1.0 Images of Children: Children's Intelligence and IQ Tests

Intelligence testing raises political, personal, and social issues. For example, intelligence test scores help identify the extremes of intelligence, but using them to selectively place children in special education classes is a controversial practice.

2.0 Piaget's Theory and Concrete Operational Thought

Concrete Operational Thought. Piaget's concrete operational period extends from about seven years of age to the beginning of adolescence. Thought is characterized as reversible and decentered but is limited to reasoning about the concrete world. Conservation tasks can be solved: The child realizes that the amount of a substance does not change by changing any of its superficial characteristics. Thought is made up of operations that are mental actions or representations that are reversible. Children can correctly solve classification tasks for the first time.

Piaget and Education. Three of Piaget's ideas have been applied to education.

Piagetian Contributions and Criticisms. Piaget made four major contributions: First, he made brilliant observations of children, and his observations have been replicated repeatedly. Second, his ideas about what to look for in development are noteworthy. Third, his theory led others to focus on the qualitative nature of changes in mental development. Fourth, he produced imaginative ideas about how change occurs (e.g., the concepts of assimilation and accommodation). Four aspects of Piaget's theory have been criticized. First, his theory suggests that certain characteristics of a stage should emerge at the same time, but they do not. Second, small changes in procedure have large effects in children's responses and affect the stage to which a child is assigned. Third, training studies have demonstrated that a child apparently at one Piagetian stage can be taught to respond at the level of a higher stage, something not allowed within Piaget's framework. Fourth, some cognitive abilities seem to emerge earlier than Piaget believed, and their subsequent development may take longer than he thought. That is, a younger child can do more and an older child can do less than Piaget believed.

3.0 Information Processing

Memory. Long-term memory improves during middle and late childhood and can be enhanced by the use of control processes such as rehearsal, organization, and imagery. The keyword method uses imagery to enhance memory. Other factors such as age, attitude, motivation, and health also influence memory.

Metacognitive Knowledge. Metacognition entails an understanding of one's own ability to think and reason. It benefits learning in school settings.

Cognitive Monitoring. Cognitive monitoring is a process of knowing what you are doing, what to do next, and assessing one's overall understanding of a problem or situation. The source of much cognitive monitoring for children is other people; however, various programs have been designed to promote this skill in children. An illustrative example is reciprocal teaching.

Schemas and Scripts. Knowledge about aspects of the world allows us to make inferences about information. Knowledge is thought by some to be organized in structures called schema. Schema for events, such as visiting a restaurant or a doctor's office, are called scripts. Scripts emerge early in life, perhaps by one year of age.

Critical Thinking. Critical thinking entails a deeper, rather than surface, understanding of problems, open-mindedness about approaches and perspectives, and reflective thinking rather than dogmatic acceptance of ideas. To improve this skill, children need to develop problem-solving strategies, improve their mental representations, expand their base of knowledge, and be motivated to use such newly developed thinking skills.

4.0 Children and Computers

Positive Influences of Computers on Children. Computers can serve as positive influences in children's lives by functioning as personal tutors (e.g., computer-assisted instruction), creating opportunities for experiential learning, and enhancing writing and communication skills.

Negative Influences of Computers on Children. Computers can provide negative influences in children's lives by producing regimented and dehumanized classrooms, unwarranted sharing of curriculum, and increased rather than decreased social inequality.

5.0 Intelligence

Intelligence is an abstract ability that is measured indirectly. Intelligence tests estimate children's verbal ability, problem-solving skills, and ability to learn from and adapt to everyday life.

One Face or Many? This question asks whether intelligence is composed of a general or a specific ability. Binet's original intelligence test in 1905 was designed to identify those children in French schools who should be placed in special classes. Binet developed the idea of mental age. The ratio of mental age to chronological age eventually developed into the intelligence quotient (IQ). Standardization of the Binet showed that this test produced a normal distribution of scores for the population. The contemporary Stanford-Binet provides separate scores for verbal reasoning, quantitative reasoning, abstract/visual reasoning, and short-term memory.

Like Binet, Wechsler viewed intelligence as general in nature, but the Wechsler scales are divided into verbal and nonverbal categories. These are further subdivided to reflect specific aspects of intelligence. Wechsler devised the WAIS (for adults), the WISC (for children), and the WPPSI (for children 4 to 6½ years).

Sternberg has developed a triarchic theory of intelligence in which the component is the basic unit. Sternberg distinguishes among componential, experiential, and contextual intelligence. Gardner has developed a theory of intelligence based on seven different intelligence types, including intelligence about one's body and social relations.

Culture and Ethnicity. There are cultural ethnic differences in intelligence test scores. Ethnic research needs to increase its emphasis on diversity within ethnic groups and on the processes that explains ethnic differences rather than focuses on the differences between ethnic groups. Early intelligence tests favored White, middle-class, and urban individuals. Alternatives and supplements to standardized intelligence tests have been proposed. Another alternative to standardized intelligence tests are attempts at producing culture-fair intelligence tests; however, attempts to produce such tests have not usually been successful.

The Use and Misuse of Intelligence Tests. Intelligence test results should be combined with other information about a person to be used effectively. The misuse of the intelligence tests entails the belief that IQ score indicates a fixed and unchanging index of a person's intelligence.

6.0 The Extremes of Intelligence

Mental Retardation. Mental retardation is indicated by subaverage general intellectual functioning existing concurrently with defects in adaptive behavior. It appears during the developmental period. Some forms of mental retardation, such as Down syndrome, are biologically based. Other forms, such as cultural-familial retardation, may be environmental in origin.

Giftedness. Gifted children are often identified by well-above-average performance on IQ tests. A longitudinal study of gifted children by Terman found that these people have more intellectual accomplishments, more satisfying personal lives, and better health than a control group.

Creativity. Creativity is the ability to think in a novel or unusual way and is not identical with intelligence. One view is that creativity may involve divergent rather than convergent thinking. Daniel Perkins proposed a snowflake model of creativity and applied it to education.

7.0 Language and Development

Vocabulary and Grammar. Children in middle and late childhood begin to think more analytically about words and increase the size of their vocabulary. These children also make advances in grammar.

Reading. There are three traditional methods for teaching children to read: the ABC method, the whole-word method, and the phonics method. A combination of the whole-word method and the phonics method is usually taught in American schools; however, reading is much more than the sum of these approaches.

Bilingualism. Bilingualism is an issue in language development with implications for education and public policy. Debates exist about whether non-English-speaking children should be taught English as a foreign language or as a second, equal language.

8.0 Achievement

Need for Achievement. David McClelland argued that need for achievement reflects a desire to accomplish something or to reach a standard of excellence. To increase the achievement motivation of their children, parents need to set standards, model achievement-oriented behaviors, and reward children for their achievements.

Intrinsic and Extrinsic Motivation. Intrinsic motivation is behavior that is motivated by self-determination and an underlying need for competence. Extrinsic motivation is behavior that is influenced by external rewards. Incentives are external cues that stimulate motivation. Care must be exercised in the use of incentive because extrinsic rewards can weaken performance on intrinsically motivated tasks. Recognizing that effort is important is a key to good performance in school.

Mastery Orientation versus Helpless Orientation. A helpless orientation is one in which children appear trapped by the experience of difficulty and attribute their difficulty to inability. A master orientation is one that describes children who are task oriented and who focus on learning strategies. They report being challenged and excited by difficult tasks rather than being threatened by them.

Achievement in Ethnic Minority Children. Research on the achievement of minorities generally has failed to consider social class, a factor more important than race. In addition, there is considerable diversity within ethnic groups. Although American children generally are more achievement oriented than children in other countries, they have not compared favorably with Japanese children in recent years. For example, the level of mathematical skills in school children appears substantially higher in Japanese children than in American ones. The difference has been explained in terms of the time spent on the activities, the amount of practice, and the level of attention of the children.

Key Terms

1.0 Images of Children: Children's Intelligence and IQ Tests
intelligence test

2.0 Piaget's Theory and Concrete Operational Thought
concrete operational thought
operations
reversible mental action
logical reasoning
classification skills

3.0 Information Processing
long-term memory
control processes or strategies

rehearsal
organization
imagery
keyword method
metacognitive knowledge
cognitive monitoring
reciprocal teaching
schema
script
critical thinking

4.0 Children and Computers
computer-assisted instruction
experiential learning

regimentation
dehumanization

5.0 Intelligence
individual differences in intelligence
general versus specific ability
mental age (MA)
intelligence quotient (IQ)
normal distribution
Stanford-Binet test
Wechsler Scales (WAIS, WISC, WPPSI)
triarchic theory of intelligence
componential intelligence
experiential intelligence
contextual intelligence
component
Gardner's seven types of intelligence
culturally biased test
culture-fair test
System of Multicultural Pluralistic Assessment
(SOMPA)
Kaufman Assessment Battery for Children
(K-ABC)

6.0 The Extremes of Intelligence
mental retardation
organic retardation
cultural-familial retardation
gifted child
convergent thinking
divergent thinking
creativity
snowflake model of creativity

7.0 Language and Development
grammar
ABC method
whole-word method
phonics method
bilingual education

8.0 Achievement
achievement motivation (need for achievement)
intrinsic motivation
extrinsic motivation
helpless orientation
mastery orientation

Guided Review

1.0 Images of Children: Children's Intelligence and IQ Tests

1. Intelligence testing raises issues that are _____, _____, and _____ in nature.

political, personal
social

2.0 Piaget's Theory and Concrete Operational Thought

1. _____ _____ thinking appears at about age seven or nine. Thought is made up of _____, mental actions that are reversible.

Concrete operational
operations

2. The ability to _____ is an operation that allows one to divide things into different sets and subsets on the basis of _____ characteristics. This allows the child to create or understand the relationships in a _____ _____.

classify
several

family tree

3. From the Piagetian perspective, three principles can be applied to the problem of education. First, the most important issue concerns _____. Second, children acquire _____ information, but also must _____ things as well. Third, children come to school with a _____ to learn. This was acquired through _____ _____ with the environment, and school must not dull the _____ to learn with a _____ curriculum.

communication, new
unlearn
motivation
spontaneous interaction
eagerness, rigid

4. Four findings raise questions about Piaget's approach to cognitive development. One is that development is _____ as synchronous as Piaget proposed. Two is that _____ changes in procedures produce _____ changes in children's apparent abilities. Three is that children can be trained to reason at a stage _____ than the one appropriate for their age. Fourth is that abilities develop _____ and over a _____ period of time than Piaget supposed.

    not
    small
    large

    higher
    earlier, longer

5. The example of the Kpelle farmers illustrates that _____ _____ plays a role in cognitive development _____ to the expectations of Piaget.

    formal education
    contrary

3.0   Information Processing

1. Important issues regarding the information processing abilities of elementary school children concern memory, _____, schemas, _____, and _____.

    metacognition
    scripts, critical thinking

2. _____ _____ _____ increases during middle and late childhood, in contrast to short-term memory. Long-term memory depends on both _____ _____ and _____ characteristics.

    Long-term memory

    control processes, learner

3. Rehearsal, organization, and imagery are learning activities that fit the category of _____ processes, ones that require _____ and _____. They are under the learner's _____ and are _____. They are also considered to be _____.

    control, work
    effort, control
    conscious, strategies

4. Extended processing of to-be-remembered material after it has been presented is called _____. _____ is more frequently used spontaneously by children in middle childhood or older.

    rehearsal, Organization

5. A control process that makes use of mental, usually visual, associations is called _____. A specific type of imagery used to teach children lists, such as states and their capitals, is the _____ method.

    imagery

    keyword

6. Learner characteristics include age, _____, motivation, and _____.

    attitude
    health

7. Children's previously acquired _____ has an impact on memory. In a study comparing the memory for chess board arrangements by chess-playing children and novice adults, the chess-playing children were _____ than the adults.

    knowledge

    better

8. _____ knowledge concerns the mind and how it works, and is accumulated through experience and stored in long-term memory.

    Metacognitive

9. When children assess what they are currently doing, determine what they need to do next, and evaluate the effectiveness of their problem-solving strategies, they are engaging in _____ monitoring.

    cognitive

10. When students take turns leading a group that is trying to learn a concept, and use different strategies to teach that concept, they are participating in _____ teaching.

    reciprocal

11. Active organizations of past experiences are called _____.

    schema

12. When children hear stories they learn to expect a beginning, a middle, an end, a main character, and a plot because they recognize a _____ schema.

    story

13. Schema for events are often called _____, and may appear by the age of _____ year(s).

    scripts
    one

14. Critical thinking involves dealing with _____ meanings of problems, being able to _____ _____ _____ different approaches and perspectives, and to understand and evaluate rather than to merely accept and carry out.

    deeper
    remain open to

15. According to psychologists such as Sternberg, education should include both acquiring _____ and learning _____ _____. More attention needs to be paid to teaching _____ _____ skills in schools using these skills in _____.

    information, thinking skills, information-processing, life

4.0 Children and Computers

1. Some of the positive attributes of the use of _____ by children include their ability to serve as personal tutors, their motivational effects, and their social impact.

    computers

2. _____ _____ instruction uses the computer as a _____.

    Computer-assisted, tutor

3. To improve children's planning and problem-solving abilities, educators have used the _____ component of the _____ computer software.

    turtlegraphics, Logo

4. The computer is especially helpful in improving the _____ and communication skills of children.

    writing

5. Negative effects of computer usage by children include the _____ of the classroom, _____ curriculums, and _____ _____ regimentation in the classroom.

    dehumanizing, restricted
    too much

6. Computers may introduce further _____ differences into education because of their _____.

    class
    costs

5.0   Intelligence

1. One definition of _____ is having verbal ability, problem solving skills, and the ability to learn and adapt in everyday situations. Psychologists who study intelligence are interested in _____ _____.

   intelligence

   individual differences

2. The first intelligence test was constructed by _____ and _____. The tasks on the tests ranged from the ability to _____ _____ to defining _____ _____.

   Binet
   Simon, draw designs, abstract concepts

3. Binet called the concept that describes the level of a child's intellectual functioning the _____ _____. It was based on the _____ of _____ a child of a given age could answer.

   mental age
   number, items

4. The formula for calculating the IQ from the mental age was _____ age divided by _____ age multiplied by _____.

   mental
   chronological, 100

5. The assumption is that the distribution of intelligence in the population is _____.

   normal

6. The revised IQ test is now called the _____ _____. The _____ revision of the Stanford-Binet analyzes individual's responses in _____ separate area scores.

   Stanford-Binet
   fourth
   four

7. The other most widely used individual tests were developed by _____. It includes both _____ and _____ components.

   Wechsler
   verbal, performance

8. The WISC is the _____ _____ _____ _____ _____, the WAIS is the Wechsler _____ _____ _____, and the WPPIS is the Wechsler _____ and _____ _____ _____. The first of these is applicable to children between the ages of _____ and _____. The last is used with children between _____ and _____ years of age.

   Wechsler Intelligence Scale for Children, Adult Intelligence Scale, Preschool, Primary Intelligence Scale, 6, 16, 4, 6½

9. Sternberg developed the _____ theory of intelligence. Analytic thinking and abstract reasoning are termed _____ intelligence. Creative thinking is called _____ intelligence, and practical knowledge is called _____ intelligence.

   triarchic
   componential
   experiential
   contextual

10. Howard Gardner has developed a theory of intelligence based on _____ different kinds of intelligence. He believes that each of these kinds of intelligence can be destroyed by specific _____ _____ and that each shows up in both the _____ and in _____ _____. Critics of this approach point out that _____ occur in domains other than _____.

    seven
    brain damage
    gifted
    idiot savants
    geniuses, music

11. There _____ significant cultural and ethnic differences in performance on intelligence tests. Compared to White students, Black students score about _____ to _____ points _____ on standardized intelligence tests.

    are

    10, 15
    lower

12. Different ethnic groups demonstrate varying strengths in verbal abilities, numerical and spatial abilities, and reasoning abilities. Jewish children and Black children do their best on _____ abilities. _____ children score higher on numerical and spatial abilities, and _____ _____ children score higher on spatial and reasoning abilities.

verbal
Chinese
Puerto Rican

13. Ethnic differences in intelligence may be due largely to _____ differences. Scarr found that when children from disadvantaged Black families were adopted by more advantaged middle-class families, their scores on intelligence tests resembled national averages for _____-class children.

socioeconomic

middle

14. Norms for the early intelligence tests were based almost entirely on _____-class, White standards.

middle

15. Two types of cultural bias can be item _____ and _____.

content, language

16. A test that gives no advantage to people with a particular social background is called a _____ _____ test. It is also possible to devise a test with items _____ to the members of the group being tested.

culture-fair
familiar

17. There are no _____ items in the Raven Progressive Matrices Test in an attempt to be culture-fair. Yet, individuals with more _____ tend to score better.

verbal

education

18. The System of Multicultural Pluralistic Assessment (SOMPA) was designed for _____ _____ children from __ to __ years of age. The SOMPA consists of verbal and nonverbal intelligence measured by the _____, social economic background of the family, social adjustment to _____, and _____ health.

low-income, 5, 11
WISC-R

school
physical

19. The Kaufman Assessment Battery for Children (K-ABC) is an example of a _____ _____ test. It can be given to children from the age of 2½ to _____.

culture-fair
13

20. Intelligence tests should not be used as the sole _____ of _____. The scores achieved by an individual on an IQ test should also not be thought of as a _____ indicator of his or her intelligence.

indicator
intelligence
fixed

6.0 The Extremes of Intelligence

1. A low IQ and difficulty adapting to everyday life is the currently accepted definition of _____ _____. An IQ score below _____ is usually the criterion.

mental retardation
70

2. Brain _____ or an extra chromosome in the case of _____ syndrome can cause _____ _____. These are considered _____ causes of retardation.

damage, Down
mental retardation
organic

3. Cases of mental retardation that do not have a known organic cause are called _____ _____. Children with the type of retardation termed cultural-familial frequently come from _____ environments.

cultural-familial
impoverished

4. A child with a well-above-average intellectual capacity is termed _____.

gifted

5. _____ performed the classic study of gifted children. The children in his study had remarkable _____ and _____ success, and evidenced _____ emotional problems than their less gifted peers.

Terman
academic, material
fewer

6. The gifted children in Bloom's study who became stars devoted _____ amounts of time to training and practice.

enormous

7. Parents of gifted children often feel _____ about them. One of their concerns is with the effects of _____ relationships. Another important thing for parents to remember is that _____ children's _____ and _____ development lags behind their intellectual development.

ambivalent
sibling
gifted
social, emotional

8. Defining creativity is _____, and it appears only weakly related to _____.

difficult
intelligence

9. Creativity is most closely related to _____ thinking, the ability to produce _____ _____ to one question. The _____ thinker is the person who selects the _____ answer typically required by many _____ intelligence tests.

divergent
many answers
convergent, correct
standardized

10. Daniel Perkins' _____ model of creativity has been applied to education.

snowflake

7.0 Language and Development

1. During the elementary school years, children become more _____ in their approach to words, associating words with the _____ to which they belong. They show similar gains in understanding grammar, as evidenced by their use of _____ and _____ phrases.

analytical
category
comparatives
subjective

2. The _____ method of teaching reading stresses the sounds   **phonics**
    that letters make when they are in words. When children learn to
    read with the _____ _____ method, they learn   **whole-word**
    associations between words and their meanings. The now obsolete
    _____ method emphasizes the memorization of the _____   **ABC, names**
    of the letters of the alphabet. The current approach is to use
    some combination of the _____ and _____ _____   **phonics, whole-word**
    methods.

3. Children in America who do not learn English as their first
    langauge experience are _____.   **bilingual**

4. Children enrolled in bilingual education programs learn concepts in
    their native language until they are in the _____ or _____   **first, second**
    grade, at which point they begin to learn things in English.

5. Investigations have shown that _____ does not interfere with   **bilingualism**
    performance in either language.

6. The _____ _____ is one of the few countries in the   **United States**
    world in which most high school graduates know only their own
    language.

8.0 Achievement

1. The need for _____ is defined as the desire to accomplish   **achievement**
    something, to reach a standard of excellence, and to expend effort
    to excel.

2. _____ view of achievement motivation is that it varies   **McClelland's**
    between individuals and can be measured. It is thought to develop
    out of interactions between the child and _____. _____   **parents, Independence**
    training and high _____ for achievement foster its   **standards**
    development.

3. Motivation that is based on an underlying need for competence is
    called _____ motivation. Extrinsic motivation refers to   **intrinsic**
    behavior supported by _____.   **rewards**

4. External cues that stimulate motivation are called _____. One   **incentives**
    recent study showed that the application of _____ incentives   **external**
    and rewards can decrease _____ if the task was already   **performance**
    _____ motivated.   **intrinsically**

5. Schunk found that either _____ cues, such as information   **external**
    about peer performance, or _____ cues, such as goals,   **internal**
    improved performance in a math problems task. Children that
    received _____ produced the highest level of performance.   **both**

6. An important influence of internal causes of achievement is
    _____, a controlled process.   **effort**

7. Children with a _____ orientation react to challenges by questioning their _____, whereas children with a _____ orientation react to challenges by focusing on their _____ _____.

helpless
abilities, mastery
learning strategies

8. Students with a _____ orientation earn higher grades than those with a _____ orientation.

mastery
helpless

9. _____ _____ is a better predictor of achievement orientation than _____. _____-class individuals do better in achievement-oriented situations than _____-class individuals.

Social class
race, Middle
lower

10. Generally, American children are very _____-oriented. However, specifically with respect to mathematics, they are clearly being surpassed by _____ children.

achievement
Japanese

11. It appears that the most likely explanation for the apparent cultural difference in mathematics ability results from the differences in the amounts of _____ and _____ children in the two countries get in mathematics. The _____ did not differ. The _____ mothers had a generally higher level of schooling. The _____ children are not more intelligent. The Japanese teachers have _____ experience. However, the Japanese school week is _____, as is the school _____. Japanese teachers spend _____% of the time on mathematics as opposed to _____% for American teachers. Japanese children are _____ likely to be paying attention to the teacher. Japanese children get _____ homework.

time, practice
curricula
American
Japanese
less
longer, year
20
20
more
more

Key Terms Matching Exercise

1.0 Images of Children: Children's Intelligence and IQ Tests (Term 1)
2.0 Piaget's Theory and Concrete Operational Thought (Terms 2–6)
3.0 Information Processing (Terms 7–18)
4.0 Children and Computers (Terms 19–22)
5.0 Intelligence (Terms 23–39)
6.0 The Extremes of Intelligence (Terms 40–47)
7.0 Language and Development (Terms 48–52)
8.0 Achievement (Terms 53–57)

---

1. intelligence test

a. The ability to systematically evaluate possibilities and deduce a correct answer

2. concrete operational thought

b. Concrete operations in Piaget's theory; mental actions that allow a child to do mentally what was done before physically that are reversible

3. operations

    c. In Piaget's theory, the term refers to various forms of mental action that older children use to solve problems and reason logically

4. reversible mental action

    d. An ability to divide things into sets and subsets and reason about their interrelations

5. logical reasoning

    e. Measures of verbal ability, problem-solving skills, and the ability to learn from and adapt to daily experience

6. classification skills

    f. In Piaget's third stage of development, children approximately 7 to 11 years old can perform operations; logical reasoning replaces intuitive thought as long as the principles can be applied to specific, concrete examples

---

7. long-term memory

    a. An ability to create a mental picture of an object or event

8. control processes or strategies

    b. Learning and memory strategies that draw heavily on information-processing capacities and are under the learner's conscious control

9. rehearsal

    c. Memory storage for considerable periods of time

10. organization

    d. In Piaget's theory, a biologically based tendency to integrate knowledge into two interrelated cognitive structures

11. imagery

    e. Extended processing of to-be-remembered material after it has been presented; a control process used to facilitate long-term memory

12. keyword method

    f. Imagery strategy, combining two concrete words that stand for two other words in a visual image

---

13. metacognitive knowledge

    a. A schema for a typical sequence of actions or events in a particular situation

14. cognitive monitoring

    b. Structures of knowledge about aspects of the world, such as objects, concepts, events, and knowledge

15. reciprocal teaching

    c. The process of taking stock of what you are currently doing, what you will do next, and how effectively the mental activity is unfolding

16. schema
17. script

    d. Knowledge of one's own thinking processes

    e. Despite varying definitions, the common element is the individuals grasp the deeper meaning of problems, keep an open mind about different approaches and perspectives, and decide oneself what to believe

18.	critical thinking	f.	An instructional procedure to develop cognitive monitoring; it requires that students take turns in leading the group in the use of strategies for comprehending and remembering text context that the teacher models for the class

---

19.	computer-assisted instruction	a.	Variation in intellectual abilities that are commonly assumed to be normally distributed
20.	experiential learning	b.	Controversy about whether intelligence is a general ability or a set of specific skills
21.	regimentation	c.	The computer is used as a tutor to individualize instruction; the concept is to use the computer to present information, give students practice, and provide additional instruction if needed
22.	dehumanization	d.	To impose uniform and rigid conditions of learning
23.	individual differences in intelligence	e.	To deprive of human qualities or characteristics
24.	general versus specific ability	f.	Hands-on experience as a basis for understanding

---

25.	mental age (MA)	a.	Symmetrical frequency distribution, with a majority of the cases falling in the middle of the possible range of scores and fewer scores appearing toward the ends of the range
26.	intelligence quotient (IQ)	b.	Theory that there are three types of intelligence: componential intelligence, experiential intelligence, and contextual intelligence
27.	normal distribution	c.	Widely used individual tests, comprised of the WAIS-R, WISC-R, and WPPSI
28.	Stanford-Binet test	d.	Binet's measure of the level of a child's intellectual functioning
29.	Wechsler Scales (WAIS, WISC, WPPSI)	e.	Originally defined as $(MA/CA) \times 100$; however, now defined in statistical terms as a deviation score
30.	triarchic theory of intelligence	f.	The American version of Binet's original test of intelligence that may be given to individuals from toddlers to adults

---

31.	componential intelligence	a.	Analytical thinking and abstract reasoning
32.	experiential intelligence	b.	Practical knowledge
33.	contextual intelligence	c.	Insightful and creative thinking
34.	component	d.	Basic unit of intelligence, a basic unit of information processing in Sternberg's theory

35. Gardner's seven types of intelligence

36. culturally biased test

e. Intelligence tests that do not attempt to eliminate cultural bias

f. A theory of intelligence that assumes seven different components: verbal, mathematical, ability to spatially analyze the world, movement skills, insightful skills for analyzing ourselves, insightful skills for analyzing others, and musical skills

---

37. culture-fair test

38. System of Multicultural Pluralistic Assessment (SOMPA)

39. Kaufman Assessment Battery for Children (K-ABC)

40. mental retardation

41. organic retardation

42. cultural-familial retardation

43. gifted child

a. Child with well above average intellectual capacity or a superior talent

b. Subaverage intellectual ability caused by genetic disorders or brain damage

c. Significantly subaverage general intellectual functioning existing concurrently with deficits in adaptive behavior and manifested during the developmental period

d. An improved version of culture-fair tests that can be given to children from 2½ to 12½ years of age

e. Form of mild retardation with no detectable brain abnormality but at least one parent or sibling who is also mentally retarded

f. An intelligence test for children 5 to 11 years old that encompasses information from four aspects of a child's life

g. Intelligence tests that attempt to eliminate cultural bias

---

44. convergent thinking

45. divergent thinking

46. creativity

47. Snowflake model of creativity

48. grammar

49. ABC method

50. whole-word method

a. Method of teaching reading that emphasizes memorizing the names of the letters of the alphabet

b. The formal description of rules for syntax

c. Many-faceted phenomenon, involving, among other things, the production of novel ideas or products

d. Type of thinking that produces one correct answer

e. Type of thinking that produces many different answers to a single problem

f. Method of teaching reading that is based on learning direct association between words and their meanings

g. A model of the creative process that has been applied to educational settings

51. phonics method	a. Need and motivation to strive for success; viewed as a property of the individual, remaining constant over different domains and time
52. bilingual education	b. This describes children who seem trapped by the experience of difficulty; they attribute their difficulty to a lack of ability
53. achievement motivation (need for achievement)	c. Method of teaching reading that stresses the sounds that letters make when in words
54. intrinsic motivation	d. This describes children who are task oriented; they focus on their learning strategies rather than on their ability
55. extrinsic motivation	e. Programs for students with limited proficiency in English that instruct students in their own language part of the time while English is being learned
56. helpless orientation	f. Behavioral influence by underlying needs for competence and self-determination
57. mastery orientation	g. Behavioral influence by external rewards

Key Terms Matching Exercise
Answer Key

1. e	10. d	19. c	28. f	37. g	46. c	55. g
2. f	11. a	20. f	29. c	38. f	47. g	56. b
3. c	12. f	21. d	30. b	39. d	48. b	57. d
4. b	13. d	22. e	31. a	40. c	49. a	
5. a	14. c	23. a	32. c	41. b	50. f	
6. d	15. f	24. b	33. b	42. e	51. c	
7. c	16. b	25. d	34. d	43. a	52. e	
8. b	17. a	26. e	35. f	44. d	53. a	
9. e	18. e	27. a	36. e	45. e	54. f	

Self-Test A

1. As a child Robert Sternberg was afraid of the IQ test; however, as an adult he developed a theory of intelligence. This illustrates the _____ aspect of intelligence testing
   a. political
   b. social
   c. personal
   d. achievement

2. A child is given the conservation of liquid task. The child argues that the liquid in the two containers is the same because although one is taller, the other is fatter. This is an example of
   a. decentration
   b. reversibility.
   c. egocentrism.
   d. classification.

3. One characteristic of concrete operational thought is
   a. decentration
   b. centration.
   c. abstract reasoning.
   d. the personal fable.
4. A logical child who requires real objects for the basis of her reasoning is
   a. sensorimotor.
   b. preoperational.
   c. concrete operational.
   d. formal operational.
5. Knowledge relevant to a task
   a. provides a better filter.
   b. allows shallower processing of information.
   c. totally explains age differences in performance on information-processing tasks.
   d. makes information processing more efficient.
6. If young children retain information better when it is related by a script, which list would be easiest for a preschool child to learn?
   a. cat, pig, deer
   b. hamburger, pizza, steak
   c. ball, bat, glove
   d. couch, desk, table
7. All of the following constitute positive influences of computers on children's lives with the exception that computers
   a. can act as personal tutors.
   b. can produce regimented classrooms.
   c. can motivate students.
   d. comprise multipurpose tools.
8. Which of the following is a difference between the Piagetian approach and the psychometric approach to intelligence?
   a. Psychometricians argue for a genetic component to intelligence; for Piaget it is just experience.
   b. Piaget argues for a genetic component to intelligence; for psychometricians it is just experience.
   c. Psychometricians are interested in qualitative changes; Piaget, in individual difference.
   d. Piaget is interested in qualitative changes; psychometricians, in individual differences.

9. What was the task required of Alfred Binet?
   a. He was asked to come up with a general theory of intelligence.
   b. He was asked to design a test that would identify students who would not benefit from regular classes.
   c. He was asked to determine the relationship between intelligence and creativity in French school children.
   d. He was asked to design achievement tests that measured the reading and mathematical abilities of school children.
10. Jonathan has a mental age of ten and a chronological age of eight. Jonathan's IQ would be
   a. 125.
   b. 113.
   c. 100.
   d. 80.
11. How does the Wechsler scale differ from the Binet?
   a. The Binet provides a measure of general intelligence; the Wechsler does not.
   b. The Wechsler provides a measure of general intelligence; the Binet does not.
   c. The Wechsler measures both verbal intelligence and performance; the Binet does not.
   d. The Binet measures both verbal intelligence and performance; the Wechsler does not.
12. Traditional intelligence, such as analytic thinking and abstract reasoning, is what Sternberg terms
   a. experiential intelligence.
   b. componential intelligence.
   c. contextual intelligence.
   d. formal intelligence.
13. All of the following may be biological causes of retardation except
   a. being raised in an impoverished home.
   b. an extra chromosome.
   c. a defect in metabolizing a certain amino acid.
   d. brain damage during delivery.

14. Mentally retarded children who have IQs in the range from 50 to 70 generally have retardation caused by
    a. cultural-familial factors.
    b. brain damage.
    c. genetic factors.
    d. metabolic difficulties.
15. Terman's research found that gifted children had
    a. a higher suicide rate.
    b. more emotional problems.
    c. less social maturity.
    d. fewer emotional problems.
16. A group of children is asked to think of as many different solutions to the question "How can our school raise money for athletic equipment?" They are being tested for
    a. intelligence.
    b. convergent thinking.
    c. divergent thinking.
    d. internal motivation.
17. In teaching children to read, what is the currently accepted method?
    a. ABC method alone
    b. whole-word method with phonics method
    c. whole-word method alone
    d. phonics method alone

18. The major debate regarding bilingualism concerns
    a. the scientific quality of studies of bilingual education.
    b. the best way to conduct bilingual education.
    c. whether children should learn a second language.
    d. the negative consequences of bilingualism for achievement motivation.
19. Motivation based on a personal desire to excel is called
    a. cognitive motivation.
    b. extrinsic motivation.
    c. intrinsic motivation.
    d. reinforced motivation.
20. Children who are frustrated by difficulty and who say that they lack ability exemplify
    a. a helpless orientation.
    b. a mastery orientation.
    c. intrinsic motivation.
    d. extrinsic motivation.

Self-Test Answers
Test A

1. c	4. c	7. b	10. a	13. a	16. c	19. c
2. a	5. d	8. d	11. c	14. a	17. b	20. a
3. a	6. c	9. b	12. b	15. d	18. b	

Critical Thinking Exercises

Exercise 1

In Chapter 10 you learned about preoperational thinking. In Chapter 13 you now are learning about concrete operational thinking. In Chapter 16 you will learn about formal operational thinking. After you review the appropriate sections in these three chapters, indicate which of the following cases best illustrates *concrete operations*. **Hint:** There is more than one example of concrete operational thinking. **Circle the letter of the best answer and explain why it is the best answer and why each other answer is not as good.**

A. Katie is asked, "Do you have a brother?" She says "Yes." Then she is asked, "Does he have a sister?" She answers, "No."
B. Ray says, "A fly is like both insects and birds. It's like birds because it flies, but it's like insects because it has six legs."
C. Tim is working on analogies. He declares, "Biking is to pedaling as riding in a car is to stepping on the gas pedal because they both make the vehicle go!"
D. Bobby states, "I understand how this nickel and these five pennies are the same as this dime."
E. Her teacher asks Mary, "How can the scale be brought back into balance?" Mary replies, "The only way to do that is to remove the weight that made one pan sink lower than the other."

Exercise 2

Santrock addresses numerous issues concerning the cognitive development of elementary school children in Chapter 13. Use that information to determine which of the following statements is not contradicted by specific evidence or argument in the chapter. **Circle the letter of the best answer and explain why it is the best answer and why each other answer is not as good.**

A. The issue of individual differences is relevant to all approaches of intelligence.
B. Concrete operations is made up of unlimited, reversible mental actions.
C. Instruction in information processing at the elementary school level is so poor that children do not improve their logical or analytical skills during this time.
D. Children entering the elementary school grades have their own ideas and information about various concepts.
E. The introduction of culture-fair tests eliminated nearly all cultural bias in the testing of and research on individuals from different socioeconomic and ethnic backgrounds.

Exercise 3

Read the following passage titled "Achievement in Math Requires Time and Practice: Comparisons of Children in the United States and Japan." On the basis of this information, indicate which of the following statements constitutes an assumption rather than an inference or an observation. **Circle the letter of the best answer and explain why it is the best answer and why each other answer is not as good.** (Hint: There is more than one assumption.)

A. There are no genetic differences between Japanese and American children that could influence mathematics achievement.
B. The differences between Japanese and American children's scores are smallest for first-grade girls.
C. The difference in achievement is caused by the amount of time spent in school.
D. Differences in achievement are not associated with differences in teacher experience.
E. Japanese and American children are equally motivated to achieve in mathematics.

Achievement in Math Requires Time and Practice:
Comparisons of Children in the United States and Japan

Harold Stevenson and his colleagues (1986) recently conducted a detailed investigation of math achievement in first- and fifth-grade children from the United States and Japan. The final sample includes 240 first graders and 240 fifth graders from each country. Extensive time was spent developing the math test that was given to the children, the children were observed in their classrooms, and additional information was obtained from mothers, teachers, and the children themselves. As shown in Table A, the Japanese children clearly outscored the American children on the math test in both the first and fifth grades. And, by the fifth grade, the highest average score of any of the American classrooms fell *below* the worst performing score of the Japanese classrooms.

TABLE A	*Average Mathematics Achievement by Japanese and American Children*	
Country	Boys	Girls
Grade 1		
Japan	20.7	19.5
United States	16.6	17.6
Grade 5		
Japan	53.0	53.5
United States	45.0	43.8

From H.W. Stevenson, et al., "Achievement in Mathematics" in H.W. Stevenson, et al. (eds.), *Child Development and Education in Japan.* Copyright -c- 1986 W.H. Freeman and Company. Used by permission.

What are some reasons for these dramatic differences between American and Japanese children's math achievement? Curriculum did not seem to be a factor. Neither did the educational background of the children's parents. And neither did intelligence; the American children sampled actually scored slightly higher than the Japanese children on such components of intelligence as vocabulary, general information, verbal ability, and perceptual speed. Possibly the Japanese teachers had more experience? Apparently, this was not the case, since in terms of educational degrees and years of teaching experiences, no differences were found.

The amount of time spent in school and math classes probably was an important factor. The Japanese school year consists of 240 days of instruction and each school week is 5½ days long. The American school year consists of 178 days of instruction and each school week is 5 days long. In the fifth grade, Japanese children were in school an average of 37.3 hours per week, American children only 30.4 hours. Observations in the children's classrooms revealed that Japanese teachers spent far more time teaching math than did American teachers; approximately one-fourth of total classroom time in the first grade was spent in math instruction in Japan, only approximately one-tenth in the United States. Observations also indicated that the Japanese children attended more efficiently to what the teacher was saying than American children did. And Japanese children spent far more time doing homework than American children—on weekends, 66 minutes versus 18 minutes, respectively.

And in another recent investigation, Chinese children were assigned more homework and spent more time on homework than Japanese children, who, in turn, were assigned more homework and spent more time on homework than American children (Chen & Stevenson, 1989). Chinese children had more positive attitudes about homework than Japanese children, who in turn had more positive attitudes about homework than American children.

The conclusion: Learning requires time and practice. When either is reduced, learning is impaired.

Research Project 1 Conservation Tasks

The purpose of this exercise is for you to see an example of a preoperational and a concrete operational reasoner. Pair up with another class member and test two children, a four- to five-year-old child and an eight- to nine-year-old child, using several of Piaget's tasks. Administer two conservation and two classification tasks to each child, and then compare the children's responses with each other and attempt to interpret those responses in view of Piaget's theory. In order to test the two children, you will need to clear this through the human subjects review board at your school and get a signed informed consent form from the children's parents. A description of the tasks, the data sheet for recording the observations, and a list of questions to answer follows.

Conservation Task 1: Conservation of number task. Make two sets of ten identical items with each set a different color (e.g., one set of ten blue poker chips and one set of ten white poker chips). First place one row of same-colored ten items in front of the child. Ask the child to make an identical row with the other set. Ask the child if the two rows have the same amount of items or if one row has more. Do not go on until the rows are identical in number and arrangement and the child agrees that the two rows are the same. Now spread one row out and push the other row together so that the display looks as follows:

OOOOOOOOOO

o o o o o o o o o o

Ask the child if the rows are the same or if one row has more. Ask the child why it is the same or why one has more and which one, if either, has more. If the child says one row has more, ask the child where the more came from. Record all responses.

Conservation Task 2: Conservation of liquid task. Pour into two identical glasses an identical amount of juice. Ask the child if the two glasses have the same amount, and adjust the volume in each glass until the child agrees that both have the same. Now pour the liquid from one glass into a taller, thinner glass. Ask the child if the amount of juice is the same in both glasses or if one has more. If the child thinks one has more, ask which one. Have the child justify the judgment of having the same or different amount. Record all responses.

Classification Task 1: Classification of groups. Present the child with cutouts of big and small triangles, circles, and squares. Some of the shapes should be red, some blue, and some green. Ask the child to put together those things that go together. Record how the child sorts the objects. Now ask the child if there is another way to put the objects together. Record the second sort.

Classification Task 2: Present the child with a set of wooden beads, with ten red and two blue. (You can substitute poker chips or M&Ms.) Ask the child if there are more red beads or more blue beads. If the child were to make a train with the red beads and another train with the blue beads, which train would be longer? Now ask the child if there are more red beads or more wooden beads. If the child were to make a train with the red beads and another train with the wooden beads, which train would be longer?

	Child 1	Child 2
Task	Sex __ Age __	Sex __ Age __

Conservation Task 1:
Creation of row
Response
Justification

Conservation Task 2:
Response
Justification

Classification Task 1:
First ordering
Second ordering

Classification Task 2:
Response : red > blue?
Response: red > wooden?

Questions:

1. Which tasks did the four- to five-year-old child solve? How would you characterize the nature of the child's responses to the questions?
2. Which tasks did the eight- to nine-year-old child solve? How would you characterize the nature of the child's responses to the questions?
3. How would you characterize the differences between the performance of the younger and older child on these tasks?
4. What do these observations tell you about Piaget's theory? How would the children be classified into Piaget's stages based on their responses to your problems?

Research Project 2 Creativity

This exercise illustrates structured interview methods and a test of creativity. Give a creativity task to two children, one age five and the other age ten. In order to test the two children, you will need to clear this through the human subjects review board at your school and get a signed informed consent form from the children's parents.

Evaluate the children's responses with the hypotheses that there may be both age differences and individual differences in creativity. Two tasks are to be presented to each child. Be sure to keep a "straight face" during the child's response period and to treat both children the same. Use the following data sheet and data summary sheet for collecting and summarizing data. Answer the questions that follow after completing the interviews of the children.

Child 1:   Age ___ Sex ___
_____

Task one: What are some unusual ways to use a spoon?

Task two: How many objects can you name that are red?

_____

Child 2:   Age ___ Sex ___
_____

Task one: What are some unusual ways to use a spoon?

Task two: How many objects can you name that are red?

_____

Data Summary:
1.   Count the number of responses for each child for each task. Enter into the following table.

Task	Child 1	Child 2
1		
2		

2.   Without looking at the data first, create a scale measuring the originality of the responses and score the responses for originality.

Questions:

1.   Which child had the larger number of responses for task one? For task two?
2.   Which child had more original response for task one? For task two?
3.   Overall, which child seemed to provide more creative responses? To what would you attribute this? How does your finding fit with information on creativity presented in the text? Do you think your particular tasks were appropriate for eliciting creative responding in children? Why or why not?

Essay and Critical Thinking Questions

Comprehension and Application Essay Questions

We recommend that you follow either our guidelines for answering essay and critical thinking questions, or those guidelines provided by your instructor in preparing your response. Your answers to these kinds of questions demonstrate an ability to comprehend and think critically about concepts and topics discussed in this chapter.

1. Discuss examples of political, social, and personal uses of intelligence tests.
2. Explain the four characteristics of concrete operational thought according to Piaget.
3. Discuss at least three findings that challenge Piaget's theory about cognitive development.
4. Explain why and how information processing psychologists distinguish among control processes, metacognitive knowledge, and learner characteristics.
5. What is critical thinking? What are important critical thinking processes? Why is critical thinking important to education and everyday life?
6. Explain the pros and cons of computers in the lives of elementary school children.
7. Provide examples from your own school experiences to explain the knowledge versus process views of intelligence.
8. Summarize the issues and findings entailed in Terman's longitudinal study of gifted children.
9. What is bilingual education? What is known about bilingualism? How successful have bilingual education programs been?
10. What is achievement motivation? Discuss either the parental practices that promote achievement motivation or the helpless and mastery orientations toward achievement.

Critical Thinking Questions

Your answers to the following kinds of questions reflect an ability to apply your critical thinking skills to a novel problem or situation that is *not* specifically discussed in this chapter.

1. This chapter indicates that critical thinking is important to education and everyday life. Apply your knowledge about the scientific base of child development by designing a study to determine the relationship between learning to think critically in school and a happy and successful everyday life: (a) What specific problem or questions do you want to study? (b) What predictions would you make and test in your study? (c) What measures would you use (i.e., observation, interviews, and questionnaires, case studies, standardized tests, physiological research, or a multimeasure, multisource, and multicontext approach) and how would you define each measure clearly and unambiguously? (d) What strategy would you follow—experimental or correlational, and what would be the time span of your inquiry—cross-sectional or longitudinal? (e) What ethical considerations must be addressed before you conduct your study?
2. According to Chapter 1, five issues define the nature of development: (a) biological, cognitive, and social processes, (b) periods or stages, (c) the issue of maturation (nature) versus experience (nurture), (d) the issue of continuity versus discontinuity, and (e) the issue of stability versus change. Indicate your ability to think critically by (a) perusing this chapter for two examples of each of the five defining issues and (b) explaining how and why each of your examples illustrates one of the five defining issues.
3. Chapter 2 presents six different theoretical approaches (i.e., Freudian, cognitive, behavioral and social learning, phenomenological and humanistic, ethological, and ecological), but notes that no single approach explains the complexity of development. Indicate your ability to think critically by interpreting Robert Sternberg's profound interest in intelligence tests in terms of each of the six theoretical approaches.
4. One aspect of thinking critically is to read, listen, and observe carefully, and then ask questions about what is missing from a text, discussion, or situation. For example, your author suggests that developing and using critical thinking skills is a desirable developmental outcome. Indicate your ability to think critically by selecting any topical presentation in the textbook and evaluating it in terms of the author's guidelines for critical thinking.
5. Santrock places several quotations in the margins of this chapter. One by Ralph Waldo Emerson says, "The reward of a thing well done is to have done it." Another by Francis Bacon says, "Knowledge is power." Indicate your ability to think critically by (a) learning about the author and indicating why this individual is eminently quotable (i.e., what was this individual's

contribution to human knowledge and understanding), (b) interpreting and restating the quote in your own terms, and (c) explaining what concept, issue, perspective, or term in this chapter Santrock intended this quote to illuminate. In other words, about what aspect or issue in development does this quote make you pause and think reflectively?

Self-Test B

1. Which of the following is not characteristic of concrete operational thought?
   a. reasoning
   b. reversibility
   c. the ability to classify
   d. animism
2. The concrete operational thinker
   a. can consider all the possible social structures that might evolve.
   b. is able to mentally reverse an action.
   c. is concerned about being the center of everyone's attention.
   d. can form and consider a hypothesis.
3. A child is given the conservation of liquid task. The child argues that the liquid in the two containers is the same because you only poured it, and you could pour it back. This argument is an example of
   a. decentration.
   b. reversibility.
   c. egocentrism.
   d. classification.
4. According to Piaget, one of the important goals for teaching children should be
   a. rewarding correct responses.
   b. eliminating punishment from the schools.
   c. redesigning the curriculum so that children learn more useful content.
   d. learning how to communicate with the child.
5. Which of the following is a criticism that has been leveled at Piaget's work and theory?
   a. The stages of thought turned out to be unitary.
   b. Children cannot be prematurely pushed from one stage to another by training.
   c. Small procedural changes appear to change the child's cognition.
   d. Some cognitive abilities appear much later than Piaget described.

6. A child is given the task of memorizing the states and their capitals. The child repeats over and over, "New York, Albany; California, Sacramento; Oregon, Salem . . ." This is an example of which of the following?
   a. semantic elaboration
   b. organizational processes
   c. imagery
   d. rehearsal
7. What characteristic of the learner contributes the most on memory tasks?
   a. attitudes
   b. motivation
   c. prior knowledge
   d. rehearsal
8. Tarek, age four, knows that when you go to the store, you walk around, pick up something, stand in a line at the front of the store, give a lady some money, the lady gives some money back, and then you leave with the item you picked up. This is an example of
   a. short-term memory.
   b. long-term memory.
   c. a script.
   d. cognitive monitoring.
9. Which of the following major issues discussed in this chapter is most likely to be favorably influenced by hands-on experience with computers?
   a. development of concrete operational thought
   b. intelligence
   c. language development
   d. achievement motivation
10. Thomas has a mental age of seven and a chronological age of 14. What is Thomas's IQ?
    a. 200
    b. 103
    c. 78
    d. 50

11. The WPPSI is designed for use with
    a. adults.
    b. normal school-aged children.
    c. preschool-aged children.
    d. infants.
12. What term is used in Sternberg's theory for creative thinking?
    a. tacit knowledge
    b. componential intelligence
    c. contextual intelligence
    d. experiential intelligence
13. Which theorist is associated with the position that intelligence does not involve a general factor, but includes intelligences such as body knowledge, or social knowledge?
    a. Gardner
    b. Sternberg
    c. Wechsler
    d. Spearman
14. A test that is standardized on one group and then is used to evaluate a group that is substantially different from the original group could be said to have
    a. cultural bias.
    b. validity.
    c. culture-fairness.
    d. test-retest reliability.
15. Tania is given the problem 8 + 9 = ? to solve. This task requires which of the following skills?
    a. memory
    b. divergent thinking
    c. creativity
    d. convergent thinking
16. Perkins devised the snowflake model to help understand
    a. the effects of computers on children.
    b. information processing.
    c. achievement motivation.
    d. creativity.

17. Bilingual education
    a. entails learning two languages in school.
    b. is appropriate only for elementary schools.
    c. produces divergent thinkers.
    d. allows students to learn in their native language.
18. In cartoons you sometimes see the rider of a donkey dangling a carrot in front of the beast. In the language of this chapter, the carrot is a(n)
    a. achievement motivator.
    b. intrinsic motivator.
    c. extrinsic motivator.
    d. all of the answers are correct.
19. Juanita studies hard for a test because she is intrigued by the information and wants to understand it. Bill studies hard for the test because he wants to get a good grade in the course. Juanita's motivation is _____ and Bill's is _____.
    a. intrinsic, intrinsic
    b. intrinsic, extrinsic
    c. extrinsic, intrinsic
    d. extrinsic, extrinsic
20. Children in the United States trail children in Japan in mathematical skills because
    a. Japanese children get more practice in math.
    b. Japanese teachers are better prepared in math than American teachers.
    c. Japanese parents in the study had more education than the American parents.
    d. Japanese children had a higher intellectual level (IQ).

Self-Test Answers
Test B

1. d	4. d	7. c	10. d	13. a	16. d	19. b
2. b	5. c	8. c	11. c	14. a	17. d	20. a
3. b	6. d	9. a	12. d	15. d	18. c	

Objectives

1.0 *Images of Children: Children's Understanding of Injustice*
1.1 Explain how researchers determine whether children understand concepts such as conflict, socioeconomic inequality, and civil rights.

2.0 *Families*
2.1 Describe changes in the amount of time that parents spend with their children during middle childhood as compared to the preschool years.
2.2 Compare and contrast issues that arise between parents and young children, and parents and elementary school children.
2.3 Explain how children's cognitive development during middle childhood may make parenting easier than it was or will be at other times in children's lives.
2.4 List issues related to school and to discipline, and indicate how discipline by parents changes as children develop.
2.5 Define and distinguish between unilateral and coregulated control, and list guidelines for coregulation by parents.
2.6 Explain why more elementary and secondary school children than infants and preschool children live in stepfamilies, describe typical patterns of adjustment to stepfamilies, and identify factors that produce individual differences in children's adjustments to stepfamilies.
2.7 List problems encountered in stepfamilies and strategies for building strong stepfamilies.
2.8 Define latchkey children, describe the problems they face when parents are away, and identify parenting strategies and styles that may diminish or heighten the difficulties faced by latchkey children.

3.0 *Peer Relations*
3.1 Indicate how much time children spend and what they do with their peers during middle childhood.
3.2 Define and distinguish among popular, rejected, and neglected children, indicate the risks faced by children of each category, and discuss factors that predict whether rejected children become delinquents or drop out of school.
3.3 Explain how to train neglected children to interact with their peers.
3.4 Define prosocial behavior, and evaluate the claim that it may be more important to focus on the aggression of rejected children than to improve their social skills.
3.5 Define social cognition, list Dodge's five steps in social cognition, and indicate how social cognition changes during middle childhood.
3.6 Explain how social cognitive skills influence peer relations.
3.7 List and explain the functions of friendship for elementary school children.
3.8 Sketch the development of friendship according to Selman.
3.9 Describe the role that intimacy and similarity play in friendships during middle childhood.

4.0 *Schools*
4.1 List the ways in which schools socialize children, and describe how going to school changes children's lives.
4.2 Explain what it means to say that children's learning is integrated, and compare and contrast the two classrooms described by Katz and Chard.

4.3 Discuss how teachers produce favorable student outcomes according to Gage's research and Erikson's theory.

4.4 Explain the concept of aptitude-treatment interaction (ATI), and contrast low- and high-achievement-oriented students.

4.5 Indicate the evidence for the claim that schools are middle-class institutions that favor middle-class students.

4.6 Indicate evidence for the claim that teachers treat ethnic minority and majority children differently, and discuss the role that teachers' expectations play in the school experience of lower-class and ethnic minority students.

4.7 Evaluate attempts to promote equality in education for ethnic minorities through desegregation.

4.8 Describe a jigsaw classroom, and list pros and cons of its use with socially and ethnically diverse children.

4.9 Indicate the evidence for Ogbu's, Spencer's, and Dornbusch's claims that schools are racist institutions.

4.10 Summarize how James Comer would improve the quality of education for inner-city children.

5.0 *The Self*
5.1 Indicate how elementary school children describe themselves.

5.2 Define and distinguish between social aspects of the self and social comparison in the self understanding of children.

5.3 Define perspective taking and explain how it contributes to self-understanding.

5.4 Define and distinguish among Selman's five stages in the development of perspective taking.

5.5 Distinguish between self-understanding and self-esteem.

5.6 Define and distinguish between the Piers-Harris Scale and Harter's Perceived Competence Scale for Children, and indicate how they represent conceptual and methodological improvements in the study of self-esteem.

5.7 List parenting attributes associated with boys who have high self-esteem, and speculate whether these attributes are the same or different for girls.

5.8 Describe the self-esteem of ethnic minority children compared to White children, and discuss the pros and cons of ethnic pride and high self-esteem.

5.9 Indicate why and how one might modify children's self-esteem.

5.10 Define Erikson's concepts of industry and inferiority, and discuss experiences that promote a sense of industry.

6.0 *Gender*
6.1 Define gender-role stereotypes, list the stereotypes of feminine and masculine individuals, and indicate factors that favor or minimize stereotypical differences between women and men.

6.2 Summarize gender similarities and differences.

6.3 Indicate the gender-role stereotypes for achievement, distinguish between instrumental-achievement and expressive-affiliation, and describe and evaluate programs to develop and support talented young women.

6.4 Define sexism, describe past conceptions of masculinity and femininity, and indicate evidence for claims of sexism today.

6.5 Compare and contrast past concepts of femininity and masculinity with the concept of androgyny.

6.6 Define and distinguish among Bem's gender-role orientations: androgynous, feminine, masculine, and undifferentiated, and discuss the value of each for adapting to different social contexts.

6.7 Compare and contrast gender roles in America, China, Egypt, and Russia, and assess the prospects for equal status between men and women in these countries.

6.8 Indicate Pleck's criticisms of the concept of androgyny, and explain why he favors the term **gender-role transcendence**.

6.9 Indicate and discuss gender-related research findings that have implications for three types of public policy.

6.10 Describe the evidence for the claim that gender-related attitudes and behavior of females and males are similar across different ethnic groups.

7.0 *Moral Development*

7.1 Define and distinguish among the stages and substages of preconventional, conventional, and postconventional levels of moral development, and describe observations that indicate their presence in the moral reasoning of children.

7.2 List and describe three criticisms of Kohlberg's work and theory.

7.3 Define and distinguish between a justice and a care perspective.

7.4 Indicate and explain criticisms of Gilligan's analysis of moral development, summarize Gilligan's reply to her critics, and evaluate whether she has addressed the criticism.

7.5 Define altruism, and describe its developmental path from the preschool through the middle childhood years according to Damon.

7.6 Define and distinguish among equality, merit, and benevolence as bases for altruistic sharing, and describe the evidence that indicate obedience to adult authority is not a primary factor in children's sharing.

Summary

1.0 Images of Children: Children's Understanding of Injustice

In make-believe situations that entail conflict, socioeconomic inequality, and issues of civil-political rights, children recognize injustice and produce interesting solutions.

2.0 Families

Parent-Child Issues. Parents spend less time with children during middle and late childhood. Parents remain important socializing agents and confront new parent-child issues and changing forms of discipline. These issues include modesty, bedtime, temper, fighting, eating, autonomy in dressing, and attention seeking. During the elementary school years, new issues such as chores, self-entertainment, and monitoring arise. In middle and late childhood, school-related matters take on central importance. Discipline changes during elementary school as it become easier to reason with children. There is less physical punishment. Deprivation of privileges, appeals to self-esteem, and guilt are more likely to be used. During these years, there is a coregulation process as control shifts from parent to child.

Societal Changes in Families. Two important changes in families include stepfamilies and latchkey children. Remarriage after divorce occurs often and can result in many different kinds of families with attendant complications and conflicts. Relationships within the stepfamily are often conflict ridden, strained, and distant. Over time, preadolescent boys seem to improve more than do girls in stepfather families. Adolescence is an especially difficult time to enter a stepfamily. William Gladden provides guidelines for parents and children in stepfamilies. Latchkey children, who spend much time alone and undersupervised after school, may be vulnerable to problems.

3.0 Peer Relations

Peer Popularity, Rejection, and Neglect. Peer interaction increases during elementary school. By seven to eleven years of age, children spend 40 percent of their time with peers. Peer popularity in school is related to reinforcing others' behavior, listening carefully to peers' conversations, being happy, showing enthusiasm and concern for others, and having self-confidence without conceit. Neglected children are not actively disliked, but have no friends; rejected children are disliked by their peers. To improve the peer relations of neglected and rejected children, some advocate training in prosocial skills whereas others recommend reducing the children's aggression.

Social Cognition. Social information processing skills can affect peer relations. Intention or motive is attributed to others' behavior, and misinterpretation can lead some children to respond aggressively. Social knowledge or availability of scripts for developing friendships also affect a child's ability to develop peer relations.

Friends. Friendships are specific attachments to a peer and have similarities to parent-infant attachment; however, they often are not permanent. Friendships serve six different functions. Intimacy in friendship develops with age; adolescents know more intimate things about their friends than do elementary school children. Friends are also similar to one another in interests, values, and attitudes.

4.0 Schools

By the time that they graduate from high school, children have spent more than 10,000 hours in school. During middle childhood, the classroom is still the major context for children.

The Transition to School. One concern is that schooling proceeds mainly on the basis of negative feedback to children, a factor that may impair self-esteem. It is desirable to have an integrated elementary school curriculum.

Teachers. Positive teacher traits are enthusiasm, planning ability, poise, adaptability, and awareness of individual differences. Erikson believes that good teachers have the ability to produce a sense of industry rather than inferiority in their students. The characteristics and style of the teacher and student characteristics interact. Some teachers are more comfortable with a flexible curriculum than others. Some students profit more from a highly structured classroom than do other children. This is a reflection of the aptitude-treatment interaction.

Social Class and Ethnicity in Schools. Teachers and administrators are predominantly White and middle class and may have lower expectations for children who are lower class or non-White, an example of institutional racism. Teachers with lower-class origins appear to perceive their lower-class students more positively than do middle-class teachers. The jigsaw classroom may reduce racial tension by reducing class competition and promoting cooperation.

5.0 The Self

The Development of Self-Understanding. In middle and late childhood, the child's ability to understand how he or she is viewed by others increases a dimension of self-concept. Children shift away from defining themselves in terms of external characteristics and move toward defining themselves in terms of internal characteristics. Self-understanding increasingly entails social comparison.

The Role of Perspective Taking in Self-Understanding. Perspective taking is the ability to assume another's point of view and understand his or her thoughts and feelings. Robert Selman described a five-stage theory of perspective taking. At age three, children are egocentric; however, by adolescence they display an in-depth ability to take another's perspective.

Self-Esteem. Whereas self-understanding entails a cognitive representation of oneself, self-esteem that develops during this time encompasses an evaluative or affective self-appraisal. The terms self-concept and self-esteem are sometimes used interchangeably. They can be assessed with Harter's Perceived Competence Scale for Children, a measure with four components. Parental attributes are associated with children's self-esteem. Ethnic pride and self-esteem involves both benefits and costs to individuals. Improving children's self-esteem must involve interventions that get at its sources.

Industry versus Inferiority. Industry versus inferiority is the critical developmental task of middle and late childhood according to Erikson. Children become interested in making and doing, and they master many skills.

6.0 Gender

Gender Stereotypes, Similarities, and Differences. Gender stereotypes reflect broad impressions about males and females. Most stereotypes are so general that they are ambiguous; however, stereotypes are found throughout the world. Research indicates that differences between the sexes have been exaggerated. Moreover, all differences are averages, much overlap exists, and differences may result from biological influences, social influences, or both. There are a number of physical differences between the sexes; however, cognitive differences are either small or nonexistent. Males are more active and aggressive than females, but females better read emotions, more often display helping behavior, and have wider social networks than males. Overall, there are more similarities than differences between females and males.

Gender-Role Classification: Femininity, Masculinity, and Androgyny. In the past, masculine traits were more valued by society, and sexism was widespread. Alternatives to traditional views of masculinity and femininity emerged in the 1970s. The concept of androgyny challenges the view that well-adjusted children behave in sex-appropriate ways and suggests that masculinity and femininity are independent dimensions rather than polar opposites. Gender-role measures now classify individuals as masculine, feminine, androgynous, or undifferentiated. One alternative to androgyny is gender-role transcendence, but it also draws attention from the imbalance of power between males and females.

Gender and Social Policy. Gender-related findings have implications for social policy regarding children. Three notable areas include stereotypes and the media, education, and child care. Changes are needed in the way that media, teachers, parents, and society view gender roles.

Gender and Ethnicity. Many similarities exist between females of different ethnic groups and between males of different ethnic groups, but small differences can be noteworthy. Researchers have begun to focus on the positive aspects of minority females and males, although relatively little research has been conducted in this domain.

7.0 Moral Development

Kohlberg's Theory of Moral Development. Kohlberg's theory of moral development entails three levels of moral reasoning, with two stages at each level. At the preconventional level, a child's reasoning about moral issues is based on expected punishments or rewards based on the standards of other people, parents, or the rules of religion or society. At the postconventional level, the individual reasons about moral issues based upon an internal moral code. Kohlberg found that higher levels of moral reasoning appear with age.

Kohlberg's Critics. Kohlberg's theory has been criticized on several grounds. First, moral thought is not the same as moral behavior, and some argue that Kohlberg has placed too much emphasis on reasoning, and thereby neglected moral action. Thus, moral reasons can be a shelter for moral behavior. Second, Gilligan has criticized Kohlberg for interviewing only males in developing his theory and has suggested also that his view omits a concern for caring relationships as a key ingredient in moral reasoning. Third, Kohlberg's view has been criticized as being too individualistic and culture specific. It is argued that morality should be construed as a matter of the individual's accommodation to the values and requirements of society.

Altruism. Altruism is an unselfish interest in helping someone else. William Damon indicates that altruism develops in an orderly way. Up to three years of age, sharing occurs for nonempathic reasons. At about age four children begin to share as a result of empathic awareness and adult encouragement. Elementary school children begin to show an objective sense of fairness and an understanding of the principle of equality. By middle to late childhood, the principles of merit and benevolence are understood.

Key Terms

1.0 Images of Children: Children's Understanding of Injustice
injustice

2.0 Families
coregulation
stepfamily
latchkey children

3.0 Peer Relations
neglected children
rejected children
prosocial behavior
social cognition
intimacy in friendships
integrated learning
aptitude-treatment interaction (ATI)

4.0 Schools
desegregation
jigsaw classroom
institutional racism
school-governance team

5.0 The Self
self-understanding
social aspects of the self
social comparison
perspective taking

self-esteem
Perceived Competence Scale for Children
industry versus inferiority

6.0 Gender
gender-role stereotypes
instrumental-achievement
expressive-affiliation
feminine
masculine
sexism
androgyny
undifferentiated
gender-role transcendence

7.0 Moral Development
moral reasoning
internalization
preconventional reasoning
punishment and obedience orientation
individualism and purpose
conventional reasoning
interpersonal norms
social system morality
postconventional moral reasoning
community rights versus individual rights
universal ethical principles
justice perspective
care perspective

altruism
equality
merit
benevolence

Guided Review

1.0 *Images of Children: Children's Understanding of Injustice*

1. Phyllis Katz used hypothetical or _____ situations to
demonstrate that elementary school children understand concepts
such as _____, socioeconomic _____ and _____
rights. Children's solutions to these problems often entailed
_____ resources and work, and prohibitions against _____.

pretend

conflict, inequality, civil

sharing, aggression

2.0 *Families*

1. When children move into the elementary school years, parents
spend _____ time with them. The size of the drop in
attention seems to be inversely correlated with _____.

less
education

2. During the early childhood period the focus of parent-child
interactions are issues such as _____, _____ regularities,
_____ of temper, _____, _____, _____ in
dressing, and attention _____. During the elementary school
years, about age _____, new issues emerge such as doing
_____ and the possible _____ for them, _____, and
_____ outside the home.

modesty, bedtime
control, fighting, eating,
autonomy, seeking
seven
chores, payment,
entertainment, monitoring

3. During middle and late childhood _____-related matters
become prominent. Problems in this area are the main reason for
_____ help.

school

clinical

4. In some ways discipline is easier from the elementary years on
because the child can _____. The _____ can understand
the reason for disciplinary rules. The incidence of _____
punishment decreases after the beginning of elementary school.

reason, adolescent
physical

5. The transition between the _____ parental control of the
preschool years and the reduced supervision of the _____
years is a period of what has been called _____. During this
time parents should _____, _____, and _____ the
child, effectively using all direct contacts, and strengthen the
child's self-_____ skills.

strong
adolescent
coregulation
monitor, guide, support

monitoring

6. The way in which parents interact with children and in which
children interact with their parents is influenced by _____
each attaches to the other.

labels

7. Parents of elementary school children have more _____ than
   when the children were younger. The reduction in child rearing
   demands that occurs during _____ and _____ childhood
   may be accompanied by the mother's decision to return to a
   _____.

experience

middle, late

career

8. Two prominent societal changes in families concern _____ and
   _____ children.

stepfamilies
latchkey

9. In comparison to studies of the effects of divorce, studies of
   _____ are relatively _____.

stepfamilies, rare

10. Entering a stepfamily often produces _____ problems for
    _____ and _____.

behavior
girls, boys

11. Relationships with the _____ are more strained than those
    with the _____ parent. Relationships with the stepfather tend
    to be _____.

stepparent
biological
distant

12. William _____ has identified frequently encountered _____
    in stepfamilies, and suggested _____ for building a strong,
    positive stepfamily.

Gladden, problems
strategies

13. Children who return to an empty home after school are called
    _____ children. Elkind worries that latchkey children get too
    much _____. They are more likely to get into _____;
    however, the degree of developmental risk to latchkey children is
    largely _____.

latchkey
responsibility, trouble

undetermined

3.0 Peer Relations

1. The proportion of peer interaction at age 2 is ___%, by 4 it
   was ___%, and between 4 and 11 it increases to more than
   _____%. Boys, more than girls, prefer _____ sports but both
   list _____ _____, _____ _____, and _____
   as important. Groups tend to be _____-sexed.

10
20
40, team
general play, going
places, socializing, same

2. Giving _____ enhances popularity in children as does _____
   to others, showing _____, being _____, and self-
   _____.

reinforcement, listening
enthusiasm, yourself
confidence

3. _____ children have few friends, but _____ children are
   more likely to be _____, _____, and overtly disliked by
   peers.

Neglected, rejected
disruptive, aggressive

4. Both _____ and _____ children _____ _____
   trained to interact with their peers more effectively. One issue is
   whether neglected children should focus on increasing their
   _____ skills or decreasing their _____ and _____
   behavior.

neglected, rejected, can
be

prosocial, aggressive,
disruptive

322

5. Children's _____ cognitions about their peers become increasingly important for understanding peer relations.

social

6. Dodge's analysis of children's understanding of social situations reflects an _____ _____ approach. According to Dodge, inappropriate aggression is frequently the result of a deficit in _____ detection. The work of Dodge can be interpreted as showing that aggressive children incorrectly attribute hostile _____ to peers.

information-processing

intention

intentions

7. Inability to interact appropriately with peers may mean that a child does not have a _____ for forming a friendship. Further, it has been found that boys without peer adjustment problems were superior at a number of _____, _____ skills than maladjusted boys.

script

social, cognitive

8. Friendship serves six different functions that include companionship, _____, physical support, _____ _____, social comparison, and _____ and _____. Friendships begin to be prevalent during _____ and _____ childhood.

stimulation, ego support
intimacy, affection
middle, late

9. Of the two most important components of a friendship, one is _____, and the other is that friends tend to have _____ physical characteristics and _____.

intimacy, similar
attitudes

4.0 Schools

1. The 13 years of schooling that the typical American child receives amounts to over _____ hours of classroom time. In school, there are _____ that define and limit behavior.

10,000
rules

2. Early experiences in school expose the child to primarily _____ feedback. Consequently, children's _____ _____ is lower in the later part of elementary school than early in elementary school.

negative
self-esteem

3. Teachers tend to segregate the curriculum and teach one topic at a time rather than _____ experiences like they appear in the real world.

integrate

4. _____ symbolize authority, establish the classroom climate, and influence the interaction between children.

Teachers

5. Teacher traits associated with _____ student outcomes include enthusiasm, ability to plan, poise, adaptability, warmth, and a willingness to accept individual differences.

positive

6. Erikson believes that good teachers should be able to produce a sense of _____ instead of _____ in their students. They recognize _____ and help children _____ _____ about themselves, thus building self-esteem.

industry, inferiority
effort, feel good

7. Recently, educational experts such as Cronbach and Snow have argued that teaching effectiveness should be studied by looking at the aptitude by treatment _____. In an aptitude-treatment interaction, _____ refers to potential. Treatment refers to the _____. Students with high achievement orientation do well in a _____ classroom whereas those with low achievement orientation do better in a _____ classroom.

interaction
aptitude
technique
flexible
structured

8. Schools have a _____-class bias. Middle-class teachers have _____ expectations for children from low-income families than for middle-class families. It appears that teachers with _____ _____ backgrounds might make better teachers in low-income schools.

middle
lower
lower-class

9. In addition to _____ class, another variable that influences children's difficulties in school is _____ background. For example, teachers expect and _____ achievement more often for _____ and _____ students.

social
ethnic
reward
White, Black

10. _____ by itself is not sufficient to promote understanding between different races.

Desegregation

11. The _____ classroom was one attempt to produce cooperation in learning among children in a multiracial classroom.

jigsaw

12. John _____ argues that ethnic minority children have _____ educational opportunities, teachers who have _____ expectations for students, and encounter _____ stereotypes.

Ogbu
inferior, low
negative

13. According to Margaret Beale Spencer, schools manifest _____ racism. James Comer's solution to the problem of _____ minority students involves formation of a _____ _____ team.

institutional
ethnic
school-governance

5.0 The Self

1. In middle and late childhood, self-understanding shifts from defining oneself using _____ characteristics to defining oneself using _____ characteristics.

external
internal

2. Definitions of self in the middle and late childhood period are based on psychological as well as _____ characteristics.

social

3. When children define themselves as Girl Scouts or Boy Scouts, they are making reference to _____ groups in the self-description.

social

4. Children over the age of seven often use _____ _____ in the way that they describe themselves.

social comparisons

5. _____ _____ is the ability to assume another person's perspective and understand his or her thoughts or feelings.

    Perspective taking

6. Six- to eight-year-olds are usually in the social-informational state of perspective taking according to Robert _____.

    Selman

7. Children in the mutual perspective taking stage are usually between the ages of ___ and ___.

    10, 12

8. Children's _____ _____ skills can increase their self-understanding, improve their peer group states, and increase the quality of their friendships.

    perspective taking

9. _____ _____ is the evaluative and affective dimension of self-concept.

    Self-esteem

10. _____ _____ is also called self-worth or self-image.

    Self-esteem

11. Recently theorists have recognized that self-esteem may be _____ specific rather than a _____ judgment about the self.

    domain, global

12. The _____ _____ Scale has been used to measure a child's overall self-esteem.

    Piers-Harris

13. Harter's _____ _____ _____ _____ _____ is a measure that consists of four components of self-esteem.

    Perceived Competence Scale for Children

14. The four domains measured in Harter's Perceived Competence Scale for Children are _____ _____, physical competence, _____ competence, and social competence.

    self-worth cognitive

15. Parents who express affection, show concern about their children's problems, get along with each other, set clear and fair rules, and allow freedom within limits have children with _____ self-esteem.

    high

16. Recent research comparing minority children with nonminority children has shown that the _____ children have higher self-esteem.

    minority

17. Susan Harter believes that self-esteem is best strengthened in children by intervening at the level of its _____.

    causes

18. The psychosocial crisis in Erikson's theory during this period is _____ versus _____. _____ becomes a very important setting for resolving this issue.

    industry, inferiority, School

6.0 Gender

1. Broad categories that convey impressions about males and females
    are termed _____ _____ stereotypes. Such stereotypes
    are both _____ and subject to _____ change.

    gender-role
    ambiguous, cultural

2. Although gender-role _____ are common throughout the
    world, it is important to focus on genuine gender _____ and
    _____.

    stereotypes
    similarities
    differences

3. Gender differences are based on _____, and there is often
    much overlap between _____ and _____ even though
    there is an _____ difference between them.

    averages
    males, females
    average

4. According to a classic study by Maccoby and Jacklin, females are
    more _____ than males, and males are more _____,
    _____, and better at _____ _____ skills than females;
    however, recent evidence suggests that the _____ differences
    between females and males is decreasing.

    verbal, mathematical
    aggressive, visual-spatial
    verbal

5. Nonoverlapping gender differences exist for areas of _____;
    however, many measures _____ _____ reveal gender
    differences on measures of achievement-related behaviors.

    achievement
    do not

6. _____ results in the negative treatment of individuals on the
    basis of sex.

    Sexism

7. An instrumental orientation is a _____ gender-role orientation
    that focuses on the attainment of goals and emphasizes the
    person's accomplishments.

    masculine

8. An _____ orientation is a feminine gender-role orientation
    that emphasizes the facilitation of social interaction,
    interdependence, and relationships.

    expressive

9. _____ _____ is a masculine gender-role orientation that
    includes the components of leadership, dominance, independence,
    competitiveness, and individualism.

    Self-assertion

10. Integration is a _____ gender-role orientation that includes
    the components of sympathy, affection, and understanding.

    feminine

11. An _____ individual has both self-assertive and integrative
    characteristics.

    androgynous

12. Sandra _____ classified gender-orientation into four
    categories: masculine, _____, androgynous, and _____.

    Bem
    feminine, undifferentiated

13. When a child has neither masculine nor feminine characteristics,
    the child is said to have an _____ gender-role orientation.

    undifferentiated

14. Children who are _____ are the least competent. They are
    the least socially responsible, they have the least self-control, and
    they receive the poorest grades in school.

    undifferentiated

15. Joe _____ argues that the concept of _____ should be
    replaced by the concept of _____ _____ _____
    —the belief that people should be judged as individuals.

    Pleck, androgyny
    gender-role
    transcendence

16. Gender-related research with important implications for social
    policy concern gender-role stereotypes and the _____,
    _____, and _____ _____.

    media, education
    child care

17. Studies of gender and ethnicity require considering _____
    separately from _____.

    females
    males

18. Ethnic minority females have experienced _____ and
    developed _____ strategies in the face of adversity. This
    finding is _____ for ethnic minority males.

    discrimination
    coping
    true

7.0 Moral Development

1. Kohlberg stressed that moral development is based on moral
   _____ and unfolds in _____. He used the _____ for
   much of his research into the moral reasoning of children, and
   based much of his theory on the key concept of _____.

   reasoning, stages
   interview
   internalization

2. In his view, a child without internalized moral values who bases
   moral judgments on consequences is operating at the _____
   level. One who has internalized an authority's standards of moral
   behavior is operating at the _____ level. One who develops a
   personal moral code after exploring alternative moral options is
   operating at the _____ level.

   preconventional

   conventional

   postconventional

3. In the first stage of Kohlberg's theory, moral judgments are based
   on the presence or absence of _____. In the second stage
   judgments are based on the presence or absence of _____. In
   the third stage judgments are based on other people's _____
   such as those of the _____; in the fourth stage, they are
   based on _____. A person operating at the fifth and sixth
   stages of moral reasoning based judgments on a _____ moral
   code accepted by the community or one that is _____.

   punishment
   rewards
   standards
   parents
   law
   personal
   individualized

4. Kohlberg has found that advancement through the stages is related
   to _____ and occurs in a particular _____.

   age, sequence

5. Some critics of Kohlberg's work have argued that he did not pay
   enough attention to moral _____. Quite simply, moral
   _____ does not always ensure moral _____.

   behavior
   reasoning, behavior

6. Gilligan has offered a second criticism of Kohlberg's theory. She argued that the Kohlberg data are very _____ _____.   sex-biased
Gilligan proposed that there are two perspectives in moral reasoning. The _____ perspective focuses on the rights of the   justice
individual, whereas the other view of moral reasoning is the _____ perspective.   care

7. A third criticism is that moral development is more _____ _____ than Kohlberg's approach suggests.   culture-specific

8. _____ is an unselfish interest in helping someone.   Altruism

9. At about four years of age _____ awareness along with parental encouragement results in more frequent sharing behavior.   empathetic

10. _____ is the first principle of sharing that elementary school-aged children use regularly.   Equality

11. By the mid- to late elementary school years, children also use the principles of _____ and _____.   merit, benevolence

12. _____ means giving extra rewards for hard work and _____ means giving special considerations for individuals in disadvantaged conditions.   Merit, benevolence

Key Terms Matching Exercise

1.0 Images of Children: Children's Understanding of Injustice (Term 1)
2.0 Families (Terms 2–4)
3.0 Peer Relations (Terms 5–11)
4.0 Schools (Terms 12–15)
5.0 The Self (Terms 16–22)
6.0 Gender (Terms 23–31)
7.0 Moral Development (Terms 32–48)

---

1. injustice

a. A family composed of at least one parent who had previously been in another marital relationship

2. coregulation

b. Children who return to an empty home after school, and spend time unsupervised by parents or other authority figures

3. step-family
4. latchkey children
5. neglected children

c. Children who are ignored by their peers
d. Children who are disliked by their peers
e. A violation of what is right or another person's rights

6. rejected children

f. Gradual transfer of control from parent to child, a transition period

7. prosocial behavior
   a. Socially desirable behaviors such as sharing, helping, and cooperating

8. social cognition
   b. Idea that the outcome of a particular educational intervention might depend on the level of the students and vice versa

9. intimacy in friendships
   c. The elimination of racial separation in public settings such as schools

10. integrated learning
   d. An education process that minimizes tightly scheduled and discrete time blocks devoted to a single aspect of a school's curriculum

11. aptitude-treatment interaction (ATI)
   e. Knowledge about the social world and one's interpersonal relationship

12. desegregation
   f. Self-disclosure and the sharing of private thoughts

---

13. jigsaw classroom
   a. The basic component of an educational intervention program by James Comer that makes up a team of individuals who have a say in how a school is run

14. institutional racism
   b. Distinguishing and comparing oneself to others in a similar social milieu

15. school-governance team
   c. Incorporation of references to social groups in one's self-descriptions

16. self-understanding
   d. Discrimination of prejudice based on race that is supported, or at least not discouraged, by institutions such as schools

17. social aspects of the self
   e. Procedure designed to make learning a cooperative effort among children

18. social comparison
   f. The substance and content of a child's self-conception; the cognitive representation of self

---

19. perspective taking
   a. Erikson's fourth stage of development occurs approximately during the elementary school years; children's initiative brings them in contact with a wealth of new experiences; moving toward middle and late childhood, children direct their energy toward mastering knowledge and intellectual skills

20. self-esteem
   b. Broad categories that reflect our impressions and beliefs about males and females

21. Perceived Competence Scale for Children
   c. Describes masculinity as concerned with attainment of goals and an emphasis on the individual's accomplishments

22. industry versus inferiority
   d. One is able to assume another persons perspective and understand his or her thoughts and feelings

23.	gender role stereotypes	e.	Value that children place on themselves and their behavior
24.	instrumental-achievement	f.	Measure of self-concept emphasizing the assessment of the child's sense of competence across different domains

---

25.	expressive-affiliation	a.	Individual whose psychological makeup includes both masculine and feminine aspects of behavior
26.	feminine	b.	Discrimination based on sex, especially against women
27.	masculine	c.	Possessing the characteristics generally attributed to a woman
28.	sexism	d.	Describes femininity as concerned with facilitating social interaction, interdependence, and relationships
29.	androgyny	e.	Individual who does not perceive himself or herself as either masculine or feminine
30.	undifferentiated	f.	Possessing the characteristics generally attributed to a man

---

31.	gender-role transcendence	a.	The belief that a person's competence should be judged on an individual basis rather than on the basis of gender orientation
32.	moral reasoning	b.	An aspect of moral development that concerns children's knowledge and understanding of moral principles and moral issues
33.	internalization	c.	In Kohlberg's theory of moral development, the child who shows no internalization of moral values
34.	preconventional reasoning	d.	Moral thinking based on punishment
35.	punishment and obedience orientation	e.	Moral thinking based on rewards and self-interest
36.	individualism and purpose	f.	Incorporation of both knowledge and cultural tools of thinking

---

37.	conventional reasoning	a.	Moral judgments based on trust, caring, and loyalty to others
38.	interpersonal norms	b.	In Kohlberg's theory; characterized by morality that is internalized and based on the development of a moral code derived from an active exploration of alternative moral courses and options
39.	social system morality	c.	Moral judgments based on recognition that laws are important for society but recognition that the laws can be changed through consensus

40. postconventional moral reasoning

    d. Moral standard based on human rights that apply equally to all people

41. community versus individual rights

    e. Moral reasoning in which the individual abides by standards that have been internalized, but are dictated by others

42. universal ethical principles

    f. Moral judgments based on law, justice, and duty, with no recognition that laws can be changed

---

43. justice perspective

    a. Being treated the same as everyone else and having the same status or privileges

44. care perspective

    b. In Gilligan's theory of moral reasoning, people are viewed in terms of their involvement with other people; the focus is on their communication with others

    c. In Gilligan's view of moral reasoning, people are differentiated from other people and seen as standing alone; the focus is on the rights of the individual

45. altruism

46. equality

    d. A tendency toward doing charitable and kind acts, especially toward disadvantaged individuals

47. merit

    e. To earn or deserve something

48. benevolence

    f. Performance of behaviors designed to help another individual without regard to potential external reward

Key Terms Matching Exercise
Answer Key

1. e	8. e	15. a	22. a	29. a	36. e	43. c
2. f	9. f	16. f	23. b	30. e	37. e	44. b
3. a	10. d	17. c	24. c	31. a	38. a	45. f
4. b	11. b	18. b	25. d	32. b	39. f	46. a
5. c	12. c	19. d	26. c	33. f	40. b	47. e
6. d	13. e	20. e	27. f	34. c	41. c	48. d
7. a	14. d	21. f	28. b	35. d	42. d	

1. Which of the following statements about the relationship between step-children and step-parents is true?
   a. The relationship between stepfather and child is distant and somewhat unpleasant.
   b. The relationship between stepmother and child is distant and somewhat unpleasant.
   c. The relationship between the child and the stepfather involves an extensive but abrasive set of interactions.
   d. The relationship between the child and stepmother is warm and affectionate.

2. Which of the following is not a potential problem for latchkey children?
   a. They may get into trouble without limits and parental involvement during latchkey hours.
   b. They may be forced to grow up too fast.
   c. They may be required to take on responsibilities before they are ready for them.
   d. They may thrive on the responsibility and become more mature and independent.

3. Which of the following has not been associated with peer popularity?
   a. using reinforcement
   b. showing conceit
   c. showing enthusiasm
   d. showing concern for others

4. Deficiencies in which of the following information-processing strategies can lead to inappropriate aggression in some boys?
   a. interpretation of social cues
   b. selecting an optimal response
   c. response search
   d. enactment

5. Friendships differ from the parent-child bond in what way?
   a. parents are a source of security in upsetting circumstances, friends are not.
   b. Separation from parents arouses anxiety, separation from friends does not.
   c. The parent-child bond is permanent, friendships are not.
   d. Children develop a sense of trust in their parents, not in their friends.

6. At what age do children become capable of autonomous interdependent friendships?
   a. early childhood
   b. early adolescence
   c. late childhood
   d. late adolescence

7. In evaluating academic self-image of children, it was observed that in first grade
   a. girls rate themselves as less smart than sixth-grade girls.
   b. boys rate themselves as less smart than sixth-grade boys.
   c. girls are more concerned with achievement than boys.
   d. boys are more concerned with achievement than girls.

8. Which of the following is an example of an integrated approach to the curriculum?
   a. Nabil reads every day from 10:00 to 10:30 and then does math.
   b. Mark goes to the library once a week to check out a book.
   c. Carmen writes and reads in all subject areas.
   d. Mary writes for only 20 minutes a day when she and her classmates work on penmanship.

9. All of the following traits in a teacher relate positively to the student's intellectual development except
   a. impulsiveness.
   b. enthusiasm.
   c. adaptability.
   d. awareness of individual differences.

10. Individual differences between children and the kinds of classroom experiences that they can profit from is termed
    a. appropriate environment.
    b. high aptitude.
    c. aptitude-treatment interaction.
    d. expressive orientation.
11. A classroom where children are dependent on each other for their learning is called
    a. flexible classroom.
    b. open classroom.
    c. traditional classroom.
    d. jigsaw classroom.
12. The Perceived Competence Scale for Children was developed by
    a. Erikson.
    b. Harter.
    c. Skinner.
    d. Maccoby.
13. According to Erikson, the developmental task of the elementary school years is
    a. trust versus mistrust.
    b. identity versus identity confusion.
    c. industry versus inferiority.
    d. social competence.
14. Which of the following is a way in which males differ from females, according to research evaluated by Maccoby and Jacklin?
    a. Males are more verbal.
    b. Males are more competitive.
    c. Males are more dominant.
    d. Males are more mathematical.
15. Jimmy is a sympathetic, warm, affectionate, analytical, forceful, little boy. His sex role orientation is best labeled as
    a. masculine.
    b. feminine.
    c. undifferentiated.
    d. androgynous.

16. Self-assertion is to _____ as masculinity is to femininity.
    a. integration
    b. expressive orientation
    c. instrumental orientation
    d. nurturing
17. Kohlberg's theory of moral development concentrates primarily on which of the following?
    a. moral feeling
    b. moral reasoning
    c. moral behavior
    d. moral action
18. If a child is presented with a moral dilemma and responds by arguing that the person should choose a course of action that avoids punishment, which of Kohlberg's stages would be represented?
    a. Stage 1
    b. Stage 2
    c. Stage 3
    d. Stage 4
19. If a child is presented with a moral dilemma, and responds by arguing that the person should choose a course of action so that people will not think badly of them, which of Kohlberg's stages would be represented?
    a. Stage 1
    b. Stage 2
    c. Stage 3
    d. Stage 4
20. Children share things for all of the following reasons except that they
    a. feel obligated to share.
    b. are concerned for others.
    c. are obeying adult instructions.
    d. want to have their own way.

Self-Test Answers
Test A

1. a	4. a	7. d	10. c	13. c	16. a	19. c
2. d	5. c	8. c	11. d	14. d	17. b	20. c
3. b	6. b	9. a	12. b	15. d	18. a	

Critical Thinking Exercises

Exercise 1

The study of cognitive development and intelligence has provided a model for studying other aspects of psychological development. For example, researchers have applied the methods and theories originally devised to study children's minds to aspects of children's personality and social development. This exercise requires you to identify the approach to intelligence that seems to have been most influential in research on each topic below. Present reasons for each of your choices, and also indicate which approach appears to have been most widely used in the works on personality and social development presented by your author. **Note that this exercise differs from previous ones in that you do not have to identify a best answer; to the contrary, you should develop arguments for each item!**

A. aptitude-treatment interaction
B. social cognition
C. Perceived Competence Scale for Children
D. masculinity, femininity, and androgyny
E. moral development

Exercise 2

Review the brief description of Bronfenbrenner's ecological model of sociocultural influences that appears in Chapter 2. When you have done so, determine which of the following findings reported in Chapter 14 is correctly matched with one of the systems described in the model. **Circle the letter of the best answer and explain why it is the best answer and why each other answer is not as good.**

A. Microsystem: Children spend less time with their parents because they are spending more time with their peers.
B. Mesosystem: Children from middle-class families enjoy school more than children from lower-class families.
C. Chronosystem: The gender roles that children are encouraged to adopt today are more diverse than those prevalent a decade ago.
D. Macrosystem: Peers influence children's development by accepting, neglecting, or rejecting each other.
E. Exosystem: Adolescents who have stepparents are more likely to experience problems in close relationships outside the family.

Exercise 3

In this chapter Santrock describes attempts to define and measure gender roles. Which of the following statements constitutes an assumption made by gender role researchers, rather than an inference or an observation? **Circle the letter of the best answer and explain why it is the best answer and why each other answer is not as good.**

A. Girls should grow up to be feminine and boys should grow up to be masculine.
B. Gender-role stereotypes are more harmful to females than to males.
C. Femininity and masculinity are separable aspects of personality that have their own unique characteristics.
D. Androgynous individuals are more flexible and mentally healthy than masculine or feminine individuals.
E. Rather than merge gender roles, females and males should transcend gender-role characteristics.

Research Project 1 Children's Attitudes Towards School

After acquiring parental approval and a signed informed consent form, ask three students (one in first or second grade, one in third or fourth grade, and one in fifth or sixth grade) about their attitudes towards school. Then answer the questions that follow.

Questions	Child 1 Grade __ Sex__Age __	Child 2 Grade __ Sex__Age __	Child 3 Grade __ Sex__Age__
Do you like school?	Y/N	Y/N	Y/N
Do you like your teachers?	Y/N	Y/N	Y/M
Do you like the other students?	Y/N	Y/N	Y/N
Compared to other students, how well do you do in school? (better, average, worse)	B/A/W	B/A/W	B/A/W
How do you do in each of the following subjects? (Good, Fair, Poor)			
Math	G/F/P	G/F/P	G/F/P
Reading	G/F/P	G/F/P	G/F/P
Art	G/F/P	G/F/P	G/F/P
Physical education	G/F/P	G/F/P	G/F/P
Social Studies	G/F/P	G/F/P	G/F/P
Music	G/F/P	G/F/P	G/F/P
Spelling	G/F/P	G/F/P	G/F/P
Writing	G/F/P	G/F/P	G/F/P
What do you like best about school?			
What do you like least about school?			
Do you expect to go to college or other school after you get out of high school?			

Questions

1. In general, what are the attitudes toward school? Do students view themselves as successful students?
2. Do attitudes change as students get older?
3. What subjects are rated highest?

Research Project 2 Gender Roles and Television

In this project, you will be required to evaluate three prime-time television shows for gender role stereotyping. Pick three shows between 8:00 and 9:00 EST that children might watch. For each show record the following information: (1) number of male and female main characters; (2) occupations of main male and female characters; (3) thematic connections between males and females (e.g., female in distress and male as rescuer); (4) personality characteristics of one male and one female from the show (use the Bem androgyny scale to determine masculinity, femininity, or androgyny). Use the following data sheet to record information. Then answer the questions that follow.

Program _____ Male _____ Female _____

Number

Occupations

Connections

Sex Type

___

Program _____ Male _____ Female _____

Number

Occupations

Connections

Sex Type

___

Program _____ Male _____ Female_____

Number

Occupations

Connections

Sex Type

___

Questions:

1. In the shows you watched, were more main roles taken by males or females? What kinds of occupations did the males have? What kinds of occupations did the females have? Were there status differences in the occupations of the males and females? What were they?
2. What kinds of themes connected the males and females in the television programs you watched? Were the themes stereotyped for male-female relationships?
3. What were the sex-typed categories of the males portrayed on television: (masculine, cross-sexed, androgynous)?
4. What were the sex-typed categories of the females portrayed on television: (feminine, cross-sexed, androgynous)?
5. What do you think these models are teaching children about what it means to be a male or a female in our society? Do you think these models are a fair representation of the way women and men act in the real world?

Research Project 3 Gender and Age Roles in Magazine Advertisements

This project explores gender and age stereotypes in magazines. You are to look at one widely circulated magazine and evaluate how ads depict males and females of various ages. Evaluate physical appearance, personality, and behaviors. Use this chart to help you organize your impressions, and then answer the questions that follow it.

Magazine Title _____ Issue date _____ Number of Ads _____

INFANTS: **BOYS**   **GIRLS**

physical appearance:

body message:

clothes:

facial expressions:

personality:

intelligence:

activities:

verbal comments:

sexuality:

other:

YOUNG CHILDREN: **BOYS**   **GIRLS**

physical appearance:

body message:

clothes:

facial expressions:

personality:

intelligence:

activities:

verbal comments:

sexuality:

other:

OLDER CHILDREN: **BOYS**   **GIRLS**

physical appearance:

body message:

clothes:

facial expressions:

personality:

intelligence:

activities:

verbal comments:

sexuality:

other:

ADOLESCENTS: **BOYS**   **GIRLS**

physical appearance:

body message:

clothes:

facial expressions:

personality:

intelligence:

activities:

verbal comments:

sexuality:

other:

YOUNG ADULTS: **MEN**   **WOMEN**

physical appearance:

body message:

clothes:

facial expressions:

personality:

intelligence:

activities:

verbal comments:

sexuality:

other:

MIDDLE ADULTS: **MEN**   **WOMEN**

physical appearance:

body message:

clothes:

facial expressions:

personality:

intelligence:

activities:

verbal comments:

sexuality:

other:

ELDERLY ADULTS: **MEN**   **WOMEN**

physical appearance:

body message:

clothes:

facial expressions:

personality:

intelligence:

activities:

verbal comments:

sexuality:

other:

___

Tally up the number of persons in each age group that appeared in ads; determine what percentage of ads had each age group depicted:

	Total No. Persons in Ads	*% of Ads with this Age Group*
INFANTS		
YOUNG CHILDREN		
OLDER CHILDREN		
ADOLESCENTS		
YOUNG ADULTS		
MIDDLE ADULTS		
ELDERLY ADULTS		

Questions:

1. Are all age groups represented in advertisements? Who is underrepresented and overrepresented? Why?

Essay and Critical Thinking Questions

Comprehension and Application Essay Questions

We recommend that you follow either our guidelines for answering essay and critical thinking questions, or those guidelines provided by your instructor in preparing your response. Your answers to these kinds of questions demonstrate an ability to comprehend and think critically about concepts and topics discussed in this chapter.

1. Explain how researchers determine whether children understand concepts such as conflict, socioeconomic inequality, and civil rights.
2. Explain the kinds of school and discipline problems that parents confront with their children, and how parents change their disciplinary practices as children grow older.
3. What are latchkey children? What kinds of problems do they face when parents are absent? How can parents diminish or heighten the difficulties faced by latchkey children?
4. Compare and contrast popular, rejected, and neglected children.
5. Explain how children can learn to be more popular with their peers.
6. Explain how entering school changes children's lives.
7. Explain what is meant by saying that schools are middle-class institutions that favor middle-class students.
8. Compare and contrast the self-esteem of ethnic majority and minority children. Also discuss the pros and cons of ethnic pride and high self-esteem.
9. Explain Bem's four gender-role orientations, and discuss the value of each for adapting to different social contexts.
10. Explain Kohlberg's theory of moral development, and indicate three criticisms of his approach.

Critical Thinking Questions

Your answers to the following kinds of questions reflect an ability to apply your critical thinking skills to a novel problem or situation that is *not* specifically discussed in this chapter.

1. This chapter devotes much attention to gender roles. Apply your knowledge about the scientific base of child development by designing a study to determine the developmental outcomes for individuals who enter occupations that are gender "inappropriate": (a) What specific problem or questions do you want to study? (b) What predictions would you make and test in your study? (c) What measures would you use (i.e., observation, interviews, and questionnaires, case studies, standardized tests, physiological research, or a multimeasure, multisource, and multicontext approach) and how would you define each measure clearly and unambiguously? (d) What strategy would you follow—experimental or correlational, and what would be the time span of your inquiry—cross-sectional or longitudinal? (e) What ethical considerations must be addressed before you conduct your study?
2. According to Chapter 1, five issues define the nature of development: (a) biological, cognitive, and social processes, (b) periods or stages, (c) the issue of maturation (nature) versus experience (nurture), (d) the issue of continuity versus discontinuity, and (e) the issue of stability versus change. Indicate your ability to think critically by (a) perusing this chapter "Social Development in Middle and Late Childhood" for two examples of each of the five defining issues, and (b) explaining how and why each of your examples illustrates one of the five defining issues.
3. Chapter 2 presents six different theoretical approaches (i.e., Freudian, cognitive, behavioral and social learning, phenomenological and humanistic, ethological, and ecological), but notes that no single approach explains the complexity of development. Indicate your ability to think critically by analyzing the concept of self in terms of each of the six different theoretical approaches.
4. One aspect of thinking critically is to read, listen, and observe carefully and then ask questions about what is missing from a text, discussion, or situation. Alternatively, critical thinking also involves asking why the material is included in the text. Indicate your ability to think critically by (a) explaining why Santrock devotes more space to gender issues in this chapter than to any other issue in any other chapter even though he does not relate these issues to themes of

development during middle and late childhood, and (b) justifying your recommendation about where, and how extensively, these topics ought to be discussed.

5. Santrock places several quotations in the margins of this chapter. One by Ralph Waldo Emerson says, "A man's growth is seen the successive choirs of his friends," and another by William Lloyd Garrison says, "My country is the world; My countrymen are mankind." Indicate your ability to think critically by selecting one of the quotes and (a) learning about the author and indicating why this individual is eminently quotable (i.e., what was the individual's contribution to human knowledge and understanding), (b) interpreting and restating the quote in your own terms, and (c) explaining what concept, issue, perspective, or term in this chapter that Santrock intended this quote to illuminate. In other words, about what aspect or issue in development does this quote make you pause and think reflectively?

Self-Test B

1. How do researchers learn about children's understanding of concepts such as conflict and civil rights?
   a. Researchers ask the parents about their children's understanding of such concepts.
   b. Researchers ask children to complete questionnaires.
   c. Researchers pose problems to children and ask them to devise solutions.
   d. Researchers watch how children interact while in the classroom and on they playground.

2. Discipline used by parents of elementary school-age children is least likely to contain which of the following?
   a. deprivation of privileges
   b. physical punishment
   c. comments designed to increase the child's sense of guilt
   d. reasoning with the child

3. The process of coregulation, and the major shift to autonomy usually occurs about age
   a. 7 years.
   b. 9 years.
   c. 12 years.
   d. 15 years.

4. In a step-parent family, the child's relationship with the stepmother is frequently
   a. the same as their relationship with the step-father.
   b. warm and accepting.
   c. distant and unpleasant.
   d. extensive but abrasive.

5. Wally comes home from school every day and takes care of himself until his parents come home from work at six. During the summer, he is home alone all day. This is a description of
   a. an abandoned child.
   b. permissive-indulgent parenting.
   c. an insecure attachment.
   d. a latchkey child.

6. Which of the following activities is least characteristic of girls' play with peers?
   a. team sports
   b. socializing
   c. going places
   d. general play

7. Children who are actively disliked by their peers are termed
   a. neglected children.
   b. rejected children.
   c. latchkey children.
   d. withdrawn children.

8. Knowledge of a script that will allow one to become friends with another is an aspect of
   a. social information processing.
   b. social knowledge.
   c. perspective taking skills.
   d. communicative skills.

9. Friends are often similar in all of the following except
   a. age.
   b. sex.
   c. attitudes toward school.
   d. ability.

10. By the time they graduate, children will have spent about how many hours in school?
    a. 7,000
    b. 9,000
    c. 10,000
    d. 20,000
11. According to research, the type of feedback most frequently observed in the classroom during the early grades is
    a. negative feedback for both boys and girls.
    b. negative feedback for girls, positive feedback for boys.
    c. negative feedback for boys, positive feedback for girls.
    d. positive feedback for both boys and girls.
12. Which of the following adjectives is likely to be used by a lower-class teacher to characterize a lower-class student?
    a. lazy
    b. rebellious
    c. happy
    d. fun-loving
13. An activity that combines the study of fractions with the study of scale models illustrates the concept of
    a. aptitude-treatment interaction.
    b. a jigsaw classroom.
    c. integrated learning.
    d. equality in education.
14. Do children in middle childhood describe themselves by saying things such as "I play sports?"
    a. Yes, because children this age often describe themselves by mentioning external characteristics.
    b. No, because children this age often describe themselves by mentioning internal characteristics.
    c. Yes, because self-descriptions indicate evidence of self-understanding.
    d. No, because they are unable to make social comparisons.

15. The ability to understand another person's thoughts and feelings best describes
    a. self-understanding.
    b. perspective-taking.
    c. social comparison.
    d. gender role orientation.
16. Nadia is a sensitive, compassionate, individualistic, and self-reliant little girl. Her sex-role orientation is best labeled as
    a. masculine.
    b. feminine.
    c. undifferentiated.
    d. androgynous.
17. An androgynous individual is one whose psychological makeup
    a. includes both masculine and feminine aspects.
    b. is masculine if the individual is female.
    c. is feminine if the individual is male.
    d. is low on both masculine and feminine aspects.
18. Reasoning about a moral dilemma based on reference to the law, and that one must obey the law, would be considered
    a. preconventional.
    b. conventional.
    c. postconventional.
    d. nonconventional.
19. If a child responds to a moral dilemma by saying, "You should do what will make you feel best, what gets you the most," the individual would be considered to be in Kohlberg's
    a. Stage 1
    b. Stage 2
    c. Stage 3
    d. Stage 4
20. Which of the following criticisms of Kohlberg's theory of moral development is most strongly associated with Carol Gilligan?
    a. sex bias
    b. too difficult coding scheme
    c. cultural specificity
    d. lack of concern with moral behavior

Self-Test Answers
Test B

1. c	4. d	7. b	10. c	13. c	16. d	19. b
2. b	5. d	8. b	11. a	14. b	17. a	20. a
3. c	6. a	9. d	12. c	15. b	18. b	